Words and Things

ROGER BROWN

Words
and Things

THE FREE PRESS, GLENCOE, ILLINOIS

The Free Press
A Division of Macmillan, Inc.
866 Third Avenue, New York, N.Y. 10022

Maxwell Macmillan Canada, Inc.
1200 Eglinton Avenue East
Suite 200
Don Mills, Ontario M3C 3N1

Macmillan, Inc. is part of the Maxwell Communication
Group of Companies.

Printed in the United States of America

printing number

6   7   8   9   10

Library of Congress Cataloging-in-Publication Data

Brown, Roger
Words and Things: An Introduction to Language

Design by Sidney Solomon
Library of Congress Card Catalog No. 58-9395
ISBN 0-02-904810-9

To my father and mother

Preface

In 1951 the Social Science Research Council brought together three linguists and three psychologists interested in language behavior for a summer seminar at Cornell University. As is usual with interdisciplinary seminars, no very specific outcome was envisaged—beyond the always desirable "interaction." For once, however, subsidized interaction proved to be lively, grew autonomous, spread rapidly, and ended in the foundation of a new area of research—"psycholinguistics." Within a few years there appeared several good books on psycholinguistics, a general review of the subject was published as a special supplement to the *Journal of Abnormal and Social Psychology,* and an increasing number of young research scientists came to identify themselves as psycholinguists.

Descriptive linguistics was a great find for American psychology. Our first admiration was for the impeccably behavioristic methods of the linguist. Then came the great excitement of finding that this "new" science had turned up phenomena with which psychology was long familiar—perceptual constancy, acquired perceptual distinctiveness, sensory generalization, the importance of differential reinforcement, positive and negative transfer in learning. It looked as if the findings of linguistic science could be readily "translated" into psychology, greatly enriching the painfully thin chapter on language behavior. The discovery of these results gave psychology the thrill of a massive independent confirmation.

More slowly, we began to absorb the really new things linguistics had to say about language and behavior in general. During the decades of concentrated work on conditioning and instrumental learning psychologists generally assumed that language required no direct study. Language behavior was understood to be the class of responses produced by the muscles of articulation and, as such, it would conform to the general laws of response acquisition which could be more conveniently discovered in the salivary reflex of the dog and the bar pressing of the rat. There was, of course, some uneasiness about this assumption. I heard it expressed once by a distinguished learning theorist who said: "What I can't understand is why animals don't talk," but for the most part psychologists voiced no doubts.

There is a refrain running through descriptive linguistics which goes like this: "Language is a system." "System" is a word that conditioning theorists only use in the last chapters of their studies when they "extrapolate" the results with bar pressing to human thought, personality dynamics, and social change. We all understand that talk about how "conditioned responses get organized into a system so as to yield complex mental processes" is an incantation to preserve our sense of relevance. Consequently it has taken psychologists a long time to realize that the linguist means something when he says: "Language is a system." Very simply, he means that when someone knows a language he knows a set of rules: rules of phonology, morphology, reference, and syntax. These rules can generate an indefinite number of utterances. Learning a language is more than the rehearsal of particular sentences. From particular sentences we induce a governing set of rules and the proof is that we can say new things, never heard and never rehearsed, which nevertheless conform to the rules and are comprehensible to people who know the rules. The most important thing psychology is likely to get from linguistics is the reminder that human behavior includes the response that is novel but appropriate.

Properly classified, linguistics seems to be a subdivision of cultural anthropology, for the linguist describes one kind of cultural system. In the organization of a university, however, the linguist is often placed in one of the language-and-literature departments where his immediate colleagues are literary men not likely to share his interest in laws of behavior, his horror of subjectivism and culture-bondage, and his concern with methodology. In that position the linguist may suffer from what I. A. Richards once amusingly diagnosed as an Ishmaelite Complex: he sulks in his tent and dreams of world conquest. It is understandable that this Ishmael should enjoy his contact with the behavior sciences since they honor his work and share his point of view but there is a price to be paid for this fellowship.

For many years linguists have absolved themselves of responsibility for the most difficult questions concerning language behavior by relegating such problems to the province of psychology, sociology, and anthropology. By narrowly restricting the phenomena in which he would permit himself to be interested, the linguist kept his achievement agreeably close to his objectives. In acknowledging that his study is one of the behavior sciences the linguist takes upon himself the great burden of those sciences. All the little ravelled ends of linguistic methodology—class variations in speech, alternative phonemic solutions, the role of meaning in morphemics—lead out to the general study of human behavior. What kind of a scientist is it who would fail to pursue the leads of his own research?

"Psycholinguistics" has never seemed to me to be a good name for the empirical study of language behavior. In the first place the word has an absurd but intrusive false etymology; it sounds as if a "psycho-linguist" ought to be a deranged polyglot. More seriously, the name appears to limit the field to the traditional objectives of linguistics and that is not desirable. In fact, the range of research already belies the name for many studies are now called "psycholinguistic" which make no use of descriptive linguistics. Rather, we aspire to a "psychology of language." Descriptive linguistics now seems to make the best single contribution to this field, but there are also notable contributions from general and social psychology, from anthropology, sociology, acoustics, literary criticism, mathematics, and philosophy.

My own interest in the study of language began in philosophy

classes with Professor Charles Stevenson and in a psychology seminar with Professor Edward Walker at the University of Michigan.
The first exciting contacts with linguistics came through Professors
Charles Fries, Hans Kurath, and Kenneth Pike at Michigan. The
chairman of the department of psychology at Michigan, Professor
Donald Marquis, first suggested that I prepare a course in the
psychology of language and gave me an opportunity to offer it in
his department. At Harvard I joined the Cognition Project, which
is inspiringly directed by Professor Jerome Bruner, and found in
the theoretical ideas of that Project an excellent analytic tool for
the study of language. Harvard showed its customary hospitality to
new fields of scholarship by creating a committee to administer a
Ph.D. in psychology and linguistics. The four graduate students
who undertook that program have all collaborated with me on one
or another of the research projects reported in this book. They are
Miss Jean Berko, Donald Hildum, Eugene Gordon, and—the first
man to take this new degree—Dr. Eric Lenneberg. Among the undergraduates at Harvard there have been several who elected to
write Senior Honors theses on research problems in the psychology
of language, and I am grateful for my contacts with these young
men. They are James Beck, Raymond Leiter, and John Loeser. All
of the people named in this paragraph have helped to shape *Words
and Things*.

Cambridge, Massachusetts is a good place to live for one interested in the psychology of language. In the recent past it was
the home of two great pioneers in this field—George Kingsley Zipf
and Benjamin Lee Whorf. Such eminent men as Professors Joshua
Whatmough and Roman Jakobson offer superlative linguistic instruction at Harvard. Among the psychologists at Harvard are
Professor John Carroll, who was the chairman of the original "psycholinguistics conference" at Cornell, and Professor George Miller,
who wrote the fine textbook that I have used in my course on the
psychology of language. In the Harvard Department of Social Relations Professors Gordon Allport, Clyde Kluckhohn, and Henry Mur-
ray have all made valuable contributions to the empirical study of
language. The Massachusetts Institute of Technology in Cambridge is a great center for studies in acoustical phonetics and the
mathematical theory of communication. At both Harvard and
M.I.T. many of my young colleagues and friends are working on

language—Dr. Susan Ervin, Professor Dell Hymes, and Dr. Eric Lenneberg at Harvard; Professors Noam Chomsky, Davis Howes, and John Swets at M.I.T. Among the recent visitors to Cambridge have been Professor Charles Morris, a "founding father" of the psychology of language, and Professor Solomon Asch whose studies of metaphor and of the doctrine of "suggestion" have an honored place in this field. It is a great privilege and inspiration to live in this community.

The Harvard Laboratory of Social Relations gave financial support for many of the experimental studies reported in this book. Two journal editors, Professor Bernard Bloch of *Language* and Professor M. Brewster Smith of the *Journal of Abnormal and Social Psychology* have been especially generous in publishing our studies and particularly helpful in criticizing our presentations. I also wish to thank John Wiley and Sons, Inc., for permission to quote extensively from my chapter "Language and Categories" which appears as an Appendix in *A Study of Thinking* by Jerome S. Bruner, Jacqueline J. Goodnow, and George A. Austin. Material from this Appendix appears in Chapters I, III, VI, and VII. Figure 1 in Chapter VI is reprinted with permission from the same source. Finally, I am indebted to the learned lady who typed this manuscript, Mrs. Martha Robinson.

ROGER BROWN

Cambridge, Massachusetts
October 7, 1957

Contents

Words and Things

Introduction

"A CHILD OF ELEVEN or twelve, who some years before had been seen completely naked in the Caune Woods seeking acorns and roots to eat, was met in the same place toward the end of September 1797 by three sportsmen who seized him as he was climbing into a tree to escape from their pursuit." In these words Dr. Jean-Marc-Gaspard Itard began his first report on the education of the wild boy found in the Department of Aveyron. The discovery of a human creature who had lived most of his life outside of all human society excited the greatest interest in Paris. Frivolous spirits looked forward with delight to the boy's astonishment at the sights of the capital. Readers of Rousseau expected to see an example of man as he was "when wild in woods the noble savage ran." There were even some who counted on hearing from the boy mankind's original unlearned language—they conjectured that it was most likely to be Hebrew. The savage of Aveyron disappointed all of these expectations. He was a dirty, scarred, inarticulate creature who trotted and grunted like a beast, ate the most filthy refuse, and bit and scratched those who opposed him.

(3)

In Paris he was exhibited to the populace in a cage, where he ceaselessly rocked to and fro like an animal in the zoo, indifferent alike to those who cared for him and those who stared. The great psychiatrist Pinel, who taught France to treat the insane as patients rather than as prisoners, was brought to examine the boy. After a series of tests Pinel pronounced him a congenital idiot unlikely to be helped by any sort of training.

Many came to believe that the so-called savage was merely a poor subnormal child whose parents had recently abandoned him at the entrance to some woods. However, a young physician from the provinces, Dr. Itard, believed that the boy's wildness was genuine, that he had lived alone in the woods from about the age of seven until his present age of approximately twelve, and there was much to support this view. The boy had a strong aversion to society, to clothing, furniture, houses, and cooked food. He trotted like an animal, sniffed at everything that was given him to eat, and masticated with his incisors in the same way as certain wild beasts. His body showed numerous scars, some of them apparently caused by the bites of animals and some which he had had for a considerable time. Above all, a boy of his general description had been seen running wild in the same forest some five years earlier.

Dr. Itard had read enough of Locke and Condillac to be convinced that most of the ideas a man possesses are not innate but, rather, are acquired by experience. He believed that the apparent feeble-mindedness of the boy of Aveyron was caused by his prolonged isolation from human society and his ignorance of any language and that the boy could be cured by a teacher with patience and a knowledge of epistemology. Itard asked for the job. He had been appointed physician to the new institute for deaf mutes in Paris and so asked to take Victor there to be civilized and, most interesting for us, to learn the French language. Permission was granted and Itard worked with the boy, whom he called Victor, for five years. Itard had little success in teaching Victor to speak for reasons that are discussed in Chapter V of this book. However, he had considerable success in teaching Victor to understand language and, especially, to read simple words and phrases. The doctor's methods of instruction were founded on an analysis of the basic psychology of language which is the same as the analysis on which the present book is founded. A short description of Itard's progress in language instruction will therefore serve as useful introduction to the point of view from which *Words and Things* has been written.

In teaching Victor to understand speech, Itard found that he must, in the beginning, set aside the question of meaning and simply train the boy to identify speech sounds. In the first period after his capture Victor paid no attention to the human voice but only to sounds of approach or movement in his vicinity—noises that would be important to a creature living in the forest. Itard devised an instructive game for teaching Victor to distinguish one vowel from another. Each of the boy's five fingers was to stand for one of five French vowels. When Itard pronounced a vowel, Victor was to raise the appropriate finger. Victor was blindfolded and the vowels were pronounced in an unpredictable order so that if the boy made correct responses it must be because he could distinguish the vowels. In time Victor learned to play the game, but he was never very good at it. Thus Itard decided that the boy's vision was more acute than his hearing and thought he might be taught to read more easily than he could be taught to understand speech.

Again Itard came up with an ingenious game designed to teach Victor to identify the forms of the written and printed language, even though he could not yet understand their meanings. The same collection of words was written on two blackboards, making the order of words on one board unrelated to the order on the other. Itard would point to a word on his board and it was Victor's task to point to its counterpart on the other board. When the boy made a mistake, teacher and pupil "spelled" the word together; Itard pointed to the first letter of his word and Victor did the same with his supposed match, and they proceeded in this fashion until they came to two letters where Victor saw a difference. After a time Victor could read quite a large number of words, some of them very much alike. As yet, however, this was not reading with understanding but simply the identification of empty forms.

The time had come to teach Victor something about the meanings of words. Itard arranged several objects on a shelf in the library, including a pen, a key, a box, and a book. Each thing rested on a card on which its name was written, and Victor had already learned to identify the names. Itard next disarranged the objects and cards and indicated to Victor that he was to match them up again. After a little practice the boy did this very well. Itard then removed all the objects to a corner of the room. He showed Victor one name and gave him to understand that he was to fetch the object named. Victor also learned this very quickly, and Itard grew increasingly optimistic.

The next test went badly at first. Itard locked away in a cupboard all of the particular objects with which Victor had practiced, but made sure that there were in his study other objects of the same kinds—other pens, keys, boxes, and books. He then showed Victor a word, e.g., *livre,* and indicated that the boy was to bring the referent. Victor went to the cupboard for the familiar book and finding the cupboard locked had to give up the task. He showed no interest in any other book. The same failure occurred with the other words. Victor had understood each word to name some particular thing rather than a category of things.

Itard then spread out a variety of books, turning their pages to show what they had in common. He indicated that the word *livre* could go with any of them. After this lesson, when shown the word *livre,* Victor was able to fetch a book other than the specific book of his training. However, he did not correctly constitute the book category at once, for he brought a handful of paper at one time and a pamphlet and magazine at another. As his errors were corrected, however, he learned to distinguish books from other sorts of publications and also to recognize such categories as are named *key, pen,* and *box.* The crucial test for understanding of the referent category was always Victor's ability to identify new instances.

Itard next approached the difficult problem of conveying an understanding of words that name qualities and relations rather than objects that have size, shape, and weight. He took out two books, one large and one small, and Victor promptly labelled each with the word *livre.* Itard then took Victor's hand and spread it flat on the front of the large volume showing how it failed to cover the full surface. The same hand spread out on the smaller book did cover that surface. Victor then seemed puzzled as if wondering that one word should name these two different objects. Itard gave him new cards labelled *grand livre* and *petit livre* and matched them with the appropriate books. Now came the test to see whether Victor had learned specific habits or had abstracted a general relationship. Itard produced two nails, one large and one small, and asked that the cards *grand* and *petit* be correctly assigned. Victor learned this relationship and others besides.

Itard had another good idea for verbs that name actions. He took a familiar thing, e.g., a book, and made it the object of some action—pounding it or dropping it or opening it or kissing it. In each case he gave the boy the appropriate verb in the infinitive form. The test was for the boy to label such actions when their object was changed, e.g., to a key or a pen. This too Victor learned.

The end of all this imaginative teaching was that Victor learned to read with understanding quite a large number of words and phrases. He would obey simple written commands and also use the word cards to signal his own desires. In addition to all this he assumed the manners and appearance of a civilized young man. However, Itard's final word was discouraging. Although Victor had been greatly improved by education, diminishing returns on his efforts convinced Itard that the boy was performing to the limits permitted by his intellectual endowment and these limits, unfortunately, were subnormal.

Reference and Categories

When Dr. Itard wanted to give Victor some idea of the meanings of words, he hit upon a way of showing that each word stood for something, that each word had a referent. This is the sort of thing each of us would do to convey to a small child the meanings of his first words; it is also the usual recourse in trying to communicate with a foreigner who understands no English. The use of language to make reference is the central language function which is prerequisite to all else. It is the beginning of the psychology of language and is, accordingly, the focus of this book.

What Victor learned about reference was at first too specific. Words do not name particular things as Victor thought; they name classes or categories. Someone who properly understands the word *book* is prepared to apply it to any and all particular books. I see in the room where I sit a novel in a highly colored dust jacket and quite near it one numbered volume of a sober encyclopedia; on the floor is a Penguin paperback, and asleep in the hall the tele-phone directory. Although they differ in many respects, all of these are, nevertheless, books. They have the printed pages and stiff covers that define the category.

Actually we do not badly stretch the notion of the category if we treat even a single particular book as a category. The single book, the single anything, is a category of sense impressions. Victor must have seen the book that was used in his early training on many occasions, in various positions, and from different angles. At one time a book is a rectangular shape lying on a table; at another time the same book is only the back of a binding on the library shelf. While it is possible to say that these various experiences constitute a category, that category must be distinguished from the sort named by *book* in general. The various appearances of one book have a continuity in space-time that makes us think of them as one thing preserving its identity through change. The various individual books around my room do not have this kind of con-tinuity. So let us agree to call all referents categories but to dis-tinguish the particular referent from the general by calling it an "identity" category.

Itard's later training procedures show that not all referents are objects with size, shape, and weight. Actions like dropping and kissing are referents and so are such qualities as large and small or red and green. Clearly too, these referents are categories. The act of dropping changes many of its characteristics from one occasion to the next but preserves something invariant that defines the ac-tion. Any sort of recurrence in the non-linguistic world can become the referent of a name and all such recurrences will be categories because recurrences are never identical in every detail. Recurrence always means the duplication of certain essential features in a shifting context of non-essentials.

It is quite easy to see that the referents of words are categories but somewhat less easy to see that language forms, the names of referents, are also categories. Variations in the production of a language form are probably more obvious in the written or printed version than in the spoken. Differences of handwriting and of type are so great that it is actually difficult to specify what all the ren-derings of one word have in common. Even the individual letter is a category of forms changing considerably in their numerous productions. Variations in pronunciation are also certainly ubiquitous but our early extensive training in disregarding the dimensions of speech that are not significant for distinguishing English words causes us to overlook them. So long as phonetic essentials are preserved we identify utterances as the same, although they change greatly in loudness, pitch, quaver, breathiness, and the like. From acoustic studies we know that even one speaker "repeating" the same vowel does not produce identical sounds. Itard's productions of the French vowels cannot have been identical from one time to another and neither, we may be sure, were the "matched" words he wrote on the two blackboards. In these first games Victor was learning to categorize the empty forms of language, to pick out the essential recurrent features and to overlook the non-essential variations.

In this book you will be asked to think of linguistic reference as the coordinate recurrence of categories, one a linguistic form and the other not. Reference is not always as deliberate and explicit as it was in Itard's games. Most children learn their native language without a great deal of deliberate tuition. They somehow pick it up around the house and in the streets. Occasionally an adult takes the trouble to say: "This that I hold in my hand is called a *book*," but more often there will be no explanatory sentence and no helpful act of pointing. It is just that some kind of book will usually be around when *book* is said and children form the association. Reference may be said to exist wherever occurrences of a name are coordinate with occurrences of some other kind.

Since both referents and names are to be treated as categories in this book we need a rule by which the reader can tell when to think of a word as a linguistic form and when to look through the word to its referent. The rule has already been used: the italicized form *book* is to be thought of as a word while book without italics is to be thought of as the referent. In addition to this rule we need some descriptive terms (a metalanguage) for talking about categories. A terminology that is well suited to this purpose has been developed by the Harvard Cognition Project and is set forth in the book *A Study of Thinking* by Bruner, Goodnow, and Austin (29).

The following presentation of our descriptive metalanguage is based on that book. The important terms are placed in quotation marks on their first appearance.

Metalanguage for Talking About Categories

A "category" is a class, a grouping of objects or events. An "attribute" is any dimension on which objects and events can differ. The objects called *livres* by Itard, and *books* by us, have such attributes as color, size, number of pages, kind of binding, and title. Individual books vary on these and on many other dimensions.

In Aristotle's classic discussion of categories a distinction is made between the essential or defining attributes of a category and the accidental or non-defining attributes. Victor at first understood the word *livre* to name a particular book and so acted as if the color and binding and title of that book were essential attributes of the referent named *livre*. However, Itard thought of all these characteristics as accidental; the only essentials being the printed pages and hard covers common to all the books in his study. It rather looks as if Victor understood that printed pages were essential before he understood about hard covers since he at first took newspapers and pamphlets for books.

Aristotle's distinction between essential and accidental attributes is a kind of ideal logic of categories that is not very well suited to the psychology of categorizing behavior. Consider the nature of the binding on a publication. The very hardest bindings are probably found on books alone but there are bindings of an intermediate stiffness which are found on both paperback books and certain magazines. The comparative stiffness of the covers of a publication will help me to decide whether it is a book or a magazine but there is no value of this attribute that is found in all books and in no non-books. This attribute is neither strictly essential nor strictly accidental. It will be useful to replace that dichotomy with a continuum; following the precedent of the authors of *A Study of Thinking* we shall speak of the relative "criteriality" of an attribute for a category. When some value of an attribute is used as a basis for inferring the category membership of an object then that attribute is to some degree criterial for the categorization. To the degree that an attribute can change in value without affecting categorizing judgments, it is not criterial for the categories in question. The stiffness of the binding certainly has some criteriality for distinguishing books from magazines; one sort of binding is much more likely to go on a book than on a magazine. On the other hand the occurrence of printed pages is not criterial for the distinction in question since it is common to both books and magazines.

It is important to make a distinction between "potential criteriality" and "actual criteriality." On one of the first few pages of every book the year of publication is marked whereas magazines have on the cover or on an early page a more complete date of publication—month and year or even day, month, and year. In addition a magazine is likely to list its volume and number. This fact about magazines and books stems from a defining difference in their manner of publication. Magazines are periodicals, members of a series to which new members are added at regular intervals. Books are either one-time publications or, if they sell many copies, aperiodic recurrent publications. This is a difference of potentially perfect criteriality between magazines and books. However, it is not a difference of which Victor was aware; in his categorizing behavior he made no use of the date-of-publication attribute. Therefore the attribute had no actual criteriality for him. We shall use actual criteriality to describe the use of an attribute in some person's categorizing behavior. Potential criteriality is a matter of existent conditions rather than of anyone's psychology.

Some further examples will help us to develop agility in handling the notions of category, attribute, and potential and actual criteriality. Consider the category we would call *1954 American pennies* as opposed to the category we would call *1944 American pennies*. The date on the coin is an attribute of potentially perfect criteriality, a defining attribute. The brightness of the coins has some potential criteriality. The 1954 pennies tend to be brighter than those coined in 1944. However, there will be some 1954 specimens that have knocked about a great deal in a short time and grown dingier than certain 1944 specimens that have led a secluded life in someone's bank. If, in categorizing pennies, I were sometimes uncertain of the date I would probably give consideration to the brightness of the coin in deciding whether it was of 1954 or 1944. Brightness would then be an attribute having actual criteriality for me.

Think of the ways in which animals are identified. The elephant's trunk is an attribute having potentially perfect criteriality and usually having high actual criteriality. The cerebral index of a chimpanzee could be used to distinguish the chimp from a man but this attribute is, in fact, seldom used. We ordinarily rely on more available attributes (hairiness, facial contours, etc.) though these may have a slightly lower potential criteriality.

Non-criterial attributes are not all of the same sort. An attribute that assumes more than one value for the members of one category, and which assumes the same values for another category, is non-defining and "noisy." In distinguishing books from magazines the quality of the paper making up the pages is such a noisy attribute. There are books with glossy pages and there are slick magazines, as well as both books and magazines printed on rough stock. The color of the covers is probably also a noisy attribute for distinguishing books from magazines. Both kinds of publication have drawn on the full color spectrum. If, to cite another example, one were learning to distinguish different makes of automobile by sight the color of the car would again be a non-defining and noisy attribute. The designation *noisy* is well chosen for the attributes we are discussing because noise in its literal sense is often a distraction from a task and noisy attributes are similarly a distraction in the business of category formation. When Victor had to learn to recognize books in general he probably found it confusing that they should greatly vary in color and that certain non-books (magazines) should vary in the same way.

When an attribute has the same value for all the members of more than one category it is non-criterial for the categories in question but also "quiet." Both books and magazines are bound together on one side and open on the other side. This attribute is of no use in distinguishing books from magazines since it is the same for both. However, it is a quiet non-criterial attribute. When makes of automobile are to be distinguished, the presence of metal parts is such a non-criterial quiet attribute since all makes of car have metal parts. The quiet attribute is true to its name in that it does not disturb the person learning category distinctions; its invariable and unvarying presence does not draw attention away from the potentially criterial attribute.

The criteriality of an attribute for a category is always relative to some other category or categories from which the first is to be distinguished. One dictionary defines *book* as "a written or printed narrative or record" and that is a good beginning which serves to mark off books from such other things as trees, roses, clouds, and persons. If books are to be distinguished from everything else in the world then "writing or printing" becomes a potentially criterial attribute. However, the dictionary definition will not serve to separate books from the things with which they are most likely to be confused—the newspapers, magazines, and pamphlets that Victor at first took for books. When it is a question of distinguishing one sort of publication from another then, of course, the fact of printing becomes a non-criterial quiet attribute because it is common to every sort of publication. Shifting to automobiles now, we can see that the condition of being manufactured from metal helps to distinguish automobiles in general from the other objects in the world and so is criterial when that is the problem, but the same condition is not criterial for distinguishing makes of automobile. If we change the problem in another way and try to distinguish 1935 automobiles from 1955 automobiles, then color becomes a potentially criterial attribute because some of the paler pinks and violets were not thought suitable for cars in the earlier year. Among makes of automobile today color is a non-criterial and particularly noisy attribute.

Any collection of objects or events is susceptible of a large number of alternative categorizations. Books are classified by public libraries into fiction and non-fiction; among works of fiction, a further division into mysteries, westerns, and novels apparently helps many library patrons to find what they want. High school boys who "have to write a report on a book" classify by number of pages and density of print. Teachers of literature work with such categories as the naturalistic novel, the Gothic novel, and the *roman à clef*. Someone furnishing a room might think in terms of bindings. If anyone cared to do so, books could be classified by weight, first name of protagonist, number of illustrations, average frequency of semicolons, or according to any of an indefinite number of additional schemes. All of these categorizations would work with the same population of objects. A category, in short, is a human construction imposed on an array of objects or events.

Among the various sorts of categories human beings use, it is worthwhile to distinguish several types. Probably our favorite kind of category is that in which the members all have some attribute that is never found outside the category. We prefer this variety because it puts least strain on the memory; from a single attribute one can infer category membership with perfect confidence. The preference for this sort of category is so great that categories or concepts have sometimes been defined in terms of this single variety, as, for example, "a group of entities having some common and distinctive characteristic." However, this is not the only sort of grouping principle we use. There are, in addition, "conjunctive" categories, "disjunctive" categories, and "relational" categories. A conjunctive category is defined by the joint presence of appropriate values of several attributes. A historical novel, for instance, is a fictional story set in some earlier period of time. A right triangle, to cite another example of a conjunctive category, is a three-sided, closed figure containing one 90° angle. A disjunctive category is defined by any one of a set of alternative attributes. The members of such a category do not share any characteristic attribute but they are nevertheless grouped together. The strike in baseball is such a disjunctive category, for a strike is either a pitch that is across the plate and between the batter's knees and shoulders, or it is a pitch at which the batter swings and misses, or it is a pitch the batter hits but which falls into foul territory. For purposes of the game these quite unlike events are treated as equivalents, members of a disjunctive class called *strikes*. A relational category is defined by a specifiable relationship between attributes. Within an array of quadrilateral closed figures we could establish a relational category by defining the members as those figures having a larger altitude than base; not an absolute value of either attribute but a relation between the two would define the category.

There is one additional distinction that is important for the psychology of language. Most categories have two sorts of attributes —"formal" attributes and "functional" attributes. Formal attributes are such characteristics as size, shape, color, weight, and the like; functional attributes are uses that can be made of members of a category. For example, the formal attributes of knives are a limited range of lengths, a blade having at least a minimal sharpness, and a handle. Among the functional attributes of knives are the slicing of bread and the peeling of apples. These are tasks knives can perform. Some categories are actually named for their functional rather than their formal properties, e.g., *glass cutters* and *paper weights*. This seems to happen when a function can be performed by objects that have very unlike formal attributes.

How does the behavior scientist—the psychologist, linguist, anthropologist, or what have you—determine when a subject has a category? There are several different kinds of behavior that can be used. A human subject can be asked to define a category—to name its criterial attributes. What is a book? What is an automobile? This turns out to be a rather stringent requirement. We are not able to give good definitions of very many categories. A less exacting requirement asks that a subject identify new instances of a category. Can he point out the books in this room as distinct from such other things as papers and magazines and inkwells? It is important that the instances be new to him since the identification of familiar instances might be a rote performance. When Victor could correctly identify books he had never seen, it strongly suggested to Itard that he had abstracted the criterial attributes of familiar books and could recognize them in new surroundings.

One advantage in using the identification of new instances as evidence of a category is the fact that animals other than man can be expected to meet the requirement, with the difference that their identifications cannot be verbal and will not be given on request. If you ask him, a man will tell you which of two circles is the larger and which the smaller. One must provide differential reward for a rat—feeding him, perhaps, when he jumps at a larger circle and letting him bump his nose when he jumps at a smaller circle. If he can learn to distinguish the two circles he will "tell" us so by consistently jumping toward the one that brings food. Similarly, a fish can be taught to swim toward the larger circle by selective feeding; a dog can be taught to salivate at the sight of the larger circle and not at the sight of the smaller. In short, where a man would be asked to say different words, an animal can be required to make different responses of a sort congenial to its species. However, the discriminating response alone is not evidence that the animal has a category; it must be asked to identify new instances. A rat that jumps to the larger of two circles could next be shown the larger circle plus another still larger. If the creature jumped to the familiar circle, it would appear that it had simply learned to approach a particular figure; but if it jumped instead to the new larger circle there would be a strong presumption that it had formed the category we should call *the larger of two circles.* One might go on to see whether the animal could learn to favor the larger of any two objects by training it with such varied things as boxes and nails and books. In the end it would be possible to find out whether the animal could form the categories that Victor learned to label *petit* and *grand.* In this book we shall most often use the identification of new instances as the performance giving evidence of the possession of a category. One reason for doing so is our interest in comparing the language performance of animals and man.

Plan of the Book

The ten chapters that follow are concerned with such very old problems as the nature of meaning, the language of animals, the relation between language and thought, the character of primitive language, the possibility of phonetic symbolism, and the techniques of persuasion through language. In short, a set of real chestnuts, most of them either given up for dead, or demonstrated to be pseudo questions, or officially proscribed by scholarly societies. While I admit to believing that the old questions are the best, it is not merely antiquarian interest that causes me to discuss them now. The pleasant surprise is that there is a lot of new evidence on these matters, evidence derived from psychology, descriptive linguistics, and anthropology. The questions are alive and moving toward solution in the behavior sciences.

Chapter 1. The Analysis of Speech. We begin, as Itard did, by leaving meaning aside while the sounds of speech are studied. The science of descriptive linguistics has found that all human languages are built on the same general plan. Most of the variations that occur in speech are not used to distinguish one referent from another. Only a very limited set of acoustic distinctions is used in this way. However, languages do not all recognize the same distinctions and so a person learning a second language has serious difficulty "hearing" that language as it is intended to be heard and pronouncing it as it is intended to be pronounced. The Frenchman is likely to say *zis and zat* for *this and that*, and we are likely to say *tu* as if it were *two*, and at first neither of us will hear anything wrong with his own pronunciation. The cause and remedy of this sort of difficulty become clearer when the results of descriptive linguistics are translated into the category metalanguage as they are in this first chapter.

Chapter II. The History of Writing and a Dispute About Reading. We continue Itard's sequence by moving next to the written language. It is a curious fact that the contemporary American dispute about whether Johnny can read and why not is closely connected with the history of writing systems. The earliest (pre-alphabetic) written symbols directly represented objects but for various reasons this kind of writing was not adequate for the needs of complex societies. There are great psychological economies in a phonetic writing such as our alphabet, economies that have caused phonetic writings to prevail over the older representational writings. However, the alphabet used for writing English has come to be a very irregular phonetic system. Some say that its irregularities are so exasperating that children ought to be taught to read English without any direct tuition in the sound values of the alphabet. Others say that this is tantamount to returning us to a hieroglyphic writing since it deprives children of the advantages that inhere in a phonetic writing. The question is whether the letters of our alphabet have sufficiently constant sound values to make knowing them worthwhile. If it is worthwhile knowing the usual sounds of the letters, should they be taught through explicit drill or ought exercises to be devised that will lead a child to induce the rules for himself?

Chapter III. Reference and Meaning. Itard undertook to teach the meanings of words by showing Victor examples of the things named and this is one of the ways in which meanings are commonly learned. What happens to a person when he experiences word and referent in association? Many psychologists and philosophers have reported that they form a mental image of the referent which thereafter comes to mind whenever the word is spoken and is the meaning of the word. However, we know that words name categories, and it is difficult to see what sorts of image would go with books-in-general or with keys-in-general and when it comes to animal-in-general most of us give up. We may even report, as have many before us, that we have no images at all for any words. What images, for example, have you had in connection with the last sentence? But if meaning is not an image, what is it?

Chapter IV. Phonetic Symbolism and Metaphor. What is the nature of the associations between words and referents? It is almost axiomatic with modern semantics that there is nothing natural or appropriate in such associations. They are supposed to be altogether arbitrary. Except for the trivial case of onomatopoeic or sound-imitative words it is even difficult to understand what "appropriateness" to a referent could mean. The whole notion of sound symbolism is generally taken to be a delusion of hyperaesthetical literary people. Metaphor is acknowledged to be real enough but of limited interest since it is chiefly a device of poetry. If all this is true how does it happen that *tumba* seems such a good word for a mound or swelling and *ongololo* so appropriate a name for the centipede? How is it possible for more than 90 per cent of native English speakers who know nothing of Chinese to guess that *ch'ing* means light and *ch'ung* means heavy? If metaphor is limited to poetry what do we mean when we say that a person has a "cold" manner, a "dry" wit, and "narrow" interests? Why, finally, do corporations pay a psychological consulting firm to find them a "good" name for a new product?

Chapter V. The Comparative Psychology of Linguistic Reference. It is common to cite man's ability to use language as a distinctive ability setting him off from the other animals. But is the break so absolute? Can we not find some phyletic continuity? Are there not animal communications that deserve to be called language? Certain birds are said to talk; the bees are reported to have an elaborate instinctive language; chimpanzees appear to produce sounds very like our vowels and consonants. The first four chapters have described the essential properties of human language and have put us in a position to judge whether or not animal communications are also languages. Even if the communications various animal species use among themselves are not languages, it is still possible that a gifted animal, given careful training, might learn to use a human language. What would happen, for instance, if a chimpanzee were from birth to be given more intensive and skillful training in the use of English than any child receives? Can the ape become a language-using animal? The interesting complement of this question is to ask how much of language can be learned by a human being like Victor who has in his early years been deprived of social contacts.

Chapter VI. The Original Word Game. This is the game of linguistic reference that Victor played with Itard and all children play with their parents. The rudiments of the game are the perception of speech categories, the pronunciation skill, and the identification of referent categories. This third process could also be called cognitive socialization since it involves learning to structure experience and thought as they are structured by the social group. The perception of speech in terms of a small set of distinctive features is the key to the larger and more important business of cognitive socialization. In this chapter we enjoy the benefits of our preliminary study of descriptive linguistics, for it is linguistic analysis that exposes the vital functions of speech in the socialization of the child. The Original Word Game is not given up after childhood. To be sure, the first two rudiments, speech perception and pronunciation, will have reached a level of automatic perfection but the categorizing and recategorizing of reality goes on as long as we continue to learn. All advanced education, all professional studies are in part problems of linguistic reference.

Chapter VII. Linguistic Relativity and Determinism. How do languages differ from one another? Obviously they make their words from different sound sequences. The Frenchman says *chien,* the German *Hund,* the American *dog.* In this case the words differ but the referent seems to be the same. Is this always true? Are the languages of the world a set of alternative codes for the same concepts? If so, it is a pity that the world cannot agree on a single code and so save us all the trouble of boning up on a second or third language in preparation for a trip abroad or the reading of a foreign journal or a diplomatic mission. Of course, if the referents are different, as well as the words, then each language would embody a unique point of view and the loss of any one language would mean the loss of an insight into reality.

How is thought related to language? According to the usual view language does not come into play until thoughts are formulated. If the thinker wants to communicate, he uses language as a medium, as the passive carrier of thought. There is a contrary view which holds that language is an active determinant of thought. According to this view the structure of a man's native language is a kind of mold fixing the general form of his cognitive functions. This problem of the connection between language and thought is closely related to the nature of the differences between languages.

Chapter VIII. Progressions and Pathologies. Is there a direction of advance in linguistic reference? Does impairment of language function through brain injury or schizophrenia cause a regression in reference? The authorities say that the direction of advance is from "concrete" to "abstract" reference. Aphasic patients and schizophrenics are supposed to function concretely, as do animals, primitive peoples, and children, whereas the healthy, civilized adult is said to be capable of abstract reference. Using the category metalanguage, it is possible to give precise definition to the notions of "concrete" and "abstract" reference and to examine the evidence for the doctrine of progressions and pathologies.

Chapter IX. Persuasion, Expression, and Propaganda. We hear, nowadays, that the science of propaganda has developed to the point where great masses of people can be persuaded to believe what is untrue and to perform what is immoral. This science is supposed to have swept several nations into totalitarian slavery and is said to be a potent threat to the American people. There is also some indignation at present over the unscrupulous use of advertising to manipulate consumer choices and even electoral choices. In general, modern man as a target of propaganda and advertising is pictured as a helpless dupe. This chapter argues that there is in human psychology something that checks the efforts of the unscrupulous propagandist. It is not any sort of sophisticated learning or higher education in propaganda analysis but simply our lifelong practice in learning to discern the true motives of people who try to influence us. We make a beginning at this business as children in the running propaganda warfare that goes on between children and adults. Essentially what is involved is learning to "read" behavior, and especially speech, as an expression of character. In numerous inadvertencies the propagandist is likely to "give away" his intentions and so deprive his message of persuasive power. The expressive function of language proves to be a variant of reference and susceptible of description in our metalanguage.

Chapter X. Linguistic Reference in Psychology. What are the special qualities of the language of science? Presumably it should be unequivocal and non-evaluative. The language of science ought to be purged of the ambiguities and implicit judgments that plague ordinary language. More than any other science, psychology uses terms that are close to popular parlance. Sometimes the professional borrows from colloquial speech; sometimes the professional's term is taken up by colloquial speech. The concepts and propositions of psychology are themselves psychological and social forces. Ideas about human nature and national character, for instance, though formed within the science are bound to have an influence in the world at large. As a consequence, the psychologist has an especially difficult time using language as a trustworthy instrument. In this last chapter we twist around and apply what we have learned about the psychology of language to the language of psychology.

These are the topics of the book. They sound rather "old fashioned and philosophical" for a book in behavioral science, but then a great many scientists came to their profession by way of an early interest in philosophy. Most of us once hoped that empirical study would answer or, at any rate, enrich some of those first and most tormenting questions. We have tried to feel as strongly about the lesser questions to which answers are more accessible, to get excited about a new aptitude test or a technique for improving factory morale. Clearly these are more useful endeavors than worrying about the nature of meaning and the use of metaphor. However, the old questions have a kind of "punch" that the new ones cannot match. Perhaps it is because philosophical concerns were a part of our adolescence but possibly it is because they have more to do with what man thinks about his own nature.

chapter i

The Analysis of Speech

W<small>E ARE ALL</small> aware that speech, like chemistry, has a structure. There is a limited set of elements—vowels and consonants—and these are combined to produce words which, in turn, compound into sentences. The elementary sounds do not make reference; [p] stands for nothing. Reference begins with the word and applies also to many sentences.

The analysis of speech is the business of descriptive linguistics. *Linguist* has long been a name for one who speaks many languages. The descriptive linguist of today is a social scientist who studies the structures of various languages but who may not be able to speak more than one or two. Linguistics aims at providing concepts that will serve to describe all languages and which can be used to contrast languages in regard to sound system (phonology), rules for word formation (morphology), and rules for word combination (syntax). Knowledge of the structure of a language is not the same as the ability to use the language. The latter is a cognitive and motor skill built up by a kind of practice that is not necessary to the comprehension of structure. The difference is rather like that between a knowledge of the theory of music and the ability to play the piano. For the man who speaks many languages *polyglot* is an unequivocal designation. For the student of language structure we will use the word *linguist*.

The first requirement for descriptive linguistics is an inventory of the elementary speech sounds used in all the languages of the world, an International Phonetic Alphabet (I.P.A.). It was originally intended that the I.P.A. should provide a distinct sign for every distinct speech sound. It was further intended to classify these sounds in terms of the gross physiology of their production so as to have both a symbol for the sound and a kind of articulational recipe by which one could reconstitute the sound. These original goals have proved to be unattainable for the reason that the number of physically distinct speech sounds, in even one language, is indefinitely and unmanageably large. This was a surprise to the first people who studied phonetics and is a surprise to many people today who have the common impression that there are not a great many different vowels and consonants, perhaps thirty or so in any one language, maybe as many as a hundred in all languages. In fact, it is more nearly true to say that every sound uttered is in some way different from every other. This wide divergence between impression and fact arises because what we think of as vowels and consonants are not single invariant sounds but rather categories of varied individual sounds (*phones*).

We have all learned to overlook many dimensions of variation in speech. However, speakers of different languages do not always select the same dimensions for attention and inattention. There are, in short, cultural differences in the way speech is perceived. This fact has caused linguistics to distinguish *phonetic* transcription from what is called *phonemic* transcription. Phonetic transcription is a culture-free system for recording any speech. It does not take account of all the physical differences in speech—that would be impossible. It does take account of all the differences that are significant in any language. Phonemic transcription of a language represents as different sounds only those that are thought of as different by native speakers. It reproduces the local feeling about the language. A phonetic transcription, a culture-free description, must precede the discovery of any local phonemic system. Without a phonetic alphabet the linguist would be in danger of imposing his own parochial habits of speech perception on any new language he encountered.

Phonetics and phonemics are the best developed branches of descriptive linguistics and this chapter is principally concerned with them. This will not simply involve a résumé of linguistic theory but also an attempt to translate that theory into psychological terms. The category metalanguage set forth in the Introduction is exactly suited to this task. This metalanguage also fits some of the best established facts of morphology and syntax. The chapter closes with a brief treatment of these matters.

It is conventional to enclose phonetic symbols in square brackets and that convention is followed in this book. Thus [p] is a phonetic symbol. Phonemic symbols are placed in slanted brackets, and so /p/ is phonemic. Where the sound value of the symbol is not obvious it is followed with a word illustrating the sound.

Phonetics

Speech begins as a breath pulse forced from the lungs by the short contraction of certain muscles located between the ribs. Stetson (218) has suggested that these syllabic puffs are delivered very much as one might produce brief exhalations from a bellows with a series of sharp hand jabs. At the top of the windpipe are the vocal folds and the opening in these is called the glottis. These folds are not at all like the miniature harp I pictured when I first heard of the vocal cords. They are more like a pair of lips that can close over the glottis and lock air in the chest or can retract to permit the free passage of air in breathing. In intermediate positions the folds are set in vibration to produce the complex musical tone that is the beginning of phonation. Adjustments of air pressure and vocal fold tension alter the pitch and loudness of this tone.

The complex musical tone generated by the folds is modified in its transmission through the cavities of the throat, nose, and mouth. These act as a set of filters, selectively transmitting those partials of the tone to which they are tuned. The tuning of the filters is changed by adjusting the shape and size of the cavities. If this filtering action is the only factor modifying the glottal tone the result is called a vowel. In other cases the breath pulse is stopped or diverted—sent hissing through some narrow passage or suddenly released with a small explosion. The interruptions are produced by causing the moving parts (lower lip and tongue) to articulate with the fixed parts (upper lip, teeth, hard gum ridge, hard and soft palates, etc.). Whenever the breath pulse is impeded in this way we call the result a consonant. The consequence of all these gymnastics is a vibration of the air that can be heard.

In classifying the vowels it is customary to distinguish at least three attributes: the portion of the tongue acting as a mobile articulator, the height to which the tongue is raised, and the shaping of the lips. There is some disagreement as to the number of values to be recognized for each attribute. Three elevations of the tongue are customary but Bloch and Trager (20) interpolate intermediate positions to yield seven. These are named, like Lloyd Warner's social classes, low, higher-low, lower-middle, mean-middle, higher-middle, lower-high, and high. The tongue itself is usually charted into front, middle, and back regions. Two shapes of the lips, rounded and unrounded, are standard. Three tongue regions, seven elevations, and two lip shapings in all possible combinations of three yield forty-two possible vowels. In addition, however, all of these vowels can be nasalized by dropping the nasal flap. The apex of the tongue (farther forward than the front— the very tip) can be independently active during the pronunciation of a vowel. It may turn up toward the teeth or even curve backward producing the retroflex vowel. Then, of course, the vowel may be whispered rather than voiced. Vowels may, and do, vary in length and in tone. We have not yet exhausted the attributes that can be used to characterize vowels. The number of values to be recognized for each attribute seems to be an arbitrary decision since the number possible is indefinitely large.

Consonants are produced by the articulation of mobile parts and fixed positions, five of the former and six of the latter. There are then thirty conceivable positions of articulation. Actually, however, only a few of these occur. The lower lip does not reach back to scrape the hard palate and the tongue tip does not contact the velum. The eight realized positions are: 1) bilabial (two lips), 2) labiodental (lower lip, upper teeth), 3) dental (tongue tip, upper teeth), 4) alveolar (tongue tip, gum ridge), 5) cacuminal (tongue tip, hard palate), 6) palatal (tongue front, hard palate),

7) velar (tongue back, soft palate), and 8) uvular (tongue back, uvula). In these eight positions of articulation it is possible to interrupt and release the breath in a variety of ways. These are the four types of articulation: the plosive (stop), as in [p]; the spirant (fricative), as in [f]; the lateral, as in [l]; and the trill, as in Italian [r] of *rialto*. The combination of eight positions and four types of articulation yields a potential of thirty-two consonants. It is possible to distinguish the flap (as in British *very*) from the trill and so create a fifth articulation type. Nasalization is another at-tribute usually added. Then the entire set can be voiceless rather than voiced. The anthropologist adds that the Hottentots produce clicks and smacks which, like our *tsk! tsk!* are produced by in-spiration of air rather than expiration. We had taken exhalation for granted, but it now appears that this was a culture-bound notion. The attributes and attribute values needed to characterize the consonants are, like those needed to characterize the vowels, indefinitely numerous.

There is no end to phonetic transcription so long as its goal is taken to be the unique specification of every unique sound. Heights of the tongue might assume a thousand values; regions of the tongue might be subdivided forever; lip roundings, pursings, and pinchings discriminated endlessly. Each of the positions and types of articulation can be fractionated. Some phonetic transcriptions are narrower than others but none is ultimately narrow.

Kenneth Pike (182) has attempted to extricate phonetics from this dilemma. He redefines the goal as follows: "The articulatory procedure, therefore, does not attempt to describe an infinite variety of sounds and articulatory positions, but only those above the perceptual threshold; the number which can be perceptually discriminated is not infinite." Pike recognizes that perceptual thres-holds are affected by linguistic background, and that the ear able to hear all his distinctions will have to be phonetically trained. Each discriminable vocal sound can be described, in Pike's system, with a formula which is also a set of directions for producing the sound. The vowel [o], for instance, is written: "MaILDeCVveIpvrc APplalʲtlwmovtnranshsrʲlisAPpsabʲtlmctnransnsfTpgagʲtlwvtitʋransn sfSrpFSv." This formula tells the initiate that the productive mech-anism is an air stream produced by the lungs in an egressive direc-tion while the controlling mechanism is a valvate stricture of the velic or subvalvate esophageal variety. The preceding sentence translates only the first ten letters of the formula. The Pike system is able to provide unique formulas for millions of distinct phones. Pike writes, in conclusion, "Of course, even an analphabetic system is limited to noting those elements which are above the perceptual threshold of the observer; it is suggestive, but by no means exhaustive."

Thus Pike has undertaken to provide a system that can be used to describe all the *discriminable* phones—still a very large population. The more usable and familiar phonetic alphabets comprise about fifty symbols and a dozen diacritica. They are able to record all the vowels and consonants that are used to distinguish meanings in any known language. This is a far smaller group than the total number of discriminable phones. A phonetic writing must provide symbols for recording the sounds of a new language without prejudging the question as to which of these sounds are equivalent for speakers of the language and which are distinctive. It must record any speech difference that natives might consider distinctive. Consequently, more detailed transcriptions are better than less detailed transcriptions but they are also more difficult. In most cases the more modest phonetic alphabet will suffice. As mentioned earlier, a phonetic transcription of some kind is prerequisite to a phonemic transcription that classifies the sounds of the language according to the *Sprachgefühl* of native speakers.

Phonemics

The phoneme is often called the smallest unit of speech that "makes a difference" to a listener or speaker. Linguistic scientists have developed intricate but generally reliable techniques for discovering these units in any speech corpus. However, there is some disagreement about minor points of procedure and a great deal of disagreement concerning the psychological status of the phoneme. In my opinion the phoneme is best handled in psychology as a cognitive category.

The Phoneme as a Functional Category. Imagine that we have undertaken a study of the metal currency of a country. Imagine further that we have a collection of coins belonging to that currency and that some of these coins are large and some small, some have a rough outer perimeter and some are smooth, some are dull and some shiny. Such coins could be categorized in a number of different ways. On first impulse we would probably divide them into large and small coins since the size attribute is highly criterial in identifying American coins: it is predictive of their exchange value. However, in this new society, whose coinage we have sampled, size might not predict exchange value. If we observed buying and selling in this society we might discover that all coins with rough perimeters are treated as exchange-equivalents distinct from a second group having smooth perimeters. In working out the coinage system it would be our concern to establish functional categories first, to find out which coins were equivalent in that they could be used to buy the same things and could be exchanged for one another. When we had established the functioning categories for the society in question we would seek to discover the attributes people used for anticipating the functional value of a coin. In our imagined coinage system it would appear that the character of the perimeter is the criterial formal attribute. Size is evidently a noisy non-criterial attribute.

Phonemes like coins are functional categories. The linguistic scientist who studies the speech of an unfamiliar preliterate people resembles the coin classifier. He too collects a group of specimens (a speech corpus). As in the case of the coin classifier, the linguist has two tasks: to discover the local functional categories and then to discover the attributes by which natives recognize equivalents. With the coins the first step entailed an impartial description of the attributes of the sample—size, contour, and surface shading. The first step with a speech corpus is a phonetic transcription that recognizes all the formal differences that are likely to be used in the local categorization. Just as the American coin classifier must guard against his tendency to assume that size will be a criterial attribute, so the linguist whose native language is English must guard against a tendency to assume that voicing, for instance, will be a criterial attribute. Each analyst seeks to find the local categorization not to impose his own categorization on the local materials.

The phonetic transcription of the corpus of speech should be as narrow as one can manage. Since the transcription will not be ultimately narrow (a symbol for each unique sound) there are sure to be some recurrent phonetic sequences. Distinguishable sounds will sometimes be found imbedded in such recurrent contexts. These sounds are the focus of the first stage of phonemic study.

Are two discriminable phones, A and A', that occur in identical phonetic contexts, categorized together or separately categorized by a native speaker? Notice that, if the object language were English, A and A' might correspond to [p] and [b] in *pan* and *ban* with the prime mark indicating the voice that is added to the bilabial plosive [p] to make [b]. Alternatively, A and A' might correspond to [p'] and [p] in which the second phone is unreleased as it sometimes is in *nip*. The same word is, however, sometimes pronounced with a released aspirated [ṗ] of the kind heard in *pin*. Either form of [p] is possible in final position. Our *Sprachgefühl* classifies the [p]'s together—indeed we may never have noticed their difference—but we consider the [p] and [b] to be altogether different. Now we are concerned with A and A'. The phonetician has distinguished between them since he writes them differently. What of the native speaker?

It is difficult to know just what question to ask. If a man in a pith helmet were to ask you, as a native speaker of English, to tell him whether there was any difference between two sounds, and if he then painstakingly enunciated [p]'s, released and unreleased, you might well report the difference though noticing it for the first time. Any set that puts the informant on his mettle, that puts a premium on acuteness, is undesirable. What we want is his acculturated ear. We want a casual, habitual judgment, not an auditory difference limen.

Harris (88) suggests that the phonetician produce A in its phonetic context (ABC) and then ask the native speaker whether A'BC is a repetition of ABC. In effect one asks if the utterances are the same but without focusing on the particular sound. If the utterances were *pan* and *ban* no speaker of English would accept them as equivalent. If the utterances were *nip* (unreleased) and *nip* (released) they would be accepted as equivalent so long as the informant did not feel that his powers of auditory discrimination were being tested. Alternatively the linguist might pronounce ABC and ask informants to repeat the utterances several times. If any of the "repetitions" turned out to be A'BC we should know that the native speaker accepts A' as equivalent to A. The parallel with coin classification is a very close one, for the repetition procedure is a speech equivalent of giving and receiving change.

As an alternative to the repetition procedure the linguist might observe usage of ABC and A'BC to see whether they correlate with the same or different non-linguistic circumstances. In the simplest case ABC and A'BC would be denotational words, used in pointing at different persons or objects. The informant would take one boy by the hand and say, "This is my son ABC and this," taking the other boy by the hand, "is A'BC." Of course this procedure is liable to serious misconstruction. A single pointing has no unequivocal meaning. Do I point to a glass, a glass of milk, milk, a container, or a thing? By careful attention to repeated pointings and namings, however, the linguist may discover whether ABC and A'BC name different categories for native speakers. Pike (185) reports that one of his best checks on a phonemic analysis comes from the reaction of natives to his speech. If they roar with laughter when he is serious, or if they are insulted when he is being pleasant, the inappropriate reaction can sometimes be traced to the pronunciation of A in a context that calls for A'.

Using several of these operations to check on one another the linguist obtains a set of phonetic categories. The phones within a category are said to be in free variation with one another. Each category is given a symbol. These symbols have no exact phonetic value; they stand for classes of phones. The categorial [p] stands for both released and unreleased varieties. The original phonetic transcription made by the linguist was also necessarily categorial. The categories were his, rather than those of the native speakers and they were smaller categories than the new variety. Still these new phonetic categories are not phonemes.

The coin parable offers no exact analogy for the second step in phoneme identification. What happens, essentially, is that some of the classes of freely varying phones can be classified together to yield a higher order category—the phoneme. Classes of phones that can be so united are called allophones (or varying forms) of one phoneme. There are two criteria for this procedure: *articulational similarity* and *complementary distribution*. These are described below.

Among the categories of free variants there will be some that share distinctive features of articulation. This is true of the [p] of *pan* and the [b] of *ban*. It is also true, in English, of the prolonged [o:] heard in *toad* and the shorter vowel of *tote*. As native speakers of English we think of these two cases as quite different. The two consonants are distinct from one another; the vowels are the same, except for an insignificant difference in duration. The phonetician does not yet know that we think of them this way, that we make two phonemes of the consonants and only one of the vowels. There is no *a priori* reason why we should think of them this way. In some other languages vowels of different length are different phonemes whereas voiced and voiceless forms of a consonant are one phoneme. From the phonetician's point of view there are here two pairs of sounds that resemble one another, a pair of bilabial stops and a pair of rounded, back vowels. The two stops are not in free variation; native speakers do not offer *pan* as a repetition of *ban*. The two vowels are not in free variation; native speakers do not pronounce *tote* with a long vowel nor *toad* with a short. What difference can the phonetician find in the two cases that will lead him to categorize the vowels together and the consonants separately?

The two vowels are in complementary (or mutually exclusive) distribution while the consonants are not. When the [o] precedes a voiced consonant it is longer than when it precedes a voiceless consonant (*poke-pogo, rope-robe, moat-mode,* etc.). The two [k] sounds of *keep cool* constitute a pair of consonants in complementary distribution. In your own articulation you will notice that the [k] of *keep* is farther forward (pre-velar) than the mid-velar [k] of *cool*. When similar categories of phones are in complementary distribution they are allophones of a single phoneme. Perhaps allophones are best thought of as varied forms of one basic sound. The basic sound is modified by its various phonetic contexts. The pre-velar [k] anticipates the front vowel of *keep* and the mid-velar [k] the back vowel of *cool*. The particular allophone of a phoneme to be found in a given context is predictable from the context (e.g. shorter vowels before voiceless consonants, longer vowels before voiced consonants).

This leaves us with [p] and [b] as distinct phonemes. Although they have very similar articulational features they are not allophones of one phoneme because they are not in complementary distribution. Like free variations, like the aspirate and non-aspirate

[p], the sounds [p] and [b] occur in identical phonetic contexts. The difference is that while *pan* is not accepted as a repetition of *ban,* native speakers will accept *nip* with aspirate [p] as a repetition of *nip* with non-aspirate [p].

What part does linguistic meaning play in the procedure for determining phonemes? An off-hand characterization of the phoneme will sometimes describe it as the minimal speech element capable of signalling a difference of meaning. An equally off-hand comparison of our English examples suggests that *pan* and *ban* differ in meaning while the two *nips* do not. Some of us, if pressed to define "a difference of meaning," might translate the phrase as any difference in an auditor's total response. This position is untenable since certain free variants and misplaced allophones will alter meaning in this sense. *Nip* with released [ṗ] strikes me as rather jaunty while the unreleased *nip* is distinctly constricted and tight-lipped. This slight semantic shift would turn up in a sufficiently detailed record of my total responses to the words. However, the difference does not prevent me from recognizing the two pronunciations as the same word. We have no use for total responses. Like Heraclitus' streams and the sounds of speech they probably do not repeat. We want the kind of categorial reaction elicited by the repetition procedure. The informant brings his own understanding of equivalence and difference of meaning to the task. There is no need in this procedure to specify any actual meaning; nor is there any necessity to define the nature of meaning.

In the procedure for the discovery of phonemes there are two principal stages. The categorization of free variants is worked out from direct behavioral study of native speakers. The collection of allophones into a phoneme relies on distributional characteristics within the speech sample and on a judgment of articulational similarity *made by the linguist* rather than a native speaker. This procedure leaves the psychological status of the phoneme in some doubt. If the phonemes are classes of elementary sounds which are equivalent for native speakers, the linguist's judgment of articulational similarity surely ought not to play a part. In English the initial consonant of *hit,* [h], and the final consonant of *sing* [ŋ], are in complementary distribution. Yet, these are not considered to be allophones of a single phoneme because they lack articulational similarity. This lack is a judgment made by the linguist. How can one be sure that the linguist's notion of similarity jibes with that of native speakers? Is this not a point in the procedure where the possibility arises of imposing a system on native speakers instead of discovering the system they unconsciously use?

Why cannot phonemes be discovered by exclusive use of the repetition procedure? Suppose we expand that procedure so as to allow for the comparison of phones occurring in different contexts. If the linguist asks informants for repetitions of *tote* he probably will not hear the long [o:] in these productions and so could not assume that the two [o]'s are categorized together. If the linguist pronounces *tote* in the usual way and then offers *tote* with a long [o:] as a repetition the native speaker may possibly notice the departure from conventional practice and reject the "repetition." On the other hand he is far more likely to accept it than would be the case if the change were phonemic as in *boat* or *toot* or *toad*. Conceivably, then, allophones might be distinguished from phonemes by the comparative willingness of native speakers to accept one sound as a repetition of another. No such procedure has been worked out as yet.

The practical purpose of a phonemic analysis is often the creation of an alphabet for a previously unwritten language. It would be possible to assign a letter to each category of free variants and thereby create a writing system that would differentiate all utterances the native speaker distinguishes. However, a simpler alphabet will accomplish the purpose. Because they are in complementary distribution, a set of allophones can all be assigned the same letter. It is not necessary to assign different letters to the allophones since an allophonic difference is never the only feature differentiating utterances the native speaker finds different in meaning. The long and short [o]'s in English can be written with one symbol because there are no English words distinguished by vowel length. The differences between allophones are always redundant and so need not be represented alphabetically. However, not all categories in complementary distribution can be represented by a single letter. The native speaker of English will balk at using one letter for [h] and [ŋ] because they are too unlike in sound. Using the combined criteria of complementary distribution and articulational similarity, linguists have found that they obtain a set of speech elements for which an alphabet can be designed that will be ac-

ceptable to native speakers. The native speaker can learn his letters
and spell almost at once. This means he finds it natural to use one
symbol for all the allophones of a phoneme and that he recognizes
the allophones as recurrences of one basic form. The feeling of the
native speaker for all allophones is typified by the remark of a
speaker of Spanish who said, with reference to his allophones, [z]
and [s], "Well, [z] is the way [s] sounds in some words." The
ultimate criterion for including allophones within one phoneme is
the acceptability to the native speaker of the assignment of a single
symbol to these allophones for the purpose of spelling his language.

    The letters of an alphabet transcribe with more or less precision
the vowels and consonants in speech, but there are other phonemes
that are not written alphabetically. These may appear as the
printer's space (juncture), or as diacritica in a guide to pronunciation (stress), or as punctuation at the end of a sentence (intonations). In English the utterance *market* is not acceptable as a
repetition of *mark it*. The second utterance involves an external
open juncture (symbolized [+]) which is lacking in the first.
This phonemic difference signals a very great difference in meaning. In English the utterance *pérmit* (stress on the first syllable)
is not a repetition of *permít* (stress on the second syllable). The
former word is a noun, the latter a verb. In many languages
(Chinese, Mixteco, Navaho) there are tone phonemes. In Mixteco,
for instance, a given sequence of segmental phonemes pronounced
with a low tone means *mountain* while the same sequence means
brush when pronounced with a medium tone. A syllable does not
have a fixed lexical meaning unless its tone is specified. The absolute pitch of individual syllables is not a significant feature of English speech, but the contour of relative pitch levels across an utterance is significant. We can change the utterance *Tom is here* from
an exclamation of surprise to a statement of fact by altering the
intonation contour. Pike (184) proposes that all the significant
contrasts of English are accomplished with four levels of relative
pitch. The secondary phonemes (juncture, stress, tone, intonation)
together with the more familiar segmental phonemes comprise the
total significant features of speech.

    Attributes which serve to differentiate phonemes in one lan-
guage may differentiate allophones or even free variants in another language. In English most of our consonants can be paired

as voiced and voiceless phonemes [b], [p]; [d], [t]; [g], [k]; [z], [s]; [v], [f]. Pittman (187) reports that in the Oto language (Oklahoma) these consonant pairs are in free variation. Either member of a pair may indifferently be pronounced in the same context to produce the same utterance. On the other hand, the degree of aspiration of a plosive, which is either an allophonic or free variant attribute in our language, is phonemic in other languages. The length of the vowel was once a phonemic distinction in English and is so today in many languages.

The fact that the phonemes of one community may be the allophones or free variations of another community has important implications for the teaching of languages. Particular problems of speech perception and production can be predicted from a knowledge of the phonology of the old and new languages. The English Language Institute at the University of Michigan, under the direction of Charles Fries (67), has developed a training manual designed to teach English to students who natively speak Spanish and a quite different manual for students whose native language is Chinese. Each manual is based on a comparative study of the two languages concerned. For the Spanish speaker it is important to know that his language does not separate the phones [s] and [z] into separate phonemes. Consequently he will have trouble pronouncing and, especially, hearing the difference between such English words as *rice* and *rise* or *ice* and *eyes*. Chinese speakers, especially those from the Yangtse River area, do not use [l] and [n] initially to contrast words and so confuse *light* with *night* and *line* and *nine*. In general, where two languages give different categorial status to a phonetic distinction problems of perception and pronunciation can be anticipated. Thus the English Language Institute lesson books contain pronunciation drills which contrast the sounds that will be difficult for the group of students for whom the book is designed.

What cues are used by native speakers in categorizing elementary speech sounds? In their definition of the phoneme Bloch and Trager (20) write, "The sounds which constitute a single phoneme are phonetically similar, in the sense of sharing some feature of articulation or some combination of features (resulting in a characteristic auditory effect) absent from the members of all other phonemes." The parenthetically mentioned "characteristic auditory effect" has not been demonstrated for native speakers and is certainly not guaranteed by the linguist's judgment of articulational similarity. The first step toward such a demonstration has been taken in the experimental search for acoustic features characteristic of the various phonemes of English.

Acoustic Attributes of the Phonemes of English. The individual phoneme is a category that is not ordinarily analyzed. One does not experience [p] as a bundle of attributes—plosive articulation, in bilabial position, without the voice. Most speakers know nothing of articulational positions or acoustic formants. The decomposition of phonemes is the peculiar occupation of phoneticians. If the analysis is acoustic they require elaborate physical apparatus to discover their attributes. The analyses of the elementary speech units are, like the analyses of chemistry, the business of specialists using laboratory apparatus.

The most useful visual translation of the acoustic patterns of speech is achieved by the sound spectrograph. This mechanism is a set of filters covering the range of frequencies that are produced with any sizable strength in speech—usually from 20 to about 3500 c.p.s. The first filter might transmit frequencies from 20 to 70 c.p.s., the second frequencies from 70 to 120 c.p.s., the third frequencies from 120 to 170, etc., in units of 50 cycles. The entire range could be covered with about 70 filters. The output of each filter controls the intensity of an individual light. The brightness of this light is proportional to the energy transmitted by the filter. The lights are arranged side by side in order of increasing frequency of filter tuning. Light sensitive paper moves past the battery of lights at a steady rate. On this paper the frequencies appear in vertical arrangement with their relative amplitudes indicated by the degree of darkening of the paper. Passage of time is indicated by horizontal distance along the paper. The 50 cycle filters described here would provide a rather detailed picture of the acoustical properties of a flow of speech. Filters more broadly tuned would yield less detail.

The glottal tone is a practically uniform distribution of power among an evenly spaced series of frequencies up to about 3500 c.p.s. In shaping the mouth and throat to pronounce a vowel we tune these cavities to transmit particular frequency bands. Other frequencies present in the glottal tone will not reach the outer air.

The vocal filters thus impose a pattern on the glottal tone. If the acoustic result is then passed into a spectrograph the pattern will emerge in the black and white of the spectrogram. The spectrograph does not modify the tone it receives because its filters (unlike those of the vocal system) cover the entire frequency range. Covering this range with a series of filters simply makes it possible to distinguish the relative amplitudes of the frequency bands present in the original tone.

Most acoustic studies have dealt with English vowels, and we shall concentrate on these. The decomposition of the vowel is made visible in the spectrogram. Analyses of vowels can be checked by using any of several devices for synthesizing speech. It is even possible to paint the attributes that are hypothesized to be criterial and to have this pattern transformed into sound.

If a single speaker pronounces the vowels of English we find that each vowel can be uniquely characterized by the placement of its first two formants. The formant is a frequency band of concentrated energy in the vowel spectrum; it appears as a dark bar on the spectrogram and is assigned the value of its center frequency. It is common to plot vowel charts with the frequencies of formant 1 on the ordinate and the frequencies of formant 2 on the abscissa. Any single pronunciation of a vowel can then be placed on the chart by the intersection of its values for the two formants.

One's first thought is that these two formants are the criterial attributes of vowel phonemes. While repeated pronunciations of a given vowel may vary in other respects they will retain the same defining values for the first two formants. This appealing solution fails, however, when we examine an adequate sample of the sounds included within any single vowel phoneme. To attempt to describe a phoneme from a single pronunciation of a single speaker is rather like formulating notions of national character from a brief encounter with one foreigner. The potential criteriality of various acoustic attributes for any phoneme can only be discovered from a representative sample of the phonetic events included within the phoneme. That means sampling repeated pronunciations by a variety of speakers of all the allophones of a given phoneme.

A single speaker will vary his pronunciation of the same allophone. Potter and Steinberg (189) asked a trained phonetician to produce repeatedly, all in the same environment, a set of vowel allophones—the vowels of *heed, hid, head, had, hod, hawed, hood, who'd,* and *hud.* There were no exact acoustic duplicates for any given allophone even when only the first two formants were plotted. Each vowel was, however, a well-defined area with no overlap between areas. This result suggests that the single allophone, at least, may be specified in absolute acoustic terms—not, to be sure, by particular frequencies, but by a rather narrowly circumscribed range of frequencies. However, this is still too simple a formulation. Potter and Steinberg had two untrained speakers repeat the allophones. The areas were now larger with one speaker showing some overlap of [e] and [æ].

The second important source of variation is that between speakers. Vowels are pronounced by both soprano and bass and are somehow recognized in both cases. What attributes are preserved in this shift? Joos (118) was one of the first to recognize how great a problem this posed for the acoustic definition of the phonemes. He pointed out that, "The acoustic discrepancies which an adult has to adjust for when listening to a child speaker are nothing short of enormous—they commonly are as much as seven semitones." Comparing vowel charts for several speakers, Joos noted that while the absolute placement of vowels varied, the relative position in the vowel pattern was constant. Joos suggested a completely relativistic definition of the individual vowel. "On first meeting a person the listener hears a few vowel phones, and on the basis of this small but apparently sufficient evidence he swiftly constructs a fairly complete vowel pattern to serve as background (coordinate system) upon which he correctly locates new phones as fast as he hears them." This definition would make the individual vowel a relational category, defined not by absolute acoustic values but by its position relative to the other vowels of the same speaker. It is surely true that knowledge of the total vowel repertoire of a speaker will aid an auditor in the recognition of a particular vowel but, as we shall see, such knowledge is not always necessary.

Two recent studies of vowel allophones nicely complement one another. In one, several speakers were asked to pronounce printed syllables in which different vowels appeared between unchanged consonants. In the other, allophones were synthesized and a group of judges was asked to identify them. The probability of identification for each synthetic vowel was determined. Potter and Steinberg

(189) gave a set of printed syllables to men, women, and children to be pronounced. The variation in the vowels was much greater than that observed for a single speaker. The vowel areas shade into one another. There are normative ranges for each kind of voice with the formants for the adult male voices lowest, the female adults next, and the children highest. This is also the order in which the average fundamental frequencies rise. Examination of the spectrograms indicates potential criteriality in the absolute placement of the formants if this placement is normalized with reference to the fundamental frequency. Thus if a male speaker's formant pattern for [æ] is raised to the degree that his fundamental tone is lower than a female speaker's, and if a child's is correspondingly lowered, the three patterns are nearly identical. It seems possible, then, that vowels might be identified by the placement of the first two formants corrected for the speaker's fundamental tone—all without reference to the remainder of the speaker's vowel repertoire. It remained to determine whether this potential criteriality could actually be utilized.

R. L. Miller (161) used the 100 component harmonic tone synthesizer to produce many of the formant patterns Potter and Steinberg obtained from their subjects. Nine judges were asked to identify the sound as one of eleven vowels identified by symbol and a printed example of its use in a word. Although some of the allophones are different from those used by Potter and Steinberg, the vowel boundaries generally correspond closely with those obtained in the former study. Experimenting with different formant patterns, Miller found some that were invariably identified in the same way and others on which the judges disagreed. These latter transitional patterns correspond to the areas of overlap in the vowel production charts of Potter and Steinberg. The 100 component synthesizer makes it possible to combine a given formant pattern with fundamental tones characteristic of either a man, woman, or child. Miller found that the categorization of the formant pattern changed as the fundamental shifted. As the fundamental was raised the vowel boundaries of the judges rose correspondingly. It seems to be clear, then, that absolute placement of formants 1 and 2, normalized with reference to voice fundamental, is successfully used to identify vowels in isolation.

While formant position is clearly criterial for isolated vowels it is just as clear from Miller's study that no vowel can be identified with a particular pair of values for formants 1 and 2. Even with the correction for fundamental frequency each vowel is a region whose boundaries are not sharp but are shaded into adjoining vowels. Some patterns will always be identified in the same way, but as one moves away from these there is a gradient of probability with one vowel declining and another increasing until another region of certainty is reached.

It is important to recognize that the sharpness of the probability gradients, the clarity with which category boundaries are defined, is a function of the attributes plotted. Suppose one asked subjects to draw lemons and oranges and then plotted only two dimensions of their pictures—color and size. In the resultant space there probably would be a region sometimes intended to be a lemon and sometimes intended to be an orange. If now a third attribute of somewhat lower criteriality—shape, perhaps—were added to the plot there would be fewer points in the resultant space with indeterminate category membership. It is similarly true that addition of a third formant helps with vowel identification (particularly for the vowel of *bird*). Miller, furthermore, found the comparative intensities of the first two formants to be a criterial attribute. Scientists at the Haskins Laboratory (Cooper, De Lattre, Liberman, Borst, and Gerstman) have undertaken a program to rank order the cues to phoneme identification. It may be that when this work is complete the vowels will have become certain rather than probabilistic categories.

Studies of the acoustic character of English vowels usually elicit pronunciations by showing the subjects a printed English word in which the desired vowel occurs. Thus for the vowel [æ] subjects might be asked to pronounce *gag*. In repeated pronunciations the experimenter obtains a range of free variants. He can examine this range of acoustic attributes characteristic of the category of free variants acceptable as [æ] in the context "g–g." He cannot discover, from such data, the attributes of the English vowel phoneme because the vowel of *gag* is only one allophone of this phoneme. The [æ] of "bad" sounds quite unlike the [æ] of *"gag"* and certainly has different acoustic properties. The acoustic research so far discussed has been limited to the study of single allophones of English vowel phonemes. To summarize, the allophone is a category of free variants mutually substitutable in given contexts and in complementary distribution with other categories of free variants to which it shows some articulational similarity. Acoustic specification of a phoneme can only be accomplished by sampling all of its member allophones. We may be sure that it will be more difficult to identify the criterial acoustic attributes of phonemes than it has been to identify these attributes for allophones.

In recent years there has been an imaginative attempt to specify the criterial attributes of phonemes without reference to specific formant frequencies: the work of Jakobson, Fant, and Halle, set forth in *Preliminaries to Speech Analysis* (113). Impressed with the binary computer as an analogue to the human nervous system, these authors propose that any phoneme can be uniquely characterized with a set of two-value attributes. An attempt has been made to describe these "distinctive features" in both acoustic and articulational terms. For example, the Grave-Acute feature has reference acoustically to predominance of one-half of the spectrum over the other. If the higher frequencies dominate the feature is acute; where the lower frequencies dominate it is grave. In articulational terms the grave feature is generated by a larger or less comparted mouth cavity, while the acute feature originates in a smaller or more divided cavity. The English phonemes /u/, /o/, and /f/ are grave, and /i/, /e/, and /s/ are acute. The features Vocalic-Non-vocalic, Consonantal-Non-consonantal, Compact-Diffuse, Grave-Acute, Flat-Plain, Nasal-Oral, Tense-Lax, Continuant-Interrupted, and Strident-Mellow have been used to describe the phonemes of English. Each phoneme appears as a bundle of concurrent features. Many of these features are derived from more traditional articulational and acoustic studies. The idea that they all operate in a binary fashion is an added elegance. As yet this exciting proposal has not been tested widely enough to tell whether it will solve the problem of phoneme specification.

The allophone and phoneme are the elementary categories of speech. Included within one allophone are speech sounds that prove to be mutually substitutable in given phonetic contexts. Included within one phoneme are allophones that the native speaker finds it natural to spell with the same letter. Acoustic analysis of the vowel allophones of English is advanced to the point where several of the more criterial attributes are known. The allophones are still probabilistic categories but this may be a result of incomplete analysis. It is possible that each allophone will be uniquely characterized by the conjunction of a large number of attributes. Acoustic analyses have only begun to sample the population of sounds included in the phonemes of English. It is very likely that these phonemes will not all be the same kind of category. There may be simple conjunctive cases. There may also be probabilistic and disjunctive categories. Although the job of acoustic analysis is incomplete one very important point has been established and should be reiterated. All known speech is susceptible of analysis into a small number of recurrent categories.

Functional Attributes of the Phonemes of English. When a subject is asked to identify a set of vowels all of which appear in the same phonetic context (e.g. *hid, hud, hod*) he has only the acoustic attributes of the vowels to guide him. Ordinarily, however, our recognition of a speech sound is facilitated by the context in which it occurs. If the acoustic attributes do not enable us to choose between several possible vowels the context may render one of them more probable than the others. The probability of finding one phoneme and no other in a given context describes the potential criteriality of the context for that phoneme. For some contexts in a language there are always some phonemes so improbable that the linguist has called them "impossible." If we treat these combinations as one extreme on a continuum of probabilities of occurrence, it is possible to combine the descriptive linguist's work on phonemic structure with the information theorist's work on transition probabilities. Both of these have described functional attributes of specific sounds.

No system of speech makes use of all possible phoneme combinations in the manufacture of words and morphemes. No orthography puts its symbols together in all possible ways. There are always combinations that do not occur. Benjamin Whorf (247) has constructed a formula describing phoneme combinations that are "possible" in the English monosyllabic word. The formula allows for a great variety of English monosyllables, but it also clearly rules out many conceivable possibilities. There is, for instance, no provision for syllables beginning with /zr/, /sr/, /vd/, or /ŋ/ because such syllables do not occur in English.

What is the status of the combinations that are not allowed? Whorf rules out any suggestion that the prohibited combinations are humanly unpronounceable with data showing that most of the things English will not allow are practiced in some language or other. In addition, he calls attention to the "unspeakable" combinations that we do manage—*sixths, glimpsed,* and the like. It seems that the formula summarizes cultural practice rather than human necessity.

However, Whorf writes as if there were a kind of necessity in this practice. Of course this necessity would be cultural rather than human. Whorf sees an imperative in the formula. "A new monosyllable turned out, say, by Walter Winchell or by a plugging adman concocting a name for a new breakfast mush, is struck from this mold as surely as if I pulled the lever and the stamp came down on his brain." Whorf allows that Winchell might coin the word *thrub,* since it is tolerable by the formula, but that Winchell will not coin the word *srub.* There is then a behavioral disposition created by familiarity with the combinational possibility structure of a set of phonemes or letters. We may suppose that there is also a perceptual disposition to hear "possible" morphemes and words.

The linguistic distinction between possible and impossible phoneme combinations can profitably be displaced by a continuum of more or less probable combinations. Whorf, at least, accomplished the "impossible" when he wrote *srub* and now we have done it too. I asked thirty native speakers of American English to invent new one-syllable English words. Most of these inventions were "possible," according to the Whorf formula, but two, *Bz* and *Zl,* were not. An "impossible" word is occasionally created in the comic strips. My favorite example appears in Al Capp's *Li'l Abner.* There is a man in this strip who brings catastrophe wherever he goes. Capp draws him with a miniature cloud over his head, a cloud that follows him about dripping a perpetual rain. This character is an outcast. People flee at his approach. Capp has aptly named him *Joe Btfsplk. Joe* for the pitiable, human aspect; *Btfsplk* for the unspeakable fate he suffers. When phoneme combinations fall below a certain level of probability they fall under the linguist's ban as "impossible." However, such combinations are more accurately described as highly improbable.

Shannon and Weaver (205) have introduced the "transition probability" in their book on the mathematical theory of communication. Any sequence of English letters (or phonemes) is followed by a variety of letters (or phonemes) with varying frequencies in

English usage. The probability of various transitions can be calculated. For convenience of presentation, in describing transition probabilities we will use English letters rather than phonemes as our units. What will be said of letters applies also to phonemes.

Consider the letter T. Suppose we know all the letters that follow *T* in written English and know also their relative frequencies of occurrence. We might write each letter on slips of paper, making the number of slips for a letter proportional to the frequency with which the letter follows *T*. Then if we were to add a second letter to follow *T* by drawing at random from the slips of paper we should be likely to draw *H*, less likely to draw *R*, and most unlikely to draw *P, B, F, V, Z, M, N*, etc. Suppose that *H* is drawn, we might then use this new letter as context and again draw a letter to follow. The drawing would, of course, be made from a new collection of slips representing the relative frequencies with which *H* is followed by various letters in written English. Proceeding in this way with each successive letter we should construct a second order approximation to English which is a sequence of letters built on the transition probabilities for successive sequences of one letter.

As the amount of antecedent context used increases, one speaks of third order, fourth order, nth order approximations to English. A first order approximation would be constructed by drawing letters and the printer's *space* according to their relative frequencies in ordinary text. The zero order approximation is constructed by drawing at random from the letters and space with no allowance for the relative frequencies of the language.

It would be prohibitively laborious to make all the tabulations necessary to construct these various orders. The expedient used relies on the behavioral disposition created in a person by his acquaintance with the combinational probability structure of his native language. Several people cooperate to build the sequence a letter at a time. For a third order approximation one person would be asked to add a letter to the first two. The next person would be given only the last two and would again add a third. Each person, as a speaker of English, is presumed to choose in accordance with the transition probabilities of the language.

A variation on the method for determining transition probabilities is the method by which context probabilities can be determined. A subject is provided with surrounding context rather than with antecedent context alone and he is asked to provide as many letters as are required to fill the context. Thus in C O N − E X T the letter *T* will have a very high probability of occurrence in English while all other letters will have a very low probability. Speakers of English might be expected to reveal their knowledge of the language's combinational probability structure in the responses they would make with this procedure. This same knowledge should affect the perception of speech whenever the audible pattern is not perfectly unambiguous.

The effect of expectancies (derived from experience with English) on the identification of syllables has been demonstrated in an experiment by Brown and Hildum (27). As stimulus materials they used ten sets of syllable triplets. These appear in Table 1.* Within a triplet-set all three syllables have the same vowel and final consonant but the three have different initial consonant clusters. One syllable begins with an initial cluster that results in an *English word* (e.g. /θrol/ or *thrall*). Another syllable begins with a cluster that is possible (Jones [119]) in initial position in English but which does not yield a conventional word (e.g. /prol/). This is called, in Table 1, an *English not-word*. A third syllable begins with a cluster that never occupies initial position in English (e.g. /zdrol/). This is called a *not-English syllable*. In short, a triplet-set is constructed by combining a particular −VC context with initial consonant clusters that are not equally probable in English.

---

*Adapted here by permission of *Language*.

TABLE 1. THREE KINDS OF SYLLABLES

English Words	English Not-Words	Not-English Syllables
/θrol/	/prol/	/zdrol/
/skeyn/	/kleyn/	/pweyn/
/sluwp/	/θruwp/	/pšuwp/
/kliyk/	/triyk/	/šliyk/
/trays/	/skays/	/fways/
/preyt/	/dreyt/	/sreyt/
/θrowv/	/slowv/	/vmowv/
/glib/	/spib/	/tlib/
/kliyv/	/θriyv/	/gniyv/
/spuwf/	/gluwf/	/čluwf/

All subjects in the experiment were native speakers of English. Group I consisted of Harvard undergraduates who had never studied any aspect of descriptive linguistics. Group II consisted of very advanced students of linguistics, most of whom were acquainted with at least one non-Indo-European language.

The groups heard the thirty syllables pronounced in a random order and under less than perfect acoustic conditions. Group I had been told that it would hear thirty English monosyllabic words. They were warned that the words were so uncommon that no one could be expected to recognize more than a very few of them. Group II had been told that it would hear thirty syllables made up of English phonemes but that not all of the syllables were conventional English words. By virtue of both training and instructions, then, Group I should have brought to the task expectancies derived from English phonology whereas Group II should have had less precise expectancies.

With the ten conventional English words Group I made correct identifications about 70 per cent of the time. With the *English not-words* Group I did much less well, making only about 37 per cent correct identifications. With the *not-English words* the performance of Group I fell to only 10 per cent correct identifications. It appears that syllable identification is a function of expectancies as well as stimuli. When the stimuli are not perfectly clear, as in the present experiment, the expectancy is very important. So long as the expectancies of Group I were appropriate to the syllables there were many correct identifications. When the expectancies became misleading, with the *not-English syllables,* there were very few correct identifications.

Analysis was also made of the erroneous responses of Group I. In general, when these subjects made a mistake they were likely to think the syllable heard was a conventional English word. This is, of course, in line with the expectancies created by their experimental instructions. The mistakes varied in degree, in the number of phonemes changed by comparison with the syllable actually pronounced. When the mistake was a big one, involving two or more phonemes, the resultant identification was almost invariably a conventional English word. However, when the mistake was minimal, a single phoneme, the resultant identification was almost as likely to be not a word as to be a word. It would seem that when the listener strayed by as much as two phonemes from the presented stimulus he was following the lure of a conventional word. With a minimal error he seems to have been sufficiently confident of what he has heard to break with the expectation of a word.

Finally the mistakes involving substitution of one phoneme for another were analyzed in terms of the number of distinctive features changed by comparison with the original phoneme. These errors were usually minimal, involving a change in only one distinctive feature (e.g. /p/ to /t/ or /k/). Changes of two features were much less common and changes of three features still less common. This result suggests that a distinctive-feature analysis of English phonemes correctly represents their relative similarity for the ear of a native speaker. Mistakes of two or more features almost invariably resulted in a conventional English word. A change of only one feature resulted in an identification that was not a word more often than in an identification that was a word. This result conforms to the rubric proposed in the last paragraph; the probability that a mistake will be a word increases as the magnitude of the perceptual mistake increases. With an error of only one feature in one phoneme the identification is more often not a word. This conforms to the real character of the syllable triplets, two-thirds of which are not words.

In summary, when subjects uninstructed in linguistics (Group I) hear speech that they expect to be in their native language their perceptual identifications are directed by their knowledge of sequential probabilities in the language as well as by the acoustic stimulus. Expectancies appropriate to the material presented result in correct identifications. Misleading expectancies result in erroneous identifications. Minimal errors (changes of one phoneme and of one feature within a phoneme) are most common. More serious errors are correspondingly less common. As the magnitude of the error increases, its probability of occurrence (in a set of syllables supposed to be English words) also increases. It is as though the identification is a joint product of expectancy and stimulus. Where the one is weak the other must be strong.

The preceding interpretation of the results for Group I is consistent with all that we know about phonology, auditory perception, and the statistical structure of language and, therefore, seems plausible. However, the data for Group I alone do not exclude an alternative explanation that is equally consistent with what is known about speech. Perhaps the experimenter, a native speaker of English, unintentionally pronounced the improbable sound combinations with less clarity or force than the probable combinations. His solemn vow that he did not do so is unimpressive when set against the known power of the phonological mold to twist men's tongues. It would be nice to know that all the syllables were equally identifiable for an unacculturated listener. This would provide a base line of syllable identifiability with expectancies exerting no systematic effect. We do not have such a base line but we do have in Group II, listeners whose perceptual habits should be less parochial than those of Group I, listeners who are somewhat culture-free as a result of linguistic training and special instructions. With the *English words,* which both groups expected, Groups I and II made identical scores. This fact suggests that their auditory acuity was about the same. On *English not-words* Group II had nearly four times as many correct identifications as did Group I and on *not-English words* their percentage was more than eleven times as great. Whatever the relative audibility of the syllables may have been it was the same for both groups. The fact that the group trained and instructed to listen for improbable combinations recognized many more of such combinations than did Group I suggests that the latter was indeed led astray by expectancies derived from its experience of English. Analysis of the errors of Group II reveals further consequences of the weaker English expectancies. The erroneous identifications of Group II were much less likely to be words than were the mistakes of Group I. This likelihood is not related to the magnitude of the mistake as in Group I. Group II is like Group I in that the number of mistakes is inversely related to the magnitude of the mistake. It is as though the identifications of Group II were largely determined by the stimuli. Since they had been set to expect just about anything expectancy played little part in their identifications.

One of the "impossible" initial consonant clusters used in this study yielded atypical results. The cluster [šl] which appears in /šliyk/ (*shleek*) was recognized more often than the other impossible initial clusters. It is the authors' guess that this cluster ought not to be classified with those that are impossible in English. Probably /šliyk/ should be considered an *English not-word* rather than a *not-English syllable.* The Yiddish word *schlemiel* is fairly often heard in American English speech (especially among college students). If the stimulus materials had included the cluster /šm/, which is also described as one that does not occur initially in English (Jones [119]), we believe that it would have proved to be even more advanced than [šl] in the direction of familiar English. Again there are several common Yiddish words and also, of course, Al Capp's *shmoo.* Indeed, this initial cluster seems to have picked up a semantic. It is irreverent, a kind of jocular slur. I recently heard a conversation in which one colleague said, "I don't care about your theory, I've got data." The other replied, "Data-shmata, I like my theory." From the experimental results with /šl/ it seems likely that changes in the phonology of a language may be detected in psychological studies of syllable identification.

Knowledge of combinational probabilities must be a great help in listening to ordinary speech. When the speech is really English the most probable guess will most probably be correct. The potential criteriality of each context-attribute for a phoneme is the probability of finding the particular phoneme and no other in that context. The surrounding context /sk–æp/ predicts /r/ almost perfectly. The context /t–n/ has a lower potential criteriality for a whole group of vowels since we have the words *ten, tin, tan, ton, tune, tone, teen.* The context has some criteriality, however, since no consonant is likely to appear in the vacant position.

Phonetic context must ordinarily be an important factor in the identification of phonemes. Why, then, worry about the acoustic attributes of phonemes in isolation? The acoustic experiment is reminiscent of the visually reduced situations in which depth perception has sometimes been studied. Only when such monocular cues as superposition and relative size have been eliminated can the contribution of binocular disparity be studied. The acoustic experiments could be justified on the ground that their simplifications are essential if the role of the stimulus is to be determined. There is at least one very important reason for determining this role. To use contextual attributes in the identification of phonemes one must have learned something about the probabilities of various phonemic sequences. Probabilities cannot be learned until recurrences can be recognized. To learn the frequency with which a sequence occurs the sequence must be identified and distinguished from other sequences. It follows that the acoustic attributes of speech have priority over the contextual. The child must learn them first.

In ordinary conversation, however, the functional attributes are important and may serve to convert some phonemes from probabilistic to certain categories. If the acoustic attributes admit of several alternative categorizations the functional attributes are likely to provide a basis for choosing between these interpretations. In the stream of speech the functional and acoustic combine to define phonemes and, in defining phonemes, they define the larger reference-making utterances.

Reference-Making Utterances

The reference-making utterance is more easily defined by example than by principle. The word *pail* has a referent but its constituent phones do not. Words, sentences, and paragraphs are all likely to have referents as are the linguist's morphemes and phrases. Allophones, phonemes, distinctive features, and phones will not have referents. There is no semantic common denominator contributed by /p/ to *pull, pig,* and *up.* These few examples will bring us to an understanding about the reference-making utterance that is adequate for present purposes.

Linguistic analysis of meaningful units of speech is not as advanced as the analysis of speech elements. The sentence and paragraph are conventional units in some written languages but are not used in descriptive linguistics. The word has long defied precise definition. Of the units used by the linguist the morpheme is most important and nearest a clear operational definition. The postulates of morphemics are too involved and controversial to be discussed in detail but the main points can be described in a few words.

The morpheme is a unit reminiscent of the word but not to be identified with it any more closely than the phoneme is to be identified with the letter of the alphabet. The morpheme is the minimal semantic unit. The free morpheme can occur alone in the language. Speakers will sometimes pause after a free morpheme before continuing their discourse. The free morpheme is a word not susceptible of analysis into smaller semantic units. The words *dog, house,* and *man* are all free morphemes. However, a plural form like *dogs* is not a single morpheme word as it analyzes into the free form *dog* and the bound form -*s*. A bound form like -*s* never occurs in isolation but it has a semantic content—in this case the idea of plurality.

Like phonemes, meaningful utterances have two kinds of attributes. Formal acoustic attributes include the segmental phonemes, the allophones, and the secondary phonemes—the whole substance of the utterance. Functional attributes are the phonemic contexts in which an utterance may occur. The potential criteriality of such a functional attribute is the probability of utterance occurrence in a given context. These two kinds of attributes are described below.

Acoustic Attributes of Reference-Making Utterances. The first principle of systematic morphemics (Nida [169]) is the statement that forms which possess a common semantic distinctiveness and an identical form in all their occurrences constitute a single morpheme. Identical form means the same phonemes in the same sequence (not necessarily contiguous), for phonemes are the attributes of morphemes and of all meaningful utterances. The individual morpheme, as the word or phrase, is specified by the conjunction of particular phonemes in a particular sequence. The category can be changed by altering a phoneme or disturbing the sequence.

It is a little difficult to accept the phoneme as an attribute. We have grown accustomed to it in the role of category. The internal complexity of the phoneme is now so clearly in mind that it is difficult to accord it the simplicity of an attribute. There is, of course, quite as much complexity in such familiar attributes as the color red, the form of the circle, the tactile experience of hardness. To be categorized as red a color must fall within critical ranges on the dimensions of hue, brightness, and saturation. Similarly an English consonant must satisfy conditions of formant placement and comparative intensity to be classified as /p/. As attributes of apples and of *apples* redness and /p/ lose their internal differentiation. The morpheme, unlike the phoneme, is a category that is analyzed by the native speaker, at any rate by the literate native speaker of a language with a syllabic or alphabetic writing.

There is also a potential criteriality in the particular allophone form assumed by a phoneme. Consider the English morphemes *need* and *neat*. These two are distinguishable in speech by their distinct final consonants—a phonemic difference. In addition the vowels are different. Both are allophones of /i/ but the [i] of *need* is more prolonged than that of *neat*. The distinction is allophonic and therefore predictable from phonetic context. The long vowel always precedes a voiced consonant and the short vowel a voiceless consonant. It follows that any two words for which vowel length is a potentially criterial attribute are also distinguished by their final consonants. The consonants are predictable from vowels. However, the converse is not true. There are pairs of words distinguished by the consonants /d/ and /t/ which are not distinguished by vowel length (e.g. *dill-till, drain-train*). We don't know what use is actually made of such allophonic variations in the identification of morphemes. It seems likely, however, that this feature would be used where the final consonants were not clearly produced and the context gave no cue.

Functional Attributes of Reference-Making Utterances. Phonemic equivalence does not guarantee that two utterances will have the same meaning. The English suffix *-er* in *runner, dancer,* and *teacher* has not the same meaning as the *-er* of *taller, older,* and *stronger.* The former is used to designate the performer of an action; the latter designates a higher degree of some quality. The difference of meaning that is not phonemically signalled is conveyed by functional attributes. The agentive *-er* is affixed to verbs while the comparative *-er* is attached to adjectives. This systematic difference in context keeps the meaning clear. The sequence *-er,* appearing in isolation, is ambiguous.

There are also words in English that are phonemically identical but distinct in meaning. Phonemic equivalence is not, of course, the same as identical spelling. Since stress is not represented in conventional print such pairs as *permít* and *pérmit, présent* and *presént* look alike. However, they differ in the stress phoneme. The word *board* as in *board of wood* is a true homophone of *bored* as in *bored with psycholinguistics.* These two are spelled differently, but the difference between *board of wood* and *board of directors* is not marked in writing or in phonemic sequence. The two meanings have been distinguished by placing each word in a highly criterial context. Those are different boards that are likely to occur in the phrases *board of wood, board of directors,* and *bored with psycholinguistics.* The functional attributes sort out different meanings for phonemically identical words.

Transition probabilities can be computed for meaningful utterances by a method like that used with phonemes. One can test any fraction of a context as a functional attribute of a morpheme, word, or phrase. The potential criteriality of the context corresponds to the probability of finding one particular form in the context. Thus the sentence frame *Now is the time for all good————to come to the aid of the party* is so criterial for *men* that the acoustic cues are really redundant. When utterances have identical acoustic attributes but different meanings the importance of the functional cues is especially clear. More usually, however, functional attributes join with acoustic cues to identify the utterance.

Higher Order Categories: Parts of Speech

If we were to record a very large sample of English speech we should find that there are some morphemes or words that occur in the same context. In the linguistic frame *The————is good* we might find *book, tree, house, speech,* and many other words. Appearance in a given linguistic frame provides a basis for categorizing together a collection of words.

Fries (67) uses the linguistic frame to define four large functional classes which correspond roughly to the conventional parts of speech—noun, verb, adjective, and adverb. Beginning with a large sample of telephone conversations he finds many words in the frame *The————is/was good.* All of these are nouns. Fries goes on to define Form Class 1 as "a body of words that belong to the same part of speech by virtue of the fact that they can all fill this particular position." It is not necessary to find a word in this context to identify it as a member of Form Class 1. A native speaker of English can judge whether any English word is a possible entry in this test frame. This possibility has nothing to do with semantic suitability but rather with grammatical acceptability. Thus the utterance *The* devil *is good,* is perverse in sentiment but quite possible grammatically.

The functional definition of the part of speech is, in some ways, an improvement on the older semantic definitions. According to these, the noun, for instance, is the name of a person, place, or thing. Persons and places can be reliably identified but *thing* is clearly a word for whatever is neither person nor place and yet a noun. It is difficult to find thing attributes in virtue and truth yet both are nouns. On the other hand, as Fries notes, *blue* is the name of a color but is not a noun in the phrase *a blue tie*. Functional rather than semantic attributes seem to provide the ultimate criteria for recognizing English parts of speech. It is even doubtful whether semantic common denominators exist for the parts of speech.*

Functional classes sometimes have common stimulus attributes— a characteristic suffix or vowel. In English, however, nouns have no distinctive phonemes nor have verbs, adjectives, or adverbs. With regard to stimulus attributes these are elaborately disjunctive categories. Some nouns end with *-al* (*arrival, refusal,* etc.); others with *-ure* (*departure, failure,* etc.); others with *-ance* (*acceptance, acquaintance,* etc.) and there are many other common noun suffixes. In addition, there exist countless nouns that exhibit no characteristic suffixes—*house, man,* etc.

Both Harris (88) and Fries (68) think of word classes in terms of what can and cannot happen in the word combinations of a language. This is again a possibility-impossibility dichotomy, like that found in Whorf's formula of English phoneme combinations. It may again be desirable to substitute a probability continuum for the linguist's dichotomy. The English speaker's judgment that *very* cannot possibly fill the gap in *The————is good* may derive from the very low frequency of such an occurrence. Members of a part of speech may be words that attain to a certain minimal probability of occurrence in a given language frame. I think, however, that something a little different is involved in these judgments of grammatical possibility or impossibility that define the parts of speech. The recognition that *The* devil *is good* constitutes a possible English utterance probably does not depend on actual experience of this utterance. The judgment would surely be made even if the word *devil* had never been heard in that frame. *Devil* will have been heard in such frames as *The————is bad,* or *The————visited them.* In these frames such words as *man,*

---

*An empirical study of the semantics of the English parts of speech is described in Chapter VII of this book.

woman, dog, mayor, etc. have also appeared. The general functional equivalence of *devil, man, woman, dog,* and *mayor* would lead one to extend this equivalence to the frame *The————is good.* If *man, woman, dog,* and *mayor* have actually been heard in this frame then it will be consistent to believe that *devil* is acceptable in the same position. I might write *The* very *is good* one hundred times and still it would not seem acceptable in the sense that *The devil is good* is acceptable. That is surely because *very* is organized into one functional class and *devil* into another on the basis of my total experience of the language rather than from a direct counting of occurrences in a particular sentence. The frame sentence is a useful test for part-of-speech membership but the judgment of possibility or impossibility on which the test depends is not founded simply on experience of the test sentence but on functional categories abstracted from total experience with the combinational probabilities of the language.

The traditional parts of speech are not the only higher order functional categories. Utilizing the notion of contextual probabilities it would be possible to categorize words or morphemes in infinitely various ways. One could put together all the words satisfying a particular level of probability for any set of contexts. In most cases these classes would have no semantic value for the native speaker. In other cases one might find that he had functionally isolated the names of living creatures or perhaps the class of proper nouns or the class of verbs of action or verbs of being. I would expect all such semantic categories to be susceptible of functional definition by the method of contextual probabilities. Indeed, I think functional categories are suggested to us by semantic categories. Proper nouns are names of identity categories. Living creatures have certain attributes separating them from non-living objects. Even the parts of speech may have begun as semantic classes, now grown fuzzy and inconsistent through historical change to the point where semantic attributes are only probabilistic in their association with the form classes.

Summary

All human speech can be analyzed into a set of distinctive sound elements—the phonemes. The descriptive linguist undertakes to dis-

cover the phonemic distinctions of a given language from the behavior of native speakers of that language. For this purpose he
needs, in the first place, a system of phonetic transcription that
records all of the conceivably distinctive features of the native
speech. It is not useful to record all of the attributes of speech
because, in these terms, each utterance would be unique. Phonemes
are discovered from a phonetically transcribed collection of utterances by 1) grouping together the free variants—phones that were
transcribed as distinct but are accepted by native speakers as
"repetitions" of one another; 2) provisionally grouping together
those classes of free variants that have a high degree of articulational similarity; 3) keeping together those classes that are in complementary distribution and separating those that are not. The
result is a categorization of elementary sounds which is the functioning categorization for native speakers; in short the phonemes.

Native speakers identify their phonemes by acoustic and functional attributes. The search for the acoustic invariants of English
vowels is still in progress but it is already clear that these are not
formants at particular frequencies. They may be relations between
formants. The identification in the laboratory of isolated vowels is
much harder for the speaker of English than the everyday identification of vowels in context for the reason that context makes
one phoneme more probable than another. Very improbable sequences are likely to be mistakenly identified even under mod-
erately good acoustic circumstances.

Phonemes do not make reference. The larger units of speech
that do make reference—the morpheme, word, and phrase—have
phonemes for their attributes. At a still higher level of description
words or morphemes are grouped into classes of syntactical equivalents. For some of these classes there are roughly coordinate semantic categories.

chapter ii # The History of Writing and
a Dispute About Reading

T HE BEGINNINGS OF speech are lost in pre-history but the alphabet is a historical invention. For this reason it is customary to say that speech is a more ancient form of language than is writing. This conclusion is not so certain if writing is understood to include the systems that preceded the alphabet. These systems were composed of characters that made direct reference to objects, persons, and events. The individual symbol had a semantic rather than a phonetic value. There is no way of knowing whether speech is older than these reference-making characters, for while ancient inscriptions are sometimes preserved, speech is not. Curiously enough all of this history and pre-history is quite intimately connected with a present-day dispute about the proper way to teach American children to read. It has been said that contemporary methods of teaching reading deprive children of the great advantages that first accrued to mankind with the invention of the alphabet. This chapter begins with an explanation of these advantages and proceeds to a discussion of the reading controversy.

A Psychological History of Writing

Paleolithic man, whose chipped stone implements have been found in various parts of Europe, was also paleographic man whose drawings have been found in the Altamira caves of Spain and in caves on the banks of the Dordogne in France. There is no direct evidence of speech during this period—somewhere between 35,000 and 15,000 B.C. However, it may also be inappropriate to speak of the cave pictures as writing. There is no way of knowing for what purpose they were produced—whether with magical, aesthetic, or communicative intent.

The inclination to call the cave pictures writings stems from the fact that they are significant markings. They have a reference. They stand for something. This is true of modern writing. However, a man as remote from our time as we are from the Paleolithic might not recognize our writing as significant and certainly would not immediately be able to discover its meanings. We, however, can decipher some of the Paleolithic scratchings because they are representational. Several of the pictures were accidentally found by children playing in the caves. While they cannot have identified the pictures they saw as bison, as mammoth, or saber tooth tiger, they knew certainly that they were confronted with animals.

Dating from later periods (though still long before the Christian era) are the pictograms or representational writings found in Egypt, Scandinavia, China, America, and most of the rest of the world. These are often very numerous. We can decipher many of them at once. The sun ☿ the moon ☽ and man ⚣ are unmistakable.

The pictogram is entirely independent of speech. It stands in direct relation to a class of non-linguistic objects or events. The pictogram has a semantic rather than a phonetic value. In addition, it is representational. The symbol manifests one or more of the criterial attributes of the signified non-linguistic referent. Sketches of the sun and moon lack the luminosity of their originals but preserve their contours. In our writing today we have some symbols that are semantic but not representational. The number 5, for instance, stands directly for an idea but does not represent that idea. We have seen 5 so often that we may have come to think of it as having a phonetic value. But this is not the case. The number 5 can be pronounced *fünf* or *cinq* or *cinque* as well as *five*. The word *five* is a phonetic symbol; the number 5 is semantic but not representational, the mark $\cancel{||||}$ is both semantic and representational.

The Economy of Representation. It would seem to be desirable for a semantic symbol to be representational since a picture is more easily understood than an arbitrary mark. If the first writings had been arbitrarily associated with their referents they might never have been deciphered. At best a great deal of tiresome trial and error would have had to precede accurate comprehension. By contrast, it is sometimes claimed, the representational symbol can be understood at once by everyone. Probably this statement exaggerates the psychological economy of representation. The drawing $\uparrow$ is not, after all, very much like a man. It does not have the color, size, weight or tridimensionality of a human being; there is only a rough equivalence of relationship between the lines of the figure and the trunk and limbs of a man. Can we be sure that we would know at once the meaning of this picture if we had not learned that stick figures conventionally preserve skeletal relations while neglecting other characteristics? Very likely it is necessary to learn by experience what kinds of attributes are likely to be represented in symbols of this kind. Even if such experience is necessary, however, the representational symbol has an advantage over the arbitrary symbol. Once we have seen several stick figures or contour drawings we should be able to decipher, on sight, indefinite numbers of new drawings constructed on the same principles.

A symbol cannot represent its meaning to someone who has no experience with the thing signified. The writer and his reader must see the same world in the same way. When man was creating writing he was probably living in a group resembling the simpler preliterate societies of today. Characteristically, these small primitive groups are very limited in geographic range, which means that these people, existing in mutual dependence, see the same flora and fauna and the same caves, storms, and stars. Furthermore, it is characteristic of such a society to be relatively lacking in social differentiation. To be sure we always find age and sex roles, are likely to find warriors, hunters, chiefs, and the like but there will be no such elaborate differentiation as that of the modern state which subdivides endlessly into occupations and professions. A variety of social positions and roles means a variety of special experiences. Those in our society who know about cyclotrons may not know about the unities of dramatic action, the instrument panel of a jet plane, or the difference between cool and hot jazz. To the degree that social roles are uniform people may be expected to have common experience and to categorize this experience in similar fashion. If we extrapolate these characteristics of geographic and social homogeneity back in time to the earliest societies we must attribute a homogeneity of experience to the people within any one society. The simplest rule of semantics for such a society would be that of linking an object with a representation of itself. Where everyone operated with the same non-linguistic categories it would be possible to construct symbols immediately recognizable to everyone who had learned a few simple conventions of symbol construction.

Quite naturally, there are many ancient pictograms that we cannot decipher today on sight. When we don't have the referent category a symbol cannot represent it to us. As the early societies expanded and differentiated there must have been increasing numbers of people who were in this same position with respect to many of the symbols of their society. Included in the Egyptian hieroglyphics are pictures of religious ceremonies that probably could not be understood by any but the priestly class familiar with the rites pictured. The word *hieroglyphic* means, of course, sacred writings. Some of the ancient pictograms of animals may have had meaning only for hunters while pictograms of special tools may not have been decipherable to any but the professional users of the tools. As the ancient societies became increasingly complex it must have been increasingly difficult to employ symbols that represented their meanings to everyone.

Many of the ancient drawings are mistakenly deciphered by naïve interpreters today, not because the object represented is unfamiliar but because the symbol relies on a cognitive association we do not make. What is a picture of a white bird in flight likely to mean? My informants, thinking of a dove, generally reply, "Peace." The American Indians who used this drawing were not acquainted with Noah's dove and the dove of peace. To them the bird meant haste. Peace was, of course, represented by a pipe. The reference for such drawings is not the thing pictured but an idea associated with that thing. Drawings of this type are conventionally called ideograms rather than pictograms.

The ideogram is a useful device for symbolizing abstract ideas that cannot be pictured. One cannot draw haste or peace or life or death or soul. For soul the Egyptian drew a bird with the head of a man. Presumably the bird is suggestive of flight and the human head makes this flight non-avian. Now that we know its translation this drawing seems apt but it is unlikely that we should have hit upon the translation without help. Homogeneity of experience should make for common mental associations, and so it may be true that the ideograms were more easily understood in the past than they are today. Probably, however, there was less certainty about these representations of abstract ideas than about the concrete pictograms.

The expanding size and complexity of ancient societies and the expanding repertory of abstract ideas must have limited the usefulness of representational writings. We may guess that the communication economy involved in a clearly recognizable picture was not very great in the ancient Oriental writings—Sumerian, Egyptian, Hittite, and Chinese. There was a clear tendency for some symbols to become increasingly schematic and unlike their referents. It is believed that the letters of the Roman alphabet are such "fallen away" representations. Details tended to disappear or, if they survived, to be "sharpened." The drawing of a bird might lose all detail until there was only a single curve, retained and simplified from the original curve of the wing. This end product would appear to be a perfectly arbitrary designation for a bird. The fact that this schematization process was tolerated implies that the ancient societies did not rely on the representation being immediately recognized. Probably the characters had to be learned as conventional designators. The business of learning to write must have been onerous. There could be as many characters as there were ideas and all these to be learned by rote. A new economy was needed to replace the waning economy of representation. The new economy that developed involved relating writing to speech.

The Phonetic Principle. Nothing direct or certain is known about the origins of speech. Since writing began as representation there are many who believe that our other methods of communication must have started in the same way. Gesture may have begun as the imitation of non-muscular movement, position, and contour. The sign languages we know, those of the Plains Indians, the Trappist monks, and Australian aborigines, include many recognizable imitations. Our first utterances may have mimicked non-vocal sounds. If these referent sounds were familiar within a community the onomatopoeic vocalization could have been easily understood. As we shall see in a later chapter, there are some representational words in present day languages but there is no evidence that they were the beginning of all speech. However, if we must have some myth about the origins of communication I will imagine that primitive man began by representing the world with all his muscles—gesturing, speaking, and drawing. Only the drawings survive.

If an individual has a certain number of ideas to communicate by speech, there are several methods he might use. Each idea could be linked with a distinctive sound. The linkages could be arbitrary or representational. Alternatively the number of sounds could be combined so that each idea would be designated by a unique combination. It would even be possible to use a single sound and repeat the sound a unique number of times for each idea. With a large number of ideas this last system would soon become unwieldy. At the other extreme it would not be possible to find representational sounds for most ideas. Even the requirement of an arbitrary sound for each idea would soon involve us with sounds difficult to discriminate from one another. The earliest speech we know, and indeed all known speech, avoids the two extreme procedures. There is always a number of elementary speech sounds fewer than the number of ideas expressed. The elementary sounds are combined in sequences of varying length to designate ideas.

Writing first became dependent on speech for the sequential arrangement of its characters. With the earliest pictograms and ideograms the symbol sequence often reproduces the chronology of the referent events. If a hunter fasted, and then gathered his weapons, and then killed a bison these events would be pictured in that order. At a later time the characters followed the sequence in which the ideas conceived would be expressed in speech. When this is true Gelb (71) calls the characters logograms to indicate that they stand for words more directly than for things or ideas. The logogram, however, is still a semantic character and the great advantage of alphabetic writing is the fact that the elementary characters are phonetic rather than semantic.

The kind of change that introduced the phonetic principle into orthography may be illustrated with a story from Gelb's discussion of Sumerian. The Sumerians used the word *ti* for *life* but had no written sign for this idea. It is a difficult idea to represent. As it happened, the spoken form *ti* had two meanings in Sumerian. *Ti* was a homophone meaning *arrow* as well as *life*. The arrow is easily represented as ⟶. At some point it occurred to the Sumerians to use this same sign ⟶ to designate *life*. This is a shift to the phonetic principle in writing. The written character is now invariant with respect to sound but variant in meaning. It is as if the character ☿ were used to stand for the English word *son* as well as for *sun*. The written form is generalized along a dimension of sound rather than meaning 'and so becomes derivative from speech. In this process of phonetic extension the character altogether loses its representational value.

Phonetic characters were only very gradually introduced into the ancient writings. The pictograms, ideograms, and logograms survived along with the newer phonetic forms. There was no abrupt revolution. However, the direction of change was from the semantic to the phonetic character. Among phonetic writings syllabaries sometimes came before alphabets. The syllable, coinciding as it does with the breath pulse, may have a kind of perceptual salience that makes it the "natural" phonetic unit of speech. The vowels and consonants, however, are a much smaller set of speech elements and this makes for a simpler writing. Eventually they were separated out and coordinated with written characters to make an alphabet.

The great economy of phonetic writing can be understood if we recall that everyone learns to speak before learning to write. Speech is always constructed of a limited set of elementary sound classes (vowels and consonants). Meaningful units of speech are sequences of the elementary sounds. In learning to speak one learns the unique vocal combination for each referent. Quite certainly one does not consciously analyze these sequences but learns each one as a complete whole. This learning of semantic rules is not entirely nonsense learning. As we shall see there are many systematic features. With full allowance for these, however, the learning task remains immense. If now the written form of this language were to employ a distinct character for each idea, attaining literacy would require a second great learning period. There would be a complete new set of semantic rules to be grasped; a set independent of those involved in speech. If, however, a written character is assigned to each of the elements of speech the individual who has learned to speak can learn to spell by memorizing a simple alphabet and learning to analyze familiar phonetic combinations into their elements. When he can substitute letters for sound elements, he will be able to spell. The combinational problems having been solved for speech, they will automatically be solved for phonetic writing. Everyone who has learned to speak—and that is very nearly everyone—can now easily learn to read and write and spell.

The result of our reasoning seems to be an obvious untruth. For English speaking children do not learn to read and write in a few easy hours. Spelling is so complex a skill that only the athletes of literacy who train to win spelling bees become really proficient. All of this is because English orthography (like French but unlike Italian or Spanish) has fallen away from an early happier state. George Bernard Shaw was always extremely angry about English spelling. In a preface to R. A. Wilson's *Miraculous Birth of Language* (249) he set forth his views:*

> Professor Wilson has shewn that it was as a reading and writing animal that Man achieved his human eminence above those who are called beasts. Well, it is I and my like who have to do the writing. I have done it professionally for the last sixty years as well as it can be done with a hopelessly inadequate alphabet devised centuries before the English language existed to record another and very different language. Even this alphabet is reduced to absurdity by a foolish orthography based on the notion that the business of spelling is to represent the origin and history of a word instead of its sound and meaning. Thus an intelligent child who is bidden to spell debt, and very properly spells it d-e-t, is caned for not spelling it with a b because Julius Caesar spelt the Latin word for it with a b.

In the history of the English language spelling has changed less rapidly than speech. Many of the spellings of Middle and Old English are preserved in the living language although the pronun-

---

*Quoted with the permission of The Philosophical Library.

ciations of the words have drastically changed. In France the natural inertia of spelling has been reinforced by the efforts of the French Academy to maintain "the perfect language" in the state of perfection it attained some centuries ago. Some of the non-phonetic aspects of our own writing are the contributions of pedantic scribes. As a consequence of all these factors we have in English a writing system with so many inconsistencies that we do not have the full advantage of a phonetic orthography.

Methods of Learning to Read

Imagine that you are teaching the primary grades in America and you will find even more cause than Shaw had to be angry about our writing system. Your pupils are first graders, varying somewhat in mental age but probably averaging six years. They have been speaking English for about four years. According to Smith (215), they are likely to have well over 10,000 words in their recognition vocabularies. You must teach them to read and then to spell. If our writing were consistently phonetic you could simply teach them the letters of the alphabet corresponding to each sound, give them a little practice in analyzing words into sound elements, and they would have reading vocabularies as large as their speaking vocabularies. Their 10,000+ words could be read with comprehension, or at any rate with all the comprehension attached to the spoken words. The child would spell out each new word, recognize the result as one of his 10,000 familiar speech forms and understand the written version as he understands its spoken equivalent. In fact, however, things are not so easy and this is clearly illustrated by the letter A. The name of that letter is *ay*. This is sometimes the sound of the letter in an actual word (as in *ate* or *ape*) but the letter is more often pronounced (as it is in *at* or *and*) as a short vowel. Which of these phonetic values should you teach? Even if you teach both there are horrible errors to be anticipated when your pupil finds A in *boat, peak* and *beauty*. As for B, the name of the letter (*bee*) begins with the most common phonetic value of the letter but also includes a vowel that is not ordinarily associated with the letter (as it is not in *but* or *bill*). Then, ought one to tell children about *doubt* and *debt* in which B has no sound?

Some letters have names which do not even contain the sound most commonly associated with the letter. The sound of *H* is usually that heard in *he* but that sound is not contained in *aitch* the name of the letter. Neither is the sound of *W* in *double you*. The names of letters in the English alphabet are never the same as the sound most commonly associated with the letters and, furthermore, for most letters there is more than one common sound value. The English alphabet is so inconsistent in its phonetic values that it might be a good idea to teach the system as if it were not phonetic at all.

Phonetic training with the alphabet seems to work very well in European countries. In Germany and Italy children are said to become literate in their first two years of schooling. The spelling bee is not a popular contest in these countries for the reason that nearly everyone can spell most words. After World War II, the American occupation forces in Germany tried to introduce the spelling bee as part of the democratization program but they failed because of the uniformly high level of spelling prowess. Lessons in the phonetic values of letters work very well in Europe, but perhaps that is because the languages involved have more consistent phonetic spellings than has English. A method well adapted to Italian is not necessarily well adapted to English. To be sure, reading has been taught by this method in America and England but the results in spelling accuracy and reading skills are not dazzling. It may be that there is a better method to use with English.

Look-and-Say. About thirty years ago the majority of American teachers decided there was a better method and they gave up or minimized the older alphabetic and phonetic methods. The new technique is called the look-and-say method. The fundamental idea is to treat each word as a unique visual pattern, rather as if our writing system were semantic with a different form for every meaning. The fact that these forms are constructed of a small set of recurrent letters is not stressed because the sound values of the letters are not constant. Writing is put in direct contact with meaning and its relation to speech is not taught because that relation has grown too ambiguous to be useful. Training begins with the short common words that the first grade child has long had in his speaking vocabulary. Characteristically each word is mounted on a card with a picture of the object named. The teacher flashes the card, pronounces the name repeatedly and calls attention to the picture. Vocabulary necessarily builds slowly since each word-referent association must be independently memorized. However, it is customary to begin with the words most frequently seen in printed English. From such a list of common serviceable words simple stories have been composed which a child can read while his vocabulary is still small.

The look-and-say method has often been described as a scientific method founded on psychological research as the old-fashioned phonetic methods were not. Perhaps the most often cited experiments are those done by Cattell in 1885. He showed by two lines of evidence that a familiar word is read as a whole rather than by spelling out its letters. In reaction time experiments the response of naming a short word is very nearly as quick as that of naming a single letter. This suggests that word recognition is a unitary act very much like letter recognition. Cattell also showed, using the gravity chronometer for quick exposures, that the time required to read letters that do not make words is about twice the time required to read letters that do make words. This result also suggests that the word is recognized as a whole pattern rather than as a combination of letters. Javal found in 1878 that an adult reader's eyes do not move steadily along a line, passing from letter to letter, but rather move saccadically, i.e., in a series of jumps. Erdmann and Dodge (62) demonstrated that the fixation pauses are the times of effective exposure in reading. Evidently the adult reader recognizes a number of word shapes in a single glance. If this is the method of the accomplished reader why train the novice to analyze words into letters? These researches suggested to educators that adult reading techniques might be used from the first.

The look-and-say method also found justification in theoretical psychology. After the First World War Gestalt psychology began to influence American work. The Gestalt point of view, developed by Max Wertheimer and his students Kurt Koffka and Wolfgang Köhler, was more closely linked than associationistic behaviorism with highly developed forms of human perception and problem solving. Gestalt theorists stressed the importance of an overview of the whole as a prerequisite to the meaningful, intelligent solution of problems. They insisted that rote memorization of meaningless parts was not an important kind of human learning. Since the new method for teaching reading dealt with words, the meaningful wholes of which letters are meaningless parts, it seemed to be in accord with Gestalt theory.

Finally, the look-and-say method seemed better suited than phonetic drill to a new philosophy of education that held it more important for children to be happy and wise than for them to be well stocked with every kind of information. The ability to spell out words is not the most important aim of training in reading. What we need is more adults who read with interest and understanding and who seek out high quality reading matter. It seemed likely to many teachers that phonetic drill would cause children to develop an enduring distaste for reading. Stopping to spell out letters would slow them up, break the line of thought, leave them bored and inexpert. Dealing with meaningful materials and whole stories from the beginning, a child trained by the look-and-say method would be more likely to understand what he read and to develop into an avid adult reader.

For all the reasons I have given most American teachers turned away from old-fashioned phonetic methods. But now, some thirty years after the change, they are being scolded for having made a frightful mistake. Their most censorious critic is probably Rudolf Flesch. His book, *Why Johnny Can't Read* (66) was an American best seller for many weeks. Because the book has been a best seller, academic folk, educators and psychologists, have been inclined to ignore it or to depreciate it as a cheap effort to scandalize the public. Certainly Dr. Flesch presents his evidence like a prosecuting attorney. There is plenty of rhetoric and an occasional tendency to stack the cards. Generally, however, the argument is sound. So we will take Flesch seriously, but also study the teachers' rebuttal.

For and Against Phonetic Training. If you test reading prowess you find that it consists of many skills which are not necessarily in correlation. The particular skill in which America's Johnny is supposed to be deficient is the ability to sound out new words, to read aloud material he has not seen before. If each word is taught as a unique visual pattern it follows that one will only be able to read the words on which specific training has been given. These will not be very numerous for Johnny since it is common nowadays to set 1,300 words as a reading goal for the first three years of instruction. Some parents have found that Johnny reads well within this list but can do nothing at all with new words. This is distressing since he cannot very well have classroom training on all the words he will eventually need to read. Seashore and Eckerson (202) state that adult recognition vocabularies run well over 100,000 words. At the rate of 400 new words a year, it will take Johnny 250 years to reach his parents' level. There was something in the old system of training that taught you how to read new words as well as the old ones used in your lessons.

Of course, if you are taught sound values for letters you can sound out new words a letter or two at a time and so do a reasonably good job of reading new material. But is this reading? The proponent of word recognition methods may see nothing useful in being able to *pronounce* new words that are not understood. The usefulness of being able to sound a new word depends on the state of the reader's speaking vocabulary. If the word that is unfamiliar in printed form is also unfamiliar in spoken form the reader who can sound it out will not understand the word any better than the reader who cannot sound it. Even so the ability to pronounce the new word (however ineptly) has some advantages. If the word is encountered in private reading it can be carried by pronunciation to parent or teacher for definition. However, the real advantage in being able to sound a word that is unfamiliar in print, only appears when the word is familiar in speech. The child's letter-by-letter pronunciation, put together by spelling recipe, will, with the aid of context, call to mind the spoken form. There will be a click of recognition, pronunciation will smooth out, and meaning will transfer to the printed form. The ability to sound out new words is not simply a pronunciation skill; it is a technique for expanding reading comprehension vocabulary to the size of speaking comprehension vocabulary. This is a considerable help since speaking vocabulary is likely to be ten times the size of reading vocabulary for the primary school child.

It is not quite fair to say that the child trained to whole word recognition has no techniques that can be used for recognizing new words. He will have learned something about the probabilities with which words follow one another in English, something of the sequential probabilities of the language. Suppose a child who has learned to recognize words as unique patterns has never seen the word *lion* though he has often spoken it. If he comes upon that

word in the sentence *The lion is in the zoo,* he can guess such probable insertions as *monkey* or *tiger* or, sometimes, *lion.* He cannot
look to the word for help in choosing between these alternatives.
Since the word is a totally new pattern there is nothing to be
learned from it. The words he guesses (like *tiger* and *monkey*) may
not look or sound at all like *lion.* They will resemble *lion* only in
that they are sometimes found in the same sentence contexts. A
child who has learned how to sound his letters will also have
learned something about English sequential probabilities. In addition, however, he has a second set of cues—the rough sound of the
word—to help him choose among possible alternatives. It is not that
the child who recognizes whole words is without resource when
faced with new words but rather that he has one less resource than
the child who knows how to sound his letters. Much of our growth
in reading vocabulary comes by working out unfamiliar words.
Surely two methods of word attack are better than one. Admittedly
there are inconsistencies in English spelling but it remains a
phonetic system with inconsistencies—not a semantic system.

What substance is there in the supposed experimental and
theoretical support for the look-and-say method? Consider first the
Cattell experiment showing that letters making words are read
more rapidly than letters that do not make words. This result has
been interpreted as a proof that adults read the "whole word
picture" rather than individual letters. We can propose another
interpretation. Printed English has a high level of redundancy.
When every other letter of a running text has been deleted, a practiced reader of English will still be able to reconstruct most of the
original (Shannon [204]). Perhaps Cattell's subjects were able to
read letters in words more rapidly than letters not in words because in the former case unobserved letters could be guessed from
those that were identified while in the second case this was not
possible. Letters in words follow sequential probabilities familiar
to readers of English while letters at random are all equally probable at every juncture. It is quite possible therefore, that Cattell's
subjects were reading individual letters rather than "total word
pictures" and were able to report more letters than they could
possibly identify at very brief exposures because the additional
letters could be inferred from those observed. Reading research of

the last fifty years (254) indicates that while the general shape of a word has some cue value, the clear view of letters is a more important factor in word identification. Phonetically trained readers probably need to see all the letters in the beginning. As they store the sequential probabilities linking English letters fewer visual cues are needed. The adult reader is able to identify many words at a glance but it may be that this ability is best developed out of letter-by-letter reading.

Consider now the presumed support deriving from Gestalt theory. The words "wholist" and "meaningful" are very frequently used by Gestalt theorists to characterize their own position in contrast with that of the associationists. It is not surprising, therefore, that, on a cursory reading, the Gestalt work should seem to favor the reading method that deals in "meaningful" units—*whole* words. I think, nevertheless, that this is a misconstruction of Gestalt theory. Words differ from letters or other phonetic elements in that they have reference to non-linguistic objects or events and, in this sense, words are "meaningful." In the writings of Gestalt psychologists, however, the word "meaningful" is more nearly synonymous with "systematic" than with "referential." "Meaningful" learning is learning that fits into a structure. Meaningful material is material in which there are systematic relations among the elements. Words are larger units than letters since words are compounded of letters and so, in a sense, words are "wholes." When Gestalt theory calls our attention to "wholes" it is to the system that determines the character of its parts. Are words the relevant "wholes" for someone learning to read?

Perhaps an example of a Gestaltist analysis of a learning problem will make clear what is meant by systematic, wholist learning. George Katona (121) presented the following series of numbers to be learned: 5 8 1 2 1 5 1 9 2 2 2 6. Katona had subjects study the series until they could perfectly recall it. One week later he asked them to reproduce the series but no one could do so. With another group of subjects the same numbers were learned together with the principle of their organization: the difference between 5 and 8 is 3, between 8 and 12 is 4, between 12 and 15 is 3, between 15 and 19 is 4, and so on. This principle was demonstrated by showing the numbers as follows:

Subjects learning the series in this fashion could grasp it very quickly and, indeed, could quickly learn a much longer series organized according to the same principle. One could easily construct such a series that would take a very long time to memorize by rote but which could be retained after a single exposure by someone familiar with the organizing principle. Katona, furthermore, found that his second group retained the series after an interim of a week.

When materials to be learned constitute a system it is possible to predict some of the materials from knowledge of others. Systematic learning occurs when principles are discovered which make it unnecessary to memorize detailed materials. The relevant whole for these numbers is not the total series containing the individual numbers but is, rather, the principle governing the series. Systematic learning gives insight in that it provides principles (not always verbally formulated) from which specific materials can be derived. In learning to read there seems to be more insight provided by phonetic rules than by the look-and-say method. Learning to recognize the total appearance of a given word teaches nothing about recognizing other words. Each part is independent of all others. Learning is a process of memorization. When recurrent sound-letter matchings are learned we acquire a set of principles telling us how to pronounce indefinite numbers of new words; we learn the sound system of English writing. The fact that it is a very complicated and sometimes inconsistent system does not prevent it from being a system. Gestalt theory, then, would seem to favor the insightful phonetic method.

The use of whole words as teaching materials is as possible in phonetic training as in look-and-say recognition training. The best techniques for teaching phonetic generalizations (hereafter to be called the phonic methods) do work with whole words. Phonic training calls the attention of the student to words in which there are recurrent letters or groups of letters and correlated recurrent sounds. One might begin with a set of words all having the same initial letter in printed form and the same initial sound in spoken form: such a set as *mother, man,* and *milk.* From these words a general rule emerges: For the letter *m* make the sound heard initially in *mother.* A teacher using the phonic method will usually begin with the consonants since these have more consistent phonetic values than the vowels. With the vowels it is usual to teach the short forms first (as in *had, hen, hid, hod, hut*) since these are more common in English than are the long vowels (*hate, heed, hide, hoed, mute*). Still later come such contingent rules as the following: The sound /k/ is spelled *k* before *e* or *i* but it is spelled *c* before *a, o,* or *u* and *ck* after a short vowel. Finally there are some spellings for which no rule can be found and these are probably best taught last. All of the phonetic generalizations can be abstracted from words. They need not be taught by pronouncing individual letters. Certainly they will not be taught by reciting the alphabet. The names of letters (as opposed to their common phonetic values) must eventually be memorized since it is customary to spell by naming letters rather than by sounding them. But recitation of the alphabet is no part of good phonic preparation for reading.

If it is true that phonetic generalizations can be taught with whole words it is also true that pupils who are taught to recognize whole words can incidentally form phonetic generalizations and it is certain that most of them do so. This means that pupils do not dichotomize into two groups reading by entirely different methods. However, there are differences between the teacher who works by a phonic method and the teacher working by a look-and-say method. The phonics teacher will draw general rules out of words and she will explicitly state these rules from the first, encouraging her students to use them. The look-and-say teacher will provide materials from which general phonetic rules can be abstracted but, in the beginning, she will leave it to the student to find these rules. For the first year or two, at least, he must learn his phonetic generalizations incidentally, without explicit formulation by the teacher. Later on, the look-and-say teacher may institute some direct phonetic training. Oddly enough she has always been inclined to do so with backward children who need remedial reading help. The need for a phonetic attack on new words is generally recognized by educators of the look-and-say persuasion but, for one reason or another, they believe the necessary generalizations should be incidentally learned or, if directly taught, postponed until the second or third grade. What are the reasons for this belief?

Dolch and Bloomster (55) have said: "It is true that the use of phonics means the use of generalizations, *that generalizations are best learned inductively,* and that sight words are the basis of inductive reasoning."* The italicized portion of this sentence is hardly a common sense observation. Why does the scientist write out his laws, the chef his recipes, the professional golfer his instructions for the novice if not to spare the rest of us inductive labor? We benefit from the experiences of our predecessors by reading the generalizations they formed. It may be that the Darwinian theory of evolution is best learned inductively—best in the sense of most unforgettably. But if it had to be learned that way most of us would live without a theory of evolution. On the face of it a generalization is more rapidly and certainly learned when it is explicitly stated. In addition there are experimental results to show that incidental learning is slow and uncertain by comparison with directed learning. The educator who would claim that phonetic generalizations are better learned by incidental induction than by direct formulation with examples, assumes the burden of proof. His claim does not conform to popular belief nor has it been demonstrated in the laboratory. If you really want your pupil to learn a phonetic rule it seems sensible to tell him the rule.

Some educators think it best to teach phonetics directly, but argue that such training ought not to be used before the second grade. Until that time, it has been claimed, children have insufficient mental maturity to make use of abstract phonetic principles. Dolch and Bloomster found that first grade children taught by a look-and-say method failed to form phonetic generalizations which they could use in attacking new words. The authors conclude that a mental age of seven years, which usually means second grade standing, must be attained before a child can benefit from phonic training and that all such training ought to be postponed until he has reached that age. Quite obviously their results do not demonstrate that first grade children are unable to benefit from phonic training since the children of the study were not given *explicit* phonic training. First grade children know the rules of games that

---

*Italics my own.

are fully as complicated as the rules involved in spelling. Further-more, they are rather accomplished speakers of English, which means they have formed many concepts and learned complicated grammatical conventions. It seems unlikely that spelling rules are beyond them.

Empirical Evidence. We are not entirely dependent on theo-retical argument and indirect evidence in deciding on the possi-bility of benefiting from direct phonic training in the first grade. In Scotland, children enter school at five years of age and begin the study of reading (by a phonic method) almost at once. In a study of the Committee on Reading of the Scottish Council for Research in Education (43) children beginning the second year of school were given two American tests, the Metropolitan Reading Readi-ness Test and Primary I Battery, Form A, from the Metropolitan Achievement Tests. The mean chronological age of the children was 6.3 years, approximately the age at which American children begin the first grade. The mean readiness score of the Scottish children was 90 which is 16.33 points above the norm for American children of the same age and I.Q. On the reading test their grade score was 7.5 which is at least a year above the norm for American children of the same age. It seems to be clear that children can gain from phonic training even before the first grade, and it would appear that a good way to build reading readiness is by instruction in reading.

There is also some experimental evidence on the relative merits of direct and incidental teaching for the development of phonetic knowledge. The basic design is always the same: One group is trained for a time using a phonic method and a more-or-less com-parable group is trained for the same period by some non-phonic method. Finally, both groups are given the same tests of reading achievement, and performances are compared. The studies vary greatly in the adequacy of their controls and in sample size. In summarizing this evidence Flesch ignored the significance levels of the differences found (as the authors themselves often do) and he missed several studies. Still, I find his general summary about right. Phonetic knowledge is more reliably acquired from direct tuition than by incidental induction from reading whole words.

Perhaps the three best studies are those of Agnew (3), Russell (198), and McDowell (157). Agnew compared all of the third graders in Raleigh, N. C., with a sample of 300 from Durham. In Raleigh a look-and-say method was used and in Durham a consistent, intensive phonetic instruction. The Durham children were reliably superior on oral reading, pronunciation, sounding letters, and pronouncing new words. Russell compared phonics-trained children with those trained by other methods at the end of the first year of reading instruction. His groups were equated for mental age. The classes that had received intensive phonetic training were significantly superior on eleven of twelve tests and particularly so in spelling, word recognition, and the sounding of letters. The subjects in the third research (McDowell) were fourth grade students from the Catholic schools in Pittsburgh. Five of the schools had, for three years, used intensive phonetic training while the other five had used a more general reading program in which phonetic training was one of many kinds of instruction provided. The classes that had been given intensive phonetic training came out ahead on two tests—alphabetizing and spelling. Direct phonetic instruction produces superior skill in spelling, oral reading, sounding letters, and whatever aspects of reading call for phonetic knowledge. Incidental learning does not work as well.

We might have hoped for really conclusive evidence on the relative merits of the teaching methods from a comparison of reading achievement in the days when phonetic drill predominated with achievement today. However, there are no perfectly comparable data. Summarizing the best ten studies, Gray and Iverson (80) decide that there has been no significant change in silent reading achievement in the past two or three decades. These authors add that average achievement in oral reading is not as high today as it was formerly because of radical changes in emphasis in teaching from oral reading to silent reading.

There remains one possible reason for avoiding intensive phonetic instruction and this reason is stronger than the others. We are asked to remember that the ability to sound out new words is not the only goal of reading instruction. In going after that objective with specific intensive training teachers may neglect reading speed, reading interest, and comprehension. There is some evidence in the experimental work that this can happen. Mosher and Newhall (163) and Tate (221) found look-and-say trained children slightly, but not significantly, superior to children trained by phonic methods on such tests as reading speed and silent comprehension. Agnew, in the study mentioned earlier, found the look-and-say trained children to be slightly more rapid readers. McDowell, in the study of Catholic schools, found the look-and-say classes superior on many tests but particularly so on paragraph comprehension, reading rate, and use of the Index. The sum of these results is that intensive phonetic instruction may take so much classroom time that other skills are slighted (e.g., use of the Index). Apparently, in recent decades, American education has been less concerned with phonetic knowledge than with other aspects of reading. Perhaps the loss in spelling and oral reading is more than compensated for by gains in comprehension and speed. However, on the basis of the experimental literature these gains appear to be slight, even doubtful. Gray and Iverson, in their comparison of past and present reading achievement, are more certain that phonetic skills have declined than that other skills have improved.

Perhaps the most important test of the look-and-say methods is the volume and character of the reading done by those who learned to read in this way. If look-and-say has produced a generation that reads more books than past generations we will not worry if they also spell less expertly. Certainly more books are sold today than thirty years ago, about 68 per cent more than in 1929 according to the United States Department of Commerce. However, people today are spending more money on all of the mass media—on radio, television, and movies as well as books. Book sales today account for only 9 per cent of all recreational expenditures whereas in 1929 they represented 13.5 per cent, i.e., the rate of growth in book sales has been less than for competing means of communication. Does this change in book sales represent a debit or a credit for new methods of teaching reading?

There are many who will reject the volume of book sales as an index of interest in reading. How many routinely acquired books-of-the-month go unread? The volume of book reading, not book buying, is the relevant datum. Gray and Iverson report that comparative studies of sixth, seventh, and eighth grade pupils—thirty years ago and today—show no increase in reading. From the sixth to the twelfth grade the average number of books read in a month is now, as in 1925, about 1.5. Furthermore the chronological pattern of reading interest is much the same. It rises in the primary grades, reaches a peak in junior high school, and then falls off sharply in senior high school. The curve begins to rise a little earlier today than formerly but otherwise is about the same. As for today's adults, most of whom were taught by the new methods, according to DuShane (59), the American Institute of Public Opinion found that only 17 per cent were currently reading a book. The comparable figure in 1937 was 29 per cent. Perhaps the schools are doing well to maintain even this level since reading has today the fierce competition of television and movies. On the other hand, it must be acknowledged that children's books are much more attractive today than formerly and this change, rather than the change in methods of reading instruction, may be responsible for maintaining children's interest. It is disappointing to find educators taking their stand on the claim that children today read as well as children have ever done. From the certain fact that this century has seen more discussion and research on reading than all prior centuries we should have hoped for something more than holding the line.

What to Do Now? The temperate, reasoned conclusion to this discussion, as to so many others, is that we won't know the answers until we have more and better research. The evidence certainly is not complete. We need longitudinal studies of matched groups of pupils trained by phonic and non-phonic methods, studies comparing oral reading of new words, reading speed, interest, and comprehension. But the call for more research is a stale tune from the psychologist. There are some people, living in the real world, who have a reading class to teach today and another one tomorrow. What would you do, Mr. Psychologist, if you had to act today? The answer must lie in a combination of methods. I would begin phonic instruction in the first grade, not with recitation of the alphabet, but by extracting generalizations about the more consistent consonants from whole words in which the consonants appear. I would continue to stress meaning—combining the word with a picture when possible. I would do some flash card training with whole words, choosing for this purpose the common short words like *and, but, the,* etc. I would teach these words as total patterns because they are so common in English that it will greatly speed reading if they can be read in a glance. In addition these words, some of the oldest in the language, have many phonetic inconsistencies and so make poor material for first phonetic training and yet they cannot very well be postponed if children are to read stories. Therefore, I would teach them by the look-and-say method. In my phonic instruction I would use only those words that are familiar to the child in spoken form so that he might have the thrill of recognizing and understanding his first halting pronunciations. I would rely on the satisfactions involved in such recognition to make reading interesting. This procedure that I have espoused involves more phonics at an earlier age than is now customary in American education. In taking such a stand I am sorry to be allied with unreasonable parents and enemies of progressive education. If we have all arrived at somewhat similar views on this issue I think we got there by different routes and our ways are likely to diverge again.

Probably some parents are angry because they feel guilty about not doing much reading themselves. For some reason the act of reading is held to be virtuous in its own right. If that statement needs documentation it can be found in Berelson's article on "What Missing the Newspaper Means" (16). There is supposed to be a virtue in reading that does not accrue to listening or viewing and the printed word enjoys a kind of approval that is not given to radio or television. This feeling is very common among college teachers who would feel personally discredited by the presence of a television set in their homes. Probably it is nonsense to enthrone one medium (the book) and despise another (the television). There is enough trash to go around. I don't think it can be shown that quality content is limited to one rather than another. Certainly there is nothing in the nature of the medium that prevents radio or television from being highbrow. However, whether sensible or not, reading is held to be a virtuous act (more or less regardless of the content) while viewing and listening are relaxing but a waste of time. The parent who is guiltily conscious of the fact that he does rather more viewing than reading may be distressed to see Johnny going to hell in the same way. His guilty anger can be handily displaced to the teacher and the look-and-say method that prevents Johnny from being a reader. The teacher has a strong point when he argues that children are not going to be eager to learn to read if they live among people who seem to get along very nicely without opening a book. If the Johnny of such parents has trouble with reading surely the parents ought to inquire into the extent of their own responsibility. Whether they choose to regret his backwardness and feel guilty about it is a matter between them and their culture.

The teacher has reason on his side again when he refuses to be overwhelmed by a parent's memories of his own great interest and rapid progress in reading as taught by the phonic method. There is more than one variable here. Such parents may be of superior I.Q. and have had higher mental ages than their classmates or the whole reminiscence may be rosy tinted by nostalgia. Neither should the teacher change his methods because some parent —often a college professor—tells him of his great success in teaching Johnny to read at home by using a phonic method. I have heard wonderful stories of this kind with children learning to read at four years of age, chronological age that is. But the child of a college professor probably has a high I.Q. and so may have a mental age of five or six when he is four years old. Such a child might be particularly apt at learning phonics or most anything else. The methods of the public schools cannot be geared to them. There are great individual differences in the abilities of pupils in the primary grades. Most of them will learn to read by present methods. Most of them will make phonetic generalizations for themselves whether or not the teacher points them out. I think, however, that more of them would learn to read better and sooner with more explicit phonic instruction.

Summary

To learn a written name for each referent category is a big job and writing systems all provide some kind of short cut to this knowledge. The earliest systems took advantage of the psychological economy in representation. The symbol manifested some criterial attributes of the referent and so suggested the referent. For various reasons this economy had a quite restricted usefulness, probably more restricted as societies grew in size and complexity. The written form of a language provides names for the same referents as does the spoken form, and the spoken names are generally learned first. This fact makes another economy available to a writing system. The phonetic writing, whether syllabic or alphabetic, translates recurrent speech elements into written characters and combines the characters into names as the sounds are combined in speech. When one learns such an alphabet or syllabary he ought to be able to read, write, and spell all the names that are familiar to him in spoken form. It is an irony of history that this economy, which made the invention of the alphabet so important to mankind, has been partially lost to such languages as English and French. English orthography is today a very inconsistent phonetic system. This fact has suggested to many American educators that literacy in English ought to be taught without explicit reference to the phonetic values of the letters. However, the evidence indicates that teachers do better to call attention to the phonetic system that exists, even though it is exasperatingly irregular.

chapter *iii* Reference and Meaning

I*N* READING, WHEN I come upon an unfamiliar word or phrase I have a sensation of derailment. Some process that usually flows along smoothly has been interrupted. Some expected click of my mechanism has failed to occur. It has always seemed to be the principal task of a psychology of language to discover the nature of this click. The meaningful linguistic form must set off some characteristic immediate effect in the person who understands. What is the substantial nature of this effect?

This question has usually taken psychologists back to the process of reference. Whatever the nature of the comprehension effect it often seems to be created in a person by his experience of linguistic forms in association with referent categories. When a man hears the word *dog* in conjunction with dogs he learns to hear and read the word with comprehension. What the comprehension effect may be it is difficult to tell for this effect is hidden away inside the organism. However, when a man has absorbed a reference there are also certain changes in his observable behavior and these have suggested the nature of the comprehension effect.

(82)

There are two major changes in overt behavior that follow the experiencing of a linguistic form used to name referents, and there are two principal notions about meaning that are founded on these changes of behavior. In the first place, a man who has heard dogs named becomes able to identify dogs for himself and to distinguish them from other kinds of things. It is natural to suppose that this performance is possible because the man has formed a mental image of the dog which he can match against any animals presented to his vision. The next step is to suggest that the meaning of the word *dog* is this same mental image; the click of comprehension is the image that the word evokes. However, there is a second change of behavior to be seen in the man who has heard dogs named. He begins to respond to the word as he formerly responded to the referent, to treat the word as a sign of the thing. If, for example, he has always run away from the animal he may now run when someone simply shouts out the word. Ordinarily when we understand words in reading or in listening to speech we do not make any obvious response like running away but perhaps we do make some internal sign reaction, perhaps the click of comprehension is some subtle response of a muscle or gland. It will be argued in this chapter that neither of these notions of meaning is acceptable. If there is an immediate effect that constitutes understanding of a meaningful form that effect must be neuro-physiological. There is nothing in consciousness or in behavior that is set off whenever the comprehended form occurs. Psychological semantics must operate for the present with regard to the two kinds of overt action that are produced by reference and leave the "click" to neurology.

Naming and the Mental Image

Experiencing the word *triangle* in conjunction with instances of the triangle category teaches a human being to use the word to name figures of this kind. When he has fully grasped the category he will be able to name new instances, distinguishing them from squares and ellipses and everything else. Presumably this ability to extend the name to new instances derives from a knowledge of the criterial attributes that define triangularity. We seem to be able to understand this performance by analogy with a familiar process of perceptual matching. If I am to meet someone whom I have never seen at the railway station it will be useful to carry with me a picture of that person. I can recognize him by comparing the pictured face with the faces of the people leaving the train and I will eventually find that correspondence of essential attributes which identifies my quarry. We can conceive that a man is able to name triangles in analogous fashion by comparing the temporary image in his peripheral eye with a permanent image in his mind's eye. If there is correspondence in criterial attributes the percept will be labelled with the name of the category.

A man who has taken in the connection between *triangle* and triangles is not always occupied putting the two together. When he reads *triangle* in a book or hears it in a lecture he does not point to a referent figure. Still we are sure he understands the term because he has the ability to name triangles when that action is called for. What goes on in him, we wonder, when he is quietly understanding what he hears or reads? If his ability to name triangles can be explained by attributing to him a mental image then perhaps it is this image that constitutes understanding of the word. Created in him by direct sense experience of triangles, it comes to be elicited by the word *triangle*. The image appears whenever the word occurs. It cashes the symbol. The image is the click of comprehension.

There are many difficulties with this theory but only three will be considered here. The first problem is created by the fact that linguistic forms refer to categories not to unique points in space-time. All of the pictures with which we are acquainted seem to be pictures of particular objects on particular occasions. What would a mental picture of a category look like? This difficulty applies even to proper names when we remember that they also name categories, *identity* categories. The second and third problems derive from empirical data rather than from logical considerations. A great many people have reported that they lack mental images for terms which they certainly understand and can use correctly in labelling referents. Of the people who do report mental images most do not report the kind of image that could explain the ability to identify referent instances.

How Can an Image be Generic? The philosophers and psychologists who believe that meaning is a mental image have always had trouble describing the images for general terms like *triangle* or *animal*. Locke (149) thought that the idea of triangle must be "neither equilateral, equicrural, nor scalenon but all and none of these at once." This description appears to have troubled Berkeley (17) since he wrote: "I readily agree with this learned author (Locke), that the faculties of brutes can by no means attain to abstraction. But then if this be made the distinguishing property of that sort of animals, I fear that a great many of those that pass for men must be reckoned into their number." Berkeley shows what the difficulty is, using the idea of animal as an example. "The constituent parts of the abstract idea of animal are body, life, sense, and spontaneous motion. By body is meant, body without any particular shape or figure, there being no one shape or figure common to all animals, without covering either of hair or feathers, or scales, etc. nor yet naked; hair, feathers, scales and nakedness being the distinguishing properties of particular animals and for that reason left out of the abstract idea. Upon the same account the spontaneous motion must be neither walking, nor flying, nor creeping it is nevertheless a motion, but what that motion is, it is not easy to conceive." In the metalanguage we are using, the problem is to decide what values of the noisy non-defining attributes of a category are to appear in the generic image. It would seem that any picture of an animal must have a shape and yet there is no shape that is not noisy for the animal category. If the generic image is four-footed how is it that we can identify man as an animal; if it is short-necked how can we identify the giraffe?

Ordinary pictures are of particular persons, places, or things. The image theory of meaning ought, therefore, to be more acceptable for proper nouns than for general terms like *triangle* and *animal*. The theory should be examined at this strongest point.

The determinateness of the proper noun is not so great as is commonly supposed. The name *Abraham Lincoln* seems to us to name just one man from the millions who have lived. The name *Ralph Jones*, however, seems indeterminate. We are sure that there are a number of Ralph Joneses now living but which of these may be intended in the present case, it is impossible to say. Looking back at *Abraham Lincoln* it is clear that there are or have been men known by this name other than *the* Abraham Lincoln. *The*

Abraham Lincoln can only be *that* Abraham Lincoln who is best known to all of us. In this case our knowledge of American history makes one proper name determinate but does not help with another.

There are several ways in which one might indicate a specific referent for the name *Ralph Jones*. If the name is used in company that includes someone named *Ralph Jones* it will ordinarily refer to that man. If there were a Jones family known to all of us the name *Ralph Jones* might clearly refer to the eldest son of that family. Finally, the name can be made determinate by means of a specifying verbal context. The Ralph Jones who lives at 100 E. 120th Street in New York City is a particular man.

A word that is not a proper noun, such as *man,* can be made determinate in the same ways as *Ralph Jones*. One can point or say "that man who just spoke to you." The word *man* then becomes fully as particular in its reference as would *Ralph Jones*. But the word *man* in the question, "How does man learn to use language?" is very general, referring to the entire class of human beings. Both *Ralph Jones* and *man* have particular and general potentialities. However, the general mode is more characteristic of *man* than of *Ralph Jones*. We seldom use *Ralph Jones* in its general mode while *man* is often so used. Notice, however, that if Ralph Jones were the protagonist of a famous novel we might say "the Ralph Joneses of this world" to designate the class of human beings possessing the salient traits of the fictional character. Whenever a famous person bears a name the name can be pluralized to identify a class of similar individuals, as has been done with *Babbitt, Bovary,* and *Uncle Tom*. Ordinarily, however, we predicate nothing of the class *Ralph Jones* but much of the class *man*. This is probably the cause of the feeling that *man* is a general term while *Ralph Jones* is particular.

Suppose that the name *Ralph Jones* appears, as it usually would, in a verbal context that clearly determines its referent to be a particular man. Can we construct the image that will be the meaning of this word? If we have known Jones for some years his appearance may have changed greatly, his cellular substance has changed altogether, there is only a kind of structural-functional continuity. Clearly the name *Ralph Jones*, though identified with a particular man, names a category of appearances, an *identity* category. Our visual experience of the man is a vast collection of snapshots and we naturally wonder which of these is to represent him in the mind's eye when we hear his name. The fact is that concrete proper nouns involve the same sort of difficulty for an image theory of meaning as do general terms. An utterance naming a completely specified referent would have to run on and on in this fashion: "Ralph Jones on Christmas day at 9 in the morning seen in right profile under artificial light by eyes naturally 18/20 corrected to 20/20, etc., etc."

The difficulty that bedevils the image theory is that Ralph Jones, the man, can change many of his attributes without affecting the propriety of the designation—*Ralph Jones*. He is himself whether shaved or unshaved, bathed or unbathed. It would seem, however, that any visual representation of him must be either the one or the other. Since these are non-defining noisy attributes of the category *Ralph Jones* we do not know what value to give them in the generic representation. Other attributes, if changed, will alter the propriety of the designation *Ralph Jones*. A certain relation of facial features, a narrow range of heights, weights, and skin colors, are attributes essential to Ralph Jones. Clearly these must appear in his essential image. But with which noisy attributes are they to be combined?

The generic image might strike a kind of average of the noisy attributes associated with the individuals included within a category. We can imagine this representation to be constructed like one of Galton's (69) composite portraits. Galton obtained a generic photograph of epileptics using a single sensitive plate. Each subject sat at the same distance from the camera with his full face turned toward it. The same region of the plate was exposed for the same very brief time to each successive face. Lines and features common to all or many subjects grew dark with repetition while occasional attributes were scarcely noticed. The result was a composite portrait of many individuals. We can, alternatively, imagine the generic image to assume the modal attributes of the members of a class. If Ralph Jones has usually worn his brown suit he will so appear in his imaginal representation. If equilateral triangles are more common than any other variety then this will be the form of *the* triangle.

The trouble with the composite portrait notion is that a portrait truly representative of the membership of a referent category will almost always be a hopeless jumble. Ralph Jones has been seen from many angles and in many positions. Superposition of snapshots of Jones standing and sitting will not produce an intelligible composite. My mind reels at the thought of a composite portrait for triangle or animal. As for virtue, justice, or charity, they will not sit for their portraits.

The trouble with the notion of a portrait in which each noisy attribute assumes its modal value is that such a portrait does not represent the full range of variation in the membership of a category. If Ralph Jones wears a brown suit in my mental image how am I to recognize him in his blue suit? The answer seems to be that I know that the suit he wears is no part of the essence of Ralph Jones. It is necessary to supplement the image with knowledge of what is essential and what is not. Berkeley (17) and John Stuart Mill (158) both thought that an image (or idea) must be particular but that it could represent an abstract or complex idea if attention was somehow attracted to the essential attributes and withheld from those that are accidental. Among the subjects of Francis Galton was a young lady who dealt in such specific images for general terms. Galton said to her, "I want to tell you about a boat" and stopping there, he asked for her images in connection with his remark. These came in a bubbling freshet. She had seen "a rather large boat, pushing off from shore, full of ladies and gentlemen, the ladies dressed in blue and white." Galton's philosopher friends were not so naïve. Their images refused to be committed as to whether the boat was a skiff, a wherry, a barge, launch, or punt. Their boat was logically sound but probably would not float. I find it easier to believe in the young lady's boat than in that of the philosophers.

In thinking about abstract images I have been discouraged by a personal introspective blank. However, such representations are familiar as percepts. In children's alphabet books "A" is for the essential not the particular "apple." In dictionaries the illustrations of aardvark and zebra are of generic animals. In the illustrations of the dictionary we can see how it is possible to direct attention to essential attributes and to convey the information that certain attributes of the particular representation are accidental for the category. Consider, for example, the problem of representing the eyes of a generic animal. Should they be open or closed? In life the two conditions alternate with both a brief and prolonged periodicity. A composite portrait will be heavy lidded but awake. If they are open in all the animals one pictures (as in the dictionary) then it will be understood that the attribute is of no use for distinguishing between them and may be overlooked. The wide open eye of the picture now does not mean that this animal is commonly in that state but rather that this feature of his facial expression is not useful for identifying his category membership. Other features of the animals pictured in the dictionary are significant; the number of legs, arms, and wings; the difference between hair, scales, and feathers; the total bodily contour. To these we attend. Equating attributes in an array of images is certainly not the only way to cause us to disregard their values. A feature sketched with conspicuous carelessness or perhaps only schematically described will also be understood to be insignificant.

Bishop Berkeley and John Stuart Mill, with a little help from the dictionary, give me some notion of the generic mental image. It is a particular image with attention directed to the attributes essential to the category. The other attributes which are necessary to complete the image are somehow known to be accidental. I don't say I have such images but I am prepared to believe it if others tell me they have them.

The Empirical Study of Mental Images. To what degree are these conceivable images reported to be the meanings of words? In 1903 Alfred Binet (18) published his *L'Etude de L'Intelligence,* the report of a series of studies of the thought processes of his two little girls, Armande and Marguerite. He tells the following incident concerning Armande, "I tell her the name of F . . . this is the name of someone familiar, whom we have known as a servant for six or seven years, and whom we still see occasionally, perhaps five or six times a year. Armande, after making an effort to picture F . . . to herself, gives up and says: 'There are only thoughts, I cannot picture anything at all to myself.'" Both girls reported ideas and thoughts but very few images.

In Germany Watt (237) worked with the method of controlled verbal associations. Subjects were to react to a first word with a second related in some particular way to the first—as superordinate, subordinate, or coordinate. Watt asked for an introspective report of each of four stages in the process: (1) the preparation for the experiment; (2) the appearance of the stimulus word; (3) the search for the reaction word; and (4) the arrival of the reaction word. His subjects found that the *Aufgabe* somehow directed their thoughts and caused different reaction words to arise with different directions. But there were no images to carry these dispositional states.

Woodworth (253) in America asked questions of his subjects. For example, "Should a man be allowed to marry his widow's sister?" It was not the answer to the question that interested him but the process of understanding the question. He asked for introspective reports on this process with particular reference to images. But images were often not reported and indeed Woodworth could not observe them in himself.

As all psychologists know, Edward Bradford Titchener's consciousness was a flood of brightly colored, often audible, and sometimes scented imagery.* No word, however, abstract, failed to evoke an image. "Meaning," for instance, was "the blue-gray tip of a kind of scoop which has a bit of yellow about it (probably a part of the handle) and which is just digging into a dark mass of what appears to be plastic material." He suspected the origin of this image to be the numerous injunctions delivered to him in his youth to "dig out the meaning" of Latin or Greek phrases. There are many other delightful pictures from Titchener: "horse is to me a double curve and a rampant posture with a touch of mane about it; cow is a longish rectangle with a certain facial expression, a sort of exaggerated pout."

Titchener's students also had mental images and so did their students. In the researches of Clarke (40), Comstock (44), Crosland (45), Gleason (74), and Okabe (171) one finds the assurance that nothing was found in consciousness which could not be analyzed into sensation, image, or affection. I believe in the sincerity

---

*I am not in this discussion attempting to evaluate Titchener's context theory of meaning (227). Nor am I attempting to decide whether thought is imaged or imageless. It is rather my purpose to examine the usefulness of the notion of mental image in explaining linguistic reference and as a theory of linguistic meaning. The data gathered for the controversy over imageless thought are quoted to this end. The best discussion of the imageless thought controversy appears in George Humphrey's *Thinking: an Introduction to its Experimental Psychology* (101).

of these careful scientists but I must also believe Binet (18), Watt (237), Woodworth (253), Bühler (30), and the others who report no images. Can it be that the click of comprehension is an image for some and not for others?

Titchener is one of the few men who has ever claimed to see an image of Locke's abstract triangle. The master imager describes it as "a flashy thing, come and gone from moment to moment: it hints 2 or 3 red angles, with the red lines deepening into black, seen on a dark green ground. It is not there long enough for me to say whether the angles join to form the complete figure or even whether all 3 of the necessary angles are given." But now we notice a startling thing about this image. It is not the particular image with essential attributes selected for attention that John Stuart Mill had led us to expect—nor is it a composite portrait. The essential attributes of the triangle concept are not clearly represented. Titchener is uncertain whether the angles join and even whether there are 3 angles. This is a personal Titchenerian triangle. And so with his other images—the horse that is a rampant posture, the cow that is a pouting rectangle. Titchener's is an existential psychology. He reports what he sees with his mind's eye, not what the word logically means. But have these images the properties we require of linguistic meanings?

Linguistic symbols are generally thought to acquire meaning by constant association with their referents. The mental reference aroused by the symbol should concentrate on the essential attributes of these referents, the attributes which experience has shown to be invariably present. The images reported by Titchener, and most of those reported in the laboratory, are not such clear distillations of experience. In some cases the image derives from a single accidental experience. Titchener's image of "but" was of the back of the head of a speaker who often used this word while Titchener sat behind him on a platform. In other cases it is a kind of physiognomic impression—the pout of the cow—having no relation to the functional importance of the referent and never mentioned in any definition of it. In fact the images reported are connected with the eliciting words by what appears to be a capricious variety of associations. The image may assume any form whatsoever. Why are such images unacceptable as the meanings of words?

The meaning-image must be representative of the class of referents to which a word is applied in order to fill the function for which it is required. If the image is not an essential picture but some kind of vagrant associate what becomes of the explanation of the reference-making performance? With his image of the triangle Titchener must be expected never to apply the word to any percept, for he will find none to agree with that mobile, flashing, and non-triangular triangle.

The accidental image is in every way inadequate to explain naming behavior. It is unlikely, for instance, that any of us will say that we "see" Titchener's image of the triangle and yet we will call the same entities by this name as he would have done. Accidental images vary from one individual to another and yet these individuals may agree perfectly in their naming behavior. Students in Titchener's seminars agreed with him in finding imagery to be the contents of consciousness but they did not agree on the specific images. The diversity was so great as to suggest no agreement at all on the meanings of words. Language is a cultural possession, shared by members of a society. The variable accidental image will never explain how we are able to agree in labelling the objects about us nor can it explain how we are able to communicate with one another.

In response to the serious criticisms of an image theory of linguistic meaning Pillsbury and Meader (186) demoted the image to a less central role. For them, meaning was the "type" that lay behind the word. This "type" was a neurological reaction to a word —a reaction not necessarily represented in consciousness. William James (115) had many years before rejected the absurd assumption that "ideas in order to know, must be cast in the exact likeness of whatever things they know, and that the only things that can be known are those which ideas can resemble." He held the image to be functionally the least important aspect of thought and relied heavily on the "submaximal excitement of wide spreading associational brain tracts." Titchener, himself, moved in this direction when he admitted the ellipsis of imagery in rapid reading with automatic neurological connections taking over.

The resort to neurology is a defeat for the image theory of meaning. The defeat is accomplished by an initial assumption and a stubborn fact. The assumption is that each comprehended utterance must elicit some immediate and reliable reaction from those who understand it. The fact is that suitable images are not reported for most utterances. Therefore, the theory retreats into the organism to find immediate, reliable neurological reactions to utterances. The pressures that drove the structural psychologist to neurology lay in waiting for the conditioning theorist's first attempt to explain meaning.

Meaning as a Particular Response

In 1913 John Watson mercifully closed the bloodshot inner eye of American psychology. With great relief the profession trained its exteroceptors on the laboratory animal. In his presidential address before the American Psychological Association (235) Watson introduced his colleagues to the work of Pavlov. The Russian study of salivary reflexes in dogs provided a new objective method for investigating the laws of association. This classical conditioning technique appeared to be a particularly apt model for the process by which a word acquires meaning.

The classical conditioning procedure is, in a very general way, coordinate with the reference-making procedure. Two stimuli are repeatedly presented either simultaneously or with a very brief interval between them. When this happens in linguistic reference one of the stimuli is usually spoken or written by a human being. The purpose of the reference-making procedure is to teach another human being to use the language form to name instances of the referent. Attention is focused on the transfer of the naming response from tutor to pupil and on the ability of the pupil to use the name in distinguishing instances of the referent from other things. Conditioning is a method developed for dogs and applicable to all animals. Consequently, the subject is not required to speak or write. In place of a referent there is an unconditioned stimulus that reliably elicits some response from the animal (e.g., hydrochloric acid eliciting salivation). In place of a linguistic form there is a conditioned stimulus (e.g., a bell or buzzer) that does not originally elicit the unconditioned response but comes to do so after repeated pairing with the unconditioned stimulus. The focus of attention is the response which is transferred from one stimulus to another. There is no chance that the animal will learn to name the referent or unconditioned stimulus since the parallel to the name is a conditioning bell not an animal vocalization. In short, classical conditioning is like the business of naming referents in that both procedures present stimuli in association. The two procedures differ in that the purpose of reference is to transfer a name from one person to another while the purpose of conditioning is to transfer a response from one stimulus to another.

Linguistic reference can accomplish changes in behavior that resemble the changes produced by classical conditioning. Suppose someone is well acquainted with the thing-or-event that we call *rain* but has not yet learned its name. If he is out-of-doors in the rain this person may raise his umbrella or run for cover. If he is indoors and sees the rain through a window he may decide not to go out or, if he must go out, to wear his raincoat. If he is indoors and hears the rain on the roof he may behave much as if he saw it through the window. When this person learns that the word *rain* refers to rain he will, of course, become able to apply the name to its referent. In addition, however, there will be a transfer of behavior from the referent to the name. Suppose someone standing near a window says to him: "It's raining outside" or simply: "Damn! Rain!" These utterances will cause our subject to act as if he had himself seen the rain. There has been a transfer of response from the sight of rain through a window to the saying of *Rain* by someone standing near a window. If someone in the attic calls down the stairs: "I hear rain on the roof," it is as if the subject himself had heard the rain. If, out-of-doors, someone holds out a hand, palm upward, and says: "I felt a drop of rain," our subject may raise his umbrella just as if he had felt the drop. The naming of referents resembles classical conditioning in that it results in a transfer of behavior from one stimulus to another.

Clearly, there are many differences between the behavior transfer that is a consequence of taking in a reference and the transfer produced by classical conditioning. In the first place, rain is not an invariant simple stimulus but a category having many attributes— a characteristic appearance through the window, a recognizable rattle on the roof, a feeling of damp and coldness on the skin. The behavior that transfers is not a single reliable unconditioned response but a whole set of actions, changing with the attribute of the referent that is experienced and with the circumstances attending this experience. Reactions to the sight of rain are not the same as reactions to the feel of rain. Moreover, there is no single invariant reaction to the sight of rain. What one does, depends on the total situation. Rain seen through the window will cause a housewife to run about and close the windows at one time and to run out and bring in the washing at another time. The reactions to the attributes of rain are contingent on other circumstances. What transfers when one learns the name of rain is not a single invariant reaction but an elaborate behavioral disposition to react to situations which include the word *rain* as one has reacted to situations which include experience of the attributes of rain.

We know today that classical conditioning may also involve this kind of transfer of a behavioral disposition. Pavlov used a very simple unconditioned stimulus that triggers a glandular response; he restrained the dog so that other action was impossible, and he focused his attention on salivation alone. Zener (259) has shown that when these conditions are changed the classical conditioning procedure may result in the transfer of a behavior disposition rather than of a single response. Zener first replicated the Pavlovian conditioning of the salivary reflex in dogs. He used food as unconditioned stimulus (UCS) in some cases and hydrochloric acid in other cases; a buzzer was always the conditioned stimulus (CS). The salivation reflex worked equally well with the two different unconditioned stimuli. However, Zener observed other changes in behavior produced by the conditioning process that differed with the nature of the UCS. When a dog who received food as UCS heard the CS it assumed an alert expectant posture and put its face down into the food dish. This behavior was not observed in the dogs conditioned with hydrochloric acid as UCS.

Zener then changed the circumstances in which the conditioned stimulus was presented to the trained animals. In one case the animals were first fed to surfeit. Under these circumstances the animals that had received food as UCS did not assume an expectant posture; nor did they turn to the food dish. The animals trained with hydrochloric acid showed no change in behavior when surfeit. In a second case Zener removed the dogs to another table in a different part of the room. He then sounded the buzzer as before. One dog, trained with food, bounded across the room to stand expectantly over his food dish. The others looked up and stared at the dish across the room. The dogs trained with acid failed to rise or even look up on hearing the CS. We may suppose that Zener's dogs had considerable experience of food and were disposed to approach and eat when hungry, but to ignore food when surfeit. This disposition appears to have transferred to the CS. The hydrochloric acid, on the other hand, appears to have acted as all unconditioned stimuli are supposed to act; it invariably stimulated salivation. For a hungry dog, food and acid both produced salivation but when circumstances were changed it became clear that there were many contingent responses connected with food and that these had transferred in the training situation to the conditioned stimulus.

In Watson's day, however, conditioning was understood in Pavlovian terms as the transfer of a single response. Watson (236) and others (e.g., Dashiell [48]) noticed the parallels between conditioning and the use of words to name referents—the association of two stimuli and the transfer of behavior. They were inclined, therefore, to think of meaning as a response that transferred from referent to name as a consequence of conditioning. The difficulty lies in finding the response. Someone who knows that *rain* refers to rain does not always react to the word as he would to the thing itself. He does not raise an umbrella whenever someone says *rain* any more than he says *rain* whenever he sees, hears, or feels it. Overt reaction to the word as a sign of the referent is like the use of the word to name the referent, not something he invariably does but something he is able to do when it is called for. In many situations, e.g., lecture listening and book reading, he makes no overt response and yet we must suppose that he understands what he hears or reads. Conditioning theorists, like image theorists, have wondered what the click of comprehension can be. In view of the similarities between reference and conditioning they believe the click to be a response. Obviously this cannot be an ordinary overt response. It must be some kind of concealed, subtle reaction that gives meaning to words.

Meaning as an Implicit Response. The principal conscious components of word meanings were classically taken to be images. For these Watson substituted the notion of implicit behavior. Explicit behavior is readily observed. Implicit reactions are not so easily detected. They comprise movements of the larynx—short of actual vocalization—as well as miniature actions of the fingers, hands, and body as a whole. Watson definitely located these reactions in the muscles of the periphery.

Implicit responses outside the vocal apparatus have not been studied extensively. However, one interesting experiment is that of Jacobson, called "Electrophysiology of Mental Activities" (109). Jacobson attached electrodes to various muscles in the body of a subject; then allowed the subject to lie on a couch in a darkened room and instructed him to relax. While in this state the subject was sometimes asked to imagine that he was raising his right arm or even to imagine that he was swinging a golf club. On no account, however, was he to move. With these directions Jacobson obtained action currents from the muscles that would have been involved in a full scale overt performance of the commanded movement. No such action currents were obtained from other muscles in the body. When commands followed a complicated instruction to imagine some act without performing it there were implicit responses which may be described as a miniature performance.

It may be proposed, then, that meanings are implicit responses originally elicited by referents and then, through association, by words. This view is not discredited by everyday observations of the uncertainty and variation in response to language since these observations always involve overt response. The image—a faint copy of sensation—is supplanted as the kernel of meaning by the implicit response—a faint copy of overt behavior.

There are difficulties with the implicit response reminiscent of those urged against the image. While images were often reported when subjects were asked to imagine something this is not clear evidence that images ordinarily occur when signs are understood. There is the possibility that the laboratory demonstration involved special conditions not ordinarily realized. This possibility is also very strong in Jacobson's experiment. He has shown that action currents appear when a subject is wired with electrodes and instructed to imagine a movement without performing it. The subject's effort to obey in these circumstances overflows into a tension of action-relevant muscles. The action current may be the resultant of conflicting tendencies toward movement and the inhibition of movement and might not occur in any other circumstances. It has not been demonstrated that we perform a miniature replica of a movement whenever we hear a command. If the command is addressed to me, and if I am so disposed, I will overtly perform the action. If the command is not addressed to me or if I am disinclined to obey I will not execute it overtly. Whether or not my muscles will do so to a slight degree is unknown.

The utterances used in the Jacobson study were all commands. It is not clear what implicit reactions would be elicited by statements that carry no imperative. What response originally evoked by the thing apple is produced by the word *apple* in the sentence "The apple is red"? With the best will in the world it is difficult to know which muscle to twitch. Conceivably the oculo-motor muscles might react as if to move the eyes around the outline of a real apple. Jacobson observed overt actions from these muscles when subjects were asked to visualize various things. But it has not been demonstrated that there are characteristic action patterns for different words and it is difficult to imagine eye movements appropriate to abstract terms like *animal* and *triangle*.

Finally, of course, any theory that equates meaning with particular muscle actions must predict that words will lose their meaning when relevant muscles are immobilized. No theory is really willing to stand by that prediction.

Meaning as a Mediating Response. Charles Osgood (173) has revised the conditioning model, but continues to think of meaning as a particular response—a mediating response. The first principle of Osgood's theory reads: "Stimulus-objects typically elicit a complex pattern of reactions from the organism, some of which are dependent upon the sensory presence of the object for their occurrence and others of which can occur without the object being present." Thus food will elicit sequences of salivating, lip-smacking, chewing, and swallowing. Of these responses the salivation and lip-smacking could quite easily occur in the absence of the food itself, while chewing and swallowing are not likely to occur unless the organism has food in its mouth. Osgood calls the responses that are relatively independent of the eliciting object the detachable components of the total reaction.

The theory continues: "When other stimuli occur in conjunction with the stimulus-object, they tend to be conditioned to the total pattern of reactions elicited by the object, when later presented without support of the stimulus-object, these other stimuli elicit only the 'detachable' reactions." The response to the sign is identical with a fractional component of the total reaction elicited by the stimulus object. In accordance with a suggestion of Clark Hull (100), Osgood holds that the fractional response will tend to abbreviate. The more energy expended in making a mediating reaction, the less likely it is to survive the reduction process. In general the reaction will tend toward a minimum—the only limitation being the requirement that it remain discriminable. Osgood treats the mediating responses "as if they involved actual (though minimal) muscular and glandular reactions." In other words the mediating response appears to be implicit.

This is essentially Watson's position, with a few qualifications about the fractional nature of the reaction which apparently make no real difference. In fact, however, the theory (even in this incomplete exposition) has several special properties. Osgood has said that stimulus objects typically *elicit* a complex behavior pattern from the organism. The word "elicit" is used by Skinner (212) and Hilgard and Marquis (93) to refer to the highly reliable, experimentally controlled evocation of response by means of an unconditioned stimulus in the classical conditioning procedure. The appearance of the response is highly correlated with the presentation of the stimulus. Food powder elicits salivation. The elicited response is ordinarily contrasted with the *emitted* response of instrumental training. Appearance of the emitted response is not clearly correlated with any particular stimulus. Thus it would be hard to say what stimulus change is concurrent with the eventual tripping of the latch by Thorndike's cat in the problem box (223) or the pressing of the lever by Skinner's rat (212). The animal is in the same box, confronted by the same apparatus, and moved by the same drives as when it does not perform the critical action.

In one of Osgood's linguistic examples the word "elicit" seems appropriate. He describes the meaning of the word "spider" as a kind of autonomic fear reaction originally elicited by that fearful stimulus object. In his general treatment of mediating responses the word "elicit" seems appropriately used in his description of the process whereby a buzzer comes to evoke the salivation originally elicited by food and also in his treatment of the situation in which a buzzer comes to elicit autonomic fear reactions originally elicited by shock. Although these are the examples on which Osgood leans most heavily he definitely does not mean to limit his theory to situations of classical conditioning. One of his linguistic examples goes beyond such situations. The meaning of the word "hammer" is said to consist of incipient movements of grasping and pounding. These movements in overt form are said to be elicited in a child by the stimulus object hammer. This elicitation cannot be like that involved in the autonomic response to shock or the salivary response to food in the mouth.

Like most objects that might serve as referents for linguistic forms the hammer does not, on first presentation, evoke the same reaction in all human beings (as shock and food powder in the mouth may be supposed to do). If one could count on a species-wide unlearned reaction to all stimulus objects then it would only be necessary to provide linguistic signs for the various objects and we should all use our words with the same meanings, i.e., the same fractional components of innate reactions to stimulus objects. In such a case it would furthermore follow that people everywhere must have the same meanings to convey and disagree only in the arbitrary signs to be used in expressing these common meanings. This is more semantic agreement than any theory can use. For while communication must be accounted for, it is not perfect either from society to society or between individuals in one society.

Most objects are involved in a variety of reactions. In a given setting one reaction will become more probable if it has reinforcing consequences. It follows that linguistic signs will have the same meaning for different people if these people are trained to behave in the same way with the objects named. Since the selective reinforcement determining such behavior will generally be secondary reinforcement, socially mediated, it follows that meanings are a cultural acquisition. If we are correct in believing that all of us in the same linguistic community understand our words in much the same way then the reinforcement must be reasonably uniform throughout the society. At the same time it is certainly probable that there is some variation in the use of various objects and this will account for the idiosyncratic element in each man's understanding of the same utterance.

In an image theory the meaning of a word depends principally on the sensible properties of the object named since the meaning is supposed to be a representation of the object. In Osgood's theory the meaning of a word depends principally on the actions in which the object is characteristically involved. This is, at least, a desirable counterbalance to the image theory since a hammer means grasping-and-pounding as surely as it means an object with a wooden handle and an iron head.

What evidence is there for the existence of such fractional implicit responses? Jacobson's work demonstrated that some words sometimes evoke implicit responses. This study does not demonstrate that the implicit responses discovered are fractional components of reactions to stimulus objects that may be considered referents for the words used. The evidence for actual conditioning of fractional implicit reactions has all been obtained with autonomic reaction to shock or with salivation to food powder. And there are good reasons to doubt that either of these is sufficiently covert and abbreviated to be a meaning. There are many studies in which one or the other of these reactions has been conditioned to a number of different words. If we were to take these responses for the meanings of the words it would follow that the words had been given identical meanings by this conditioning procedure and that is patently absurd. It is necessary to say that these responses are at most only a part of the total mediating reaction, the remainder of the reaction not having been observed in any of these studies. In sum, there is scarcely any direct evidence for the existence of mediating responses elicited by linguistic signs.

What can be said of the plausibility of such responses? We worried a great deal about abstract words when playing the role of image-theorist. It proved difficult to conceive of an image generic enough to represent terms like *man, animal,* and *triangle.* The mediating responses to such terms are not any easier to imagine. We are involved in a great many behavior sequences with animals. What incipient tendency can be expected to survive the process of reduction? Osgood is aware of this difficulty and at one point mentions that the mediation activity aroused by such a class term as "animal" must be rather hybrid in nature. As a consequence of the inconceivability of these mediators we could not verify the theory by studying implicit reactions to words for the reason that we should not know where to attach our electrodes. Where might we be likely to find the mediating reaction to "animal"?

But we have not exhausted Osgood's ingenuity. He has recognized this difficulty and pushed the mediating response back into the nervous system where no one will undertake to look for it. Although he has generally treated mediation processes as if they were implicit responses he concludes his discussion by saying that "the mediation notion does not *require* that mediators be peripheral." Mediation is a hypothetical construct. It could be entirely cortical without invalidating behavioral implications. The theory is not to be judged on the evidence for fractional implicit responses but by the success with which it predicts—together with the rest of Osgood's learning theory—overt behavior. I have found that this success cannot, at present, be given anything approaching a conclusive evaluation.

Conditioning theories of linguistic meaning have been squeezed by the same pressures as image theories and have retreated under pressure to the same sanctuary—the central nervous system. Assuming that words must have immediate effects, and plagued by a shortage of overt effects, the conditioning theorist has revised his conception of meaning from overt response to implicit and eventually mediated response. Finally, behavioral meanings are found cheek-by-jowl with imaginal meanings inside the organism—neither revealed in action nor available to introspection.

Meaning as a Behavior Disposition

In *Ethics and Language* (220) Charles Stevenson turns away from any effort to describe the click of comprehension that occurs whenever a linguistic form is understood. I do the same.* If there are such immediate and invariable reactions they are neuro-physiological in character and had best be studied by the sciences concerned with such things. In Stevenson's view, "The meaning of a sign, in the psychological sense required, is not some specific psychological process that attends the sign at any one time. It is rather a dispositional property of the sign, where the response, varying with varying attendant circumstances, consists of psychological processes in a hearer, and where the stimulus is his hearing of the sign."

---

*Charles Morris in his book *Signs, Language, and Behavior* (170), also treats meaning as a behavior disposition.

It seems to me that when one comes to understand a linguistic form his nervous system is partially rewired (in the sense of changes in synaptic resistances or neurone process growth) so that one is disposed to behave appropriately with regard to that form. For the psychologist meaning is not any particular response. It is the disposition to behave in varying ways with regard to the form as the contingent circumstances are changed. The disposition has no substantial character other than the structure of the nervous system. It is not a leaning, a beginning, a miniature reaction. It is a response potential. A disposition is discovered by creating various contingencies and observing responses.

Within a linguistic community there are standards (not necessarily formulated) for the usage of an utterance and for total behavior with reference to the utterance. These standards define appropriate behavior, the conventional disposition. A child born into the community does not at first conform to these standards, but he eventually does so and is then said to speak and understand the language.

I am satisfied that the disposition theory gives a more sensible account of linguistic meaning than any variety of particular reaction theory. But it does not seem to be any more suggestive of experimental problems. The image and the implicit response discourage the psychological empiricist because they have been locked away where he can't get at them. The disposition theory deals with overt behavior but with such masses of overt behavior as to generate a new kind of discouragement. A man might give all his productive years to spelling out the behavioral meaning of a single utterance and find the task unfinished in the end. Very likely this is the order of complexity in behavior necessary to a treatment of linguistic meaning but how do we begin to make a study of the subject? We can see the appeal of the particular reaction theory. Better a single reaction, however elusive, than infinitely large, shifting oceans of overt behavior.

The Response Central to the Disposition. There is a way to begin. The responses of the meaning-disposition are not all of equal importance—there are responses which are functionally central to the disposition. In social psychology the "attitude" is a dispositional concept. One who has an attitude of antagonism toward Transylvanians is disposed to do many different things, depending on the attendant circumstances. If a Transylvanian moves next door he will lead the neighbors in protest. If his daughter plans to marry a Transylvanian he will oppose the marriage. No one has ever listed all the situation-response probabilities implicit in any attitude. Yet we do research with attitudes. We get along with simple, accessible responses to questionnaires.

It is customary to assume that a man who strongly favors (on paper) sending all Transylvanians "back where they came from" will generally behave in antagonistic fashion as contingent circumstances change. We believe it is possible to make extensive inferences about unrealized behavior from the single answer to the attitude questionnaire. In fact, of course, we have never made a systematic check on this belief. It may be that social psychologists have sometimes dealt with "paper attitudes" that had no action implications. We recognize that the verbal expression may not predict a general disposition when we acknowledge that a man may pretend to less prejudice than he actually practices. However, we have a large store of individually and incidentally collected evidence that the single verbal response usually predicts a large number of other responses.

For a dispositional theory of linguistic meaning attitudes are themselves fractional meanings—dispositions within larger dispositions. One man's antagonistic actions and remarks are part of the meaning *Transylvanian* has to him. Within the linguistic community these pro-and-con behaviors seem roughly to fall on an ordinal scale so that if an individual manifests behavior D he will also manifest A, B, and C, given the proper contingencies. A man who is willing to lynch Transylvanians will also oppose their election to his club. Reaction D implies A, B, and C while reaction C implies B and A. Of course these behaviors are only approximately scalable. There will be men who express extreme dislike of Transylvanians and yet treat them very well in most circumstances. Why there should be even a rough serial order among behaviors is a difficult question. It is not because the thresholds of activation for pro-and-con behaviors have a natural serial order in all human beings. The same item of behavior (biting one's thumb at someone) will scale differently in different cultures. In any case there seems always to be some notion of degree—that some behaviors are more "extreme" on a given scale and so imply a disposition to perform less extreme behaviors on the same scale.

But attitudinal, pro-and-con behaviors are only a fraction of linguistic meanings. Are the relations among the other responses of a meaning disposition such that one can infer from one to another? Clearly, we all believe that they are. A vocabulary test undertakes to discover whether an individual knows the meanings of a set of words. No test exhausts the disposition attached to any word. Vocabulary tests always deal with single appropriate responses. In a familiar kind of test the critical word is to be matched with the nearest synonym, choosing from four alternative words. When someone can make the proper match we credit him with understanding the word. Note that this judgment is not consistent with the more popular theories of linguistic meaning. No tester undertakes to find images or mediating responses. We credit the subject with more than the particular demonstrated ability. This is clear from the fact that we should be confounded to discover that someone who knew that *idiosyncrasy* meant *peculiarity* knew absolutely nothing else about either word. How surprised we should be if he could not use either word in a sentence, could not identify a single idiosyncrasy or peculiarity in anyone's behavior. The answer to the vocabulary test, like the answer to an attitude questionnaire, is believed to be diagnostic of a sizeable behavior disposition.

However, the vocabulary match could be an isolated competence. I could teach someone who did not "understand" a word of English to match *idiosyncrasy* with *peculiarity* and, indeed, I could teach him to make the matches that would produce a very high vocabulary score. Yet we are right to infer that one who can match vocabulary items will also know many additional appropriate responses. It is not logically necessary that this be so but it is empirically highly probable. As languages are ordinarily learned it will seldom happen that an individual develops these responses without also having acquired many other appropriate behaviors.

To sit with eyes converging on a book, making periodic eye movements and turning pages at regular intervals is a sign of literacy. It raises a presumption of general competence in using the language. We should be taken aback to discover that someone who sat thus by the hour could neither pronounce nor translate a word of the print he scanned. Yet we know that this skill can be assumed in the absence of understanding. Whole audiences have nodded wisely at uncomprehended Latin orations. The family dog

sometimes sprawls on the floor staring at a newspaper, and is jokingly said to be reading his paper. Jokingly, because we know that
he will fail such further tests of comprehension as a request to
paraphrase what he has read. In general, however, individuals who
appear to read will have a large repertoire of appropriate responses
involving the language. All societies will have norms for the sequence in which language skills are acquired. It follows that the
later skills generally imply earlier skills.

Now it could happen that the sequence in which language skills
are acquired is a perfectly arbitrary matter with nothing to make
one sequence preferable to another. If this were the case there
probably would be little agreement on the sequence from one
society to another. Alternatively, it may be that the learning of
some responses creates the disposition to make other appropriate
responses on which one has not had any specific training. There
may be language skills especially useful for teaching the whole
language system—skills with high transfer value. These should
tend to occur early in any society's training sequence. In empirical
studies of linguistic meanings we cannot deal with total behavior
dispositions but must concentrate on particular behaviors. For
certain practical purposes (determination of vocabulary size) it is
enough to know that individuals who possess one appropriate response will generally also possess many others. For these purposes
it doesn't matter whether the implication is strictly conventional,
a matter of arbitrary normative sequence, or whether the implication holds because the particular responses observed are able to
generate further responses without further training. For the theoretical psychology of language, however, accidental sequences are
of little interest while functional sequences are of great interest.
The science of linguistic meaning might profit from a redefinition
of its problem. The task is not to find the constant reaction that
lies behind the varying overt behavior but rather to find functionally central responses within the overt behavior.

It has been difficult to hold this discussion of reference and
meaning close to the single linguistic form and the time has come
to give it up. An attempt to understand the meaning of a single
linguistic form in isolation from the total language process would
be rather like trying to understand a single bid in isolation from
a game of bridge. The meaning of a form, its total conventional
usage, involves the full language game.

As Wittgenstein (251) has shown, there is a more than a casual similarity between language and a game. If someone wants to learn to play bridge he can do so by watching others at play. When he has learned the game he will not be restricted to the bids and moves that others have been observed to make but will be able to originate novel yet appropriate moves. He has not memorized a particular set of contingencies and actions but, rather, from observing a limited set, he has extracted rules that enable him to act appropriately in any contingency that may arise in any particular game of bridge. And so it is with speech. From observation of a limited sample of play one learns the rules of this game and becomes a kind of creative participant, extending the game along lines permitted by its structure. Psychological semantics cannot describe all the appropriate moves involving any one utterance. What it might try to do is to describe performances which indicate that general rules have been extracted and then discover the experiences that make these performances possible.

The ability to name new instances of a referent and the ability to react to a name as a sign of a referent seem to be performances that give evidence of the possession of very general dispositions. Suppose a person can correctly name a set of new instances of the triangle category, instances differing in size, color, and position and set in contrast with such figures as squares and pentagons. Such a person will usually be able to identify indefinite numbers of triangles as yet unseen. Suppose he can react to the word *triangle* as he does to the attributes of triangles themselves. He can learn new reactions to new triangles and we may be confident that these too will transfer to the name of the category. For a person with these skills the word *triangle* can be used effectively to define new terms. To be told that *lampshades* are roughly *triangular* in shape will help him to identify instances of this new category in which triangularity figures as a criterial attribute. The two central skills, ability to name instances and ability to react to the name as a sign of an instance, are both created by experience of the name in association with instances of the referent category. This is an experience that comes early to all children and these are skills that adults everywhere look for as evidence of the comprehension of linguistic forms. The reference-making procedure and the two abilities it creates are central to the language game.

I can suggest one other kind of skill which is predictive of general appropriate usage. Suppose we provide a person with a selection of sentence frames, such as "The————is good," "He ————ed," "The soup is————good," "The————was bad." We then ask him to indicate the frames in which *triangle* could possibly be inserted. If he indicates nominal positions for *triangle* then probably he has a general disposition to use this word in one vast population of frames and to exclude it from another more vast population. This skill seems to depend on two kinds of experience. The subject must have seen different words placed in the same frames and so learned that words fall into classes of functional equivalents (the parts of speech). Once that is known he will place *triangle* in the nominal class if he experiences it in one or two characteristic frames and will then have a very elaborate disposition with regard to this word. Students of language have conventionally classified this sort of disposition as belonging to grammar rather than meaning. Since I define meaning as the total disposition to make use of or react to a linguistic form, it follows that a readiness to use words in accordance with conventions about the parts of speech is a part of meaning. However, it is a part that can be distinguished from reference.

The use of a word in sentences expressing an attitude toward the referent is another part of meaning, but not a part that is uniform within a linguistic community. Agreement on norms of reference and grammar constitute the community. Within these norms individuals can construct sentences expressive of various attitudes toward the same referent and name. Their meanings are somewhat different since they are disposed to form some different utterances. But these differences lie within a larger agreement. We begin here to touch on variations in meaning within a community, variations that can cause failures in communication. Only a part of an individual's disposition with regard to a linguistic form is cultural, only a part of our dispositions are held in common. This sharing makes some communication possible between all members of the community. More communication is possible for those who have larger areas of overlap.

Summary

In the past it has been assumed that linguistic meanings are, from a psychological point of view, particular reactions set off in a person by meaningful linguistic forms. It has always been understood that the observation of others using linguistic forms to make reference helps to teach the meanings of these forms. Consequently those who have attempted to describe the meaning reaction have looked to reference and its consequences for suggestions. Some have noticed that the act of linguistic reference teaches people to use the linguistic form to name referents. That ability would seem to depend on some internal representation of the referent, some mental image. Perhaps this mental image is the reaction that occurs whenever a meaningful form is understood. Others have noticed that reference teaches a person to use the name as a sign of its referent. One reacts in certain circumstances which include the name as if these circumstances included some experience of the referent instead of the name. Perhaps there is some kind of subtle response of muscle or gland that is originally released by the referent and which, through conditioning, comes to be released by the name whenever the name is understood. The meaning reaction may be a covert response of muscle or gland. Neither of these proposals can stand up to the evidence. Both traditions ultimately agree that the essential meaning reaction must be central or neuro-physiological in character. That may be. If we focus on behavior, and leave the central reaction to others, the meaning of a linguistic form appears to be the total disposition to make use of and react to the form. Within this disposition, however, some behavior seems to be more worthy of study than does other behavior—more worthy because it is somehow fundamental in creating the full disposition. The two best examples of such behavior, in my opinion, are the two abilities with which the theories of meaning begin—the ability to name referents and the ability to react to names as signs of referents. Both of these are generated by experience of name and referent in association.

chapter iv

Phonetic Symbolism
and Metaphor

PLATO (188) SETS the problem of the dialogue
called *Cratylus* in the following words:

> Hermogenes. I should explain to you, Socrates, that our friend
> Cratylus has been arguing about names; he says that they are nat-
> ural and not conventional; not a portion of the human voice which
> men agree to use; but that there is a truth or correctness in them,
> which is the same for Hellenes as barbarians.

These words also set the problem of this chapter. In the *Cratylus*
two principles of correctness in naming are described. I call these
principles metaphor and phonetic symbolism.

Name can be understood narrowly to mean the name of a man—
a proper name. The principle of correctness in a name is then to be
found in its etymology. Agamemnon is truly named since he is
literally called "admirable for remaining" and his endurance at
Troy demonstrates an admirable steadfastness. An irreligious, evil
man would not be correctly named *Theophilus* (beloved of God)
or *Mnesitheus* (mindful of God). However, *name* also has a wider
sense by which it includes all reference-making linguistic forms,

(110)

whether proper nouns, general nouns, verbs, phrases, or whatever. Whenever any name is applied to a new referent one can ask whether this application is appropriate to its prior usage. Is *Tide* a good name for a washing powder in the light of that word's familiar application to the periodic movement of the seas? Is *underwear* a good name for the garments worn beneath one's outer clothing in the light of the familiar uses of the component forms *under* and *wear*? Is *television* aptly named considering the meanings of its Latin roots? Was Richard I properly called "the lion hearted" considering what lions are like? The etymological appropriateness of a proper name like *Agamemnon* is a special case under the general principle of metaphorical appropriateness. This principle applies whenever one name is used for two different referent categories. The later use is appropriate to the earlier insofar as the two categories share criterial attributes.

Phonetic symbolism is concerned with the association between a name and a single referent-category. This association is appropriate to the degree that the name-category shares criterial attributes with the referent-category. Socrates believed that some of the sounds of Greek speech had a shaky, quivering quality, that some had a penetrating quality, that others made him particularly aware of articulational movement. The presence of such sounds in words that labelled referent categories which also had attributes of shakiness, penetration, or movement made appropriate names of these words. The link here is between name and referent.

In this chapter we shall consider phonetic symbolism first. The principal question here has always been whether the thing exists at all. There has never been any doubt of the reality of metaphor. Indeed, it is ubiquitous in all languages. However, there are certain words in English and other languages, the vocabulary of sensation, whose metaphorical status is doubtful.

Phonetic Symbolism

Experimental studies of this subject divide into those dealing with artificial words and those concerned with natural languages. Among the studies of artificial words are some in which subjects were asked to choose appropriate meanings for the experimenter's phonetic creations and some in which subjects were asked to invent new words for meanings suggested by the experimenter. It then remains to determine the relevance of this evidence to the problem of the origin of speech and finally to determine what part phonetic symbolism plays in mature language function today.

Choosing Meanings for Artificial Words. The artificial words of these experiments are consonant-vowel-consonant forms like *mel.* A form like *mel* is a word for a speaker of English in the sense that it makes a tolerable combination of letters (or sounds). It could become a meaningful form in English more easily than such combinations as *mle* or *lme,* which violate our customs of orthography and phonology. We don't begin words with the consonant clusters *ml* or *lm* and we think of these clusters as unpronounceable. *Mel,* though not a conventional English word, is a conventional syllable (*Melba, Melville*) and could become a word.*

Mel is not a word because there are no community-wide rules of definition for this form. That is not to say that *mel* is devoid of meaning: the syllable brings many things to mind—*melody, melancholy,* etc. However, *mel* differs from a sequence like *elm* in that there are no rules of transformation for *mel.* To the question, "What is an *elm*?" there are normative replies. "It is a kind of tree." To the question, "What is a *mel*?" one might get answers but none that constitutes a social norm. There are no conventional rules of transformation, no conventional verbal definitions. In the case of *elm* there are also rules of reference relating the word to non-linguistic objects. In a park we can point out the *elms* but not the *mels.* In the sense that *mel* has no conventional definition, neither verbal nor referential, it is nonsense. And so these experimental materials might be called nonsense syllables, in agreement with Ebbinghaus (60), or artificial or potential or non-linguistic words.

Edward Sapir (200) posed the following problem concerning these nonsense syllables or artificial words. A speaker of English is told that the syllables *mal* and *mil* both have the meaning table but that one of the syllables is to symbolize a large table and the other syllable a small table. It is the subject's task to decide which syllable is more appropriate in each case. The syllables are matched

---

*Since the syllable *mel* was used in Sapir's (200) experiments it has, in fact, become a word. In the technical vocabulary of sensory psychology the *mel* is the unit of a scale of subjective pitch (219).

for initial and final consonants. They differ in the vowels inter-
polated between the consonants. It must then be the vowel that
determines the subject's decision. Sapir constructed syllables to
contrast the vowels [a] (as in German *Mann*), [æ] (of English
hat), [E] (of English *met*), [e] (of French *été*), and [i] (of
French *fini*). In addition he used syllables that contrasted consonants.

With some 500 subjects, ranging in age from eleven-year-old
children to adults, he always found impressively large agreement
on the relative size implications of the sounds studied. For the
contrast of [a] and [i], for instance, about 80 per cent of his subjects of all ages agreed that [a] should be the larger.

In 1933 Stanley Newman (168) further analyzed Sapir's data
and collected additional data on the same general plan. He placed
the vowels on a scale of magnitude and found that they fell in the
order [i], [e], [E], [æ], [a] from small to large. This sequence
is familiar to a phonetician since it closely duplicates (1) the re-
ceding positions of articulation made by the tongue within the
mouth, (2) the decreasing frequencies of vocal resonance as measured acoustically, and (3) the increasing size of the oral cavity
used in pronunciation. Adding the vowels [u] (as in English
who'd), [o] (as in English *hoed*), and [ɔ] (as in English
hawed), he found that these vowels were judged to be larger than
the five studied by Sapir. In general, larger magnitudes are associated with a large oral cavity, a low vocalic resonance, and an
articulation of the tongue toward the back of the mouth.

With consonants there were also consistent and systematic relations. It is customary to group consonants by articulatory position.
The alveolars are produced by touching the tip of the tongue to
the hard gum ridge behind the upper teeth (as in [t], [d]).
Labials are made by bringing the lips together (as in [b], [p]).
Palatals are produced by bringing the back of the tongue up to
the soft palate (as [g], [k]). Among these three positions of
articulation the order of size implication was (from small to large)
alveolar, labial, and palatal. Many English consonants fall into
pairs, of which one is voiced and the other is its unvoiced equivalent ([d], [t]; [b], [p]; [g], [k]). The voiced consonant usually
seemed the larger of the two.

Newman also had subjects contrast sounds for the dimension,

bright to dark. In part this dimension correlated with magnitude, the larger vowels being darker and the voiced consonants both large and dark. The correlation was not perfectly consistent, however. In one respect, brightness was associated with largeness and darkness with smallness; among consonants the order of articulations—alveolar, labial, palatal—runs from dark to bright.

The findings of Sapir and Newman can be illustrated with reference to the English word *God*. This word, by virtue of its sounds alone, suggests a very great magnitude. It is composed of a back vowel and two voiced consonants. I even wonder if the greater piety for me of the pronunciation *Gawd* is not partially due to the still greater magnitude of this vowel ([ɔ]). In general, the word is dark as well as large. However, the first consonant is articulated in the bright palatal position. It will not be surprising if the religious American finds the Frenchman's *Dieu* a puny unsatisfactory name for *Gawd. Jehovah,* on the other hand, is magnificently large.

The discoveries of Sapir and Newman are unexpected and fascinating. We all know about onomatopoeia—the imitation of nonspeech sound in speech. But this is not onomatopoeia. Here speech sounds suggest spatial and visual dimensions, size and brightness. We all know that in poetry the sound sometimes echoes the sense. We have heard that there are people whose senses are unified, so that they have colored hearing and what not; this is called "synaesthesia." But these are exotic phenomena, not experienced ordinarily. Even those who report them disagree among themselves. Does "trippingly on the tongue" echo its sense or not? Is a C major chord on the piano the color of old gold or of new leaves? The whole business of intersensory connections has always seemed dubious to us. And now Sapir has invented a task which most of us would undertake bemusedly—the matching of unfamiliar words to meanings—and hundreds of unsophisticated subjects of all ages have agreed very well on the answers. They were surprised, and we are surprised.

How have we come by this ability to judge the size and brightness of words? It might be that we answer by analogy with familiar English words. The vowel of the word *large* is like that of *mal* while the vowel of *little* is like *mil*. On the other hand, the vowel of the word *big* is like *mil* while *small* is like *mal*. This seems unsatisfactory. Perhaps, however, in English as a whole there are correlations between vowels and magnitudes which we have abstracted and are able to use in order to decide on the size of *mal*. The high agreement among subjects would then be just a cultural uniformity. If such associations are learned they must be learned early since Sapir's eleven-year-old subjects agreed somewhat better than his older subjects. If the associations in the language are a purely arbitrary convention it seems odd that they should be systematic, with magnitudes increasing as vowels move back in the mouth and fall in pitch. Perhaps there is something natural and inevitable in these associations of sound, size, and brightness. Perhaps all people, whatever their linguistic training, would make the same judgments. All of these matters must be deferred until we have seen more of the evidence.

In 1924 Usnadze (230) studied the process by which ten German adults selected names for a set of unfamiliar, "nonsense" drawings. He provided them with a list of nonsense words (spelled phonetically) from which a choice was to be made for each drawing. In some cases subjects found the nonsense drawing reminiscent of a familiar object and then selected the nonsense word most like the conventional name of the conventional object. This is not the process we are after. In certain more interesting cases the subject chose a name with the same *Gestalt* or form as the picture. We can't be quite sure what "similar form" in a word and a picture would be like and the author does not make this point clear. However, Usnadze's study has inspired a recent research that makes clear the nature of similar *Gestalten*.

In 1954, at Heidelberg, Wissemann (250) studied the creation of onomatopoeic words. His subjects were adults who had graduated from high school. Wissemann used three different procedures. In all cases he provided noises which were to be assigned suitable names. In some cases the names were selected from a prepared list; in other cases the subjects created the names *de novo*.

The subject was always tested individually. While he listened, the experimenter, in an adjoining room, worked with chains, a cooking pot, a spiral spring, a horn comb, and other unlikely laboratory apparatus to produce fourteen different noises. The technique for producing each noise is described in great detail. The first noise, for instance, is made by striking an iron weight of 5 kg. with a hammer weighing .5 kg. The blow is given with such force that the hammer immediately recoils to strike a second lighter blow. Forty-five double strokes a minute are prescribed. For the second noise a lacquered wooden ball (of specified weight and diameter) is rolled down a plywood board (dimensions also specified) at an inclination of 13° (from the horizontal) to drop at last into a metal box (which is 23 cm. on each side). The third task is, by comparison, rather loosely described. A *"Bierflasche"* (two-thirds full of water) is to be shaken *"so dass das Wasser bei den ruckartigen Bewegungsänderungen in der Flasche hin und her geschleudert wurde."* [For the movement of water in a bottle it is difficult to imagine a better onomatopoeic form than *geschleudert* itself.] In subsequent performances the experimenter snaps a piece of wood, pushes over a tower built of wooden blocks, and smashes a glass vessel on the floor.

There are many very interesting things in this study. For instance, one might guess that the length of an onomatopoeic name would be proportional to the duration of the noise so that polysyllabic words would represent noises of great duration. This is not the case. The number of syllables corresponds to the number of divisions heard in the noise. Syllables express the differentiation of the noise rather than its duration. Stress is used to highlight especially loud, or otherwise salient, divisions in the noise.

A noise that had an abrupt onset was usually given a name beginning with a voiceless stop consonant ([p], [t], [k]). Voiceless stops are also called plosives for the very good reason that they explode, their sound begins at peak intensity; it is not graduated. A noise having a gradual onset was usually named by a word having an initial spirant consonant ([s] [z]) and the spirant is of course a speech sound that begins gradually. The initial sounds of onomatopoeic names reproduce the stimulus gradients of referent noises.

These few results suggest the nature of Usnadze's similar *Gestalten* in names and drawings. The number of syllables might correspond to the number of perceptual sub-wholes in a drawing. The form of a visual gradient could be reproduced in sound. The sound spectrogram pictures the plosive [p] as a dark smudge that does not shade off at the edges while [s] is a gradually darkening area. The spectrogram shows how recurrence, relative strength, and rhythm in sound can be represented in a picture.

Wissemann's subjects were asked to say why they favored certain sounds in their onomatopoeic words. They were not provided with any standard terminology for making this report. It is remarkable, therefore, that most subjects agreed that the vowels should be used to express the pitch (high, middle, or low) and tone color (bright, colorless, dark) of the referent noise. These two dimensions appeared in perfect correlation, with high pitch corresponding to bright tone color. The vowels [i], [ü], and [ö] are clear and high while [u] and [o] are dark and low. Other vowels are intermediate on both dimensions.

Wissemann's findings for tone color are in agreement with Newman's results. The vowels [ü] and [ö] were not included in the American studies. Their symbolic placement with the high front [i] reinforces the view of all these authors that tongue position is a more important articulational determinant of phonetic symbolism than is lip formation. Rounded vowels are dark and low when articulated with the back of the tongue but they are bright and high when articulated with the front of the tongue. In this connection it is of some interest to recall Eberhardt's (61) results obtained by using the Sapir-Newman procedures with deaf children. While these subjects ordered English vowels in much the same way as hearing subjects they displaced the [u], judging it to be quite small. It is probable that proprioceptive cues from the rounded lips are a more salient part of the vowel impression for the deaf than for the hearing and that this rounding suggests a small magnitude.

With all their representational features the onomatopoeic words had also certain conventional aspects. This is true of the onomatopoeic words of natural languages. While roughly imitative, the words for the cry of the rooster (*cock-a-doodle-doo* in English, *kykeliky* in Danish, *kikericki* in French, *coquelico* in Spanish) are also conditioned by the individual language. They represent locally acceptable sound combinations. Many of Wissemann's subjects limited themselves in word creation to the sounds of German speech and to conventional combinations of these. Some even attached characteristic part-of-speech suffixes to their words so that they can be recognized as intended verbs or as intended exclamations.

While many of Wissemann's subjects coined words according

to the formulas of German phonology, they did not all do so. Some introduced very un-German retroflex sounds and even Hottentot clicks and smacks. It happened, occasionally, that a subject described a vowel sound he couldn't produce, e.g., a vowel midway between two familiar German sounds. There were many impossible phonetic clusters—"impossible" in the sense that they violate German phonology. It seems to have been possible for some subjects to imitate the noise in comparative freedom from their speech training. Still even the most unorthodox subject was far from realizing all the noise-making possibilities of his vocal apparatus. They all produced speech. There were no howls, croaks, or groans.

With the Wissemann study we cannot help raising the question of the origin of speech. His subjects, without any discussion or instruction, used similar principles in their invention of onomatopoeic words. Presumably they could have decoded one another's words since they were operating on the same rules of semantic representation. Indeed, they shared one semantic rule (the correlation of vowels with brightness and darkness) with Newman's American subjects. Is it possible that primal man created his first words in accordance with these same imitative rules and that these rules, being "natural" to all men, made translation of the first words easy? Wissemann's educated adults are a long way from primal man. His subjects share a language tradition. Perhaps it is that tradition which suggests the syllable as the unit of the noise and the vowel as its tone quality. Newman's subjects had a different native language but one too closely related to German for us to be sure that the brightness values of vowels are independent of language training. These problems of interpretation had better be deferred until we see what is known of phonetic symbolism in natural languages.

Phonetic Symbolism in Natural Languages. Can it be doubted that phonetic symbolism exists in all the languages we know? Consider the case of the high front vowels, [i] (as in French *fini*) and [I] (as in English *hit*). In the experiments of Sapir, Newman, and Wissemann these vowels, when they appeared in nonsense words, were judged to be small and bright. Otto Jespersen (118) believed that these vowels were significantly related in natural languages to a cluster of meanings: the qualities small, insignificant, weak, and rapid. From his great knowledge of the Indo-European languages he drew a vast collection of confirming instances. Here are some words for *little:* in German *kleine,* in French *petite,* in Italian *piccola,* in Latin *minor,* in Magyar *kis,* in Greek *mikros.* Then there is the formation of the diminutive. In English we add an [i] to make *Bobby* of *Bob* and *birdie* of *bird.* In Italian the suffix *ino,* in Spanish the suffixes *ico* and *ito* are diminutives. Jespersen had a wonderful collection of anecdotes about children who made their own phonetic alterations in conformity with the symbolism of vowels. For instance, a nephew of von der Gabelentz used the word *lakeil* for an ordinary chair, while the word for a big easy chair was *lukul,* and for a tiny doll's chair *likil.* Children often invent such words as *teeny* or *weensy* to express the smallest of the small. Then, too, there are many examples of vowel symbolism in the word inventions of adults. Television engineers call their smallest lights *inky-dinks.* In Hi-Fi language the small transmitter that specializes in high frequencies is called a *tweeter* (the transmitter for low frequencies is a *woofer*). The small canary that stars in animated cartoons is called *Tweety* (two voiceless alveolar consonants and a double high front vowel make this about as small as a word can be). Then the little patch of rapidly flickering light in the living room is the *Tee-Vee.*

These examples are drawn from many sources but it is possible that our expectations select for us the cases that fit. We may be overlooking equally numerous contrary instances. Newman systematically compared size words in English and found no evidence of vowel symbolism. He drew from Roget's *Thesaurus* all the words listed under Greatness, Smallness, Size, and Littleness. Excluding duplications, there were about 500 such words. Eleven judges then checked any words whose size implications were not clear and these were excluded from the list. Comparing the small words with the large, Newman found no significant difference in the size implications of their vowels. It is quite possible, then, that vowel symbolism does not exist in English or any other language in spite of Jespersen's numerous persuasive examples. On the other hand it may be that the correlation only holds for words very directly concerned with size. Newman's list may have been too extensive. It included many words whose association with size is remote, e.g., *decimate, descend, wretched, stalwart.*

With a slight modification Newman's method can be used to test for the existence of vowel symbolism in natural languages. To check on the size implications of his English words he listed the entire 500 under the headings "large" and "small" and asked judges to check those words whose categorization seemed inappropriate. It is better procedure to give each judge the list of words and have him classify each word as large or small without any suggestion from the experimenter. One can then compare the vowels of large and small words where the classification was perfectly unequivocal, with all judges placing the words in the same classes. It would be wise to make the vowel comparison with samples of words at varying levels of judgmental reliability. In addition the contributions of the words should be weighted for their frequencies in English (225). *Small* and *little* should be given great weight since they are common words with clear size meaning while *wretched* and *decimate* should have less weight since they are less common and have more doubtful size implications. Miss Jean Berko and I have made some of these tests for vowel symbolism in English words implying magnitude and, as yet, have found no evidence that it exists.

Even if the procedure described above should yield data showing some elements of phonetic symbolism in French, German, Italian, and the other Indo-European languages the picture would still be incomplete in one vital respect. It would be necessary to investigate phonetic symbolism in languages outside the Indo-European family. This extension would increase the generality of the conclusion but, also and more importantly, it would refine our notion of the exact character of the phonetic symbolism discovered. The Indo-European languages have a common ancestor. It is possible that any phonetic symbolism found in such languages existed also in proto-Indo-European. This phonetic symbolism might originally have been entirely accidental and arbitrary. Its naturalness for us today could be a consequence of our linguistic training. If, however, the same correlations of sound and meaning can be found in languages having no historical relation with the Indo-European family we shall be inclined to believe that they are somehow natural for the human species.

Richard Paget (176) has looked to Chinese, Polynesian, and Semitic languages, as well as the more familiar Indo-European tongues, for confirmation of his special theory of phonetic symbolism. It is Paget's opinion that the basis of symbolism is the ability of the articulational apparatus to imitate motion and contour in the external world. Communication is supposed to have begun as a system of whole body gesture representing the basic actions of primitive life. The muscles of articulation performed these gestures in miniature. The addition of phonation to these movements produced meaningful utterances in which the muscle action represented the meaning. Strictly speaking the sound is not representational in Paget's theory. The sounds are appropriate only because they are produced by imitative gestures. Thus Paget finds the proto-Polynesian words for *large* and *small, oho* and *i-i,* to be appropriate because the mouth forms large and small apertures in the two cases rather than because of the qualities of the sounds themselves. Paget examines a list of Indo-European roots (naming simple actions) and finds most of them imitative. *Angh* seems to him to be a good name for *choke* since it is produced by tightening the throat with the tongue. *Pak* is a suitable word for *bind* or *hold fast* since it is made by releasing the lips and then bringing the back of the tongue up against the palate. Looking through a dictionary of the Cantonese dialect Paget found 150 gesture words on a first reading. In modern English he examined the ninety-nine monosyllables beginning with *sp* (movement coming to a point) and found 81 per cent of them to have meanings appropriate to the gesture. In Indo-European roots, in Semitic and Sumerian languages, in archaic Chinese, in the languages of Oceania, North America, and South America, Paget found large numbers of words having gestural symbolism.

As one reads through Paget's evidence incredulity grows strong. *Gar* is appropriate to *devour* because it is a swallowing motion; *kar* is appropriate to *roll* because it involves a rolling motion. Paget alone judged whether each word was appropriate or not. It is clear that others less convinced of the theory would often not have made the same decisions.

H. Müller (165) relied on others to find the "appropriateness" in a set of words from such remote languages as Samoan, Bantu, and Eskimo. His subjects were children from six to eleven years of age. The list includes several wonderful examples. If you were to associate to the word *tumba* you would probably hit on something close to the idea of swelling or corpulence which is its translation. For *ongololo,* the centipede may not come to mind but the equivalence of form is obvious. The author concludes, from perusal of the children's protocols, that they drew from the words, meanings which were similar to their actual meanings. While Müller was not the judge of the symbolic qualities of the words he was the sole judge of the appropriateness of the meanings reported in the children's protocols. We must be skeptical, here, as with the work of Paget, though our doubts are aroused at a different point in the procedure. In these studies, and also in Heinz Werner's (240) work on physiognomic speech, there is no concern with the reliability of the judgments made and no attempt at a statistical test of a clearly formulated hypothesis.

In 1934 S. Tsuru (229) introduced greater control into the phonetic symbolism experiment. Tsuru compiled a list of thirty-six pairs of Japanese antonyms ("hot-cold," "high-low," etc.). His subjects were fifty-seven Harvard and Radcliffe undergraduates who spoke English as their native language and disclaimed any knowledge of Japanese. Seated in a group, subjects first saw a pair of Japanese words printed in Romish characters. The English equivalent pair was then written on the board, the order of the words within the pair being randomly related to the order within the Japanese pair. From the back of the room a native Japanese pronounced the words twice, reversing the order the second time. Subjects then attempted to match English-Japanese synonyms, with one minute allowed for each pair. If they had nothing to guide them to correct answers subjects should be correct only 50 per cent of the time on these 2-alternative guesses. Since they were right significantly more often than this they must have been able to find some clues to the right answers. As they had learned nothing of Japanese it would seem that phonetic symbolism must have guided them. And since Japanese is a language that is not historically related to English this would be a universal human phonetic symbolism—not simply a conventional association.

But the solution is not that easy. All the authors whose work has been described—Jespersen, Paget, Müller, Werner, and Tsuru—selected their examples in full knowledge of both the native and the foreign language terms. Among the thousands of words in the Japanese language (or the Bantu or Polynesian or any other) there will surely be some that resemble, phonetically or gesturally, their English equivalents. This will be true even though these languages are not historically related. All languages use small sets of phonemes (never more than seventy) to manufacture words. These sets overlap from one language to another. Suppose we were to put some of the same phonemes in each of two hats and then drew sequences of four phonemes from each hat. Let each hat be a language and the sequences of four phonemes one kind of word. It would occasionally happen that we should draw similar or identical sequences from both hats on a particular trial. It will likewise happen that some words of one language resemble or duplicate words with the same meaning in another language. There is no way to calculate the degree of similarity to be expected by chance. If there were we should have an exact criterion for dividing languages into families; similarity beyond chance expectancy would identify an historical linkage. If an experimenter chose to he could select the words from a foreign language that most clearly resemble equivalent terms in the native language of his experimental subjects. It would be possible for these subjects to guess appropriate meanings for the foreign words and to make correct matches within paired antonyms. However, this performance would not depend on phonetic symbolism. Subjects could simply go from the foreign word to the familiar word it resembles, and neither word need be appropriate to its referent. Of course none of our authors intended to do anything of this kind. But some of their selections may inadvertently have been made because of word-to-word resemblance rather than phonetic symbolism. Indeed, one might easily mistake such a resemblance for phonetic symbolism. It obviously isn't safe to let the experimenter pick his instances.

Tsuru was a student of Gordon Allport's and, in a study of his own, Allport (5) made a simple but important methodological improvement on Tsuru's design. He had a native speaker of Hungarian translate Tsuru's list into that Finno-Ugric tongue which is historically not related to either English or Japanese. Because the list of words was given to the translator there was no opportunity to select Hungarian words for their resemblance to English. Allport's subjects were somewhat less successful than Tsuru's original group had been with the Japanese words, but the Hungarian words were guessed with better than chance success. The Allport design was repeated in 1953 by Susannah Rich (191), who used twenty-five pairs of Japanese and Polish words, and again found success significantly above chance.

In 1955 Brown, Black, and Horowitz (26) published a study repeating the Allport design, with the addition of a new (and somewhat finicking) control and more elaborate statistical analysis of the results. They began with twenty-one antonymic pairs of English words, selected because they are familiar, sensory words ("warm-cool," "heavy-light"). They were careful to choose two words in each pair of nearly equal length. The authors were completely ignorant of the languages into which the lists were to be translated—Chinese, Czech, and Hindi. The translations were made by native speakers or scholars of the particular languages, who also recorded their pronunciations of the words. The subjects were eighty-five Harvard and Radcliffe students who were ignorant of the languages of translation. The percentages of correct response were above chance for all three languages with Czech lowest at 56.4 per cent and Hindi highest at 59.5 per cent.

These data were analyzed in another and more informative way. The simple percentage of correct answers for a total list might be compounded of some very successful pairs and some very unsuccessful pairs, or there could be the same slightly better than chance results with all pairs, or any number of other possibilities. Consequently the performance for each pair of words in each language was separately determined. For the great majority of all pairs there was a greater than chance agreement among the subjects as to the translation. In other words, subjects seemed to share a conception of which of two alternative meanings was more appropriate to a given sound sequence. In addition, however, these conceptions were correct twice as often as they were incorrect. The authors analyzed Allport's data in similar fashion and found comparable results. In 1956 Maltzman, et al. (153) obtained similar results for Croatian and Japanese words.

The Brown, Black, and Horowitz study adds three languages to the list of those for which speakers of American English have made better than chance translations. In addition the study rules out one conceivable source of this ability to translate—a source, that is, other than phonetic symbolism. Beginning with Tsuru, experimental procedure has called for pronunciation of the foreign words by one thoroughly familiar with the language. In addition the speaker has usually known the purpose of the experiment. How can we be sure that such a speaker does not give away the correct translation by the expressive quality of his pronunciations? He might introduce some haste into his pronunciation of *fast;* he might put more "weight" into *heavy* than into *light.* To eliminate this possibility Brown, Black, and Horowitz asked a control group of sixteen subjects to match words without any recorded pronunciations, using only the printed versions of the foreign words. These suggest a roughly correct pronunciation to most native speakers of English. The expressive quality of the voice was eliminated since the subjects did not know the meanings of the words they pronounced to themselves. The over-all success was slightly, though not significantly, *greater* under these conditions than in the situation where the words were pronounced aloud. Evidently the results in these studies are not to be explained by the expressiveness of the speaker.

The chain of experiments beginning with Tsuru's study has shown very clearly that native speakers of American English generally agree which of two meanings is more appropriate to an unfamiliar phonetic sequence. The question is whether these opinions are cultural or human conceptions. Do the English speaking subjects match *ch'ing* with *light* and *ch'ung* with *heavy* because the vowel in the former resembles the vowel of *light* while the vowel of the latter is nearer that in *heavy?* There is some evidence that subjects were not guided by cross language similarities in particular words. The introspections of the subjects do not mention such similarities but rather speak of general phonetic appropriateness. A most instructive pair of words occurs in the Brown, Black, and Horowitz list. A Chinese translation of *fat* is *fei* and for *thin* the word *shou.* The resemblance of *fat* and *fei* is striking. This is one of those cases to be expected by chance, in which historically unrelated languages have produced similar words for the same meaning. In this instance, however, the resemblance opposes the usual implications of front and back vowels. The high front vowel of *fei* should imply something small or thin while the low back vowel of *shou* ought to suggest something large or *fat.* The majority of the subjects (69 per cent) matched in accordance with vowel symbolism—*fei* with *thin*—and neglected the obvious similarity of *fei* and *fat.* This result suggests that the subjects were not inclined to rely on particular word resemblances.

However, the judgments of the subjects might still be cultural conceptions rather than human conceptions. Judgments may depend on general notions of phonetic symbolism which, though not consciously tied to particular words, are derived from sound-meaning correlations abstracted from many words in one's native language. Thus the vowel of *ch'ing* is like the vowels of *high, child,* and *tiny* while the vowel of *ch'ung* is like those of *low, adult,* and *large.* Introspective reports cannot be expected to reveal where the subjects' general notions of phonetic symbolism come from. They don't know.

Whether the subjects' judgments were based on particular word resemblances between English and the foreign language or whether they were based on general notions of sound symbolism abstracted from English, it would follow that English speaking subjects would agree on the likelier meaning for an unfamiliar word. Neither assumption, however, explains the fact that these judgments were correct far more often than not. With the Japanese, Hungarian, Polish, Chinese, Czech, Hindi, and Croatian languages subjects have always been right more than half the time. This fact suggests that there are resemblances between sound and meaning which are apparent to men everywhere and that these have played some part in the development of all natural languages with the result that semantic rules in totally unfamiliar languages do not seem to us to be quite arbitrary. How else explain the better than chance success? Languages like Chinese, Hungarian, and English are believed, on the best evidence, to have independent histories.

The conclusion that there is a universal phonetic symbolism playing some role in all languages is favored but not compelled by the evidence. We can't help wondering if there may not be some other basis for correct guessing. After all we do know a little something of most of those languages—a few words in a movie or a novel—a neighbor who speaks Polish to his children. Might there not be enough of such slight unrecognized learning to boost the guesses above chance success?

There is a fairly direct empirical route to the answers on the phonetic symbolism question. It is, obviously, to do comparative studies with monolingual subjects from remote language communities. Would the conception of the proper meanings for *ch'ing* and *ch'ung* be the same for German, Hungarian, Zuni Indian, Eskimo, etc.? Cultural conceptions will vary, human conceptions will not. The great defect of the experimental literature on phonetic symbolism is the neglect of international replication. Each experimenter has worked with the subjects at hand, Wissemann, Werner, and Müller with Germans; Tsuru, Allport, Rich with Harvard and Radcliffe students.

Brown, Black, and Horowitz undertook to repeat their study with monolingual Navaho Indians in New Mexico and with Chinese living in Boston. They discovered the difficulties of cross cultural experimentation but not much else. Horowitz hunted down the monolingual Navaho in his hogan and played for him the original recordings of Chinese, Hindi, and Czech words. An interpreter asked for matchings with one or another of the paired Navaho words. Not until Horowitz had returned to Boston and analyzed his data did he discover that the interpreter had misunderstood the point of the study and passed on this misconception to his subjects. They had made a complicated kind of judgment of the relative spiritual value of the paired foreign words. While revealing of Navaho values, these data do not help with Navaho phonetic symbolism.

Black and Brown obtained entrée to the Chinese community in Boston through the kind offices of Father James Chang. They contacted nine subjects through Father Chang and another ten through the director of the Chinese YMCA who made them acquainted with the Overseas Club—a group of young men who had arrived from China fairly recently. All nineteen subjects spoke the Cantonese dialect. Their knowledge of English was tested in advance by asking them to give English names for familiar objects. None of them knew very much English though there was some variation in the level of knowledge.

Many of the people in this experiment served in the back rooms of laundries or restaurants while continuing their work. There was often some question of their attentiveness and also of their understanding of the experiment. Experimenters working with an interpreter always find it difficult to be sure what the subject understands his task to be. Furthermore, the experimenters made all the tactical errors that anthropologists expect of psychologists who try to experiment in the field. For instance, the dollar an hour wage that Harvard and Radcliffe students find acceptable was insulting to the Chinese subjects. If properly approached they would donate their services as a contribution to scholarship for which the Chinese have a great veneration but if they were to be paid they expected a respectable wage.

While the authors have many reservations about their data, they are offered here as the results of the only study of this kind that has been done on phonetic symbolism. Well, not quite the only study. Sapir (200) had seven Chinese adults in his early study. However, these subjects also knew English. Still, on the contrast *mal-mil* they showed less agreement than any of the other groups tested by Sapir. The nineteen subjects of Black and Brown guessed the meanings of the same lists of Czech and Hindi words used in the earlier study with English speaking subjects.

To determine whether there was significant agreement on each pair of words the authors used a two-tailed test with a binomial distribution. Using a P of .02 there was significant agreement on only three pairs from the Hindi list and on two pairs from the Czech list. This result seems to indicate that the Chinese subjects did not share a conception of the likely translations for unfamiliar phonetic sequences. However, the result is much the same in this case as with the control group of English speaking subjects who translated without hearing the words pronounced in the earlier studies. The percentage of subjects choosing a particular word seems to remain constant as a sample is increased in size, but with only nineteen subjects these percentages are seldom large enough to be significant. Looking at the percentages without regard to significance, it seems likely that a large group of Chinese subjects would show as much agreement among themselves as did the large group of English speaking subjects.

Of the five pairs on which significant agreement was found four were correctly translated. The over-all percentages were 54.4 per cent for the Hindi and 50.6 per cent for the Czech. These are lower scores than have been reported for any English speaking subjects with any language. However, there may be an intelligence differential favoring the American college students over the Chinese immigrants and this may have resulted in some of the Chinese subjects not understanding the task and perhaps choosing arbitrarily. Ideally the foreign language subjects should also be college students.

Using an analysis of variance with the data from the Chinese subjects, and also from the earlier study with English speaking subjects, Black and Brown found that the two groups had significantly different patterns of guessing on both Czech and Hindi lists. That is, the two groups did not usually favor the same translations. With the Hindi words, however, the English and Chinese speaking groups were fairly similar, more so than with the Czech words. It is to be noted that the Chinese, like the English speaking subjects, were more successful with the Hindi words than with the Czech. Although there are these traces of agreement the results as a whole certainly do not strengthen our faith in a universal human phonetic symbolism.

There is a single result, with a particular pair of words, that is most discouraging to the universal symbolism thesis. The authors introduced Sapir's pair *mal-mil* into the Hindi list and *small-large* (in Chinese) were the proffered translations. On this pair where English speaking subjects almost universally match *mal* with *large* the Chinese responded at the chance level. Since the implications of magnitude attached to vowels are the best supported symbolic-phonetic associations in the literature this result is discouraging to the thesis that these associations are not cultural acquisitions but are natural to man.

In summary, then, what is the case for phonetic symbolism in natural languages? No sound-meaning correlation has been satisfactorily demonstrated to exist in the lexicon of any language. The examples of Jespersen are striking but not finally convincing because there was no control of the selection procedure and no statistical test of the results. Newman's careful examination of vowel symbolism in English satisfies the canons of evidence and the conclusion is negative. The more elaborate tests made by Berko and Brown also turned up no evidence for vowel symbolism in English, but, of course, only the magnitude hypothesis was checked. As yet, we shall not conclude that there are no phonetic-symbolic associations in natural languages. Even the "impressions" of so great a scholar as Jespersen are important evidence. So far as the direct check on phonetic symbolism in natural languages goes we must conclude that nothing has been established except the method (Newman's) whereby an answer can be obtained.

On the other hand, it is probable that most speakers of a given language find similar symbolic implications in an unfamiliar phonetic sequence. The results of the series of studies beginning with Tsuru and extending to Brown, Black, and Horowitz, support this conclusion. It should be stressed that these studies do not indicate that speakers of a given language can agree on an absolute, unprompted translation for such an unfamiliar word. It has only been shown that they can agree on which of two antithetical meanings such a word is more likely to have.

The data with Chinese subjects are not decisive on the matter but they do not discourage the belief, founded on the American studies, that new words have semantic leanings recognized by most of a given linguistic community. Thus one kind of phonetic symbolism is highly probable on the basis of present evidence; that there is some kind of "appropriateness" or "inappropriateness" in new names which is common knowledge within a community.

Totally problematical is the existence of a universal human phonetic symbolism. The phonetic symbolism of the English speaking community may be entirely a result of similar linguistic training. The reliable finding that guessed translations of unfamiliar words were correct more often than not would indicate that the matter is more complicated. This finding suggests that there may be sound-meaning linkages which all human beings are disposed to make and to recognize and that these linkages are found (in dilute form) in all languages with the result that subjects can do a somewhat better than chance job of translating unfamiliar words. Opposed to this view are the chance results of the nineteen Chinese subjects with words from Hindi and Czech. However, this recent attempt at cross-linguistic research had too many methodological flaws for the results to be definitive. It has shown that the answer to the questions of universal phonetic symbolism will not be easily obtained and when obtained is not likely to be a simple one. There may, after all, be some associations of sound and meaning that are universally known and others that are a cultural product.

All of the work so far has been in search of a method and, indeed, of a clearly formulated problem. These have now been found and the answers are within reach. Experiments with foreign word guessing will suggest principles of phonetic symbolism such as Jespersen's vowel-magnitude rule. Nonsense syllables can be constructed to test the knowledge of such rules in subjects from many communities. Natural words are not well suited to the study of specific principles because antonym pairs will ordinarily differ from one another in many ways. To contrast particular sounds, syllables must be constructed. Finally, natural language vocabularies can be objectively sampled to determine the extent to which a given principle of phonetic symbolism is observed within each language. The general character of the results can be anticipated. Phonetic symbolism, as a whole, will not be proved or disproved. The study of particular rules of sound symbolism may or may not reveal some that have a claim to universality. It is this which is to be determined.

The Origin of Speech. The problem of phonetic symbolism is usually linked with the more difficult question of the origin of speech. Since speech originated in prehistory, long before writing, there can be no record of the act or acts of origination. It is quite impossible to obtain a direct historical answer to the origin question but it may be that there is indirect evidence to make one reconstruction more probable than any other.

Traditional speculation on this subject has been trivialized with such sobriquets as the "ding-dong" theory and the "bow-wow" theory. The stale whimsy of this language has helped to make the whole subject distasteful. We shall avoid passing the standard theories in review but will make several distinctions among them.

Some theorists, particularly Thorndike (224), speculate that, in the beginning, symbols were arbitrarily assigned meanings. It is, then, only necessary to assume the random emission of vocalization and some such familiar learning principles as "contiguity" and "reinforcement" to explain the perpetuation and social diffusion of particular vocalizations. Other theories assume that there was originally some principle of appropriateness by which symbols were connected with meanings. The earliest speech, like the earliest writing, is assumed to have been "representational." There are three sub-varieties of the representational position. The first two of these assume some kind of imitation. The onomatopoeic theory holds that vocal sound can suggest non-vocal sound. The gestural theory holds that the articulatory muscles can imitate motion and contour in the external world. Paget (176) and Wundt (255) are the principal supporters of the view that speech originated in such gestures. The third theory holds that the intersensory connections in mankind are such that vocal sounds are inevitably associated with experiences of the other senses.

The theory of intersensory associations holds that all men know

something of the state of mind Edith Sitwell (211) credits to the
modernist poet. ". . . . (the) senses have become broadened and
cosmopolitanised; they are no longer little islands, speaking only
their own narrow language, living their sleepy life alone." Perception is not an act involving only a particular receptor but is an
affair of the whole body. Of course hearing does not involve all
parts of the organism in equal degree but reducing hearing to
audition alone means ignoring essential components. As mentioned
earlier, "synaesthesia" is the standard name for the experience of
colored hearing and other intersensory phenomena. However, phonetic symbolism ought not to be assimilated to synaesthesia for the
reason that studies of synaesthesia have typically yielded large individual differences. If there are intersensory connections which
are responsible for phonetic symbolism these must be common to
mankind generally. One can postulate the existence of such innate
connections but there is little one can offer in proof of them.

Universal intersensory connections of the sort to account for
phonetic symbolism need not be innate. They could be learned
from correlations of sense data that exist in the non-linguistic world
to which all men are exposed. I was thinking about this possibility
while sitting in a park one afternoon. Five minutes of attending to
background noise showed me that it could be true. Consider the
much discussed vowel symbolism. The front vowels with their high
acoustic formants are associated with smaller magnitudes than the
back vowels with their lower formants. In the trees about me large
black crows gave the low cry we write *caw* while smaller, quicker
birds *chirped* and *twittered* their higher notes. Small active children shouted in high voices; large, slow adults spoke in deep voices.
The sensible attributes of the non-linguistic world may tend to
cluster and man could symbolize the visible or tactile attributes of
such a cluster with auditory attributes from the same cluster. In
this way we could learn a principle of intersensory appropriateness
to use in naming.

If the first semantic utterances were in arbitrary association
with their referents it must have been a slow business learning to
understand them. If a man uttered a syllable while sitting before a
fire eating venison it would not be clear, on one hearing, what
aspect of the total situation was named by the syllable. A good
many experiences would be required before the constant element

in many situations could be linked with the syllable. The representational symbol might be more easily translated since it resembles its referent.

A representational symbol manifests one or more of the attributes criterial for the referent category. In the pictogram ⚐ certain relations of size and spatial connection are like the relations that hold between the parts of a man's body. The pictogram is not a man and, indeed, is very unlike a man. It is miniature, two dimensional, and immobile. The word *buzz* preserves something of the noise of the bee but will never be mistaken for such a noise. The word *suck* involves mouth movements somewhat like those involved in the act of sucking but the word is not such an act and will not serve to draw soda water from a straw. All of these symbols have some point of resemblance to their referent categories but they are far from being members of such categories.

Symbols resemble in all directions. The figure ⚐ and the word *buzz* are like one another in that both appear on this page. *Buzz* resembles *suck* in that both are printed with English letters. Why is not ⚐ a representational symbol of *buzz* and why is not *buzz* a symbol of *suck*? Can it be maintained that the symbols resemble their referents more closely than they resemble anything else? The figure ⚐ is more like ⚐ than either is like a man and yet the first has symbolized *man* and the second *warrior*. The word *buzz* is more like *bus* than like the sound of the bee yet *buzz* does not symbolize *bus*. Our ability to translate on sight such pictograms as ☽ or ☼ depends on our knowledge of the kinds of stimuli that serve as symbols and the kinds of stimuli that are referents. It depends also on our acquired knowledge of the attributes that establish resemblance between symbols and referents. In the pictograms used here, color and brightness and size are equated across the assortment of symbols. These common attributes establish the pictograms as a family of symbols. They do not symbolize by means of those attributes in which they resemble one another. They symbolize by means of contour in which they are unlike one another but like their respective referents. Onomatopoeic words are like one another in that all are vocally produced. They are unlike one another in duration and quality and stress pattern and it is these attributes that link them with non-linguistic sounds. The solitary representational symbol does not necessarily remind us of its referent. The resemblance is only obvious when we have learned certain conventions about symbol-referent relations.

It is not true that representational symbols can be decoded at once, without training, by everyone. It is true that they can be more easily decoded than arbitrary symbols. This is because the learning involved in decoding representational symbols can be economical and systematic. Once we have learned that pictograms reproduce in miniature the smoothed outlines of non-linguistic objects we can guess the meaning of ♉ or ⛿ without specific training on each symbol. In many cases we cannot identify the particular referents of representational symbols but can only guess at a range of probable referents. The word *cock-a-doodle-doo,* even to one who knows the principles of onomatopoeic word formation, does not inevitably suggest the cry of the rooster but that meaning is more likely than the chirp of the robin or the meow of the cat.

The economy in representational symbols is the systematic character they give to semantic rules. Naming can be systematic without being representational. Suppose that sense data in the non-linguistic world do cluster as I have suggested. Men might learn that large objects tend to make low pitched sounds, that bright colored objects tend to make sounds of a given quality and dark colored objects sounds of another quality. Suppose, furthermore, that it would never occur to anyone lacking experience of these correlations to feel that low pitched sounds, for instance, were any more appropriate as names for large objects than were high pitched sounds. Once it was learned that the name of an object would be a sound associated with that object in nature men could guess at the meanings of new names. Universal experiences can form the basis for economical naming as easily as universally obvious but unlearned sensory resemblance. In either case one names so as to take advantage of *prior knowledge—innate or acquired.*

How can we account for the vitality of the Origin question? The arguments today are not different in any important respect from those that occurred to Plato. It has often been demonstrated that the question is not susceptible of final answer. The answer, if it were certainly established, would have no practical consequences whatever. Yet the question has survived scientific obloquy and even official proscription. Philosophers and psychologists and ordinary men whose antiquarian interests are not otherwise well developed discover themselves panting after an answer to this question.

This passionate interest in the Origin of Speech has not often led to scientific inquiry. After all these centuries of concern the most obviously relevant facts have not been collected. Most commonly, men have felt one or another answer to be necessary and have then used every device of rhetoric to convince others that it is true. So long as there is no really persuasive evidence, the Origin question offers us a choice of myths and in that choice we express our convictions about the essential nature of language and of man himself. We have not wanted to discover the answer to this problem. We have wanted to establish our own answer.

The place of pre-linguistic man in the phyletic scale is between anthropoid and linguistic man. No animal has ever developed or acquired language. No healthy human being fails to acquire the language of his society. In pre-linguistic man we look for the essential difference between man and animal; we look for the essence of language and expect also to find the essence of man.

Theories of language origin are never very detailed. There is little interest in the diffusion of forms, the development of grammar, the beginnings of language families. Origin theories concentrate on one question—the appearance of the first meaningful utterance. This fact alone is enough to establish the fact that Origin theories are not ordinary historical concerns but are myths concerning the essential nature of language and meaning.

One type of theorist conceives pre-linguistic man to have been a higher anthropoid motivated by biological needs and alterable through conditioning and instrumental learning. For this theorist the problem of speech origin is the problem of explaining the accidental development of speech habits and of demonstrating the survival value of such habits. Another sort of theorist imagines pre-linguistic man to have had the impulse to symbolize and communicate. For this theorist the problem of speech origin is the problem of explaining how men found suitable representational symbols to function as surrogates for concepts. A man's position on the Origin question can be predicted far more successfully from his views on innate ideas, on the importance of art, and the existence of mind than from his knowledge of ancient history.

Despite the mythic status of this question and its resistance to solution we can look forward to an answer that is more than the projection of personal values. For the Origin question is the question of comparative psychology posed in a pseudo-historical form.

When we have discovered the critical steps by which animal communication evolves into language, we will imagine a pre-linguistic man to be the missing link in the developmental chain. When we have a satisfactory comparative psychology of language we will build a satisfactory Origin Myth. And the lack of historical verification will not matter.

The Place of Phonetic Symbolism in Language Function. Wissemann (250) has shown that subjects can, on request, construct onomatopoeic words that retain some of the attributes of referent noises. Sapir (200) and Newman (168) have shown that subjects can rank unfamiliar speech sounds on semantic dimensions that are proposed to them. Brown, Black, and Horowitz (26) have shown that subjects can choose between proposed definitions for unfamiliar words from natural languages. In all of these experiments subjects were asked to use phonetic symbolism. They proved able to do so and proved also to agree with one another on many aspects of phonetic symbolism. These experiments inspire us to ask what part phonetic symbolism plays in ordinary language processes when there is no request to exercise the function.

Bentley and Varon (15) used the syllables of Sapir and Newman as stimulus materials to which subjects were asked to provide free verbal associations. Analyzing these associations, the authors found no tendency for low back vowels to elicit large or dark ideas. Neither was there a tendency for high front vowels to elicit small and bright associations. The symbolic implications of the sounds did not guide the course of free association. Only when a scale of magnitude was proposed, and a forced choice situation created, did the vowels have symbolic values. In effect, phonetic symbolism had to be drawn from the subjects with particular directions.

Two recent studies reinforce the view that the symbolic properties of individual speech sounds are not ordinarily important in language function. Brown and Hildum (27) constructed three series of drawings and selected symbolic nonsense names for each end of each series. One series consisted of eighteen circles gradually increasing in size. The smallest circle was called *dee* and the largest *daw.* The vowels of these words have appropriate magnitude implications according to the results of Sapir and Newman. Another series consisted of arrowheads ranging from blunt to sharp. The bluntest arrow was called *bahm,* the sharpest *teece.* In the third case there were drawings of ropes stretched between two poles. The ropes ranged from slack to taut and the names were *gib* and *kip*. To check on the phonetic symbolism of these names control subjects were asked to match the names for each series with the appropriate extremes. They were all able to do so with much better than chance success. The *dee-daw* contrast was clearest, the *gib-kip* contrast least certain.

Each group consisted of twenty subjects. Each subject was shown a figure from the middle of the series and told to call it by a particular name. When the figure was a circle some subjects were told to call it *dee*, other subjects were told to call it *daw*. In every case the figure was called by one or the other of the two names associated with the series. The stimulus figure was then removed and the subject was shown the entire series from which the figure had been drawn and asked to identify the original figure in the series. The experimenters expected the subjects to be affected by the name given the figure: if the magnitude implications in the name were effective, subjects who had heard a given circle called *daw* ought to select a larger member of the series than subjects who had heard the same circle called *dee*.

With none of the materials was there any relation between the name assigned the original figure and the choice made from the series of similar figures. If we habitually expect speech to "represent" its meaning then these subjects ought to have used the name as a guide when confronted with this difficult problem of identification. If the symbolic properties of speech sound have any automatic effect the memory of the circle ought to have been differently distorted by the names *dee* and *daw*.

Most recently Horowitz (97) gave subjects an opportunity to use phonetic symbolism to facilitate a learning problem. He contrived an artificial language in which nonsense syllables were used to denote a set of geometrical figures that varied in size. Each syllable contained one vowel and these vowels covered the magnitude scale developed by Newman (168). For one group of subjects the magnitude values of the vowels corresponded to the relative magnitudes of the referent figures. For another group of subjects the correlation was perfect but negative with the "largest" vowel going with the smallest figure. A third group of subjects had to learn the language with the syllables randomly assigned to the various drawings. If subjects noticed the systematic phonetic symbolism their learning would be greatly facilitated. If phonetic symbolism has inevitable unconscious effects, the case of perfect positive correlation between sounds and sizes should be learned most readily and the perfect negative correlation least easily. As it happened there were no differences in learning time between the three groups. Apparently vowel symbolism played no part at all.

The failure to detect any effects of phonetic symbolism in situations where it is not specifically called for by the experimenter suggests that we do not usually expect speech to represent or imitate. Its dominant function is conventional reference and that is what we expect unless directed to look for something else. There may, however, be non-laboratory situations in which we are prepared for onomatopoeia and phonetic symbolism. Presumably the reading of poetry is one of these. Onomatopoeia is quite obvious in Tennyson's:

> Myriads of rivulets hurrying thro' the lawn,
> The moan of doves in immemorial elms,
> And murmuring of innumerable bees

But this sort of thing is not common. Clear cases of onomatopoeia are not often found in poetry. In Shakespeare one seeks them in vain. There are, however, many uses of a subtler phonetic symbolism in which the sound is appropriate to the sense. Macbeth's "Tomorrow and to-morrow and to-morrow," with its repetition of the dark, heavy back vowels surely suggests the sombre mood of the speaker and expresses phonetically the idea of relentless, plodding repetition. However, even in this case there are those who doubt the importance of phonetic symbolism. F. W. Bateson (12) suspects that it is a form of innocent self-deception. "To-morrow" does not strike him as especially mournful. He thinks it might easily sound quite gay in another context. Even in poetry, conventional significance is surely more important than representational sound. However, the experiments in phonetic symbolism show that we do have ideas about appropriate sounds and can use them when we are asked to do so. While it is doubtful that any *universal* phonetic symbolism exists there is, without any doubt, a *community* phonetic symbolism, shared by speakers of a given language. Thus the sound values of words *can* be used to communicate meanings. There is, in phonetic symbolism, a means of communication *available* to the poet and so I doubt that phonetic symbolism in poetry is altogether imaginary, but I do not doubt that it ordinarily assumes a subtler form than onomatopoeia.

Metaphor

When someone invents a new machine, or forms a concept, or buys a dog, or manufactures a soap powder his first thought is to name it. These names are almost never arbitrary creations produced by juggling the sounds of the language into a novel sequence. We think hard and ask our friends to help us find a "good" name, a name that is appropriate in that its present meaning suggests the new meaning it is to have.

Sometimes new words are introduced by borrowing words or morphemes from classical languages. The biological sciences have been especially partial to this practice as *photosynthesis, streptoneura,* and *margaritifera* testify. In order to savor the appropriateness of these names a classical education is required and so, for most of us, they are functionally arbitrary.

The usual method of creating a new name is to use words or morphemes already in the language; either by expanding the semantic range of some word or by recombining morphemes. Every word has a history of former meanings and, traced back far enough, an ancestor that belongs to another language. The modern French *lune* derives from the Latin *lux*. The extension of the Latin word for *light* to the moon is appropriate and may once have been experienced as appropriate. Today, however, because of phonetic change and loss of the earlier meaning, the metaphor in *lune* must be overlooked by most French speakers even as we overlook the metaphor in our *moon* which is a remote cognate of Latin *mensis* for month. Both languages arrived at their word for the moon by metaphorical means, though the metaphors are constructed on different attributes of the referent—its luminosity for the French, its periodic cycle for the English. In both cases the whole process dates so far back that the appropriateness of these names like that of *margaritifera* or *photosynthesis* is evident only to scholars.

Many new names are still very familiar in an older reference and so their appropriateness to the new referent is easy to see. There are dogs called *Spot* or *Rover;* detergents and soaps are called *Surf, Rinso,* and *Duz;* one kind of personality is said, by clinical psychologists, to be *rigid.* Compounds like *overcoat, railroad train,* and *fireplace* have familiar constituents. While the origins of these names are obvious enough they probably are not ordinarily noticed. It seems to be necessary to take a special attitude toward language, quite different from our everyday attitude, to discern the metaphors around us.

The metaphor in a word lives when the word brings to mind more than a single reference and the several references are seen to have something in common. Sometime in the past someone or other noticed that the foot of a man bears the same relation to his body as does the base of a mountain to the whole mountain. He thought of extending the word *foot* to the mountain's base. This word *foot* then referred to two categories. These categories share a relational attribute which makes them one category. Within this superordinate category, which we might name *the foundations or lower parts of things,* are two subordinate categories—the man's foot and the mountain's base. These two remain distinct within the larger category because the members of each subordinate category share attributes that are not shared with the members of the other subordinate category. The *man's foot* is made of flesh and has toes, which is not true of the base of any mountain. Thus far the relationship is like that of any set of superordinate and subordinate categories, e.g., polygons as superordinate to triangles and squares. The subordinates have something in common which makes them species of one genus but they are distinct because members of one subordinate have still more in common. Metaphor differs from other superordinate-subordinate relations in that the superordinate is not given a name of its own. Instead, the name of one subordinate is extended to the other and this, as we shall see, has the effect of calling both references to mind with their differences as well as their similarities. The usual superordinate name, e.g., *polygons,* calls to mind only the shared attributes of the various varieties of polygon.

The use of *foot* to name a part of the mountain results in the appearance of *foot* in certain improbable phrase contexts. One hears, for the first time, the *foot of the mountain* or *mountain's foot.*

Until someone saw the similarity that generated the metaphor these sayings were not heard. They cause the metaphor to live for others who have not noticed the similarity in question. The anatomical reference is called to mind by the word *foot* which has been its unequivocal name. The context *of the mountain* is one in which this word has never appeared. The phrase suggests such forms as *peak* or *top* or *slope* or *height* or *base;* it is a functional attribute of all these. Only one of these forms has a referent that is like the anatomical foot and that one is *base.* There is a click of comprehension as the similarity is recognized and some pleasure at the amusing conceit of a mountain with toes, a mountain anthropomorphized. If the metaphor was created for a poem about the mountain climber's struggle with his almost human antagonist—the mountain itself—then the metaphor might figure importantly in communicating the sense of the poem.

This metaphor blazed briefly for the person who created it and it lights up again when anyone hears it for the first time, but for most of us it is dead. This is because with repetition of the phrase *foot of the mountain* the word *foot* loses its exclusive connection with anatomy. The word may be used of mountain as often as of man. When that is true there is nothing in the phrase *foot of the mountain* to suggest a man's foot and so the phrase is experienced as a conventional name for the lower part of a mountain. Part of the phrase is accidentally homophonic with part of the phrase *foot of a man* but there is no more reason for one to call the other to mind than there is for *board of wood* to remind us of *board of directors, bored with psycholinguistics,* or *bored from within.* In the interest of univocal reference we attend to the context in which each form occurs and do not consider the meanings it might have in other contexts.

The word *foot,* in isolation, is ambiguous. It has many referents including the mountainous and the anatomical. That special attitude toward language which brings out the potential metaphors now seems to me to involve attending to forms in isolation, deliberately ignoring context. In this last sentence, for instance, consider the word *attending* and disregard its surroundings. *Attending* names at least two kinds of behavior; there is "attending a lecture" and "attending to a lecture." The latter behavior is notoriously not the same as the former. In the sentence above only the intellectual attention sense of *attending* comes to mind; the other is ruled out by context.

A metaphor lives in language so long as it causes a word to appear in improbable contexts, the word suggesting one reference, the context another. When the word becomes as familiar in its new contexts as it was in the old the metaphor dies. This has happened with *foot of the mountain*. Sometimes there is a further stage in which the older set of contexts dies altogether and also the older reference. In these circumstances one speaks of a historical semantic change in the word. The term *strait-laced* is applied nowadays to people who follow an exceptionally severe, restrictive moral code. An older sense can be revived by placing the term in one of its older contexts; "Mrs. Mather was miserable in her strait-laced bodice." In the days when people laced their clothing *strait* meant *tight* and to be *strait-laced* was literally to be rather tightly trussed up. It is not difficult to see the attributes of this condition that resulted first in a metaphor and then in a semantic change. Whether one is tightly laced into his clothing or into his conscience he will feel confined, he may strain against his bonds and burst them, or, when no one else is about, he may secretly relax them a little. The metaphor is so rich that we should not be surprised to find it in poetry as well as in the history of linguistic change.

In fact there exists a poem founded on the very similarities that caused strait-laced to change in meaning.

Delight in Disorder

A sweet disorder in the dress
Kindles in clothes a wantonness.
A lawn about the shoulders thrown
Into a fine distraction;
An erring lace, which here and there
Enthrals the crimson stomacher;
A cuff neglectful, and thereby
Ribbands to flow confusedly;
A winning wave, deserving note,
In the tempestuous petticoat;
A careless shoestring, in whose tie
I see a wild civility;—
Do more bewitch me, than when art
Is too precise in every part.
                                        Robert Herrick

Herrick lived in seventeenth century England, through the period of Puritan rule into the restoration of Charles II. F. W. Bateson (11) points out that the poem reproduced above is concerned with more than disorder of costume. It is not only the clothes but also the wearers that Herrick would have *sweet, wanton, distracted, erring, neglectful, winning, tempestuous, wild,* and *bewitching.* The poem is a plea for disorder of manners and morals as well as of dress. It is a statement of anti-Puritanism.

How does Herrick communicate these depth meanings? The poem by its title professes to be concerned with dress. The word *disorder* can be applied to dress, to manners, to politics, to morals, or even to a man's wits. The fact that we are reading a poem makes us receptive to multiple meanings but the title alone does not indicate what secondary meanings, if any, are relevant. In the first line *sweet* sounds a trifle odd since it is not often said of disorder in dress. *Sweet* starts several auxiliary lines of thought having to do, perhaps, with girl friends, small children, and sugar cane. Only one of these is reinforced by what follows. *Kindles* and *wantonness* in the second line rule out children and sugar cane. Thoughts about girls and loose behavior are supported by words like *distraction, enthrals,* and *tempestuous.* All of these words can be used in talking about clothes. However, their choice is improbable enough to call for some explanation. Since the improbable words are all drawn from a set of terms having to do with girls and their behavior a second group of consistent references is created.

A scientist might call Herrick's message ambiguous since he uses words that have several different referents and does not clearly sort these out with criterial contexts. Behind that judgment is the assumption that the poet intends, as a scientist might, to call attention to just one kind of reference. In fact, however, Herrick wanted to talk simultaneously about clothing, ladies, and morality and to do so in a very compact way. Rather than string out three unequivocal vocabularies he uses one vocabulary which is able to make three kinds of reference.

When a poet uses simile he explicitly invites us to note the similarities and differences in two referents as in "My love is like a red, red rose." When he uses metaphor a word is used in a context that calls for a different word as in "The *lion* of England" or "My *rose* smiled at me." The context evokes one reference, the word another and the meaning is enriched by their similarities and differences. *Lion* and *king, rose* and *love* concentrate on similarities. There is an extraordinary sentence of e. e. Cummings' (46) in which the difference in the two references is the main thing: "And although her health eventually failed her she kept her sense of humor to the *beginning.*" The most probable word for final position in that sentence is *end.* This is not only different from *beginning*, it is the antonym. The probability of *end* is so great that the reader is bound to anticipate it. Finding instead its antonym almost makes us feel reprimanded. Our worldly outlook has made us too prone to think of death as the end.

A playwright or novelist may communicate a second meaning by introducing action that is incongruous with the first meaning. T. S. Eliot's *The Confidential Clerk,* for instance, pretends to be a play about foundlings. The beginnings of the plot are so familiar that we already anticipate the third act resolution with a "nuss" who mixed the babies up as in the play of W. S. Gilbert. As they are introduced, each character can be assimilated to some stereotype of the stage. Lucasta Angel is a spoiled and impertinent young woman; B. Kaghan a flashy sort of practical joker; Lady Elizabeth an absent-minded dowager who dabbles in spiritualism. In the second act our conceptions of these characters and the business of the play are badly wrenched out of shape. A man named Simpkins appears and everyone begins to say and do unexpected things. Lucasta knows about her social façade and hates it; Lady Elizabeth talks seriously and movingly of God; B. Kaghan, the joker, proves to be sympathetic to the spiritual Simpkins. In order to assimilate the new information we are led to reinterpret the whole play. By the time the predicted "nuss" actually shows up we know that the biological identity, with which the author appears to be concerned, is a symbol for psychological or religious identity. The characters are trying to find out who they are but not in a sense that is answered by disclosing the name of a parent. In this play, as in many poems, latent meanings are brought to mind by introducing events that are improbable in the light of the manifest meaning.

Poetry draws attention to the formal attributes of words, their sound and shape, by using these attributes to create rhyme and rhythm. The result for many readers is a tendency to detect phonetic symbolism as well as rhyme and rhythm. Metaphor is sometimes created by setting the formal attributes of a term at variance with its functional attributes—the context. The two sets of attributes do not combine, as they usually do, to evoke a single reference. They operate independently to evoke different references which somehow enrich one another. This is also what happens when we appreciate a metaphor created as part of the general growth of the language. While the importance of phonetic symbolism in word creation and in poetry can be doubted the importance of metaphor in both of these is certain.

Metaphor in the Vocabulary of Sensation. The term *strait-laced* denotes a very complicated condition which we can analyze into named attributes. This is also true of *king, lion, rose,* and *love.* In all of these cases it is easy to talk about the shared attributes that create the metaphor. This is not the case for those metaphors that grow out of the vocabulary of sensation. Words like *warm, cold, heavy, light, bright,* and *dull* are applied to psychological qualities of temperament or intellect, to social manners, to the quality of a voice as well as to sensations. *Cold* is at once the name of a thermal sensation of the skin, of a kind of temperament or manner, and of a vocal quality. In general, terms of this kind were used to name sensations before they were extended to psychological properties of persons. The sensation reference is earlier historically and also earlier in the child's acquisition of vocabulary. These words have several distinct referent categories and so satisfy that criterion for the metaphorical term. The question is whether the referents have any common attributes. I, at least, am not able to name any such attributes. The primary references are to the basic modalities of experience. The extensions usually shift from one sense modality to another. What has thermal cold in the skin to do with coldness heard in a voice or seen in a face? Perhaps there is no common quality and the several uses of *cold* ought to be thought of as accidental homophones. Perhaps this word could just as well be applied to the personalities we now call *warm* as to those we call *cold.* There may be no aptness either way.

If the extended uses of the sensation vocabulary in English are historical accidents rather than metaphors then these extensions ought not to be regularly found in other languages so long as these languages have no historical connection with English. Asch (10) drew up a long list of words of this kind and looked at their equivalents in Old Testament Hebrew, Homeric Greek, Chinese, Thai, Malayalam, and Hausa. He found that all of these languages have morphemes that are used to name both physical and psychological qualities. They all have morphemes that designate physical-psychological pairings identical with some found in English. These results suggest that the referents have shared attributes which have caused identical metaphors to be independently discovered by different peoples. In addition, Asch found that a morpheme referring to a given physical property may develop psychological meanings that are not identical in all languages. For example, the morpheme for *hot* stands for rage in Hebrew, enthusiasm in Chinese, sexual arousal in Thai, and energy in Hausa. However, this disagreement does not suggest the operation of accidental factors since there is an undoubted kinship in the range of meanings. All seem to involve heightened activity and emotional arousal. No case was discovered in which the morpheme for *hot* named a remote, calm (in fact *cool*) manner.

Practically everyone speaks of *dryness* in a martini, *warmth* in a voice, *narrowness* of mind, and *smoothness* of manners. Do the extensions of the vocabulary of sensation really name concepts that people understand in the same way? What would happen if speakers of English were asked to identify new instances of some of these categories? Music critics often write that a singer's tone is *dry* or *cold* or *white* or *brittle*. It has been said that the application of such non-auditory terms to tone quality communicates nothing to readers who are unacquainted with the jargon of music criticism. A critic may fancy that a voice can be *dry* or *white* but his reader has no idea what is meant. In elementary composition courses students are sometimes warned against such flowery and uninformative locutions. Brown, Leiter, and Hildum (28)* asked educated but musically naïve subjects to listen to recordings of nine famous (though unknown to the subjects) operatic singers and then to select from a vocabulary of non-auditory sense terms those best suited to each voice. The authors wanted, in the first place, to see how much agreement there would be on the identification of new instances of *cool, dry, bright, thick,* etc., tone qualities. Do these

---

Adapted here by permission of *The Journal of Abnormal and Social Psychology.*

terms name concepts that are generally understood or do most speakers simply link these words with others, e.g. "a *dry* martini," "a *cool* manner"? Secondly, some of the vocabulary used seemed to be completely unfamiliar to the subjects in its application to voice quality. These terms were always familiar, however, in their primary application to sensations. If the subjects showed agreement in their extension of such terms to voices it would argue that the extensions are natural metaphors available to everyone.

The vocabulary for the experiment was drawn from the writings of two contemporary critics and from the reviews that George Bernard Shaw wrote for *London Music* in 1890. It is amusing to note, in passing, that, although Shaw wrote during the "Golden Age of Opera" when Melba, Patti, and the de Reszkes were singing in London he appears to have listened with a jaundiced ear. The words most frequently used by the modern critics were nearly all complimentary but not so with Shaw, who favored such terms as *screaming, yelling, brawling,* and *goat-bleating.*

Three of the singers whose recordings were used were sopranos; three were tenors; and three baritones. The sopranos were Maria Meneghini Callas, Maria Caniglia, and Renata Tebaldi. The tenors were Mario del Monaco, Jan Peerce, and Richard Tucker. The baritones were Gino Bechi, Lawrence Tibbett, and Leonard Warren. Within a vocal category the three singers performed the same fraction of the same operatic aria.

Subjects were provided with a list of ten antonym pairs (e.g., *"cold-warm"*) and required to apply one or another member of each pair to each voice. In addition, they had a list of twenty words which critics use to describe voices but which do not have antonyms that are so used (e.g., *"chromium," "dry," "gravelly"*). From this list subjects chose the five terms most appropriate to each voice.

In addition to comparing the descriptions of individual voices the authors compared each voice range with the other two. When baritones were contrasted with tenors and sopranos they proved to be more often called "dull," "coarse," "closed," "dark," "heavy," "rough," "hard," and "thick." This is at once a description of baritone quality and of the operatic characters played by baritones. Tenors were especially likely to be called "bright," "light," and "thin" while the sopranos were judged to be "coarse," "soft," "light," and "thin." The rather surprising application of "coarse" is explained by the fact that these were Italian dramatic sopranos whose singing showed the quality that the *aficionado* calls "guttiness." There were more adjectives distinctive for baritones than for either tenors or sopranos and that, persumably, is because the baritone is a low register voice compared here with two high register voices. It was conceivable, of course, that the two male voices would resemble one another more closely than either would resemble the sopranos. It is fitting that this should not be so since on the operatic stage tenor and soprano invariably make common cause against the baritone. The latter must find his partner in the black hearted and dark voiced contralto.

The subjects in this experiment were asked to apply sensory, non-auditory words to voice qualities. There was high agreement among them on the pairing of some words with some voices. Furthermore, many of these words were used discriminatingly; i.e., the pattern of applications to one voice differed from the pattern for other voices. We may conclude that some of these extended terms name concepts that were understood in the same way by most subjects.

Many of the words are so commonly applied to voices that the subjects are bound to have been acquainted with this usage. In these cases the referent categories could have been directly learned from designative use of the names and there is no need to assume an extension from the primary categories of sensation. There were some words, however, which subjects seem not to have heard used to designate voice qualities. They frequently complained about the vocabulary provided them, saying they would never choose words like *white* or *chromium* to describe a voice. They racked their brains for some reason for calling a voice *open* rather than *closed*. Yet even with this unfamiliar vocabulary subjects sometimes showed agreement in the identification of specific instances. Of course all the words were familiar in their primary senses and so, perhaps, their extension to voices is appropriate and obvious to everyone.

The results of Asch and Brown, *et al.,* suggest the following explanation. The principal sensory dimensions of the world are the same for men everywhere and are named in all languages. Though each of these dimensions is primarily associated with one receptor system its essential quality is inter-sensory. The quality is first detected in one sense modality and is named at that stage. Afterward the quality is detected in many other phenomena that register with other senses. The original name tends to be extended to any experience manifesting the criterial quality. And so it happens that unrelated languages extend their vocabularies of sensation in similar fashion. So it happens, too, that people in one language community can identify the basic inter-sensory qualities in operatic voices and extend their vocabularies accordingly.

We have no names for these inter-sensory qualities except the names that are also sense-specific, *cold, dry, bright,* etc. With many metaphors the shared attributes can be named without using the names of the referents involved in the metaphor. Richard is a lion because he manifests courage, majesty, strength, pride, and the like. But a voice is cold because it is cold. A single attribute links the referents and that attribute is itself one of the referents. This leaves us unable to talk about the sensory basis for the metaphor in any illuminating way. In situations like this I. A. Richards (192) sometimes invokes the notion of an emotional metaphor rather than a sense metaphor. Icicles, certain faces, and a kind of voice are all called *cold* because they arouse the same emotional reaction. There can be no doubt that these phenomena excite similar reactions (whether they are emotional or not would be hard to say). The very act of calling them all *cold* is a reaction that ties them together. The problem is to find the cause of this common reaction. The fact of the reaction does not prove that there is a single inter-sensory quality that sets it off. Temperature, manners, faces, and voices might be linked by some kind of association.

Any associationistic hypothesis must take account of Asch's findings. The associations suggested must be the sort found everywhere, not something accidental, not something cultural. The following is a crude hypothesis of this kind. Perhaps whenever people behave in an unfriendly fashion their skin temperatures fall below the level of people who behave in a friendly fashion. We should have to assume this to be true whatever form unfriendliness may assume in a given culture. The word *cold,* and its equivalents in every language, would then be extended to unfriendly people because such people are, in fact, thermally cold, not because unfriendliness looks "cold." The operational difference is that a person who had experienced thermal cold could not be expected to recognize coldness of manner unless he had experienced the association with thermal cold. If *cold* names an inter-sensory quality then it should be possible to identify *cold* manners the first time one sees them so long as the quality has been detected in other phenomena.

Mediated Associations. It is not easy to imagine direct associations that will account for the many extensions of our sensation vocabulary, and the ones imagined do not usually seem very probable. An associationistic hypothesis needs more latitude and this is supplied by imagining mediated as well as direct associations. Many substances as they grow colder (thermally) also grow rigid or stiff and slow-moving, as witness molasses, honey, putty, and the like. Suppose now that the movements and expressions of an unfriendly person also manifest stiffness and resistance to movement. Such people are slow to comply, their faces look as if "a smile would crack them." Such people might be called cold because their behavior is stiff and stiff substances are often cold. This is a mediated rather than a direct association. Thermal cold is assumed to be a dimension of experience linked with the cold receptors in the skin. However, the activation of these receptors is correlated (though imperfectly) with other kinds of experience. This correlation is the ground for extending the word *cold* to new experiences that do not activate the cold receptors. The notion that sense qualities are correlated in Nature is central to the hypothesis of mediated association. There is some evidence of such correlation in factor analytic studies of semantics.

Osgood and Suci (174) made a list of fifty adjective antonyms including such sensory terms as "sweet-sour," "loud-soft," "black-white," "sharp-dull," "heavy-light," "thick-thin," "bright-dull," and "rough-smooth." There were also other pairs on the list that did not name sense attributes, words like "good-bad," "beautiful-ugly," "ferocious-peaceful." The experimenters provided their subjects with twenty names of concepts ("lady," "boulder," "sin," "dictator," etc.) and required them to place each concept on each of fifty descriptive scales defined by the antonym pairs. The resultant matrix of choices was factor analyzed. Factor analysis is essentially a technique for pulling out correlation clusters. If several of the descriptive scales were synonymous then judgments made with one scale should be in nearly perfect correlation with the judgments made on the other scales. Scales that function as near synonyms produce a cluster of mutually intercorrelated judgments. The factor extracted from such a cluster represents the experimenter's effort to characterize the common quality of the intercorrelated scales.

Osgood and Suci extracted three orthogonal (or independent) factors and characterized them as: a) evaluation, b) potency, and c) activity. Scales that are highly loaded with the evaluation factor include: "good-bad," "beautiful-ugly," "sweet-sour," "clean-dirty," and others. Scales that are highly loaded with the potency factor include: "hard-soft," "loud-soft," "brave-cowardly," "bass-treble," "rough-smooth," and others. Scales that are highly loaded with the activity factor include: "fast-slow," "active-passive," and "hot-cold." Additional independent studies of a similar kind have yielded the same factors. Among English adjectives there seems to be a rather stable pattern of mutual implications.

The data collected by Brown, Leiter, and Hildum described earlier, were also factor analyzed. The first factor accounts for 56.7 per cent of the common factor variance. It may be called evaluation. The scales having factor loadings above .90 are "cold-warm," "hollow-full," and "like-dislike," and the single terms from the check list are "brittle," "dry," "lustrous," and "pinched." It is not possible to make detailed comparisons with the Osgood-Suci evaluation factor because the scales used in the two studies were not all the same. The scales most heavily loaded with the Osgood-Suci factor included "beautiful-ugly," "sweet-sour," "valuable-worthless," and other pairs excluded from the study of voice qualities. There is some indication, however, that the two evaluation factors would not be quite the same even if identical scales had been used. For instance, the scale "wet-dry" in the Osgood-Suci study is not loaded with the evaluation factor whereas the word "dry" is heavily loaded with evaluation in the study of voice qualities. This simply means that dryness is clearly undesirable in a voice but that, across twenty concepts, dryness is neither clearly bad nor clearly good. Changing the material to be judged somewhat alters the character of the evaluation factor but there is justification for calling both factors of evaluation, since a "good-bad" scale is central to each.

The second factor seems to be best characterized as potency. The third is more difficult to characterize, but there is some ground for thinking it an activity factor similar to that found by Osgood and Suci. The authors extracted a fourth factor but found it impossible to characterize. It is interesting to note that these four factors account for over 80 per cent of the total variance while the Osgood-Suci factors accounted for only 50 per cent. With more restricted materials and scales there is more communality.

The word clusters found by Osgood and Suci and by Brown, *et al.*, could derive from imperfect correlations in Nature among the qualities named and from mediated associations among the names. Consider two scales from the potency factor—"large-small" and "heavy-light." Imagine, as is quite possible, that these words were first encountered as names for attributes of a set of wooden blocks. If all the blocks were made of the same kind of wood the two scales would be in natural correlation; the larger the block the heavier it would be. The same sort of relationship binds "heavy-light" to "thick-thin" and to "wide-narrow." Words of this kind are ordinarily used to compare one object with others of the same type. A block is "large" relative to other blocks. As a consequence "large," "heavy," "thick," and "wide" are terms that ordinarily imply one another. And the implications spread even more widely. When it is a question of people the larger, heavier, thicker, wider adult specimens seem to be more likely to have loud bass voices than are the smaller, lighter, thinner, narrower child specimens.

Suppose, now, that a subject is asked to judge twenty concepts with respect to all these scales. A concept like "boulder" is referred to rocks and stones and, in comparison, judged to be "heavy," "large," "thick," and "wide." These terms are directly applicable to boulders. However, boulders have no voices. Where, then, does the concept belong on the "bass-treble" or "loud-soft" scales? We cannot doubt the answer. If Disney were to give a boulder a voice it would be "bass" and "loud" in contrast to the piping of a pebble. This could be a mediated association: a boulder must have a bass voice because creatures that do have bass voices are usually heavy and boulders are heavy. It is not necessary to assume that there is any subtle inter-sensory quality found in boulders and in bass voices.

Subjects in the study of Brown, *et al.*, may have felt that "thick" and "thin" simply do not apply to voices. However, "loud" and "resonant" do. Now thick people and animals and violin strings are usually loud and resonant so, if the subject is required to guess, he will call the loud and resonant voice "thick." This need not be because the voice shares some inter-sensory quality with the visual or tactile apprehension of thickness. It could be because the voice is loud and creatures who have loud voices are usually thick, a mediated association.

Some of the subjects in this study were asked to explain their word choices and the protocols support the mediated association hypothesis. Explanations generally assumed the form "I called it X because it is Y," where Y is some word ordinarily implied by X but more clearly applicable than X to the voice in question. A voice is "thick" (X) because it is "rich" (Y); a voice is "heavy" (X) because it is "deep" (Y); a voice is "closed" (X) because it is "tense" (Y). If subjects were recognizing inter-sensory qualities ought they not to say "It is heavy because it is heavy"?

To say that there is a natural correlation in the use of words like *thick, heavy,* and *large* is not the same as saying that these words name only one subtle dimension. The word clusters found in factor analytic studies ought not to be interpreted to mean that the lexicon of English is made up of countless perfect synonyms for *good-bad* or *strong-weak*. We have only to imagine a set of blocks that includes some made of balsa wood as well as some made of pine to realize that *heavy* and *large* name dimensions that are logically independent. In some naming situations the applications of these words would show no correlation, the Osgood-Suci clusters would not appear. The clusters must turn up when subjects are required to apply adjectives to concepts or voices or anything else to which some of them have no literal application. In these circumstances the subject finds a basis for choice in mediated associations which ultimately derive from the natural correlation of sense qualities. This is a situation requiring metaphorical extension and the lines predictive of that extension are laid down in our shared early experience of the implications linking words.

In the discussion of phonetic symbolism I have already suggested that sense qualities are correlated in Nature and that these correlations make one name more appropriate than another for a particular referent. If a high pitch goes with what is small in Nature then a word with high-pitched vowel formants makes a good name for a small referent. I have now further suggested that the natural correlation of sense qualities provides a basis for the metaphorical extension of the names of sense qualities. Such a name will be applied to phenomena to which it has no real application because the name usually implies some other name which does have application. So it happens that a person who busies himself with trifles may be said to have a "small" mind. This is not because his concerns are spatially small (he may spend his time polishing a Cadillac or scrubbing an elephant). It is rather because smaller things of any given type are likely to be less powerful, to have tamer consequences than larger things of the same type. A man who has a small mind concerns himself with things that do not greatly matter, things of little consequence. Ultimately then both principles of appropriateness in naming may have a common source in the correlations of sense data in the non-linguistic world.

Summary

There are two ways in which a name can be appropriate to its referent. Both name and referent are categories and it is possible for them to have similar attributes. When this is the case in speech we have the basis for phonetic symbolism. Language forms often have more than one referent and, whenever that is the case, one reference is appropriate to the other if the referent categories share criterial attributes. This is appropriate reference through metaphor. With phonetic symbolism the evidence is that speakers of a given language have similar notions of the semantic implications of various phonetic sequences. It is not known whether there are any universal principles of phonetic symbolism. Semantic change through metaphor operates continually in all languages and the creation of metaphor is a major means of poetic communication. Many, perhaps all, languages make metaphorical extensions of their vocabularies of sensation. It may be that these extensions are founded in the natural correlations of sense qualities. If such correlations exist they could also provide the basis for a universal phonetic symbolism.

chapter v

The Comparative
Psychology of
Linguistic Reference

I GRANT A MIND to every human being, to each
a full stock of feelings, thoughts, motives, and meanings. I hope
they grant as much to me. How much of this mentality that we
allow one another ought we to allow the monkey, the sparrow, the
goldfish, the ant? Hadn't we better reserve something for ourselves
alone, perhaps consciousness or self-consciousness, possibly linguistic reference?

Most people are determined to hold the line against animals.
Grant them the ability to make linguistic reference and they will
be putting in a claim for minds and souls. The whole phyletic scale
will come trooping into Heaven demanding immortality for every
tadpole and hippopotamus. Better to be firm now and make it clear
that man alone can use language to make reference. There is a
qualitative difference of mentality separating us from the animals.

The pet in the house is usually excepted from this view of
animals in general. The dog close up draws more life from us than
does the remote Chinese. We hydrate him into full mentality. He
feels, he thinks, he talks and understands, and he is devoted to us

alone. A dog can be a very satisfying creation, more governable than the people we project into life. The only difficulty is that the dog, once made human, will not resume animal status and dogs are short-lived. When the creature is squashed in the road we remind ourselves in vain that he was a dog.

Among the students of comparative psychology there are some who make a pet of every subject. They are terrible pushovers from whom animals extract complete sympathy and the benefit of every doubt. To people like this it is obvious that animals have a language but it is sometimes difficult to discover from their reports what it is in animal behavior that has suggested language. When we *can* find our way back to behavior in these reports they are useful because they seek out the most complicated and promising things animals do. They are more useful to us than the writings of the *no nonsense* behaviorist who looks the other way when the rat leaves its "T maze" lest he see something too complex to believe. Best of all, needless to say, are the studies that combine sympathy with a sense of evidence.

The literature on the comparative psychology of language is concerned with three different problems. There is, first, the question as to whether animals, living with their own kind, ever exhibit behavior that may be called referential language. Secondly, there is the capacity question. Is there any animal which, when it is given the opportunity, can acquire a human language? Finally, what of the occasional human being who is raised by animals or is somehow isolated from human linguistic behavior? Does the human talent for language result in its invention when none is taught?

Animal Languages

What kinds of animal behavior do people identify as linguistic or pre-linguistic? Since language is often equated with speech, and the most obvious attribute of speech is vocal production, vocal behavior in animals suggests language more readily than does behavior produced by any other motor system. When the sounds produced sound a little like speech they are especially likely to attract attention. If this characteristic is well developed nothing else may be required. If my dog were to pronounce my name I don't suppose I should worry about whether or not he appeared to understand it.

Non-vocal behavior, however, does not suggest language unless it seems to have "meaning." A minimal requirement of a meaningful response is that it should be selective in the stimuli eliciting it. The case for the animal is better if he demonstrates that his response can be extended to new instances of a category of stimuli. We seem then to have something like the concepts that give meaning to words.

Human language behavior has no direct instrumental effect on the inanimate world. Calling for help does not calm the sea. Words are useful only because they affect other human beings. The best understood of these effects is the case in which the word causes someone to act as if he had had direct experience of the word's referent. Consequently we are reminded of language by animal actions that have no instrumentality for the inanimate world but which cause other animals to act as if they had received the stimulus to which the action is a response.

In human beings both of these kinds of "meaningful" behavior can be created by experience of a linguistic form in conjunction with its referent. Therefore we expect animal languages to be learned in this way. A difficulty with natural animal languages is that one usually cannot tell whether the behavior has been learned or is instinctive. We expect instinctive behavior to be the same in all healthy members of an animal species and, on that account, behavior uniform in a species is not like any human language. However, human languages are shared behavior, fairly uniform throughout a society. Some comparative psychologists have simply looked for shared meaningful behavior, neglecting to distinguish species characteristics from community norms.

Allow me now to describe three cases of animal behavior that have seemed to psychologists or biologists to be referential language. These are selected to sample the phyletic scale: the bee, the jackdaw, and the chimpanzee. Afterward we shall see if there is anything in human linguistic reference that does not appear in the animal behavior.

The Bee. Karl von Frisch (234) has studied the behavior of the honeybee since about 1920. Many of his experiments were undertaken to explain the fact that when one bee has found a source of food, and returned to the hive from that source, numerous other bees shortly find their way to the same food source. The appearance of the other bees is far too rapid and regular to be attributed to happy accident. The inference of communication in the hive seems irresistible. Finder bees must somehow "tell" the secondary bees where they have been and what they found there.

There is no way to see into an ordinary hive. Von Frisch, therefore, constructed a vertical observation hive with glass walls. The behavior of the finder bee within the hive was related in systematic fashion to the location of the food recently discovered. There is a potential semantic in the dance it performs. We could learn from that dance where the nectar lies. The finder bee is closely followed in its dance by other bees which then fly fairly directly to the food source. It seems certain that the secondary bees have decoded the finder's message and used the resultant information to guide their flight.

The precise location of any food source is defined by its distance from the hive and the direction in which it lies. Both of these values are signalled by the dance of the finder bee. Consider first the dimension of distance. When the food is less than twenty-eight yards away the finder executes a round dance on the hive. As the distance increases beyond twenty-eight yards the dance begins to change its form. The bee runs a short distance in a straight line while wagging its abdomen rapidly from side to side; then it makes a complete 360° turn to the left, runs straight ahead once more, turns to the right and repeats the pattern. This waggle dance completely replaces the round dance when the food is more than 200 meters from the hive.

Within the range of distances that gives rise to the waggle dance a finer calibration of distance is revealed in the frequency with which waggles are produced in a given run and also in the number of turns made in the dance in a unit of time. Von Frisch plotted a curve relating the number of turns to the distance of the food, using some 3,885 observed dances. As the distance increased the number of turns declined. There were nine or ten turns within fifteen seconds when the food was 100 meters distant; seven turns when it was 200 meters distant; and only two turns with food six kilometers from the hive. There was some individual variability from one bee to another and, interestingly, somewhat different norms from one colony to another. This last finding suggests that we have here a species language divided into local dialects. The frequency of the waggles is a somewhat less reliable indication of distance than the number of runs. However, waggles become more frequent as the distance increases.

It is perfectly clear that there exist correlations between the finder bee's behavior in the hive and the remoteness from the hive of the food discovered. It is also clear that the differences in the behavior of the finder affect the behavior of the secondary bees. The relative importance to the secondary bees of the several indications of distance has not been determined. However, since the frequency of waggles rises as the number of turns declines there is some duplication of information. The analogy with human language is improved by the fact of a redundancy in the code.

When the food source is far enough from the hive to cause the finder to waggle dance, the direction of the food from the hive is also signalled. The direction of the straight portion of the dance is the cue. When this straight run is directly upward on the vertical hive the food lies toward the sun. A food seeker should fly into the sun. When the straight run is directly downward the food seeker should fly away from the sun. In general the line between the hive and the sun is translated into the vertical dimension on the observation hive. The location of a food source can always be expressed in terms of its coincidence with or deviation from that sun-line and the finder bee's straight run is accordingly coincident with or departed from the vertical dimension of the cone. When the food is displaced 45° to the right of the sun-line the run will be at an angle of 45° to the right of verticality.

The dependence of the directional signal on the sun is dramatically proven by the fact that finder bees coming from an identical food source will change the direction of the straight run as the sun moves across the sky. In a series of ingenious experiments von Frisch showed that the bee is oriented by his sensitivity to the polarization of light. The observation hive is entirely dark within but the sun-line undergoes translation into a gravitational vertical. The observation hive creates extraordinary conditions in that the bee must dance on a vertical surface and in the dark. The usual hive provides a horizontal surface and receives some sunlight. Under these conditions the finder bee takes his orientation directly from the sun and his straight dance is in the direction of the food source. Apparently the bee must have either a vertical surface or some glimmering of sunlight to orient his dance. Von Frisch found that finder bees in the dark on a horizontal surface dance in an irregular confused fashion.

The most delightful discovery is the bee's method of signalling a detour route. The food source was placed behind a ridge so that the bees were obliged to fly a detour to reach it. The question was: Would the bee signal the direction of the first portion of the route or the second portion? In fact it does neither but signals a bee-line, a straight line to the food. However, it signals the actual rather than the straight line distance. It has not been demonstrated that secondary bees are able to read the proper best route from this combined information, but von Frisch would not put it past them.

The Jackdaw. Konrad Lorenz (151), the Swiss naturalist, has so expertly mimicked the call note of a mother mallard as to convince a brood of mallard ducklings that he was their mother. The mallard ducklings were not deceived by the inferior imitation of a moscovy duck. They dutifully paddled after Lorenz who went on all fours to improve the credibility of his impersonation. On another occasion Lorenz called down from the sky a yellow-breasted cockatoo by sounding its flight call. He has been loved by a greylag goose and courted by a jackdaw. He has tamed the water shrew. Lorenz studies animals in their free state and is often accepted as one of the family.

The first jackdaw came to live at the Lorenz home in Altenberg more than twenty-five years ago. Today the birds fly in clouds about the town. Lorenz bought the first bird in a pet shop, and called it Jock in imitation of its own call-note. Jock so interested Lorenz that he undertook to rear a whole colony of free flying tame jackdaws so that he might study their social and family behavior. He began in 1927 with fourteen young birds. These were marked for identification but Lorenz found that he was soon able to distinguish each individual without the use of any artificial marking.

The jackdaw lives nearly as long as man. He becomes betrothed in his first year and married in his second and is monogamous for life. The jackdaw betrothal ceremony occurs a full year before sexual maturity. The male "spreads himself" before the female. His head is proudly reared in self-display. The nesting call

—"Zick, Zick, Zick"—is sounded from some dark corner or small hole. This Zick ceremony actually does not invite to nest, it is twelve months premature for that; it is rather a form of courtship. The most remarkably eloquent feature of the courtship, to Lorenz' mind, is the "language of the eyes." The male jackdaw stares lovingly directly at the female. She turns her eyes in all directions away from her suitor but darts instantaneous glances his way to check his performance. Once married, the female jackdaw greets her husband with gestures of "symbolic inferiorism." She squats before him, quivering her wings and tail. The male tenderly feeds her every delicacy he finds and the two speak in low whispers. This loving speech consists of notes heard from infant jackdaws begging for food, but reserved in the adult for tender scenes.

The flight call of the jackdaw tends to infect the others with his mood and send the lot of them swirling off into the sky. Lorenz distinguished two varieties of flight call. The ordinary note is high and light and has been transcribed as *Kia*. The other note is longer and darker; Lorenz writes it *Kiaw*. Both of these are said to have the meaning "Fly with me," not in the sense of a purposive command by the calling bird but in the sense that the call beckons to the others. *Kia*, however, is the call uttered when the bird would fly abroad and *Kiaw* is the call for homeward-bound birds. In a flock of birds there may be a competition of cries, pulling the birds in several directions at once. Eventually one becomes dominant and they sweep off, sounding it in unison.

The most notable element of jackdaw speech is the rattle of anger. The jackdaw, unlike many other birds, lacks instinctive reactions to its enemies. The naïve jackdaw will sit and wait for an approaching cat or perch on the nose of a dog. There is only one instinctive response connected with the recognition of enemies. Any living thing that carries a black dangling or fluttering object will evoke the grating rattle of warning and will be assaulted. Lorenz, himself, was painfully pecked by Jock when he inadvertently picked up a jackdaw baby. Jock, who was devoted to Lorenz, nevertheless rattled and attacked when the releasing stimulus appeared. That the stimulus need not involve a young bird was demonstrated when Lorenz became the target of a mass attack while carrying his black bathing trunks in one hand. After a rattling attack the birds are mistrustful of the person or animal who occasioned it. Lorenz believes that if you provoke the attack two or three times you have lost the bird's friendship forever. It will scold as soon as it sees you and other jackdaws will learn to do the same. Enemies are identified by the stigma of carrying a black object. The jackdaw can share its knowledge and, in effect, tell others that this is an enemy. This is the nearest thing I know among animals to a linguistically conveyed item of cultural information.

Finally, Lorenz tells of a female jackdaw separated from her mate who took to singing a melancholy ballad. The song of most birds does not employ the significant calls of the species but is a completely distinct performance. The jackdaw's song is built up from his various calls—the rattle of anger, the *Zick* of courtship, the *Kia* of flight. It is, for Lorenz, irresistibly reminiscent of the human ballad that draws on the major emotional themes of everyday life. In any case the widow jackdaw sang a song in which the *Kiaw* note was dominant, the cry "Come home."

The Chimpanzee. Yerkes, in his book *The Great Apes* (258), has distinguished the vocalization characteristics of the orang utan, chimpanzee, gorilla, and gibbon. The chimpanzee and gibbon are noisier than the others and, of these two, more is known of the chimpanzee. There are several species of chimpanzee and probably there are some differences in the vocalizations of the different species, but in most reports the animals are simply identified as chimpanzees and that must be the case here.

The vocal mechanism of the chimp is adequate for the production of a large variety of sounds. It makes possible definite articulations similar to those of human speech. In the wild state the chimp is reported by many hunters and explorers (Livingstone [148] Pechuel-Loesche [177]) to be a frequent and vigorous vocalizer. Jenks (117) writes: "By day and night the chimpanzee seems always to have something to say and one even when alone frequently makes noise enough for half a dozen animals." Köhler (128) and others say that the chimp in captivity is a quieter animal. Still Köhler (127) finds so many phonetic elements in the vocalizing of the captive chimp that he cannot suppose it to lack speech for peripheral phonetic reasons. He is sure, however, that it does lack speech.

There is some information about the detailed character of vocalization in the captive chimpanzee. Rothman and Teuber

(197) studied the chimps of the Canary Island Anthropoid Station. They report the use of a large variety of sounds, including all the vowels, but with [o] and [u] especially prominent. Learned (257) recorded the sounds of two young animals, "Chim" and "Panzee." She used a musical notation and what appears to be an imprecise phonetic transcription, and found a large number of clearly distinct utterances. Chim and Panzee made similar sounds but there were some differences between them. A comparison with three adult chimps at the New York Zoo turned up further individual differences. Apparently there is not as much species uniformity with these animals as there is with birds and bees.

There can be no doubt that some of the chimpanzee utterances have semantic value. Garner, in *The Speech of Monkeys* (70), describes the circumstances in which the chimpanzee uses its various sounds and, finding stimulus-response consistencies, he asserts that the utterances of the chimpanzee are true words. Köhler (127) denies that the chimpanzee has words but he regularly writes of chimpanzees "grumbling," "calling one another," "greeting him in the morning," etc. These translations represent Köhler's recognition of semantic features in chimpanzee vocalization. Rothmann and Teuber say that joy is expressed by repeated "Oh's," weeping involves a deep "oo" sound, and fear a high "ee."

Learned wrote descriptions of the circumstances attending each utterance of Chim and Panzee. Examining these data afterward, she found that twenty-two utterances were used with enough consistency to make translations possible. Phonetically they divide into sounds beginning with "G," those beginning with "K" whispered, with "K" aspirate, with nasals, labials, and finally those that begin with vowels. Learned makes a semantic division into sounds associated with food and sounds associated with other creatures. Most of these are described as expressing emotional states—fear, joy, alarm, excitement, etc. There are also utterances used in correlation with objects, e.g., a fruit motive and a greeting for friends.

There are not many good examples, in the literature, of chimpanzee utterances serving as signs to other members of the species. Certain calls of warning, appeals for food, and threatening barks seem to be signs. The common case is that in which many chimpanzees are simultaneously vocalizing. None may make the kind of appropriate response that indicates he has received a sign. They behave more like a rudely chattering human group than like the businesslike bee who acts at once on the sign he receives. Chimpanzee social vocalizing is often no more valuable for demonstrating the existence of signs than is a human conversation. In other situations, however, especially in their interaction with humans, there is plenty of evidence that chimpanzees can respond to signs.

Köhler writes of the chimpanzee, "It may be taken as positively proved that their gamut of *phonetics* is entirely 'subjective,' and can only express emotions, never designate or describe objects." (127) This might mean that chimpanzee utterances ordinarily express states of the speaker. They appear in closer correlation with other speaker behaviors than with stimuli external to the speaker. That is certainly true of an utterance like the fear cry whose "cause" (external stimulus) Learned is often unable to discover. The cry is always accompanied with other evidence of fear but not always by any discoverable class of stimuli external to the animal. However, Learned's report of a food bark and, more specifically, a "fruit motive" contradicts Köhler's statement. These utterances seemed to Learned to designate objects. Of course, the animal was often hungry when it saw food. However, the motivational state was not enough to produce the utterance. The response itself was most closely correlated with the appearance of food and therefore qualifies as a response designating a class of external referents. It is probably true, however, that most chimpanzee vocalizations are expressions.

Linguistic Reference and Animal "Languages." The referential forms of human language are not all vocal. Alphabetic writings have the same structure and accomplish most of the same purposes as speech but the responses involved are made with the fingers. If we were to take speech sounds as the essence of language we should have to accept the talking birds as our nearest phyletic neighbors and that is a conclusion in gross contradiction with all of comparative anatomy and psychology.

If vocalization is acknowledged to be unimportant the dances of the bee appear to be very much like referential language. The dances are selective responses made to certain features of the nonlinguistic world—food in a particular locality. In addition, the dances cause other members of the bee community to behave as if they had direct experience of the food. In short, follower bees behave as if the information possessed by the finders had been transmitted to them through the dances.

It can even be maintained that the dances are superior to ordinary linguistic reference, for they are what Carnap (35) calls a "co-ordinate language." He writes: "The method of designation by proper names is the primitive one; that of positional designation corresponds to a more advanced stage of science and has considerable methodological advantages over the former." The referents coded by the dance all have the same two criterial attributes: direction and distance from the hive. Nothing else affects the significant features of the dances, not the quality of the nectar, not the color of the flower, not even the presence of von Frisch at the food source daubing bees with paint so that he can recognize them in the hive. The dances, like the referents, have only two significant dimensions; the frequency of turns and the direction of the straight run. The dimensions of the dance are continuously isomorphic with the dimensions of the referents. This is like the relationship between the temperature of a room and the thermometer that registers it. It is superior to ordinary reference because it is systematic. Knowing that apples are called *apples* and oranges are called *oranges* does not teach anyone the name for bananas. When we know that food lying on a line between the hive and the sun causes a vertical upward dance and that food lying 45° to the right of the sunline causes a dance displaced 45° to the right of the vertical we can guess the direction the dance will take when food is 90° to the right of the sunline. There is a principle relating referents to dances so that, with its aid, we can determine either from knowledge of the other.

The dances of the bees accomplish certain things that man would be likely to accomplish with language. However, the dances are unlike language in that they are not learned. The variations between colonies noticed by von Frisch were very slight and not really at all like the language variations distinguishing human communities. For instance, speech shows gradients of differentiation both in time and space. People a thousand miles apart are likely to show greater linguistic differences than people a few miles apart. Nothing of the kind has been shown for the honeybee. The general character of the dances (the features of the dance correlated with the direction and distance of the food) is a species characteristic.

Much the most interesting of the jackdaw's calls is the warning rattle. It is elicited by a category of stimuli describable as "someone carrying a black, dangling or fluttering object." One jackdaw's rattle will cause other jackdaws to fly to the attack. These others behave as if they had seen someone carrying a black fluttering object though, in fact, they have not. The rattle is both a selective response and a sign stimulus. More interestingly the category of individuals who elicit the rattle expands, through learning, to include anyone who has in the past been seen to carry a black fluttering object and anyone who is rattled at by other jackdaws. Enemies come to be identified by past as well as present behavior and also by hearsay. The category is surprisingly like one we might call "enemies of the community."

The jackdaw's rattle is an instinctive response to the sight of a person or animal carrying a black fluttering object. Lorenz found that the jackdaws in northern Russia produced the same rattle as did his own birds. More conclusively he has raised the jackdaw in isolation from others of its kind and found that when such a bird is presented with the usual releasing stimuli it produces the calls of the species. However, there are learned components in the use of the rattle. The jackdaw learns to recognize possible enemies from their past behavior and the calls of other jackdaws.

The vocalizations of the chimpanzee are selectively used. Some seem to be primarily expressive of emotions but others designate referents. At least some of these utterances function as signs to other chimpanzees, causing them to act as if they had seen the food or the human being that set off the bark. The fact that Learned found individual differences in the vocalizations of the five animals she studied argues that some chimpanzee utterances may be acquired. On this subject we can surely take Yerkes' (256) word for it: "Assuredly many of the linguistic signs recognized in chimpanzee behavior are acquired through individual experiences."

Does nothing distinguish chimpanzee vocalizations from the referential lexicon of a language? Are the calls of the jackdaw and the dances of the bee like such a lexicon except that they are instinctive rather than acquired responses? Of course animal "languages" are different from human languages if we take account of grammar; animals do not seem to combine their linguistic responses in accordance with any rules of syntax. But we are going to stay with linguistic reference and look for differences other than the relative importance of instinct and learning.

First, a résumé of some of the characteristics of all linguistic lexicons: A lexicon provides names for a great many referent categories, in fact for most of the categories with which the community operates. A lexicon is a nearly exhaustive cultural inventory. Whenever a new category becomes important for the life of the community it is promptly named. Exactly what do I understand a linguistic name to be beyond a response that makes reference? In the first place, the names of a language are all produced by a single motor system; in the case of speech the vocal-articulational, in the case of writing or gesture the muscles of the hands and fingers. Only a few operations of this motor system (less than seventy) are significant, i.e., are associated with a change in referent category. Many other operations that occur are not significant in this sense. A linguistic name is a sequence of significant operations differing from every other name in the language by at least one such operation. The attributes differentiating referent categories are indefinitely numerous but the attributes distinguishing names from one another (e.g., phonemes or distinctive features) make only a small list. The significant attributes of names are not combined in every conceivable way. There are always conventions of phonology or orthography that exclude some combinations. When a community member undertakes to create a new name it can be predicted that this creation will be a unique but acceptable sequence of significant operations of the linguistic motor system. If an unconventional sequence is created it will seem to community members to fall outside the language and they may find it "impossible" to produce. A lexicon or collection of linguistic names is a systematic map of the community mind and animal "languages" are nothing of the sort.

We have seen in Chapter I that the essential operations in working out a phonemic system are: a) a detailed culture-free description of a large number of utterances belonging to the system, and b) judgments of equivalence and difference from community members. I think it may be just possible to devise a comparative phonemic procedure for animal languages, but nothing of the kind has yet been done.

Lorenz records the calls of the jackdaw with letters of the alphabet. He probably heard them in terms of the categories of his own speech. *Kia* and *Kiaw* are written as if they were a minimal pair of words differing only in vowel quality. No doubt these calls differ in many acoustic features. We know that vowel quality is the difference that counts for Lorenz but we do not know whether this is the difference that counts for jackdaws. In any case, the jackdaw calls are too few to subject to a phonemic procedure.

There exists no analysis of chimpanzee speech to tell us whether it has anything like a phonemic structure. The set of forms is large enough to admit of the possibility of such structure. Learned's study is tantalizing because it comes so near providing the data we should like to have for anthropoid vocalization and yet fails at several critical points. She recorded all the speech of two informants for several weeks, taking notes on the circumstances attending each utterance, but then, unfortunately, used a very broad impressionistic system of phonetic notation. The musical features of the speech were also recorded but we are not told whether these were symbolic or expressive or redundant. Her presentation suggests that particular phonetic combinations were accompanied by particular intonations. If so, there is systematic redundancy in chimpanzee speech. We do not know what features of the utterances made them distinct for the chimpanzee.

The dances of the bee are a gestural rather than a vocal language. Phonemic procedure cannot be applied but a comparable kind of structural analysis called *kinesics,* applied by Birdwhistell (19) to limited aspects of human gesture, might be adapted to the bee. The recording of the dances in terms of frequency of turns and compass direction is rather like a phonetic transcription in that it takes note of the principal differences without making any assumptions about what is significant and what is not. Genuine problems of language structure do arise from the von Frisch data. For example, the distance of the food source from the hive is related in the waggle dance to both the frequency of waggles and the frequency of runs. These two features of the dance are negatively correlated with one another. There is redundancy in the code but we cannot go so far as to call one of these features "kinemic" and the other "allokinesic." To draw that conclusion it would be necessary to know that one of the features (the kinemic) appeared elsewhere in the language as the sole distinctive difference between dances to which follower bees responded differentially. If the other feature were always redundant it could be properly called allokinesic.

Phoneticians, we know, had to give up trying to transcribe all the differences in human speech. It is, similarly, impossible to record all the differences in animal cries and movements. As we learn what differences are significant for various animal species we shall improve our notion of the features that are worth recording. To begin with there are studies of animal sensory capacities that ought to be consulted. K. U. Smith (214) has written: "Day insects are especially sensitive to differences in wave lengths of light and are capable of response to short wave lengths of light in the ultraviolet range that the human eye never sees. The mammals among the ungulate and carnivorous groups far excel the human being in detection of faint odors, particularly animal odors, and utilize these capacities in the hunt for prey and food as well as in the avoidance of enemies. The common mouse, rat, and bat display auditory acuity for high frequency vibrations that are supersonic with respect to the human ear."

Phonemes are attributes, criterial for the categorization of meaningful speech forms. They are far less numerous than the distinctions speakers are *able* to hear. Similarly, knowledge of the sensory capacities of an animal is not the same as knowledge of the attributes he uses in categorizing the responses of his species. From the human being we can get judgments of equivalence or difference as utterances are systematically varied. From the animal we must have two responses from one animal that are treated as distinct signs by another animal. To find out wherein the perceived distinction lies the sign-responses would have to change, contrasting now in one attribute, now in another, until the experimenter isolated the attributes governing the selective reactions of the second animal. There will be some natural free variation in the sign responses and these will rule out some attributes. To separate out those that recur together one might construct models of the sign response systematically varying its features. This has been done successfully by Tinbergen (226) with the fighting posture of the male stickleback fish. Using wooden models it has been demonstrated that the red blob on the underbelly of the fish is the attribute of his fighting posture that releases aggressive action in other sticklebacks.

Since we don't know how well this kind of animal phonemics

can be worked out, and since it is perhaps fanciful to imagine that anyone will take the trouble to carry it out, we shall not bother to extend the procedure to the identification of rules of phonological sequence, of redundancies and the like. It is worthwhile pointing out, however, that until this kind of structure has been demonstrated for animal languages they cannot be said to be the same as human languages. The study of the bees by von Frisch comes nearer meeting linguistic criteria than any other work in comparative psychology. It is proof of what can be done but it took some thirty years to do it.

Animal "language" responses are unlike a linguistic lexicon, also, in that they do not seem to constitute an inventory of the community mind. Bees, for instance, have many perceptual categories that are not coded by the dances. They can identify forms and colors and perfumes of flowers. The evidence of this ability is apparent in certain discriminating responses but not in the dances. As the dances are constituted there is no provision for new names. Every combination of values of the two significant attributes is allocated to some referent location of food. The dances of the bee are a closed system whereas human language is always open to extension along lines prefigured in its existent forms.

Students of chimpanzee behavior know how numerous and complicated are the categories with which these creatures operate, but most of these categories are not named in chimpanzee "speech." They are inferred from many kinds of behavior: approach and avoidance, aggression, sexual excitement, eating, climbing, etc.

Since experimental psychology began, many animals have learned many concepts but we do not know of any case in which the animal has enlarged its set of communicating forms to name the new concept. Of course the concept is manifest in some kind of discriminating response but the response is selected by the experimenter. It may be salivation, jumping, barking, or what have you. Having acquired the concept, however, the animal does not work out a means of communicating it in the response system dedicated to that purpose in his social group, as a man usually would. Though a man might be required by experimental procedure to discriminate between two classes of figures by turning a lever or pressing a button, he would not stop with that response but would also say, "It's the green squares" or "It's the larger circles." The concept is manifest in the structured response system of speech. If a concept is quite new, a name can be created for it by recombining familiar elements in accordance with known possibilities and probabilities.

In summary, a linguistic lexicon is a system of names covering the conceptual repertoire of a community. New names can be created according to principles embodied in existent names and new names are created whenever a new grouping principle is utilized by the community. Animal "languages" do not seem to constitute systems of this kind.

There are other ways in which the referential responses of animals differ from linguistic names and one of these is important. A man who knows the name for apples does not say the name whenever he sees an apple. To be sure he is prepared to name if the proper circumstances arise and our best test of his understanding is to set up such circumstances. The dances of the honeybee and the jackdaw rattle are like names in that they are elicited by selective stimuli but they are unlike names in that this elicitation is *too* reliable. No doubt the jackdaw's rattle can be upset by illness or distraction, even as can the simplest reflexes. The rattle is probably contingent on certain conditions of health and attention but these conditions are ordinarily met and the stimulus is usually able to trigger the response. A very young child sometimes produces names in this same way: referents shake them out of him like pennies from a pig bank. However except for the very first stages in linguistic function, human beings do not name in this way. Naming is contingent on more than health and attention. The adult must be asked to name something, or must be teaching names to someone, or must want to call attention to something. The contingencies governing production of the linguistic name are not like those governing animal referential response.

The follower bee reacts to the dance of the finder as if the follower had experienced the stimulus causing the dance. Because the follower reacts to the dance as a sign the dance is like a linguistic name but again it is unlike it, because the follower's reaction is *too* reliable. A human being who hears the name of some food does not usually go in search of the referent. What he does is contingent on other things in the situation and in himself. If he is hungry, likes the food in question, and takes the name for an invitation to eat, he may act as if he had seen the food itself. The contingencies governing the reaction of the follower bee are fewer and quite different.

A linguistic name is a response that can be used to designate referents and is also a stimulus that can be used as a sign of the referent. Ability to do these things is evidence that a name is understood. However, the appearance of a referent is by no means a sufficient condition for eliciting the name nor is the name sufficient to produce behavior appropriate to the referent. For the analogous performances of the bee and jackdaw the referent and its name are very nearly sufficient conditions. Whatever else is necessary is so reliably present that one can successfully predict response from stimulus which is just what cannot be done with the linguistic name. The chimpanzee, like the very young child, functions in a way that is intermediate between bee and man. He sometimes feels playful and does not react to a sign he understands. He seldom names unless he wants the referent and sees someone who can get it for him.

After all this discussion, what is the answer to the original question? Are there any natural animal languages? This answer, too, is contingent. If the essence of language is taken to be selective response to categories of stimuli then scarcely any animal lacks a language. If we add that the responses must be treated by other animals in the species as signs of the referent categories there will still be some animal languages. However, if we ask whether there is any set of responses used by animals among themselves that manifests all the properties invariably found in human languages, the answer must be no.

Animals Given an Opportunity to Learn Human Language

The animal community does not offer a language to its newborn. A test of animal *capacity* to acquire language is provided when the creature is given the opportunity to learn an existent language. What success have people had in teaching animals to use existent human languages?

Clever Hans. Pfungst's (178) story of Hans is a classic warning against enthusiastic anthropomorphism. It makes a strong case for

Lloyd Morgan's Canon—animal behavior ought to be explained by assuming the simplest psychological processes adequate to explain the behavior. The story has often been told but it is important again because of its special properties in the history of attempts at linguistic training of animals. It is an instance in which an animal was given opportunity to use human language but not required to make uncongenial vocalizations or gestures. Human speech was coded into hoofbeats for a horse.

Herr von Osten, a gentleman of Berlin, purchased Hans in 1900 and began training him a year later. Simple counting was Hans' first assignment. Von Osten would place a number of objects before the animal, then take hold of its forefoot and cause it to tap once for each object. Hans progressed amazingly. Having learned to count he went on to simple addition and multiplication. Later came subtraction and division and, eventually, the solution of problems involving factors and fractions. To the question, how much is 1/8 and 2/16, Hans could answer 4/16 by tapping first the numerator and then the denominator. Von Osten put the horse through some astounding public performances in which he would count the persons in the audience, with distinctions of sex if desired, would count their eyeglasses, umbrellas, or hats. He carried the yearly calendar in his head and could give the date of any day one might mention. He could tell time to the minute. He had a musical aptitude, including absolute pitch memory. Hans could analyze compound clangs and inform others what changes should be made in a discord in order to render it consonant. In all this there was evidence of thorough comprehension of the German language and the ability to produce the equivalents of numerals.

Von Osten opened new opportunities to Hans when he arranged an alphabetic code such that each letter was signalled by a distinctive number of hoof beats. The horse began answering questions whether they were asked or printed. "What is the woman holding in her hand?" Hans spelled out *"Schirm"* (parasol) in hoof beats. "What is this?" (showing a picture of a horse). Hans spelled *"Pferd."*

Hans became famous. His name was sung from the vaudeville stage. His likeness appeared on picture postcards, bottles of liquor, and children's toys. Some skeptics were certain that von Osten gave the animal optical or auditory signals. Others suggested that electrical wires placed under the pavement conveyed cues from von Osten to his pupil. Still others explained the whole thing as telepathy, suggestion, or "N rays" (said to emanate from the human brain). There was strong evidence against any deliberate trickery in the fact that von Osten never exhibited the horse for profit. The whole business made such a stir and seemed of such great importance to philosophy, psychology, and zoology that an investigating commission was appointed. The wonderfully comic opera constituency of this committee was as follows: Messrs. Stumpf and Nagel, professors of psychology and physiology, respectively, at the University of Berlin, the director of the Berlin Zoological Garden, a director of the circus, veterinarians, and cavalry officers. Between them these experts might be expected to know all there was to know about horse nature. The commission conducted a critical test of the trickery hypothesis. They put Hans through his paces with von Osten absent from the room. Hans did quite as well as when his master was present. In 1904 the commission wrote a favorable report, supporting von Osten's claim and absolving him of the charge of trickery.

A second commission was appointed, consisting of Stumpf and his students. One of the latter, Pfungst, devised a new critical test. Von Osten whispered a number into the horse's left ear and Pfungst a number into its right ear. Hans was then instructed to add the two. No one present knew the answer. And Hans could not provide it. He was almost always wrong. In general Pfungst showed that Hans could not perform unless someone knew the answer when the question was posed. Furthermore, the animal could be seen to watch his questioner closely. When equipped with blinders that prevented him from seeing the others Hans could not answer the question even though the answer was known to the questioner. Evidently the secret of his success was some kind of visual cue though no one had been able to detect anything of the kind.

Pfungst eventually discovered what the cues were. When the questioner asked a question he assumed an expectant posture which was maintained until Hans, in his consecutive tapping, reached the number that coded the correct answer. The questioner then relaxed his posture making slight movements of the head which signalled the horse to stop tapping. Pfungst himself made the movements unconsciously as had all of Hans' interrogators. Pfungst was able to elicit incorrect answers by deliberately producing these movements at the wrong time. With this method of responding it was, of course, possible for Hans to "know" anything his questioner knew. His failure to perform when the questioner was without knowledge reduces the whole performance to a simple kind of instrumental conditioning. The case is dramatic because our impression of Hans plummets. He had seemed to be more intelligent than most of us but has turned out to be a quite unremarkable animal. There is not even any evidence here of an ability to recognize verbal commands, let alone understand or reply to them. Still there is an interesting feature in the method. Hans's ability to use language was tested by allowing him to make responses that were a part of his usual repertoire. His essential linguistic capacities were given a fair opportunity. He was not handicapped by a requirement to form unlikely sounds or gestures.

Herr von Osten was badly shaken by the findings of the commission. He seemed at first to be thoroughly disillusioned with Hans and not a little angry. By the next day, however, he had recovered his faith and decided to prohibit further experimentation. To von Osten, at least, the horse remained *"der kluge* Hans."

Talking Birds. In 1947 O. H. Mowrer (164) purchased a collection of likely birds for studies in speech training. His subjects were a Mexican double yellow-headed parrot, an Indian hill mynah, two magpies, and eight shell parakeets. The trainer fed and watered the birds entirely by hand and while doing so spoke the words they were to learn. Roughly, the theory behind this procedure is that the bird will associate the sound of the trainer's speech with the pleasant experiences of food and water. When the bird, in its random vocalization, produces sounds resembling those of the trainer it will tend to repeat them because of their agreeable, secondarily reinforcing, effect. In this way the vocalization of the bird should "drift" in the direction of the trainer's speech. When that has been accomplished one can make feeding contingent on the utterance of either a specific word or of some sounds resembling human speech. Alternatively, one may reward only if the bird speaks when presented with a stimulus object. While Mowrer had little success with the parakeets or magpies the parrot and mynah both developed some speech. Mowrer reports that it was possible to train the birds "to indicate their wants by means of words, i.e., to say the name of whatever it is they want to eat or drink." It was also possible for the birds to learn to speak certain words or phrases in connection with particular objects or events. In this connection Lorenz tells of a gray parrot, owned by Professor Otto Köhler, that said "Good morning" and "Good evening" at the proper times. This bird, furthermore, said *"Na, auf wiedersehen"* when guests rose to leave. Furthermore, it could not be deceived by any pretence at departure but spoke its phrase only when departure was truly intended. Professor Köhler, however, was unable to train this animal to say "food" when hungry or "drink" when thirsty. Lorenz says that no one has succeeded in teaching a bird to speak purposively in this fashion. His statement is contradicted by Mowrer's results.

It would be remarkable if birds were unable to learn to use speech instrumentally since they are quite able to use other responses. In this connection, Karl von Frisch (151), for instance, had a parakeet that was not allowed to leave its cage except shortly after it had moved its bowels. This policy was, of course, intended to safeguard the furniture and rugs against the bird's careless droppings. The parakeet learned its lesson so well that whenever von Frisch approached it attempted to evacuate its bowel. Its efforts to obtain release were so strenuous that the owner feared it would do itself an injury.

Some birds have been able to learn to produce a small number of approximations to words in various languages. They have learned to use the words referentially and, according to Mowrer, expressively. The vocabulary is always small, however, and there is evidence that the words usually do not function as signs for the birds when they are uttered by others. Most importantly, no bird is known to have created novel but acceptable combinations of the words it knows. Apparently birds do not grasp the combinational structure of speech.

Gua, Viki, and Miscellaneous Monkeys. On June 26, 1931, a female chimpanzee, seven and one-half months old, was separated from its mother at the Orange Park Anthropoid Station and delivered to Professor and Mrs. W. N. Kellogg (123), to be reared as a younger sister to their nine and one-half months old son, Donald. Gua was diapered, bathed, powdered, seated in a high chair and fed with a spoon. For the nine months she lived with the Kelloggs, Gua was in every way treated like a human child. No special effort was made to teach Gua to talk but she and Donald had the same continuous exposure to human speech. Their linguistic achievements were compared to determine the importance of hereditary species characteristics in the acquisition of speech.

Almost from the first Gua had a kind of action language. When she spied a glass of orange juice on a table she approached the table and put her mobile lips up to the table edge. A gesture not difficult to interpret. At another time she took Mr. Kellogg's hand and put it on the orange juice bottle so that he might lift it to her lips. The first of these actions is a futile attempt at direct manipulation of the environment; the second, an effort to move another to give assistance. Both gestures functioned as signs since they impelled the Kelloggs to appropriate action.

Gua also vocalized. These sounds are only very roughly described by the Kelloggs but they seem to be expressive cries characteristic of the species. Their number remained the same during the 9 months residence with the Kelloggs. From the first, the cries had discernible referents. At least two of the cries acquired an extended range of usage. The food bark came to be roughly equivalent to "yes" and the "oo-oo" cry of trouble or fear came to mean "no." The food bark, for instance, was elicited by the sight of her toys and was given in answer to such questions as "Do you want some orange?" or "Do you want to go bye-bye?"

Gua did not, however, learn to say any English words. Donald, her human control, was considerably retarded in this respect and only learned six words in the nine months of comparative study. However, he babbled far more than Gua. Furthermore, Donald imitated Gua's cries and barks while Gua did not imitate in return.

In comprehension of English the Kelloggs report far more progress. Their criterion for understanding was response appropriate to the referent. This is our basis for deciding that a stimulus is a sign. Gua began to respond differentially to various utterances within a few weeks after coming to the Kelloggs and, for the first five months of their sibling association, she surpassed Donald in the number of utterances she appeared to comprehend.

There is some evidence that Gua was responding to the phonetic character of the speech she heard rather than to its intonational pattern or intensity level. She was not, however, responding to the total phonetic pattern but only to a portion of it. She would give her food bark to the query "Orange?" quite as readily as to the full question "Do you want some orange?" However, the rising intonation of the question was not essential. Gua would bark to "orange" with a falling or level intonation. She did not bark to "Grapefruit?" pronounced as a question. It seems clear that she was reacting to some phonetic characteristic in this case at least.

By the end of her nine months Gua was responding distinctively and appropriately to about seventy utterances—only slightly fewer than Donald. The absolute number has no importance since there were no clear criteria defining distinctive utterances. It may be important, however, that Gua's comprehension so outstripped her production of speech.

In one respect Gua's comprehension lagged behind Donald's. Donald began to react appropriately to word combinations he had never before heard. When Gua was told to "kiss Donald" Donald promptly put up his cheek to receive the kiss. Gua made one or two new responses of this kind but for the most part had to learn to react to new combinations of familiar elements through a process of trial and error.

In 1947 Keith and Cathy Hayes (90) adopted a female baby chimpanzee from Orange Park. They undertook repetition of the Kellogg experiment with several improvements. Gua had spent her first seven and one-half months in chimpanzee society. This might very well have handicapped her in the comparisons with Donald. Also, her humanizing was cut short after nine months. Who knows but that she might have overcome her setback if she had been given enough time? The Hayeses started to see their baby—Viki— right after her birth. They took her home at six weeks and set no limit on the duration of her stay with them. At the time of the publication of their principal report Viki had been raised as a child for three years. The Kelloggs gave Gua the opportunity to learn human speech *incidentally* in the way that children learn speech. They provided no intensive training. The Hayeses worked hard and long to teach Viki to talk, reasoning that if the chimp is like a retarded child it will need the assistance of special tutelage.

Viki had the same food bark and "oo-oo" cries as Gua. She apparently learned to understand fewer English utterances but then Cathy Hayes points out that Viki was sufficiently mischievous so that they could not be certain whether she was unable or unwilling to understand. After all, human children do not demonstrate their comprehension by obeying every command they hear.

Viki, however, learned to say three words—"papa," "mama," and "cup." She did very little babbling and these words were only attained after long, patient training in imitation, using food rewards. If you have heard Viki you may have been disappointed by her three words, which are very emperfectly articulated. "Papa" and "mama" sound much alike and are often produced voicelessly. The vowel of "cup" is quite unclear. Still, knowing beforehand what is intended it is possible to recognize the words.

Viki, like Gua, seldom responded appropriately the first time she heard novel combinations of familiar and presumably comprehended words. She would react appropriately to the command "kiss me" and also to the command "bring me the dog," but the new command "kiss the dog" brought no reaction whatsoever. The Hayes provided Viki with a set of analogous problems, "kiss me," "bring the cup," "kiss the cup," etc. She began to learn to react more quickly with the final combination. Finally, with "kiss me," "give me your hand," "kiss your hand," she obeyed the third very quickly. She seemed to be able to learn to understand new statements built on familiar models.

Garner's (70) book *The Speech of Monkeys,* published in 1892, presents a more complimentary estimate of anthropoid communication than any book published since. We are warned of Garner's susceptibility by the very first page, "From childhood, I have believed that all kinds of animals have some mode of speech by which they could talk among their own kind, and have often wondered why man had never tried it." At the same time we are informed of one aspect of his study that makes it an important supplement to the work with Gua and Viki. Garner did not require his monkeys to learn English. As a member of the more intelligent species he took the greater learning burden on himself and attempted to learn the speech of the monkeys. The Hayeses spent too many heartbreaking hours working on English pronunciation which is not after all an essential feature of human language. To give the anthropoid a fair opportunity to demonstrate his abilities it would seem desirable to work with the sounds that are congenial to him.

The difficulty is, of course, that those sounds do not constitute a language. If, however, a human being could learn to duplicate the sounds he could build a language from them and then attempt to learn it along with his anthropoid partner. Garner did not undertake to construct such a language. Nor were his monkeys raised as children. He had to settle for occasional contacts with monkeys of various species, some privately owned, some in the zoological gardens of Europe and America. Garner did, however, accomplish one aspect of the program I have outlined; he undertook to imitate the vocalizations of various anthropoids.

In the Charleston Zoo there was a brown Cebus named Jokes. Garner studied his food sound and managed to imitate it so well that Jokes came over to the bars to eat from his hand. On his third visit, when Jokes was happily chattering and playing with his fingers, Garner sounded his version of the Cebus cry of alarm or assault. Jokes sprang away, ran to his perch, then in and out of his sleeping apartment—apparently wild with fear. Nor would he become reconciled with Garner though the latter tried for two months to restore his confidence.

In the Chicago Zoo a small Capuchin was selected for study. Garner made the food sound. The Capuchin looked up and upon repetition replied with the same sound. The monkey then picked up the pan from which it drank and brought it over to the bars. Garner reports that he used the sound with similar effect for Capuchins in the New York Zoo.

Several of Garner's observations are important to a comparative psychology of language. He claims, for instance, that while most sounds are uniform within a species (quite different tongues are spoken by the Cebus, Capuchin, and Rhesus), monkeys are able to acquire new expressive sounds. In a pet shop there was a Capuchin (Puck) who always used his food bark when Garner came over to him; he was then rewarded with food. In a nearby cage sat Darwin, a white-faced Cebus. Originally shy and silent, Darwin one day came out with a sound not ordinarily heard from the Cebus. Garner says the sound came increasingly to resemble the food request of Puck. Garner fed Darwin for his efforts and eventually the Cebus produced a food request indistinguishable from the Capuchin version. Garner also holds that monkey sounds are qualified in meaning by the inflection accompanying them.

When an animal has been fed on bread and milk for a long time and is then shown a banana its food sound is altered by a banana-signifying inflection.

Are Animals Capable of Acquiring Language? No animal raised by man, however nurtured and tutored, has become a full participant in human language. The first of their difficulties, and the least interesting, is with speech production. Birds have done a better job of imitating speech than have chimpanzees and that fact is enough to show that the intellectual essence of language function does not lie here.

Animals have been more successful in giving evidence of speech comprehension than in producing speech. The section on natural animal languages concluded with the observation that animal reactions to animal signs are not governed by contingencies as are human reactions to speech. In speech, individually significant forms are altered in significance as they are placed in different linguistic combinations and as the non-linguistic environment is changed. The action implications of the command *come here*, are reversed when it is preceded by the words *do not*. The generic name *father* designates different individuals as the possessive pronouns are shifted between *my, your,* and *his*. It has been amply demonstrated that chimpanzees and many lesser animals can learn appropriate reactions to particular utterances. Students of the comparative psychology of language have concentrated on the understanding and production of isolated words and so we know very little about what animals can do with words in combination. However, there are certain experimental problems, not involving language and not even intended as language paradigms, which are concerned with this ability to react to multiple signs.

The primates have demonstrated that they can solve many kinds of multiple sign problem (87). The Weigl matching and oddity problems, to take only one example, offer the animal three non-identical stimuli, two of which are alike in color, and two alike in form. When the objects are presented on an orange tray the animal is to pick up the color-odd object but when the tray is cream colored the animal is to select the form-odd object. In this problem the appropriate reaction to each object is contingent on the color of the tray. Monkeys and chimpanzees have solved this problem and others even more complicated.

With a few notable exceptions American experiments on conditioning have neglected the problems of configurational conditioning which are most relevant to semantic structure. There is, however, an extensive output from the laboratories of Pavlov, Behkterev, Krasnogorski, and Beritov. Razran (190) has summarized and contributed to this important literature. In an experiment from Beritov's laboratory, dogs learned to go to one feeding box upon the presentation of a compound of stimuli and to another box when individual components were presented. In some early work from Pavlov's laboratory dogs learned to respond to a particular sequence of tones in a manner different from their response to any other sequence of the same tones. These experiments demonstrate contingent S-R learning but they lack the systematic character of such contingencies in human speech.

The animal accomplishments we have described all involve learning particular appropriate reactions to particular signs or combinations of signs. The limits of this learning are more likely to be set by the experimenter's patience than by the animal's capacity. To my mind, the intellectual essence of language behavior is not a matter of the number of utterances to which appropriate reactions can be trained nor even of the complication of these utterances. From experience of particular utterances and their referents a child learns to produce new responses which have not been specifically practiced but which conform to the rules of the language. He interiorizes a system for generating appropriate behavior rather than a list of rote responses. This ability to produce systematic novelties leads to the recombination of words to make new sentences, as well as to the understanding of new sentences when the elements and the model are familiar, as well as to guessing how to make a noun plural, how to put a verb in the past tense and eventually to the creation of new words that are phonologically acceptable. Most of these performances cannot be asked of an animal since they require speech which animals cannot manage. However, one could look at their reactions to language to see whether they ever react appropriately to new utterances involving familiar components. Viki and Gua are the only animals who have ever showed any ability of this kind. Again, however, there are analogous laboratory problems not involving language.

We have said that human reaction to a command like *come*

here changes when the command is prefaced by *do not*. This illustrates the fact that reaction to a linguistic sign is contingent on its linguistic concomitants. In addition, however, the prefacing words *do not* have a "characteristic" effect which is the same for any command. Whatever action is inspired by the command is not to be performed when the command is negated. This is a simple kind of systematic semantic. A human language learner, when he has experienced this effect of *do not* on a limited number of commands, knows what to do when it prefaces, for the first time, some command that is familiar without the negation. He would not have to learn this lesson for every command. Can animals similarly learn more than they have practiced?

Systematic sign contingencies can be illustrated with a study of Karl Lashley's (136) called *Conditional Reactions in the Rat*. The term "conditional reaction" suggests that contextual dependency which is the essence of language comprehension. Rats were presented with two cards and required to jump to one or the other. On the one card there was printed an upright triangle and on the other, the identical triangle was inverted. In the first stage of this experiment the animals learned to discriminate the cards (position was, of course, randomly varied) and jump to the upright triangle which led to food while the other did not. Twenty errorless trials were required as a criterion of learning and the criterion was quickly reached.

In the second stage of the experiment the same figures were presented on a horizontally striped background. In the first twenty trials with this background the animals consistently jumped to the upright triangle, demonstrating the equivalence of the triangle on the new background to the training triangle. They were now trained to select the inverted triangle and avoid the upright, a reversal of the prior training. This required many more trials than the original task but was eventually accomplished.

In the third stage the rats were sometimes exposed to the first pair of cards and sometimes to the second. They learned to respond appropriately in each case. To make a linguistic analogy that overlooks many differences, this performance is something like that involved in reacting to the commands *come here* and *do not come here*. The approach reaction evoked by the first command is inhibited by the addition of the words *do not*. In Lashley's experiment the upright triangle is approached when it appears on a plain background but this approach is inhibited by the addition of a striped ground. Some question may be raised as to whether or not this is really a case of a sign showing contextual variations in the response it elicits. The words *come here* are still identifiable units in the expression *do not come here,* but is the triangle recognized on the striped ground? May not the animals have simply learned to prefer one striped pattern to another and also to prefer one simple figure to another? The evidence that the triangle is not perceptually imbedded in the striped background is the manifestation of sensory generalization at the beginning of the second stage in training. Unless the triangle or some aspect of it had been recognized on the striped ground it would be difficult to see why the rats began the reversed training with a consistent preference for the upright figure.

Lashley made a systematic semantic economy available to his rat subjects. He trained them on a series of five problems in which cue values were always reversed when figures were shifted to a striped background. Had his animals learned this systematic principle they would have been able to respond correctly on the very first trial after the background was changed. That they did not learn it is evident from the fact that there was no significant reduction in the number of trials required to reverse the response in the second stage of training. Apparently this problem of systematic contingency was too much for the rats to solve with only five examples.

In recent years Harlow (86) has reported a series of experiments which demonstrate that monkeys and the larger anthropoids are able to form systematic sign contingencies. Harlow, himself, describes his results as the formation of learning sets or "learning how to learn efficiently." His study of discrimination reversal training closely resembles Lashley's conditional response and the systematic semantic disposition involved in negation. Harlow's subject, a monkey, sits in a cage which permits him to see a tray set before the cage and, on experimental trials, to extend one arm out to the tray. At opposite ends of the tray there are food wells and, on every experimental trial, these wells are covered by objects differing in multiple characteristics. Beneath one object, only, there is food. On successive trials the monkey can learn to recognize this object, and demonstrates this fact by lifting the positive object as soon as he is allowed to reach out to the tray. So far, this is a problem in discrimination learning. However, the experiment does not stop with one discrimination problem. There are a great many such problems and Harlow has shown that the monkey's performance improves as it proceeds with the series; it learns how to learn efficiently.

In the discrimination reversal problem monkeys were run on a discrimination problem for seven, nine, or eleven trials and the reward value of the objects was reversed for eight trials. There were 112 discrimination reversal problems. There is in this problem a systematic feature. The first reversal trial always means that the value of the objects will be reversed for seven subsequent trials. When a subject grasps this fact he should always respond appropriately on the second reversal trial. On the first fourteen problems Harlow's monkeys were correct a little less than 60 per cent of the time on this second trial. On the last fourteen problems (99-112) they were correct just short of 100 per cent of the time. The monkeys clearly learned to use the first reversal trial as a signal to reverse their object preference. Harlow repeated this problem with nine children from three to five years of age. The children's performance approached perfection in the second block of fourteen discrimination reversal problems.

A study by Riopelle and Copelan (195) modifies the Harlow procedure in such a way as to create a closer resemblance to Lashley's procedure and to the negated linguistic command. In the Harlow studies the signal for response reversal is a failure of reinforcement. In the Riopelle and Copelan study rhesus monkeys were required to reverse their choice when the tray on which the objects were presented was changed, with a yellow tray replacing the green. The monkeys learned to reverse, whatever the objects, when there was such a change of trays. The yellow tray functions here like the striped background in Lashley's study and like the negative word in a command. It should be pointed out, however, that none of these animal problems is nearly so abstract as is linguistic negation. In the animal studies only one response is reversed, jumping at a card for rats, reaching for an object for primates. The English words *do not* serve to halt or prevent any action, e.g., *do not jump . . . sit . . . sing . . . think . . .* etc. The animal problem is like negation applied to one action but with different objects of that action.

The laboratory studies of systematic contingent response have not used the same tasks and number of trials and so one cannot confidently draw conclusions about species differences in the ability to solve such problems. In the present imperfect state of the evidence this kind of task has been failed by rats, accomplished laboriously by primates, and accomplished very easily by children. This is, at least, the order of prowess to be expected for a paradigm of the systematic semantic disposition. No animal below the anthropoids is reported to have formed such dispositions in connection with language. Gua, you may recall, generally did not respond appropriately to such commands. The Kelloggs do, however, report that Gua occasionally seemed to understand a new utterance. Viki was provided with sets of utterances that were excellently chosen to teach semantic structure. She learned to obey the request *bring the cup* and then *kiss the cup.* A second set consisted of *give me your hand* and *kiss your hand.* At first, each instrumental act had to be taught in a series of trials but finally, Viki responded at once to the new command. She had learned that the response appropriate to certain forms (*cup, your hand,* etc.) is contingent on the forms with which they are combined and, furthermore, that the response should change in a characteristic fashion when the accompanying form is *kiss.* This is a systematic sign contingency.

No doubt there are many reasons why animals do not learn human language. We should like to set aside trifling causes like the lack of vocal control or the lack of sufficiently patient and skilled human tutelage, and attempt to discover if there are basic language skills which are either beyond the learning capacity of animals other than man, or especially difficult for animals other than man. I believe the systematic contingencies involved in semantic structure will prove to be among these skills.

Feral and Isolated Man

In the tenth edition of his *Systemae Naturae,* published in 1758, Linnaeus listed *Homo Ferus* (L. wild man) as a subdivision of the genus *Homo Sapiens.* The defining characteristics of feral man, succinctly listed by Linnaeus, were *tetrapus, mutus, hursutus.* There were nine historical records of wild men available to the great taxonomist. These included the Hessian wolf-boy of 1349, the

Lithuanian bear-boy of 1661, and Wild Peter of Hanover of 1724. Since Linnaeus' time about thirty additional cases have accumulated. These cases have generally conformed to two of Linnaeus' specifications: They have lacked speech and have gone on all fours. The majority have not been especially hirsute and that characteristic does not help define feral man. An attribute not mentioned by Linnaeus, but reliably found in these cases, is the depression of sexuality. It appears, like speech, to be a function that a society must develop. Within the class of feral men a distinction should be made between those known to have been nurtured by wild animals and those who lived on their own in the wilds. It must be assumed that these latter cases lived in human society until they were old enough to wander off and look after themselves. They fall between true feral man and cases of extreme isolation. It has sometimes happened that a child has been shut away from human society except for routine feeding. These cases, living with minimal human aid, are called isolated man.

Feral and isolated man interest the psychologist, philosopher, and sociologist because they provide an important natural experiment on the relative importance of genetic and environmental factors in the determination of all aspects of human behavior. The importance of feral man to the science of man was perceived long ago. Lord Monboddo proclaimed the discovery of Wild Peter of Hanover to be more important than the discovery of 30,000 new stars. Wild Peter was brought from Hanover to England by King George so that he might be used to test the doctrine of innate ideas. The king presented Peter to the enlightened princess of Wales and she placed him in charge of Dr. Arbuthnot, that good friend of Pope and Swift.

While Peter began the tradition of scientific interest in feral man, he also, unfortunately, began an equally hardy tradition of scientific difficulty in interpreting the data so obtained. There was, first of all, the problem of determining the exact circumstances of Peter's earlier life. From a number of sources it seems clear that he had lived for some time in human society. He was probably the child of a certain widower whose second wife drove Peter from the house. There was, secondly, the problem of estimating Peter's native intelligence. The behavior of feral man somewhat resembles that of the ament living in human society. If one cannot decide whether or not these cases are congenitally deficient, the results obtained are all open to the following directly opposed interpretations.

The extreme environmentalists, like Rousseau, have found in feral man proof of the infinite plasticity of man. The feral cases violate all parochial notions of human nature and prove that human nature is created in society and may take any form that society dictates. However, the extreme environmentalist cannot deny the importance of genetic factors since, as Zingg (210), remarks, there is something lacking to make this case complete—a wolf or dog who has been trained to human behavior. He can acknowledge that the character of the species sets limits on behavioral development but that, within these limits, environment is the principal factor.

The student who is inclined to give more importance to heredity will interpret the cases of feral man quite differently. He believes them all to be congenitally feeble-minded; their behavior simply demonstrates the strong determining power of innate intelligence. Aments, whether in human or wolf society, are much alike. To be sure some feral cases have recovered and demonstrated considerable learning ability, but these cases cannot have been true aments, in the opinion of the men backing heredity. Their recovery proves that when there is no genetic deficiency the most unfavorable environment has only a temporary handicapping effect. With this uncertainty about native intelligence the environmentalist cannot prove that genetically normal human specimens are rendered permanently inhuman by the lack of society in their early years. Those that remain *mutus* and *tetrapus* may be feeble-minded. Those that recover have not remained inhuman. The environmentalist points out, with irritation, the improbability that all feral cases would be feeble-minded. The heredity-man counters that the feeble-minded child is just the one to be driven out of his home or exposed to wild beasts and furthermore, not all feral men are assumed to be feeble-minded—only those who do not recover. In the opinion of the environmentalist, anyone who thinks that a child who has survived in the wilds on his own initiative could possibly be feeble-minded . . .—the man who thinks that must himself be suspected of feeble-mindedness. We tiptoe out and softly close the door behind us. Let us look at several of the best documented cases to see if they do not teach something more modest than the truth about human nature, perhaps something about the nature of language.

The Wild Boy of Aveyron. The case of Victor, the wild boy of Aveyron, has been described in the Introduction to this book. Victor was about twelve years old when he was captured in the Caune Woods and Dr. Itard tried for five years to teach him to speak and read. Victor succeeded in understanding a large number of words and phrases but he could produce no speech except the two exclamations: *"Oh, Dieu!"* and *"Lait!"* These came out, in very imperfect form, quite early in training. The discrepancy between the boy's achievements in reading and in speech production requires some explanation.

It is conceivable that Victor's mentality was adequate to the full use of language and that he was simply held back by inability to master the business of articulation and phonation. Perhaps the impulse to babble which is so evident in infants operates on a maturational timetable such that it must receive social support when the readiness is there or the impulse will die. The pecking response in chicks (175) is an example of this kind of timed skill. A bright spot elicits the pecking response in newborn chicks. When chicks were raised in the dark and fed by dropper for fourteen days it was found that they would not peck though exposed to daylight. The original study includes a dramatic photograph of a starving chick standing in the midst of a pile of grain—not pecking! Itard's experience with Victor suggests that speech in man, like pecking in chicks, may require social reinforcement at the crucial age when the impulse is ripe or else it will not develop at all. To evaluate this proposal we will look at other cases of feral and isolated man.

Kamala and Amala. Since 1850, at least, there have been constant reports of wolf-children in India. Some of the Indian people have a superstitious reluctance to kill wolves and there has also been a practice of exposing unwanted children. Most of those carried off have certainly been killed but occasionally the child is taken to the wolf den and survives for a time as an extra cub.

In 1920 the Rev. A. L. Singh (210) was told of a *manushbhaga,* a man ghost, haunting a certain Indian village. The ghost had been seen in the company of wolves going in and out of a giant dead ant hill which the animals presumably used as a den. Singh had a shooting platform built over the hill. He and some natives watched there one night and saw a procession of mother wolf and cubs, two of which looked human though they went on all fours and had long matted hair. The local natives would not dig out the hill but Singh brought in some more willing workers. The mother darted out to attack the invaders, and was killed. In the den itself they found a monkey ball of four little creatures clinging together—two cubs and two little girls.

Kamala was about eight years old and Amala only one and one-half. They were thoroughly wolfish in appearance and behavior: Hard callus had developed on their knees and palms from going on all fours. Their teeth were sharp edged. They moved their nostrils sniffing food. Eating and drinking were accomplished by lowering their mouths to the plate. They ate raw meat and, on one occasion, killed and devoured a whole chicken. At night they prowled and sometimes howled. They shunned other children but followed the dog and cat. They slept rolled up together on the floor.

Amala died within a year but Kamala lived to be eighteen. Both children's bodies were covered with sores when they were captured. Mrs. Singh healed these and softened their skins with oils and massage. She fed and bathed and caressed Kamala and evidently was the means of her socialization. The first sign that Kamala had become "involved" with a human being appeared when Mrs. Singh returned from a trip and Kamala ran to her with evident affection. In time Kamala learned to walk erect, to wear clothing and even to speak a few words.

Because Amala learned to talk a little, and promised to learn more, we cannot believe that continuous social support of infantile babbling is an essential pre-requisite to speech. Vocalization survived in her as an operant response while it did not for Victor. It is, of course, possible that Kamala lived for a longer time with adults than did Victor and so received more reinforcement for vocalizing. The situation, however, was the reverse. Victor was not found in the care of animals but was living alone. A child could survive outside of human society at an earlier age if it was in the society of some animal than would be possible if it had to shift for itself in the wilds. Victor is likely to have remained longer at home. It seems that speech is possible even when left dormant for many childhood years. Victor's failure was probably due to some specific impairment—probably of hearing. The facts on several cases of extreme social isolation will reinforce these conclusions.

Cases of Extreme Social Isolation. In 1937, in Illinois, the child Anna (49) was discovered tied to a chair in a second floor attic-like room. She was nearly six years of age, emaciated, and speechless. She had received absolutely minimal attention since her birth, had been fed almost exclusively on cow's milk, seldom moved from her chair, and never instructed in anything. Anna was an illegitimate child whose mother had hidden her away to avoid the anger of the child's grandfather.

The child was taken to a county home for retarded children and, after a year and a half there, removed to a private home. Anna lived for only four more years. In that time she learned to walk, to dress herself, to play simple games with other children, and to speak a little. She could call attendants by name and had a few sentences to express her desires. The school report on Anna expressed the opinion that she was probably congenitally feeble-minded. This diagnosis is strengthened by the fact that Anna's mother proved to be a middle-grade moron with an IQ of 50 on the Stanford revision of the Binet-Simon scale. The probability that feral and isolated children who have learned little or no speech were feeble-minded is increased by the remarkable achievements of another isolated child—Isabelle.

Isabelle was found in Ohio (50) at about the same time as Anna. Isabelle was also nearly of an age with Anna, being six and one-half at the time of her discovery. She was the illegitimate child of a deaf mute, and mother and child had lived most of the time in a darkened room away from the rest of the family. Isabelle behaved in many ways like a wild animal. She was fearful and hostile. She had no speech and made only a croaking noise. At first she seemed deaf, so unused were her senses.

Isabelle was taken away and given excellent care by doctors and clinical psychologists. Although her first score on the Stanford-Binet was nineteen months, practically at the zero point of the scale, a program of speech training was, nevertheless, undertaken. A week of intensive work was required to elicit even a first vocalization. Yet a little more than two months later she was beginning to put sentences together. Nine months after that, she could identify words and sentences on the printed page and write very well. Isabelle passed through the usual stages of linguistic development at a greatly accelerated rate. She covered in two years the learning that ordinarily occupies six years. By the age of eight and one-half Isabelle had a normal IQ and was not easily distinguished from ordinary children of her age. In this case speech behaved like many other human and animal performances; the delayed subject progressed at an accelerated rate, presumably because of her maturity.

The case of Isabelle strongly suggests that a child with good congenital intelligence can overcome the mutism caused by social isolation. It is possible that Anna would have done as well with equally expert tutelage but it seems likely that Anna was not Isabelle's equal in congenital intelligence. We do not yet know how many years of social isolation it is possible to overcome with speech training. The excellent results with Isabelle indicate that as many as six and one-half years of isolation can be made up. The moderate success with Kamala (carried on by less expert teachers) suggests that much may be done to offset even eight years of isolation from the human community.

Neither feral nor isolated man creates his own language these days, but must not such a man have done so once in some prehistoric time and so got language started? Actually the circumstances in which language must have begun represent a combination for which we can provide no instances. We have animals among themselves, animals in linguistic communities, and humans among animals, and in none of these cases does language develop. We have humans raised in linguistic communities and, in these circumstances, language does develop. What about a human born into a human society that has no language? We don't know of any such societies and so we don't know of any such individuals. But these must have been the circumstances of language origination. We shall be better able to guess what happened in these circumstances, intermediate between the primate community and the linguistic community, when we are clearer about the lines of phyletic advance that lead toward language function.

Summary

The comparative psychology of linguistic reference has been divided into three problems. We wondered first, what differences there might be between selective responses used by animals among themselves and the systems of linguistic reference used in human societies. The differences described here are: a) that animal responses are often instinctive rather than acquired; b) that no set of animal responses has been shown to have anything like a phonological structure; c) that the animal responses do not name all or even most of their shared categories; d) that the sets of animal responses are not extended to name new categories; e) that animal selective responses do not operate under the same contingencies as linguistic names. The second question we discussed concerns the ability of animals to acquire a human language when they are given the opportunity. Most of those who have worked hard on teaching language to animals have concentrated on speech production—with small success. The ability to handle systematic sign contingencies, as represented in certain laboratory problems, is probably essential to full participation in a language. This ability is either absent or very poorly developed in animals below the primates and the adult primate has much less of it than the human child. Finally, we found that man does not develop language if he grows up among animals or in isolation. Language is acquired by the human being born into a linguistic community.

chapter vi   The Original Word Game

THE ORIGINAL WORD GAME is the operation of linguistic reference in first language learning. At least two people are required: one who knows the language (the tutor) and one who is learning (the player). In outline form the movements of the game are very simple. The tutor names things in accordance with the semantic custom of his community. The player forms hypotheses about the categorial nature of the things named. He tests his hypotheses by trying to name new things correctly. The tutor compares the player's utterances with his own anticipations of such utterances and, in this way, checks the accuracy of fit between his own categories and those of the player. He improves the fit by correction. In concrete terms the tutor says "dog" whenever a dog appears. The player notes the phonemic equivalence of these utterances, forms a hypothesis about the non-linguistic category that elicits this kind of utterance and then tries naming a few dogs himself.

We play this game as long as we continue to extend our vocabularies and that may be as long as we live. However, as adults, the

(194)

task centers on the formation of the category named. All other aspects of the game have been overlearned to the point of automatic perfection. The child plays with more difficulty because he has all of the rudiments to acquire. He must learn to categorize speech itself so that he can identify equivalent and distinctive utterances in what the tutor says. He must learn the motor skill of producing such utterances so that they are recognizable to the tutor. Finally, he, like the adult, must form the referent categories. These part processes are not only analytically separable. They are actually separated in much of the child's earliest learning. In the first two years he is forming conceptions of space, time, causality, and of the enduring object. These conceptions, so brilliantly studied by Piaget (179, 182), are the basic referent categories and they are formed with little assistance from language. At the same time, through babbling and attending to the speech of others, the infant is learning to perceive and to produce speech, though as yet he may have no idea of linguistic reference. When the rudiments have been brought to a certain minimal efficiency they come together in the Original Word Game. We then find that the speech skills have a tremendous potential for assisting the formation of non-linguistic categories. The total list of such categories that a child must learn is a cognitive inventory of his culture. Speech, therefore, is the principal instrument of cognitive socialization.

This chapter is not an account of all aspects of first language learning. It is a discussion of the part played in that process by linguistic reference. Even more specifically the chapter concentrates on showing how the structure of language can facilitate the formation of non-linguistic categories. We shall begin with brief discussions of the motor skill of speech production and the perceptual skill of speech categorization. There follows a section describing the ways in which speech perception guides the formation of non-linguistic categories and another section describing the role of speech production as evidence of the possession of a category. There is a brief description of a variant on the Original Word Game in which words are defined verbally rather than by pointing to exemplars. The chapter closes by pointing out the usefulness of acquired categories and names in the formation of trustworthy expectancies.

The Motor Skill

An infant is altogether dependent on others for the satisfaction of his vital needs. His crying and kicking will not take him to food and will not constrain food to come to him. However, these actions are likely to have a socially mediated instrumental value. For the infant is the focus of a small community devoted to his welfare. This community is able and eager to satisfy his needs. He does not ordinarily have to persuade his mother to feed him when he is hungry or to change him when he is wet. Her consent is guaranteed by her concern for him. The only problem is to express the need clearly enough so that she will know what to do.

It has often been reported that infant cries of distress have the same quality whatever the nature of the distress. If this be so it would seem to follow that the communication of infant needs is very imperfect and that children are often fed when they need to be watered and bounced when they need to sleep. An experiment by Sherman (209) is usually quoted in support of this claim. Medical students, nurses, and mothers listened to the crying of infants concealed from view. The listeners tried to guess the cause of each cry. The causes were of several kinds. Sometimes a feeding was delayed; sometimes the infant was dropped a short distance or even pricked with a pin. The listeners had no success in decoding the cries. Ordinarily, of course, a mother would be aided by circumstances attending the cry. She would know whether it was feeding time or sleeping time. The Sherman study suggests that when the "situation" is blacked out infant cries are not correctly understood. It does not, of course, follow that there were no differences in acoustic quality between the cries elicited in different ways. That conclusion would have to be based on a study of acoustic records. The Sherman result only shows that such differences, if they exist, were not correctly interpreted by his subjects.

As a preliminary to his experiment Sherman made observations which show that the expressive precision of infant cries is in dimensions other than tone quality. He found it necessary to equate the experimental cries on intensity and duration and in their gradients of onset and termination. For, on these dimensions, the infant cries were isomorphic with the irritating stimuli that set them off. In general, the intensity and duration of a cry were proportional to the intensity and duration of the stimulus. Where the stimulus began gradually, as in hunger or thirst, the cry showed a similar slow gradient of onset. Where the stimulus hit suddenly with an immediate peak intensity, the cry exploded. Where the stimulus was rhythmic, as in colic pains, there was rhythmicity in the cry. Sherman was concerned with the expressiveness of tone quality and in order to study that problem he had to remove ordinarily expressive differences in duration and intensity. The occasional interpretation of Sherman's study as a proof that infant cries do not communicate is a mistake.

The isomorphism of intensity and duration provides infant cries with a natural semantic value that improves their social instrumentality. Of course the cry is not an instrumental act of the same kind as the adult request, "Please pass the sugar." It is not a conventional utterance, it contains no referential forms, and the crier presumably does not anticipate his effect. The cry is symptomatic of the vital need. It is expressive instead of referential. Its instrumentality derives from the concern of the community to use every facet of infant behavior as a clue to infant needs.

As a kind of aura to the storm of the full cry there is the whimper. If the whimper does not produce appropriate action it increases in intensity and frequency and bursts at last into the full cry. This is the punishment that awaits parents who are not alert to decode the infant's behavior. It is an avoidance conditioning situation for the adults. The warning stimulus allows time for action that will forestall the cry. As an animal will react to a buzzer so as to avoid shock so parents will react to a whimper so as to avoid screams.

The whimper assumes a relatively stable form in each infant, but not the same form in all infants. It is likely to be used a great deal, often occurring in a regular alternation with smiles and happy sounds. Adults playing with a baby are likely to take the whimper for a signal to do something else or, particularly, to bring some new object within reach. The whimper is often accompanied by reaching movements, clasping and unclasping of the hands, and turning of the head. All of these actions suggest the direction of the infant desire and increase the expressive precision of the whimper. Still greater precision is gained through the use of anticipatory criterial action in place of the generic reaching-and-grasping. A child who sees a flame across the room may make little puffing, whistling noises like those involved in blowing out a match. Where the desired object involves some characteristic action a miniature performance of that action can clearly reveal the direction of the desire. Sometimes the action is vocal as when a child makes a motor-noise playing with his toy car. The use of that noise in conjunction with the whimper of desire will serve as well as: "Give me my car." The criterial action that suggests the object of desire is a link between instrumental crying and referential speech. The action varies with the object and so, in a sense, stands for the object. This is the primal sentence frame with a constant predicate—the whimper—and varying predicate objects—the criterial gesture.

The primal linguistic form is also used by household pets. The dog's distress flows over into whining and restless roving about the house. These distress signals set a problem for the owner who cares, to find out what is wanted. The dog's actions warn of imminent yelps which will punish the owner who fails to solve the problem. Ordinarily it is not difficult to guess the animal's desire. Most dogs, and most children too, have a rather small number of messages to communicate so the alternatives are few. The behavior that communicates best is likely to be the blocked instrumental act. If the dog goes to the door we guess that he wants to be let out; if he goes to his food dish we guess that he is hungry. Where some action is especially good at suggesting the correct interpretation it is likely to become the immediate standard reaction to the desire. A cat, for instance, may learn to rattle the door latch when it wants to leave the house. The "appropriateness" of this signal is not a result of advance calculation on the part of the animal. In its effort to accomplish its desire to go out it hits on some action that effectively suggests this desire to its owners. Because this action is closely followed by gratification it is learned as the first response to the need.

Infant babbling appears, at first, to be the reciprocal of the whimper of desire. Babbling is likely to go with a contented playful mood. It commonly occurs when the child is alone in his crib or with his toys and has no one to whom to direct requests. Observing the concomitants of babbling one can understand why Suzanne Langer (134) elects to explain it as an innate impulse to play with sound, to take aesthetic pleasure in sound. However, the aesthetic pleasure or sound-play assumptions do not explain the most important thing about babbling, the fact that it drifts in the direction of the speech the infant hears.

Infants have often been heard to babble sounds not used in the speech of the community around them (151). The child in an English speaking family may produce a uvulvar [r] or a good umlaut vowel. From observations of this kind many writers have moved to the conclusion that human infants everywhere babble all the sounds needed to speak any human language. A somewhat less ambitious generalization holds that, whatever the sounds heard in babbling and they need not include all speech sounds, all infants at first draw on the same repertoire. Perhaps there is a common starting point from which babbling drifts in the direction of the speech the infant hears. Babbling would begin as a human repertoire and become a cultural pattern.

Until quite recently studies of infant babbling have been weakened by inadequate sampling and transcription. Irwin (104-106) and Irwin and Chen (107) have, for the first time, approached this problem with satisfactory techniques. These authors describe babbling at each age with a frequency polygon on which IPA symbols appear along the baseline and the height of the column above each symbol represents the frequency of that phone. For the first few months most of the sounds of adult speech are altogether absent. By the age of eleven months we usually find all of the necessary phones represented. If this profile is compared with a frequency polygon for adult American speech the two are seen to be very unlike; sounds very prominent in infant babbling are extremely uncommon in adult speech and vice versa. Conceivably the infant profile represents the starting point for all human speech and the adult profile the particular end point for individuals raised in American society. Polygons plotted for children after eleven months show an ever improving approximation to the adult profile, a phonetic drift in the direction of the local norms. The data of Irwin and Chen easily suggest a general picture of the progress of all infant babbling. We can imagine a different adult profile for each language and these ranged round the central human polygon like the points of the compass. Babbling would then drift, according to the prevailing linguistic winds, in one or another of these directions. Since studies of babbling have been restricted to the English, French, and German languages, and since most of these studies are methodologically inadequate, the circumference of the picture cannot be filled in. In addition, it would be premature to identify the profile of eleven-month-old American children as the profile of human speech potential. Probably this profile is already influenced by American speech. It may be a compromise between the American profile and the species profile. An acceptable version of the latter cannot be drawn until the babbling characteristics of infants at many ages and from many societies have been established.

To say that babbling is instinctive play is not to explain the fact of drift. For that, we need a mechanism by which society can affect the infant. The simplest assumption is selective reinforcement by adults who belong to the society. When a child babbles English sounds his English speaking parents will be pleased and will reward him with attention and smiles. Un-English babbling will get less response and so will decline in frequency. This is one of those explanations that seems obviously true until you look at the phenomenon it is intended to explain. Actually, parental reinforcement of vocalization seems not to be very selective. Practically any cheerful utterance is greeted with pleasure. Those that are not English are probably heard as though they were. When a parent imitates the baby's sounds, and parents imitate long before the infant does, they distort what he has said into an English syllable. Whatever the child may say he hears the local speech.

A likelier explanation of phonetic drift comes from Mowrer's (164) study of talking birds, mentioned earlier. Mowrer found that if the bird was to learn it must be nurtured and spoken to at the same time. Under these circumstances, Mowrer reasoned, the speech of the trainer becomes a secondary reinforcer. When the bird in isolation produces sounds it will be rewarded most by those that most resemble human speech and this generalized secondary reinforcement will increase the probability of human-like sounds until they dominate the bird's vocalization. It is likely that babbling drifts toward speech for exactly similar reasons. The advantage of this principle is that it explains how the infant can learn from his own speech play when no adult is providing selective reinforcement.

Imitation is a name for many different kinds of things. Most generally, it names a shift in one person's behavior in the direction of increased similarity to behavior of someone else when the first person has had an opportunity to observe the second. Socialization is the general name for changes of child behavior in the direction of community norms. Norms, of course, describe the usual behavior of people to whom the child is exposed. It follows that socialization is imitation in this very general sense of imitation. Babbling drift and, indeed, the acquisition of speech are, in a sense, therefore imitative processes. There is, however, a narrower sense of imitation. Sometimes when one person performs an action another person promptly produces similar action. The action of the model seems to release imitative action. This kind of behavior is seldom seen in children before at least eight months.

Before he imitates others the child imitates himself and we may guess that this self-imitation, which Holt (95) calls the circular reflex, is a prerequisite to true imitation. Holt suggests that when a sound has just been made the motor paths involved are more easily discharged than ordinarily and so the sound is likely to occur again. Piaget (182) suggests that this echolalic speech is only one example of a tendency to perpetuate pleasing effects. In speaking, the infant, of course, also provides himself with an auditory stimulus. If a circular reflex is established, so that hearing himself say "ba" he says it again, then, because of simple stimulus generalization, the sound of an adult saying "ball" should elicit this same "ba." In addition we know that the adult is likely to cut into the infant's reflex repetition of "ba" with an adult imitation "ball." In this way "ba" could become directly conditioned to "ball" as well as indirectly through stimulus generalization from "ba."

I don't think the above explanation of imitation is completely adequate nor am I satisfied with the explanations offered by Miller and Dollard (160). Their "matched dependent" form of imitation describes well enough the case in which the imitative act is selected out of rather random behavior. A small boy might one day happen to run in the wake of his older brother. If the older brother is running to meet his father who carries candy for the two boys then the younger might learn to run whenever the older does. However, the imitation that is striking in speech is not the accidental duplication of something said by a parent but rather the apparent effort to repeat what has been said by the parent. This is not a case of response selection from a random output but of a good first try. Miller and Dollard's "copying" behavior is the kind we are interested in but it is not really explained by their learning theory. The major advantage in deriving imitation from the circular reflex is that it predicts that the child's attempt will not exactly duplicate what he hears but will be the nearest sound in his own familiar repertoire. This appears to be what happens.

Church's (39) experiment with rats shows that when an animal is learning a response imitative of another animal it can also, incidentally, learn to make the response to other cues. This suggests the way in which imitative speech may turn into referential speech. The adult may say "dog" when he sees a dog. The child has learned to say "dog" or something like it whenever the adult does. He may also discover the circumstances governing the adult's utterance and, after a time, say the word on seeing the animal without waiting for the adult to speak.

Imitation can also serve to bring names into the primal sentence frame. The child looks out the window, whimpers and reaches, and on the outside the adult sees a dog. The adult offers an interpretation of the child's request, and suggests that the object is "Dog?" The child is trained to imitate this word and says it too. His response is likely to earn quick reinforcement. He may incidentally pick up the cue for the word, the sight of the dog itself. In this way he may learn to ask for the dog when he wants it and should soon learn the general lesson of naming the thing he wants in conjunction with the whimper of desire.

The Perception of Speech

It is reported by many authors that children first attend to the intensity and duration of speech, to emotional quality and intonation rather than to its phonetic characteristics (145). Meumann (145) tells a story illustrating this fact. He asked his young son: "*Wo ist das Fenster?*" and the joy pointed at the window. It rather looked as if he understood the question. Meumann then asked in

French: *"Où est la fenetre?"* and again the boy pointed at the window. The boy also pointed correctly when the question was put in English. Meumann balked at believing the boy could understand all three languages. So he asked the new question: *"Wo ist die Tür?"* And the boy pointed at the window. The child was reacting to the intonation contour that was common to all four questions. We can see how the phonetic differences in the questions might have been brought to his attention. Meumann could have required different responses, pointing to the door after one question and to the window after the other. The two questions: *"Wo ist das Fenster?"* and *"Wo ist die Tür?"* were at first perceptual equivalents. They were identified as members of one speech category, a category defined by intonation rather than phonetic features. By requiring differential response the father could have brought his son to re-examine the questions to discover unlike features that would guide him to the correct responses. Many such features are to be found near the end of each sequence. This would be training in speech perception that does not involve training in pronunciation.

The important research question is to discover how the child learns to categorize speech in terms of phonemic attributes. A child born into an English speaking community must learn to attend to the difference between voiceless [p] and voiced [b] but to ignore the difference between aspirate and non-aspirate [p]. Generally he must learn to notice phonemic contrasts but may ignore those that are not phonemic. The fact that all English phonemes can be described with a small number of distinctive features having binary values suggests that the perception of English speech might develop in a very systematic way.

Although psychologists have studied the perceptual constancies of size, shape, and color the constancy of the phoneme is a problem of which they have until recently been innocent. Among linguists, Roman Jakobson has been far in advance of others in his interest in this question. In 1941 he suggested the order in which phonemic oppositions emerge for children (111). With Halle (114) he has recently suggested such an order for the distinctive features. These authors say that the child begins in a "labial stage" in which his only utterance is /pa/. This involves the consonant-vowel contrast. "From the articulatory point of view the two constituents of this utterance represent polar configurations of the vocal tract: in /p/ the tract is closed at its very end while in /a/ it is opened as widely as possible at the front and narrowed toward the back, thus assuming the horn-shape of a megaphone. This combination of two extremes is also apparent on the acoustical level: the labial stop presents a momentary burst of sound without any great concentration of energy in a particular frequency band, whereas in the vowel /a/ there is no strict limitation of time, and the energy is concentrated in a relatively narrow region of maximum aural sensitivity."* This is the primal syllable, contrasting an ideal consonant with an ideal vowel. The next stage, according to these authors, is likely to involve a nasal-oral opposition, a distinction between /p/ and /n/. Alternatively it may involve a grave-acute distinction between /p/ and /t/. The first vowel division is said to occur on the compact-diffuse axis and the next division on the grave-acute so that the child has /a/, /u/, and /i/. The discussion goes on to outline a complete sequence of acquisition for the distinctive features. There are many questions to be asked about these proposals.

Many students of child speech have not studied descriptive linguistics and the data they present usually cannot safely be used to form conclusions about the phonemic system of the child studied. It seems to me, that the evidence in this literature is not strong enough to establish the generalizations of Jakobson and of Jakobson and Halle. Until the evidence is more complete many psychologists will hesitate to accept the Piaget-like conceptualization of the acquisition process as a set of stages through which the child must pass; they will expect the sequence to be sensitive to the particular contrasts stressed in the vocabulary offered to a child by its parents.

Jakobson and Halle (114) describe the development of distinctive features in the child's speech. However, it is not clear what relationship the authors believe to exist between these distinctions in pronunciation and the distinctions of auditory perception. Is it assumed that the child who says /pa/ hears /p/ as distinct from /a/ but hears no other distinctions? There are other possibilities. The vowel-consonant feature divides the phonemes of English into two great classes. Perhaps a child in the "labial stage"

---

*Quoted here with the permission of Mouton and Company.

distinguishes every consonant from every vowel but accepts all consonants as equivalents and all vowels as equivalent. He might "hear" two phonemes in all speech: a consonant and a vowel. Members of the first phoneme would include [b], [p], [k], [t], etc., and the second would include [a], [i], [ae], [u], etc. Such syllables as [pa], [ba], [pi], [bae], etc., would be perceptually equivalent. Continuing with this possibility, perceptual phonemics might develop with the progressive differentiation of distinctive features. Each new axis would further subdivide speech sounds and the end would come when there were enough distinctive features uniquely to characterize each English phoneme and, therefore, each meaningful utterance.

If child phonology does develop as a kind of progressive differentiation of the distinctive features, we shall be interested in knowing what kinds of experience are necessary to produce such differentiation. Suppose a child is trained to distinguish *ton* from *son*. Will this distinction bring with it the ability to tell *tune* from *soon* and *tin* from *sin?* How widely will the learning generalize? Will it extend to all contrasts of the particular phonemes or even to all contrasts involving the particular distinctive feature?

Whatever the details of the process may be there can be no doubt that the speakers of a language do learn to categorize the speech they hear in the culturally prescribed manner. It is difficult to become conscious of these perceptual habits with regard to the native language but they are quite obvious in learning a second language. If one's training has largely been in reading, the first contact with native speech is a shock. Nothing sounds at all familiar. The spoken language seems to have no more structure than "white noise." Perceiving the first language is obviously essential to speaking the language but its importance is not limited to conversation. As we shall see next, the categorical structure of the native language is the key to the entire culture.

Speech as an Attribute of a Category to be Acquired

It may be well to outline in advance the argument presented in this section. A name is itself a category, a category defined by auditory and contextual attributes. A name is, in addition, an attribute of a referent category since instances of the referent category have the property of evoking the name. The name is probably never the only kind of distinctive response evoked by a referent category but names are peculiar among such responses in that all names share a phonological and morphological structure. The names of a given language are compounded of the same small number of phonemes and, on a higher level, of morphemes combined according to rule. The naming system covers most of the culture. There is a distinctive response of this type for practically every referent category a man possesses. In general, names do not present categories in any kind of fixed relationship; they simply indicate equivalence and non-equivalence. In some cases, however, more than this is signalled. The referent category can sometimes be guessed because it duplicates attributes of the referent category (phonetic symbolism), or because its transferred meaning suggests the new category (metaphor), or because the part-of-speech membership of the name suggests the attributes that are likely to be criterial for the referent category. Finally two small experiments are described that illustrate the role of names as attributes of referent categories.

As adults we look for a referent category to explain any response that captures our attention and appears to have been deliberately produced. The presumption of a category will be especially strong if the "Other One" manifests any communicative intent. Thus a stranger who stands in front of us and makes a motion with his hands is presumed to "mean something" thereby. The most likely response to take our attention and to suggest communication is vocalization. When this vocalization is recognizably a phonemic sequence from some foreign language or an unfamiliar sequence which could be English, the presumption of a referent category approaches certainty. If a biology professor in his first lecture uses the word *coelenterate* he establishes an empty category to be filled in later. It is empty in the sense that nothing is signalled by the unfamiliar word except the existence of a category. The professor's "new word" functions as a lure to cognition. It attracts thought in a way that his other actions—wagging his head while he talks, stumbling against the platform—do not. It is not necessarily an invidious thing to say of a new study that "it is just a lot of words." Chemistry, sociology, and psychology all have their own vocabularies. The words are handed out early in the term like empty containers to be filled with experience. The pejorative sense of the students' complaint is clear in a full translation, "This course is just a lot of new sounds for familiar concepts." It is a stupid nuisance to learn new names for old meanings. The value of a neologism is that it signals a new concept to be formed. This signal has so often proved misleading that some authors do not signal their new concepts with neologisms, preferring to alter the sense of familiar words. Perhaps it is a less frankly ambitious undertaking, a more modest rhetoric.

We take a new word as a lure for cognition because in a long experience of language we have learned that such utterances are attributes of nonlinguistic categories and that these categories are ordinarily worth learning. Of course, an utterance is a category in its own right, a category defined by functional and stimulus attributes within the speech system. But the semantic utterance is also a selective response elicited by some array of nonlinguistic stimuli. For a person who does not yet categorize this array the utterance he hears from another can function as an attribute of the non-linguistic category. Ford cars produced in 1954 constitute an array of objects having certain visible attributes: a characteristic length, fender line, and distribution of chrome plate. Another attribute of this array is its ability to elicit the name *1954 Ford*. This name is likely to be heard or seen when members of the category are in one's visual field.

The linguistic name is a socially contingent attribute. It will not be heard unless someone is about who is disposed to name automobiles. In respect to this contingency the utterance is like many nonlinguistic attributes which are also contingent on particular circumstances. The characteristic front grill of the Ford is an attribute that cannot be used in categorizing automobiles unless one takes up a position from which the grill can be seen. If we face an array of automobiles at the Automobile Show their contrasting grills can be compared. If we are in the presence of an automobile-namer, contrasting names can also be compared. The utterance differs from nonlinguistic attributes in that it is not spatially localized with the car but emanates, instead, from a person. It is a functional attribute of the Ford to elicit a particular utterance from properly disposed and informed persons.

Since we are accustomed to thinking of color, size, and shape as attributes, it seems a little strange to call the name of a category an attribute. There is reason to believe that the name attribute has not always seemed so unlike the other attributes of a category. Vigotsky (232) writes: "When children are asked whether it is possible to replace the name of one object with that of another, for instance to call a cow ink, and ink a cow, they answer that it is entirely impossible, because ink is used for writing and the cow gives milk. The exchange of a name means for them also the exchange of the qualities of the objects, so close and inseparable is the connection between the two."

A child might learn to categorize the nonlinguistic world from direct contact with its sensible attributes. He would begin by categorizing in terms of those attributes that have a kind of natural prepotency for him. Perhaps visual brightness is such an attribute. It would lead him to distinguish day from night, the sun from the moon, and white from black. Probably there are some universal categories imposed on all human beings by the prepotency of certain sensory attributes. But most of the categories we possess are cultural. For these the prepotent attributes are often irrelevant and sometimes misleading. A child might not have to learn to distinguish shiny coins from dull but these categories are poor equipment for the business world. Would we group Fords together and distinguish them from Chevrolets on the basis of prepotent sensory attributes? We should be more likely to divide cars into classes defined by the color of the paint job. What of desks and tables, garages and barns, musical comedies and grand operas, Holsteins and Guernseys, schizophrenics and manic-depressives? It seems clear that most of our categorical furniture is cultural and that its presence in our minds is not guaranteed by the sensible attributes of the categories themselves. We need some sort of indication from those who participate in the culture of the things they treat as equivalents and those that are distinguished.

The semantic utterance is only one variety of response that can serve as an attribute of a referent category. In the game of Charades we project ourselves into a speechless world in which references must be guessed from nonlinguistic response. Where there is a highly criterial response the reference is easily conveyed. If one imitated a man eating something and receiving a squirt in the eye most people would know that the reference had to do with grapefruit. If one appeared to pat with affection the air at about the height of one's knee most would guess that a dog was involved. Usually, however, the criterial or distinctive action serves to identify the genus but not the species. A drinking motion is criterial for potable liquids but how does one distinguish tomato juice from orange? For problems of this kind Charades deserts the principle of reproducing the customary characteristic action involving the referent category. Instead, one inscribes in the air the contours of a tomato or breaks the word into syllables and acts out each syllable or has recourse to permitted conventional signals. Charades held to the first principle is like a science fiction world in which children are trying to discover the categories of their culture from the everyday, non-speech actions of the adults around them. It looks as if it would be a pretty difficult world.

Suppose, for a moment, that a child used the responses of his tutors as a guide to equivalence and difference in nonlinguistic reality. He could have a cue to what is edible and what is inedible by noting what is eaten and what is not eaten. Mother might be distinguished from father by the fact that his uncle kisses the one and shakes the hand of the other. The categories *bed, chair,* and *floor* could be distinguished by noting which entities are lain upon, sat upon, and stood upon. In each realm of experience we have a different set of response categories giving evidence of concepts. Using the nonlinguistic responses of others as a guide to the categories of reality we should have to learn a set of response equivalents very nearly as complex as the stimulus equivalents in the world. This point is difficult to see because we are so familiar with such response categories as sitting, standing, or kissing. The point may be clearer if we imagine a community in which kin of one sort elicit a nod of the head in their direction while kin of another sort elicit a nod in the direction of the dwelling of the wife's family. We could not discover these kinship categories until we learned to classify properly the two kinds of nod and this might take considerable learning.

In a particular case the player might notice a response on the part of his tutor—a movement of head, of eyes, and hands. His problem is to discover the defining attributes of this response so that he can identify a recurrence and use this functional equivalence as an attribute of the governing nonlinguistic concept. The difficulty is that he does not have prior knowledge of the list of attributes of nonlinguistic discriminating responses. He can scarcely hold all attributes of the first instance in mind since the attributes are not yet identified.

With regard to linguistic responses the player is in a more favorable position. From a relatively small number of experiences of speech categories it is possible to discover all the defining attributes of any future utterances—the phonemes of the language. It is, furthermore, possible to learn that any semantic utterance will be a conjunctive category defined by phonemes in a particular sequence. Once the speech system has been grasped, then, there really is no problem of category attainment so far as utterances themselves are concerned. The player of the Original Word Game who hears /kæt/ knows that these three phonemes, in the sequence given, define the speech category. He has only to remember the response in these terms to recognize new instances. The player is not, of course, in this position when he first hears speech. The point is that his experience in forming the first speech categories can bring him great secondary benefits. Incidental learning of the structure of speech can teach him to perceive new utterances in proper categorical fashion. The study of nonlinguistic responses cannot yield such benefits since these responses do not constitute a system.

The Game is not complete when the player is able to categorize the speech of his tutor. He must discover the stimulus attributes governing the tutor's verbal behavior. The child's parent will not always be nearby to tell him what is "hot." He must learn to recognize hot things by their stimulus attributes.

The utterance attribute will orient the player toward contemporaneous stimuli and will tell him when the important nonlinguistic stimuli recur. Even with these aids the categorization of nonlinguistic reality is a formidable problem. In the beginning there is no listing of attributes and no possibility of holding in mind the total nonlinguistic circumstances accompanying a given utterance. To the degree that names are appropriate to their referent categories this problem is simplified. We have seen in Chapter IV the ways in which names can be appropriate. Phonetic symbolism names the case in which the acoustic and kinaesthetic qualities of the utterance directly suggest attributes of the referent category. Metaphor is a name for the utterance that suggests its referent through a transfer of meaning and metaphorical appropriateness is probably the most important kind in the Original Word Game. Finally, a name will have membership in some form class or part of speech and these classes are likely to have a very general semantic character.* If the name is an English noun, for instance, the referent category is more likely to have some characteristic visual contour than if the name is a preposition or adverb or verb. In general the appropriate name reduces the number of hypotheses about the reference category to a relatively probable few. It operates as a kind of attribute-filter.

Because speech is a system providing attributes for the entire conceptual repertoire of a culture it would be possible to use the attributes of the utterances to represent the relations between concepts. Consider the categories of color vision. There are, as we know, millions of just noticeable differences obtainable from the color solid: seven and one-half million is estimated in the Optical Society of America's book, *Science of Color* (172). In American English, there are only about eight commonly used color names. Evidently we categorize colors. Suppose that a native speaker of English is presented with a large assortment of colors—the Holmgren yarns or the Munsell collection—and is asked to group them according to hue, making piles of those that belong together and ranging the piles in order of similarity to one another. He would probably make a small number of piles, six or eight, and arrange these with the longer wave lengths at one end and the shorter at the other, possibly making a circle to suggest that the shortest wave lengths begin to resemble the longest.

Suppose this subject were then asked to give the common names for the various points in the color solid. We should find many of these called *red*. The various pronunciations of *red* would vary but

---

*See Chapter VII.

no phonemic boundaries would be crossed. Moving along the hue dimension in the solid, we should eventually receive a "new" response, *orange*. This is clearly a new morpheme varying in many phonemes at once. Taking another direction in the solid we should arrive at *pink*, likewise a new morpheme. As each conceptual boundary is crossed there will be a phonemic change in speech. Within the concept only free variation in noncriterial attributes will occur in the subject's speech. The groupings of the nonlinguistic sorting are preserved in this labelling behavior but the distance between categories is not preserved. This could be accomplished by making the phonemic change proportional to the distance between the color groupings. For example, as we move from the longest wave lengths to those which are somewhat shorter, we ought not to squander phonemes on a great splurge of a word like *orange*. Since this category is immediately adjacent to *red*, let us give it a name in which only the vowel is changed, and that change to the vowel nearest on the vowel chart. Orange ought properly to be called [ræd]. We could then move through the vowel chart as we move through the groups of colors, keeping the phonemic change proportional to the cognitive remoteness of the categories. There would be time enough to change more than one phoneme when we moved into a new sense modality.

With very few exceptions the phonemic attributes of speech are not isomorphic with intercategorical relations. Jespersen (118) reports a case in which two children invented a language that made limited use of this higher degree of isomorphism. They used the form *bal* for place and lengthened the vowel proportionally to the size of the place. So the vowel would lengthen as they moved from village to town to city. The Guarani Indians express the past tense with the suffix *-yma* pronounced more slowly as the temporal remoteness of the event increases. In English we have the word *brunch* phonemically between breakfast and lunch, as the meal is temporally. These are rare exceptions. Speech, in general, does not use its phonemic attributes in this way. The phoneme ordinarily serves only to identify equivalent and nonequivalent stimuli.

Relations between categories are expressed by many different techniques. Consider, for instance, the sensory proximity and remoteness of hue categories. The sensory order could easily be reproduced in the word order "red, orange, yellow, green, blue, and violet." The chronological sequence of breakfast, lunch, and dinner is reproduced in this sentence. Word order is conventionally used in English to convey subject-object relations as in the familiar contrast "Dog bites man" versus "Man bites dog." Word orders are easily revised to express a variety of relations. Perhaps the most common means of indicating intercategorical relations is the use of a free or bound morpheme naming the relation. The preposition *in* describes spatial containment in the phrase *the soup in the bowl.* The affixed *-s* expresses possession in *dad's car.* The stimulus attributes of a name do not present a category in any particular relation but leave it free to be presented in infinitely varied relations through the flexible combinational resources of the language.

Speech Categories Operating as a Guide to Referent Categories. We have conducted a little experiment that illustrates the main point of this section—the use of names as attributes of referent categories. Farnsworth (64) has developed, with the Munsell Color Company, a series of eighty-five color chips equally spaced around the hue dimension. Saturation and brightness are constant. Eight alternate chips are drawn from the red-blue region of the series. There is the same very small perceptual gap between each adjacent pair of the series. The subject is shown this series of chips and told that the experimenter has a way of classifying them. It will be the subject's job to discover this classification. The experimenter moves the series behind a screen and then exposes them one at a time (in random order) naming each chip with a nonsense syllable. The subject simply watches this process until all eight have been named. He is then asked to group the chips as the experimenter has grouped them with his verbal behavior.

As Figure 1 shows there are four groups of two chips each. The groups are named [ma], [ma:], [mo], [mo:]. The difference between [a] and [o] is phonemic in English but the difference between the long and short forms of each vowel is not. To produce the proper length the experimenter thought of a voiceless consonant to follow the short form and a voiced consonant to follow the long form. Thus he pronounced [mo] by thinking *mote* and [mo:] by thinking *mode.*

FIGURE 1

Categorizations of Eight Color Stimuli in Terms of
Nonsense Names Varying in Phonetic Characteristics

```
                              :
   ma     ma    ma:    ma:    :   mo     mo    mo:    mo:
   o      o     o      o      :   o      o     o      o
                              :
```

A. English-speaking subjects

```
                    :             :             :
   ma     ma    :   ma:    ma:    :   mo     mo    :   mo:    mo:
   o      o     :   o      o      :   o      o     :   o      o
                    :             :             :
```

B. Navaho-speaking subjects

```
 ma     ma           ma:    ma:    mo     mo               mo:    mo:
 o      o            o      o      o      o                o      o
```

C. Unequal sensory distances between categories

```
:
:   Indicates point of division between categories made by subjects
:
:
```

Fifteen Harvard students whose native language is English, after hearing one series, generally divided the colors into two groups of four chips each as in Figure 1. The line of division corresponds to the line of phonemic change. They do not make a line of division where the vowel changes in length. With four repetitions the subjects persisted in their two-group classification.

In the Navaho language, vowel length is always a distinctive feature. Each vowel has a long and short form and these are different phonemes. Fifteen monolingual Navahos given the same problems of concept attainment by Horowitz (97) generally divided the colors correctly into four classes of two colors each as in Figure 1 and persisted in this division through four repetitions.

We know that English subjects are able to distinguish the prolonged vowel from the short vowel, probably as easily as the Navaho. When we rejected their two-group classifications as erroneous they eventually discovered vowel length and the proper grouping of colors. Many then remarked that they had noticed some variations in the naming but assumed they were accidental. *We could have no better statement of the cognitive status of nonphonemic variations.* They are not purposeful and significant as are phonemic changes. The Navaho subjects did not assume that the variations in vowel length were accidental. Once the English subjects learned that this dimension was significant they made no errors in identification.

The groupings produced by both English and Navaho subjects were isomorphic with the groupings they heard in the tutor's speech. Having different sets of criterial attributes (phonemes) for speech they came up with different groupings. When the English-speaking subjects were corrected they re-examined the tutor's speech and discovered the attribute to which he gave significance.

Fifteen new English-speaking subjects were shown a different series of eight colors from the Farnsworth set. In this series there are four classes named as before, [ma], [ma:], [mo], [mo:]. However, the perceptual gap between the [ma-ma:] classes and [mo-mo:] classes was four times as great as the gap between [ma] and [mo]. This situation is schematized by distance in Figure 1. When one looked at the series the two end classes were immediately seen as distinct from the four middle colors. There is a disproportionate change at the vowel-length boundary. The problem was to determine whether or not these autochthonous sensory categories would call attention to the change in vowel length and cause the subject to make four groups of the colors. Only two subjects divided the colors into four groups on the first trial. However, there were four others who did so on the second trial. Evidently the gaps in the series of eight colors helped to call attention to the difference of vowel length. Even with this strong visual encouragement, however, there were six subjects who never did believe that a difference of vowel length could make two words different and so signal a categorical distinction in the nonlinguistic world.

The fact that some English-speaking subjects, who worked with unequally spaced colors, recognized the distinctiveness of the four classes after hearing them named only once is important. This result demonstrates a facet of the Word Game that we have not discussed. It is evidently possible for nonlinguistic reality to serve as a guide to the categorization of speech. The isomorphic relationship can be useful in either direction. An inescapable visual difference leads us to look for a speech difference. We may suppose that speech has less intrinsic importance than nonlinguistic reality, and it is therefore customary to describe speech as a map and the rest of the world as the region mapped. It is clear, however, that when a dirt road turns into a four-lane superhighway we may for the first time notice the difference between a thin and thick red line on an actual road map.

The method used in these experiments is a very simple model of the Word Game. There are important differences from the Game as it is played with children. In our paradigm it is perfectly clear what entities are being named by the experimenter and it is also clear that hue is the only significant dimension for classifying these entities. When the child hears "things" named he usually will not know just where the "thing" is and which of its attributes are defining. He can use the name as an important aid to the discovery of these attributes through phonetic symbolism, metaphorical appropriateness, and part-of-speech membership. When the name alone does not suggest the criterial attributes of the referent it is customary to say something additional that will help to point them out. Sometimes, of course, one names the attributes themselves and, if the referents of such names are familiar, instances of the new category can be identified by their conjunction. More commonly one says something like: "A dog? Why, a dog is an animal"; or "A Ford? A Ford is a make of automobile." Statements of this kind place the new category under a superordinate. Their prototype is: "X is a kind of Y." This is a movement up "the ladder of abstractions," a bad direction to take, according to General Semantics, if we hope to convey the reference for a name.

The Effect of Knowing the Superordinate of a Category. What does *a make of automobile* say that *Ford* does not? Both signal a new category to be formed. Suppose that the player of this game, although he has never seen a Ford nor heard one named, has seen and heard named such other kinds of automobile as the Chevrolet, Oldsmobile, and Cadillac. From these experiences he could have learned that all automobiles run on four wheels, have some metal parts, and require gasoline. Chevrolets, Oldsmobiles, and Cadillacs share these attributes and, on that account, are members of one superordinate category—automobiles. However, Chevrolets are not so long as Oldsmobiles and Oldsmobiles are not so long as Cadillacs. In addition, each make of automobile has a characteristic grill, radiator ornament, and distribution of chrome plate. All automobiles have some sort of grill, ornament, and distribution of plate but the different values of these attributes are *noisy* for the category *automobile*. For the subordinate categories called *Chevrolet, Oldsmobile,* and *Cadillac* these values are criterial.

The Chevrolet, Oldsmobile, and Cadillac also have their subordinates. There are Chevrolets of many different colors, Chevrolets with two doors and Chevrolets with four doors, Chevrolets with metal tops and Chevrolets with cloth tops. These attribute values are noisy when it comes to distinguishing the Chevrolet from other makes of car because the attributes run a similar gamut within each category. The same attribute values are, of course, criterial for identifying particular Chevrolet automobiles. In general, categories have a common superordinate when they share characteristic attributes. The subordinates of a superordinate will be distinguished from one another by attribute values that are noisy for the superordinate.

Ford as a make of automobile is a member of a category family. One who knows the general structure of the family knows that the Ford will certainly have four wheels, that it will have a radiator ornament different from any other make of automobile, and that its color will not be an essential part of being a Ford. In short, the new category can be pretty well constituted by placement in a family; the player can know what to remember and what to overlook. As the general outlines of category families are learned new additions can easily be constituted by reference to a superordinate.

On some occasion one might choose to label the particular automobile of the previous illustration as a *convertible* rather than as a *Ford*. "What is a convertible?" A convertible is a model of automobile." With this characterization it is still expected to have four wheels; its color still will not matter but the radiator ornament also becomes unimportant. The cloth top and the number of doors take the spotlight.

Jean Berko and I have conducted a little experiment to demonstrate the effect of referring a name to a superordinate. Imagine a large number of photographs of men's faces belonging to various individuals, seen from various angles, registering various emotions. The photographs of Mr. A differ from those of Mr. B in such fixed features as size of nose, color of eyes, and height of forehead. Angle of view and expressive characteristics are noisy for this distinction. Mr. A is sometimes sad and sometimes glad, likewise B. Mr. A is sometimes seen in full face, sometimes in profile, likewise B. If one were distinguishing happy faces from sad, fixed features such as the size of nose and color of eyes would become noisy attributes while such expressive characteristics as a mouth curved up at the ends would become criterial. Actually the distinction is not quite so absolute. If A is characteristically sad, and B characteristically glad, then the expressive features will have a potential criteriality for distinguishing A from B but it will usually be less than that of the fixed features.

In our experiment we used photographs of the actor Frois-Wittmann "registering" various emotions. From the complete set we selected six pairs such that one member of each pair seemed to us to be a "cold" expression and the other "warm." We showed the first pair in the set to a subject and told him one picture showed emotion A and the other emotion B. On each subsequent pair the subject was asked to identify A and B and to tell us what characteristics of the faces guided his decision. It was a problem in category formation where the categories A and B were described as *kinds of emotions*. Other subjects were shown the same faces in the same order but they were told of one, "This is Mr. A" and of the other "This is Mr. B." Like the others they were to identify A and B in each pair and name the attributes of the faces that guided their decisions.

The faces change enough from photograph to photograph so that it is possible to believe either that they are one man posing different expressions or that they are two different men. The names A and B advertise their arbitrariness and so suggest nothing about the categories they name. For some subjects A and B were identified as subordinates of the category *emotions;* for others they were subordinates of the category *men* or, to be exact, *misters.* What did the different superordinates do to the subjects' selection of attributes in the faces?

The differences between the two groups of subjects are too large to require any tests of statistical significance. *Emotion* A was distinguished from *emotion* B in terms of expressive features like smiles and frowns. No subject mentioned any fixed feature. *Mr.* A, on the other hand, was distinguished from *Mr.* B in terms of the nose, the ears, the hairline, etc. Almost every subject relied on such features even though these are pictures of the same man. It is not surprising that these subjects also made some use of expressive features since that is the correct hypothesis and expression can have criteriality for distinguishing one person from another. However, the expressive features were used less than the fixed features by this group. The subjects distinguishing *emotion* A from *emotion* B made twice as much use of expressive features as did the subjects distinguishing *Mr.* A from *Mr.* B. We have repeated this general design with other pictures and other subjects and there can be no doubt that referring a name to a superordinate affects the constitution of the referent category.

There is a speculative addendum to this brief discussion of category families. It often happens that the structure of such a family leaves some empty positions, combinations of criterial attribute values required to maintain the symmetry of the family but not in existence and not named. In the phonological structure of a given language, for instance, there may be many stop consonants with a voiced and voiceless form for several positions of articulation; e.g., the bilabials [b] and [p], the alveolars [d] and [t]. Suppose there is, in such a language, a [g] but no voiceless equivalent. Students of historical sound change say that it is a good prediction that [k] will become a distinct phoneme in such a language. Perhaps any existent category family causes us to imagine a symmetrical pattern completing what exists more easily than we can imagine any reorganization of the pattern. Among automobile models for instance we have long had two-door hard tops, four-door hard tops, and two-door cloth tops. It is no trick to complete this 2 x 2 table of attribute values and imagine a four-door soft top. Other things equal, "imagination" may move most easily to the creation of unrealized attribute combinations that are required to complete an existent pattern. The notion of a convertible hard top might be hard to come by since it involves separating the attributes of convertibility and cloth top which have long been perfect correlates. Working for such a notion, of course, is the utility of the combination.

The imaginative creations of myth, comic strip, and animated cartoon are mostly recombinations of attribute values, criterial on one level of a category family. Members of the animal kingdom are popularly distinguished by such things as feathers, scales, wings, speech, horns, etc. Recombine some of these and you can get a feathered man (Papageno in *The Magic Flute*); a woman with scales and a tail (mermaid), a horse with wings (Bucephalus); or a man (angel); miscellaneous talking animals (Aesop's creatures and Mickey Mouse), a horse with one horn (unicorn); or a man with two (cuckold). The animated cartoon has always given animals certain human attributes; they talk, wear clothing, drive cars. It is a more recent conceit to give them the attributes of the inanimate world. Audiences are still amused by a cat that shatters like a pane of glass or melts like a block of chocolate. On the other hand the animation of the inanimate world is a very primitive process but perhaps that is because the movements of the inanimate world appear superficially to be the same as those of the animate world. No doubt the determinants of imaginative creation are very numerous but one of them, for a mind well structured into category families, may be the familiar lines of that structure.

Let us return to the Original Word Game. Discovery of the referent of a name may be aided by characteristics of the name and by placing the name under a familiar superordinate. All of this leaves the player of the Game with a hypothesis about the character of the referent. If he has enough aids the hypothesis may be a good one but it still requires testing. At this stage in the Game the name moves from tutor to player. It has functioned as a guide to the formation of hypotheses about a referent. It now functions as evidence of that hypothesis. The player does some naming on his own and the tutor checks this use of the name against his own to see whether the hypothesis about the referent is correct.

Speech as Evidence that the Speaker Has a Referent Category

The category has been defined in this book as a way of grouping an array of objects or events in terms of those characteristics that distinguish this array from other objects or events in the universe. The basic evidence for grouping an array of objects or events is some kind of response elicited by the array and not elicited by entities outside the array. The dog gives evidence of knowing the difference between buzzers and bells by salivating to the one and not to the other. The rat shows that he can distinguish circles from triangles by jumping to the one in preference to the other. The human subject satisfies the experimenter that he has grasped a concept when he selects positive instances and avoids negative instances. A human subject can also give evidence that he has attained a concept by correctly patterning his naming behavior.

Grouping entities is not sufficient evidence that a subject has a concept. The dog may have been trained to salivate to particular buzzers, the rat to jump to particular triangles, the man to name only the Ford cars on his block. I have therefore added that a concept is considered to have been attained only when a subject is able to identify new instances of it without further training. Similarly the referent of a word cannot be said to be fully understood until it can be correctly extended to entities that one has not heard labelled.

It sometimes happens that we use the same words but do not have the same categories. Consider the phrase *a great poem*. A particular teacher of literature may have a subtle understanding of the meaning of this phrase. To convey this concept to his students he uses the denotational method. The teacher sets before his pupils a series of instances of the category: the works of Shakespeare, Milton, Donne, etc. The pupils learn to refer to all of these as *great poems*. They probably are not asked to identify new instances of the concept. When I. A. Richards (192) asked Cambridge undergraduates to interpret and evaluate unfamiliar and untitled poems he tested their understanding of great poetry. They disagreed with him and with one another. Visual exposure to a set of poems cannot guarantee the abstraction of their qualities of greatness. One student might notice that most examples are in blank verse or that all involve some use of metaphor. Another student might recognize merit by the visceral disturbance it sets up, another would find nothing common to the lot but a suffocating dullness. Discovery of the common red quale in many long wave lengths seems to be fairly well guaranteed by a healthy visual apparatus but the defining attributes of great poetry do not arise from the visual system alone. They depend for their emergence on the experience, cultural membership, and intelligence of the individual. It is not surprising that individuals abstract quite different concepts from the same reading. Evidently this is very commonly the case in aesthetic matters. The general disagreement over contemporary art testifies to that. Many are discouraged by such elusive concepts and prefer to withhold judgment until an authoritative list of the great poems of the twentieth century is published. *Time* magazine is very helpful about such things. A few years ago, for instance, it referred to Artur Rubinstein as one of the four great pianists of the century and then in a footnote listed the other three in rank order. While we may not be able to agree on new instances in these areas, we can all memorize a list.

How do we identify discriminating responses in the behavior of someone whose concepts are to be discovered? To begin with, the observer makes a judgment of equivalence; the "same" response is said to be generalized to a class of stimuli. We do not often think of the rat's successful jumps or lever pressings as a category and yet it is perfectly clear that no two jumps are identical. These categories are used in a molar psychology that takes the "act" for its response unit. Consequently the categories are not defined by the particular muscles activated but by a kind of functional equivalence determined by the character of the apparatus. All jumps sending the animal hurtling through the correct door, all pressures producing a pellet—these are the categories. The formal boundaries of the categories can be changed by altering the apparatus. Moving the jumping stand nearer the screen will reduce the force of the jumps; increasing the sensitivity of the lever will lower the resistance to be overcome by the animal's push. The ultimate functional significance of these responses is their ability to produce a food reward.

Where the subject is human and the responses are verbal it is again clear that the experimenter makes a judgment of response equivalence—an array of entities is called by the "same" name. The bounds of verbal categories are set by human beings. They are not built into the apparatus but are a cultural acquisition. Not all men everywhere will agree as to which utterances are the "same." The varying utterances categorized as one word have a kind of functional equivalence in that they will produce the same social effect.

The beauty of the Original Word Game is that, when the player has a hypothesis about the nature of the referent category for a particular utterance, he himself can produce the utterance and thereby test the hypothesis. The tutor, as a representative of the culture, will categorize the player's utterances in accordance with the phonemic structure of the language. If the player gives equivalent names to members of one category and a different set of equivalent names to another category, and if he identifies new instances of each, the tutor will credit him with the references in question. These names might not be the phonemic sequences conventionally used for these referent categories. They might be baby talk names like *bow-wow* for dog. A parental tutor will sometimes allow considerable freedom in this respect, tolerating *bow-wow* until the category is formed, and then insisting on the adult label *dog*. Once the motor and perceptual skills are efficient it should be easy to shift a name. The referent categories will be the hard part of the Game.

The Game may be played concurrently with many other activities. The child and his father can play as they walk along the street, father naming, child trying, father correcting. Concepts can be learned without direct contact with ultimate attributes that may have serious consequences. The child may be told by his father when it is "safe" to cross the street. After a while the child will tell when *he* thinks it "safe," and the father will correct his usage. When the child can pattern the word *safe* as the father patterns it in his mind the father will attribute to him the concept in question. He may then allow the child to cross streets alone. The whole process of trial and correction can be accomplished using the name as a surrogate for action that would have brought the child into perilous contact with the ultimate attributes of the traffic itself. The laboratory concept-attainment experiment is likely to differ from the usual situation in that the ultimate attributes of the concept will be the experimenter's verbal behavior. A subject learns the concept so that he can anticipate whether the experimenter will identify cards as instances of the concept. There is no purpose beyond this in the learning. In the child's learning, parental speech is not usually the ultimate attribute. Beyond this there will usually be physical or social attributes of the greatest importance.

The Uses of the Named Category

The usefulness of named categories is not particularly obvious. Why should we group objects and events and, having grouped them, why should we give names to the groups? Suppose it can be shown that categories and names are important for the formation and transmission of trustworthy expectancies. The usefulness of the expectancy will probably be granted. If we can correctly anticipate what is going to happen we are better able to act so as to preserve our lives and satisfy our desires. It seems to be the chief cognitive business of every kind of higher animal to acquire trustworthy expectancies. It is not the chief business of lower animals because their simpler needs and more predictable experiences make useful instincts possible.

The following sentences are from an essay of I. A. Richards' called "Toward Practice in Interpretation" (193). "Thucydides said that his history would be 'useful to all who wish to study the plain truth of the events which have happened and which will according to human nature recur in much the same way.' 'This idea,' comments Werner Jaeger, 'is the absolute opposite of what we usually call the historical attitude nowadays. A true historian, we think, believes that history never repeats itself. Every historical event is entirely individual.'" The disagreement between Thucydides and Jaeger, as Richards points out, is a disagreement on the sense of the word *history*. If we understand history to be the stream of events appreciated in all their particulars then there are no recurrences and, therefore, no "lessons" in history. Only if we think in terms of "kinds" of events does history repeat itself. This truth about the history of nations is true also of the life experiences of individuals.

Unless we categorize, it is useless to form expectancies for there will be no recurrences. An event, in all its detail or even all of its discriminable detail, does not repeat. There is no use in remembering that event A was followed by event B because event A will never come again. However, types or categories of events do recur. It may be worthwhile knowing that an event of type A led to an event of type B because there may be new instances of both A and B.

The repertoire of categories, which is an important part of the cognitive branch of culture, consists of principles for grouping experience used in one society and its antecedents back through many centuries. When we learn all of these grouping principles we are equipped with many alternative ways of categorizing any experience. Suppose dog A bites me on the ankle. I should like to store that experience in such a way as to avoid further bites. There will be many possible forms in which to store it. I may decide that: a) chow dogs bite; or b) sleeping dogs bite (so let them lie); or c) on a hot day any dog may bite, etc. These alternative categorizations, one or more of which may be useful, are available to me because I have learned the referents of *chow dogs, sleeping dogs,* and *hot dogs* and can recognize new instances of any of these. However, my one experience affords no basis for preferring one categorization over another. I might learn which is the best categorical rule from many encounters with dogs and a number of bites but since the various categories have names there is another way.

I can bring my tentative rule to someone with a large experience of dogs and get his opinion. Do chow dogs bite? He may know that the chow is no more likely to bite than any other dog unless it is startled and then it is almost certain to bite. He suggests, in effect, that I make a new conjunctive category and learn to avoid *startled chow dogs.* This verbal advice can benefit me only because I already know how to recognize the referents of its critical terms. Because I have learned categories and their names this other man's greater experience of dogs can usefully guide my behavior. More generally I can use the accumulated knowledge of my culture only because I have learned to identify the referents for the terms employed.

Everything in the world is susceptible of multiple categorizations. When something important happens, a parent will often name the persons or objects involved and, thereby, select for a child the particular categorizations believed to be most relevant to the event. Suppose one man punches another while a child looks on. A parent may label the aggressor as an *Irishman* or a *cop* or an *old man* or a *redhead* or something else. All of these can be attributes of the same man. The selection of a name is also the selection of an attribute supposed to be predictive of aggressive behavior. The child who hears the man identified as a *redhead* will have different expectancies from the child who hears the same man identified as an *Irishman*. They will agree on what is to be expected of redheaded Irishmen but disagree on individuals who are one of these but not the other.

The participants in one language and one culture are not, of course, cognitively uniform. Consider only the business of categorizing people and forming expectancies concerning them. Each professional and occupational group has its own preferences. A psychiatrist may live in a world of schizoids, cycloids, and paranoids. There are physicians who are automatic diagnosticians, identifying people they meet as instances of high blood pressure or diabetes or peptic ulcer or colitis. My barber tells me that his first thought concerning every man on the television screen is whether or not he needs a haircut. In his novel *The Man with the Golden Arm* Nelson Algren reports on the categories of a police captain: ". . . mush workers and lush workers, catamites and sodomites, bucket workers and bail jumpers, till tappers and assistant pickpockets, square johns and copper johns, lamisters and hallroom boys, ancient pious perverts and old blown parolees, rapoes and record men, heartbroken bummies, afternoon prowlers and midnight creepers, Peeping Toms and firebox pullers." Each line of work has its own vocabulary, a corresponding repertoire of categories, and expectancies relating these categories.

There is also disagreement between individuals on the range of expectancies in which certain categories can usefully participate. Ethnic categories are familiar to nearly everyone in America. Some people think nothing can be predicted from ethnic membership while others think that many important predictions concerning character and temperament follow from ethnic membership. There is reason to believe that people who use a given categorization in many important expectancies are more skilled at identifying category instances than are people who have few expectancies about the category. Several studies, particularly those by Allport and Kramer (7) and Lindzey and Rogolsky (146), have shown that intensely anti-Semitic people are better able to identify Jewish faces from a mixed assortment of faces than are people with milder attitudes toward Jews. Intense anti-Semites hold many important expectancies of anyone known to be a Jew and so it is not surprising that they are more adept at identifying instances than are people for whom this is not an important category. In addition anti-Semitic subjects identify far more faces as Jewish (whether correctly or not) than do other subjects. *Jews* names a much bigger category for the anti-Semite than for others. This is probably a consequence of the negative character of their expectancies about the Jew; everything predicted is unsavory and calls for avoidance. Under the circumstances it would seem disastrous to overlook a single Jew and so doubtful cases are placed in the category. For any phenomenon there is likely to be, within one language and one culture, a competition of alternative categorizations, each claiming to make the most reliable and important predictions. Probably he operates best who is maximally agile at recategorizing phenomena so as to find the most reliable antecedent of each consequent that matters to him. There is a strong contrary tendency to make one categorization serve across the board. Having learned how to recognize ethnic membership, it would be handy if this single categorization would serve to predict everything important about anyone.

The various sciences claim to have arrived at categories and expectancies superior to those popularly applied to their subject matters. This claim rests on certain rules that are followed in defining categories and checking on expectancies. The business of science is continuous with our everyday cognitive business but the records are more carefully kept, more alternatives are considered and checked, and, if there is no less emotional involvement, there are more safeguards against its distorting effects. Learning the vocabulary of a science is, like the Original Word Game, far more than a problem in pronunciation. Only if the referent categories are also learned can the verbal formulations of the science guide behavior in the world outside of words.

Summary

The Original Word Game has three component processes: the categorization of speech, the categorization of referents, and the speaking skill. Invariance in speech signals some invariance outside of speech, some referent invariance. Because speech has a systematic structure it is easier to learn to recognize invariance in speech than to recognize it in other behavior. For the player of the Original Word Game a speech invariance is a signal to form some hypothesis about the corresponding invariance of referent. The speech form may guide him to a very probable hypothesis through phonetic symbolism, metaphor, or the part of speech to which the form belongs. The hypothesis can be made almost certainly correct by giving the superordinate of the new form or by naming the criterial attributes of its referent category. Whether or not his hypothesis about the referent is correct the player speaks the name where his hypothesis indicates that it should be spoken. The tutor approves or corrects this performance according as it fits or does not fit the referent category. In learning referents and names the player of the Original Word Game prepares himself to receive the science, the rules of thumb, the prejudices, the total expectancies of his society.

chapter vii

Linguistic Relativity
and Determinism

IT IS POPULARLY believed that reality is present
in much the same form to all men of sound mind. There are objects
like a house or a cat and qualities like red or wet and actions like
eating or singing and relationships like near to or between. Languages are itemized inventories of this reality. They differ, of
course, in the sounds they employ but the inventory is always the
same. The esthetic Italian deals in euphonious vowels while the
German is addicted to harsh consonant groupings but the things
and actions and qualities named are the same in both tongues. We
are confirmed in this view by our first foreign language textbooks
which present us with lists of French, German, or Latin words
standing opposite their exact English equivalents. We are encouraged by this view to believe that the world will soon recognize the
desirability and practicability of a universal auxiliary language.
Since the only barrier to international communication is a disagreement on code, this disagreement ought speedily to be resolved.

There are, of course, poetic persons who claim to find in each
language some special genius that peculiarly fits it for the expres-

(229)

sion of certain ideas. But the majority of us are at a loss to understand how this can be, since there is apparently a relationship of mutual translatability among the languages we learn. To be sure we can see that one lexicon might contain a few more items than another. If the Germans were to invent a new kind of machine, and we had not yet thought of such a machine, their dictionary would contain one more entry than ours until we borrowed the word or named the machine for ourselves. But these inequalities are in the lexical fringe. They do not disturb the great core of common inventory.

This popular view of the relation between language and thought successfully separates message and code. It does not fall into the error of believing that the names we learn as children are natural and inevitable attributes of the entities named. That kind of extreme glotto-centrism is only possible to a linguistically isolated society. The popular view has thoroughly grasped the conventionality—the cultural status—of linguistic codes. That the kinds of messages to be coded might also be culturally determined is a less familiar idea. It is downright exotic if meant to imply that notions about the physical world itself are no more than conventions.

A thoroughgoing linguistic relativity has, in recent years, been proposed by Benjamin Lee Whorf (244). It is his belief that each language embodies and perpetuates a particular world view. The speakers of a language are partners to an agreement to perceive and think of the world in a certain way—not the only possible way. The same reality—both physical and social—can be variously structured and different languages operate with different structures. If there is anything in such a view, the establishment of a universal auxiliary language must seem a remote goal. For, if Whorf be correct, the peoples of the world do not disagree on words alone, but also on what they have to say. However, Whorf's documentation of his view comes from American Indian tongues, chiefly Hopi. Perhaps linguistic relativity is true for peoples speaking totally unrelated languages, but it may have no application within the Indo-European orbit to which we and the other western nations belong.

Whorf champions a second proposition concerning language and thought which makes an even more dramatic break with popular belief than does the relativity thesis. A man's language, in Whorf's opinion, is a principal determinant of his mode of thought.

The language of a people not only embodies their world-view but also perpetuates that view. The languages of the world are so many molds of varying shape into which infant minds are poured. The mold determines the cognitive cast of the adult.

The evidence for relativity and determinism comes largely from anthropological linguistics and is extraordinarily difficult to interpret. We will examine the kinds of data presented and judge what sorts of conclusions they justify.

The Literal Translation

The Nootka language of Vancouver Island is polysynthetic (248). A single word will often express something for which a sentence is required in English. Where English arranges a sequence of free forms to say "He invites people to a feast," Nootka makes affixations to a basic verb stem to yield something that may be literally translated: "Boiled eaters go for [he] does." How very unlike our way of thinking! It is as strange as the Apache way of saying it is a "dripping spring," which Whorf (248) finds to be "as water or springs whiteness moves downward." Evidently these people do not live in the same world we do.

In elementary language classes it is well known that uncomprehending literal translations can yield quaint and comical results. To go through a German or French sentence morpheme by morpheme will often result in a rather odd English sentence. The French say *"Comment allez-vous?"* which is literally "How go you?" where we say "How are you?" They use a verb of action where we use a verb of being. Does this mean that the French are a kinetic and we a sedentary people? French teachers do not draw that conclusion but rather instruct their pupils to translate more freely. *"Comment allez-vous?"* is said to be best rendered as "How are you?" Retaining the integrity of each morpheme is to lose the sense of the whole (142). In the classroom where European languages are taught it is customary to assume that psychological processes are fundamentally the same and then to liberalize translation procedures so as to guarantee equivalent meanings. With Shawnee, Nootka, Apache, and Hopi (though never with the European languages), Whorf changed this usual procedure, insisted on a literal translation, and concluded that world views differ.

The most entertaining literal translation I know is that provided by Mark Twain for his address to the Vienna Press Club of
November 21, 1897. In German the speech is called *"Die Schrecken
der Deutschen Sprache,"* and in English "The Horrors of the German Language" (41). The following excerpts from the literal
English translation indicate how strange the German mind must be.

I am indeed the truest friend of the German language—not not
only now, but from long since—yes, before twenty years already. . . .
I would only some changes effect. I would only the language method
—the luxurious, elaborate construction compress, the eternal paren-
thesis suppress, do away with, annihilate; the introduction of more
than thirteen subjects in one sentence forbid; the verb so far to the
front pull that one it without a telescope discover can. With one
word, my gentlemen, I would your beloved language simplify so
that, my gentlemen, when you her for prayer need, One her yonder-
up understands.
        . . . I might gladly the separable verb also a little bit reform. I
might none let do what Schiller did: he has the whole history of
the Thirty Years' War between the two members of a separate verb
in-pushed. That has even Germany itself aroused, and one has
Schiller the permission refused the History of the Hundred Years'
War to compose—God be it thanked! After all these reforms established be will, will the German language the noblest and the pretti-
est on the world be.

On the basis of the premises that Whorf applies to American
Indian languages, we should be compelled to conclude that the
German has a cognitive psychology very unlike our own. Of course
we do not operate with these premises, but make liberal translations which represent the German mind to be very like our own.
What justification can there be for operating with different assumptions in the two cases?
    To begin with, American and German cultures have an obvious
close resemblance and known historical ties. There are numerous
bilingual persons and countless translated documents. The cultures
of the modern western nations differ greatly and obviously from
the cultures of the Shawnee, Hopi, and Apache. Persons truly bilingual with one of these Indian languages are uncommon, and
those who exist have often said that thinking is different in the
Indian language. It is not surprising, therefore, that Whorf works
with different premises in approaching what he calls Standard

Average European languages and the strange tongues of America and the Far East.

However, Whorf could very easily have done the wrong thing in using special premises with Indian languages. Differences of material culture and social custom do not guarantee distinct cognitive psychologies. There are few bilinguals, after all, and the testimony of those few cannot be uncritically accepted. There is a familiar inclination on the part of those who possess unusual and arduously obtained experience to exaggerate its remoteness from anything the rest of us know. This must be taken into account when evaluating the impressions of students of Indian languages. In fact, it might be best to translate freely with the Indian languages, assimilating their minds to our own. On the other hand, the error may be in our usual approach to the European languages. Perhaps Whorf's Indian premises ought to be applied to French and German and Latin,* and we should speak of the psychological differences between peoples who put adjectives before nouns and those who put them after. Our impression that the Europeans share the same cognitive psychology could be the sum of many clumsy tourist observations. We don't have the basic knowledge of psychology and language that would enable us to decide intelligently on the premises that ought to underlie translation.

The evidence of the literal translation does not establish linguistic relativity. The relativity is assumed in the premises underlying Whorf's "unsympathetic" translations. A more familiar set of premises—those used with European languages—would transform all of the translation data into evidence for an opposite thesis of linguistic absolutism. We turn, therefore, to some less equivocal data, not involving philosophies of translation.

Cases of a Name and the Lack of a Name

The discrepancy most interesting to Whorf is the case in which one language has a single category and a single name where another language has more than one category and more than one name. In Hopi there is a single word for all flying things except

---

*In his studies of communication in the sessions of the United Nations Glenn (75) has, in fact, applied Whorfian premises to European languages.

birds (246). Where we say *aviator* and *butterfly* and *airplane* the Hopi can use a single word. Here is a region of experience more differentiated by names in English than in Hopi. It is not difficult to think of other areas in which American English is category-rich. Perhaps the world of the automobile is the supreme example. We have the convertible, the club coupe, the hardtop, the sedan, the four-door, the two-door, the station wagon, the runabout, the sport car, the limousine, and many others all exclusive of the familiar trade names. It is not, however, a general property of English or Indo-European languages to be more differentiated than other languages. There have been those who held conceptual differentiation to be a sign of linguistic maturity. However, the knowledge we have of this kind of comparative linguistics does not suggest an evolutionary scale from low to high differentiation. In any comparison of two languages (A and B) there seem always to be ranges of experience more differentiated in A than in B and other ranges more differentiated in B than in A. The Laplander names far more kinds of snow; the Wintu names more varieties of cattle; the Indians of Brazil more kinds of parrots and palm trees than does the speaker of English.

Let us take the most familiar example of this kind of semantic difference and try to determine what psychological conclusions are justified. Whorf (241) notes that the Eskimo lexicon uses three words to distinguish three varieties of snow for which English does not have three single-word equivalents. We should use *snow* for all three. Does this mean that the Eskimo sees differences and similarities among snows that we are unable to see?

There is evidence to indicate that the speaker of English *can* classify snows as the Eskimo does. If we listen to the talk of small boys it is clear that they pay attention to at least two kinds of snow —the *good packing* and the *bad packing*. Whorf himself must have been able to see snow as the Eskimos do since his article describes and pictures the referents for the words.

It seems always to be possible to "name" a category that falls within our experience though we may not have a word for the category. Whorf calls the Hopi category that includes aviator, butterfly, and airplane the "flying class minus birds." Dorothy Lee speaks of one of the Wintu cattle-classes as the "speckled white and gray class." Hockett (94) translates the northern Mandarin Chinese "*gwǒ*" as "fruits-and-nuts." Murdock (167) has studied kinship terminology in 250 societies; he notes that the English word "aunt" applies to four distinct biological relationships. We don't have separate words for these while some other languages do. The absence of words is not the same as the absence of names. Murdock calls the four relationships "father's sister," "mother's sister," "father's brother's wife," and "mother's brother's wife." In all our examples of denotational discrepancy, it is not correct to say that one language has names for distinctions which another language cannot or does not name. It is always possible to name the categories in both languages so long as the nonlinguistic experiences are familiar. Since members of both linguistic communities are able to make differential response at the same points, we must conclude that both are able to see the differences in question. This seems to leave us with the conclusion that the world views of the two linguistic communities do not differ in this regard.

Although three kinds of snow, four kinds of aunt, and unlimited varieties of cattle can be named in English as in Eskimo or Wintu, the English names are phrases rather than single words. Zipf (260) has shown that there exists a tendency in Peiping Chinese, Plautine Latin, and American and British English for the length of a word to be negatively correlated with its frequency of usage. This is true whether word length is measured in phonemes or syllables. It is not difficult to find examples of this relationship in English. New inventions are usually given long names of Greek or Latin derivation, but as the products become widely known and frequently mentioned in conversation the linguistic community finds short tags for them. The *automobile* becomes the *car* and *television* shrinks first to *video* and eventually to *T.V.* Three-dimensional movies are predictably called *3-D*. In France *cinématograph* has dwindled to *cinéma* and, at last, to *ciné*. Within a linguistic subculture, words having a high frequency in local usage may abbreviate though in the larger community they remain unaltered. At Harvard, *psychology* is *psych.*, *social relations* is *soc. rel.*, and *humanities 2* is *hum. 2*. For the readers of American psychological journals *subjects* are *S's* and *experimenters* are *X's*. We shall speak of categories having single word names as more *codable* than categories named with a phrase.

Doob (58) has suggested that Zipf's Law bears on Whorf's

thesis. Suppose we generalize the finding beyond Zipf's formulation and propose that the length of a verbal expression (*codability*) provides an index of its frequency in speech, and that this, in turn, is an index of the frequency with which the relevant judgments of difference and equivalence are made. If this is true, it would follow that the Eskimo distinguishes his three kinds of snow more often than Americans do. Such conclusions are, of course, supported by extralinguistic cultural analysis, which reveals the importance of snow in the Eskimo's life, of palm trees and parrots to Brazilian Indians, cattle to the Wintu, and automobiles to the American.

I will go further and propose that a perceptual category that is frequently utilized is more *available* than one less frequently utilized. When the Eskimo steps from his igloo in the morning I expect him to see the snow as falling into one or another of his single-word-named categories. For the American who is only able to name these categories with a phrase (low codability) I do not expect such ready categorization of snows. If, however, the American were subjected to a discrimination learning experiment, if he were studying the Eskimo language, or if the perceptual structure were otherwise made worth his while, he could see snow as the Eskimo does. It is proposed, really, that categories with shorter names (higher codability) are nearer the top of the cognitive deck—more likely to be used in ordinary perception, more available for expectancies and inventions.

I expect to find the same relationship between category codability and availability within one language as in comparisons of two languages. Within one language one can compare the codability of a single category for different speakers. Suppose I point out a number of different dogs at the "Dog Show" and ask someone to tell me what he would call this class of dogs. One person may say "a breed with reddish fuzzy hair" and another may say "chows." This category is more codable for the second person and I should suppose that the classifying principle involved is more available to him. If both individuals had seen the same dog bite someone, I think that the man who says *chows* would be more likely to store the experience as something to be expected of chow dogs than would the man who must name this category with a phrase like *reddish, fuzzy haired dogs*. Many other things equal, the presence in someone's vocabulary of a one-word name for a category instead of a phrase name should indicate a superior cognitive availability of the classifying principle involved. The man who identified certain clouds as *cirrus* should be more likely to form expectancies involving this type of cloud than the man who calls them *wispy, horse-tail clouds*. The man who readily identifies a set of faces as *Jews* should be more prone to form expectancies about Jews than the man who names the same array *a lot of people, most of them are rather dark, quite a few are wearing button-down shirt collars*. One way to operationalize availability is in terms of the readiness to use a principle of categorization in forming an expectancy. This readiness can be discovered without recourse to linguistic behavior by observing the generalization of an expectancy to new instances. The man who has the word *chow* when he has seen a chow bite someone avoids members of this breed. The man who does not have the word *chow* but has seen the same dog bite someone steers clear of unlicensed dogs, or sleeping dogs, or all dogs.

The codability variable needs to be expanded in two directions. In the first place, the length of a name need not be the only index of codability. When the name is a phrase I expect subjects to hesitate before naming, to disagree among themselves on the name, and to be inconsistent from one occasion to another. When the name is a single word I expect subjects to respond quickly, in perfect accord with one another, and consistently from time to time. These expectations have been checked and the result will shortly be described. Secondly, the notion of codability can be applied to particular stimuli as well as to categories. Category codability involves the naming of a collection or class of particular stimuli. When category codability is low it has been suggested that the principle of classification is relatively unfamiliar or unavailable. Particular stimuli might also be named and a codability score assigned to each stimulus. How should the two codabilities be related to one another? We will explore these extensions of codability with reference to color perception and color terminology.

Sensory psychologists have described the world of color with a solid, using three psychological dimensions: hue, brightness, and saturation. The color solid is divisible into millions of just noticeable differences. The largest collection of English color names runs to less than 4,000 entries (152), and of these only eight occur very commonly. Evidently there is categorization of colors among speakers of English. It seems likely that all human beings with healthy visual apparatus will be able to make much the same set of discriminations. This ability is probably standard equipment for the species. Whatever individual differences do exist I do not expect to be related to culture, linguistic or nonlinguistic. This is not to say that people everywhere either see or think of the color world in the same way. Cultural differences probably operate on the level of categorization rather than controlled laboratory discrimination.

Explorations in the "Human Relations Area Files" turn up many reports of differences on this level. Seroshevskii (203), for instance, has reported that in the Iakuti language there is a single word for both green and blue. This makes the kind of denotational discrepancy with English that we have been describing. A region of experience is lexically differentiated in one culture but undifferentiated in another. If Iakuti informants were asked to name the range of colors that we call *blue* they could only do so by circumlocution, having no single word for that particular array of colors. When we are asked to name the large group of colors called by a single word "X" in Iakuti we must resort to *the blues and the greens* —a phrase rather than a word. It is presumed that these differences of codability locate differences of cognitive availability.

Suppose, now, that the task is changed and subjects speaking English and Iakuti, respectively, are asked to name individual color chips rather than classes. Let them be asked to give the usual name for each color—not feeling it necessary to give a distinctive name to each. English speaking subjects ought to find some hues that are unequivocally *blue* and others that are unequivocally *green*. These should be named promptly, with a single word and with perfect accord among subjects. They would be the stimuli having highest codability. Such stimuli will be centrally located in the categories called by the names *blue* and *green*. There would be other colors which speakers of English would name hesitantly and with disagreement from one another—some calling them *green* and some *blue*, while many would create such phrases as *greenish-blue* or *bluish-green* or *a mixture of green and blue*, or *half green and half blue*. Such low codability stimuli will be peripheral to the categories named by the single-word names which are included among the names accorded the stimuli. Concretely, for the present case, the stimuli will be peripheral to the *blue* and *green* categories; *blue* and *green* being the only single-word names assigned the stimuli. The stimuli of low codability may be central to certain other categories. They may be good instances of the category *bluish-green*. However, this category has a lower availability for the society in question than the more codable categories *blue* and *green*.

Iakuti speakers asked to name the same stimuli ought to behave somewhat differently. Their region of highest codability ought to correspond to a region of low codability for English speakers. The blue greens could be central to a highly available category for the Iakuti. They would be peripheral to available categories for English speakers and central to unavailable categories.

Some of this guesswork was put to test by Brown and Lenneberg in their "A Study in Language and Cognition" (25). The entire series of Munsell colors for the highest level of saturation ("chroma" as Munsell calls it) was shown to ten judges who were asked to map out the respective regions they would call by the names *red, orange, yellow, green, blue, purple, pink,* and *brown*. These are the color names that occur most frequently in English. The judges were also asked to select within each region a single color chip constituting the best instance of the color in question. There was very high agreement among the judges on the mapping of the color areas and also in the eight ideal instances. The eight chips most commonly selected constituted the core of a list of twenty-four test colors. The remaining sixteen chips were selected so that the total twenty-four might provide as even a coverage as possible of the color space.

The twenty-four test colors were shown to a subject one at a time. He was instructed to name the color as he would if describing it to a friend. The experimenters recorded the subject's reaction time (from exposure of the color to pronunciation of a name) and also his response. There were twenty-four subjects—all Harvard and Radcliffe students, all with normal color vision, and all speaking English as their native language.

Five measures were taken: (a) The average length of naming response to each color was obtained by counting syllables. (b) The average length was also obtained by counting words. (c) The average reaction time for each color. (d) An index of the degree to which subjects agreed with one another in naming each color. (e) An index of the degree to which subjects agreed with themselves in naming each color on two occasions.

The intercorrelations among these measures were all in the direction we anticipated when considering the possibility that codability might be measured by a variety of indices. Most of the correlations were significant, with .355 being the lowest. Colors that evoked long names (whether measured in phonemes or syllables) were named with hesitation, with disagreement from one subject to another, and with inconsistency on the part of a single subject from one occasion to another. The social norm with regard to a particular color is revealed by the data on agreement among subjects. Where there is no clear norm for naming, the disagreement within the community is matched in the behavior of a single subject by inconsistent naming from one time to another. The conflicting habits in the community may be presumed to exist within the subject and it is this internal conflict that causes a delay in reaction. These data provide excellent illustration of the interiorization of social norms.

The correlation matrix yielded a single general factor which Brown and Lenneberg called *codability*. The fourth index, the degree of agreement between subjects, had by far the largest factor loading and is therefore suggested as the best measure of codability. For interlinguistic comparisons the name-length index will serve so long as it is a matter of contrasting a phrase with a single word. When a better measure is practicable, and where the contrast involves single words on both sides or phrases on both sides, the agreement index is to be preferred. When it is a question of comparing the codability of the same category for different individuals in one linguistic community the index must be either length of name or reaction time; it cannot be agreement.

Examining the color maps of the original ten judges, Brown and Lenneberg found that the particular chips of highest codability occupied spatially central positions within the regions named by the eight color words. The chips of highest codability were in fact the ideal instances of these eight categories. Colors of lowest codability always fell within an area transitional between two regions. They occupied the anticipated peripheral loci. *Centrality* and *peripherality* of position within a category can be given a neat visual representation in the case of color since the dimensions of this region of experience are known. It is not so clear how to plot a category like chair because we are not sure of the defining attributes of this category. In one direction chairs probably shade off into couches and, in another direction, into tables. Centrality will always mean a position defined by the optimal values of the attributes determining category membership, while peripherality will mean any falling away from these values. It is proposed (with support from color categories) that central stimuli will be highly codable and peripheral stimuli less codable.

These thoughts are offered as blueprints for a set of psychological laws relating category codability to category availability and stimulus codability to category centrality. The laws are expected to hold for comparisons of different regions of experience within one linguistic community, for comparisons of different individuals from the same community for the same region of experience, and also for comparison of the same region of experience in different linguistic communities. The proposals are couched in a form that makes intercultural validity possible. They predict a relationship between variables that are defined so as to apply to any society.

A summary, then, of the so-called case of a name and the lack of a name. To begin with, this case proves to be better described as that of a short name and a long name. Length of name, in turn, yields to a dimension of codability defined by length of name, to be sure, but also by agreement and quickness in naming. Finally, it is proposed that more codable categories of experience are also more available and that more codable stimuli are centrally located in available categories.

Cases of Unlike Etymology

Paired terms from different languages with considerable but imperfect overlap in reference are very common. It sometimes happens with such pairs that the area of noncoincidence has a special status, representing older usage than the area of overlap. In such cases we speak of equivalent terms having unlike etymologies.

Hockett (94) reports that in northern Mandarin Chinese the

word for (railroad) train is *Hwoché* and that the Chinese word
analyzes etymologically into *fire* (*Hwo*) *cart* (*ché*). Our term *railroad train* has the same primary denotational range but its constituent morphemes have a totally different prior semantic from
those contained in *Hwoché*. It is conceivable that Chinese and
American thoughts about trains concentrate on different attributes
in accordance with the distinct etymologies of the names, the
Chinese seeing the steam and occasional flames, the American
noticing the tracks and the succession of cars. No such psychological conclusion is required by the linguistic difference. It is
quite possible that the words *train* and *Hwoché* are effectively cut
away from their semantic origins so that, in their primary use, they
are psychological equivalents. Hockett brings forward a nice piece
of evidence for this view. *Electric train* in Chinese is *dyànli-hwoché*
where *dyànli* means electric power. The electric train has no fire-
spitting engine. The new use of *hwoché* suggests that its etymology,
its secondary semantic, is psychologically dead. The most probable
conclusion is that the secondary semantic was once alive to guide
the construction of the new word or the extension of the old word
but that frequent usage has linked the word with its primary
semantic content and cut it free of its origins. If this be true, words
from different languages with similar denotational range but unlike
etymologies would once have marked a psychological difference
between societies but would do so no longer.

In discussing the American, and indeed, "Standard Average
European" conception of time, Whorf (245) provides a somewhat
different case of etymological differences. In the European languages it is customary to discuss time and also intensity and
tendency in words borrowed from the description of space. In
English we speak of *long* and *short* intervals of time, of *high* and
low intensity, of a tendency to *rise* or *fall*. In Hopi, time has a
vocabulary of its own—not used in spatial description. The older
senses, the spatial senses of such words as *long, short, high, low,
rise,* and *fall* are still very much alive. The temporal forms are not
compounds or modifications of the older forms (as *hwoché* is of
hwo and *ché*). Identical forms operate, at the same time, in two
spheres of experience. May it not be the case that our European
understanding of time is spatialized as the Hopi's is not?

Whorf has constructed an English paragraph to show how

ubiquitous the language of visual space is in our discussion of psychological as well as temporal matters.

> I grasp the 'thread' of another's arguments, but if its 'level' is 'over my head' my attention may 'wander' and 'lose touch' with the 'drift' of it, so that when he 'comes' to his 'point' we differ 'widely,' our 'views' being indeed so 'far apart' that the 'things' he says 'appear' much too arbitrary, or even a 'lot' of nonsense. (p. 146)

Such a paragraph does suggest a visualization of argument even as *large* and *small* suggest a spatialization of time and *high* and *low* a spatialization of intensity. The conclusion is not certain. It would be possible to use the same terms in several areas with a kind of psychological isolation so that what one understands by time is not infected with an understanding of space. Working with the same basic language, philosophers have forged varying notions of time and intensity. On the other hand, it is conceivable that the Hopi transfer spatial notions to time and intensity and psychology but do not transfer vocabulary. The matter cannot be decided with linguistic data alone. Extralinguistic psychological data are needed. Are Europeans, for instance, more prone than the Hopi to image time, to draw pictures of the Old Year or of Christmas Past? Are they more prone to image the course of an argument, the pattern of thought? Such questions are susceptible of empirical study. Whorf's comparisons, in this area, argue that such study will be rewarding.

Differences of Form Class

The words or morphemes of any language can be collected into classes of grammatical equivalents; these are called form classes.*
The best known form classes for English are the parts of speech. Nouns are words we use in some positions in word sequences but which we should never use in other positions where verbs are required (68). In French, nouns can be further subdivided into gender form classes. Nouns acceptable in the sentence frame: *Le* ————— *est bon* are not acceptable in the frame, *La* ————— *est bonne*. In Navaho there are more than twenty form classes for

---

*See Chapter I.

words naming different kinds of objects. Words of a given class are only found in sequences where the verb has the proper ending.

So long as form classes are defined in purely syntactical terms they do not suggest important cognitive differences for speakers of different languages. That suggestion appears when we add the semantic correlates of the classes. The native speaker of English is likely to think of the parts of speech in semantic terms. Nouns name substances; verbs name processes; and adjectives name qualities. In Hopi Whorf reports that the parts of speech nearest our verb-noun categories divide neatly into words naming short-term events and words naming long-term events. Both *spark* and *spasm* would have to be Hopi verbs. The genders are usually called masculine, feminine, and neuter and these are semantic characterizations. The object classes of Navaho are usually described as words naming round objects, words naming long thin objects, words naming granular substances, etc. The linguistic determinists in anthropology believe that the semantic character of the form classes fixes the fundamental conception of reality in a language community and that differences on this level correspond to different Weltanschauungen.

At the same time the science of descriptive linguistics refuses to define its word classes in semantic terms. Fries (68) has shown that for the English parts of speech such definitions are always either unclear or overextended. No one has been able to provide clear semantic definitions that will serve to distinguish every English noun from every verb, adjective, and adverb. It is notoriously true that the "masculine" and "feminine" genders include names for objects having no sex. Nor can these classes be made semantically consistent through an appeal to the sexual symbolism of the inanimate world. Languages disagree on the genders of moon, box, hat, and the like. In Navaho, too, the object classes do not show perfect semantic consistency. The word for news falls in the round object class and this is difficult to understand in a society lacking rolled up morning newspapers. In short, the semantic definitions of the form classes ignore many exceptions and are unsuitable for the purposes of linguistic science. However, the layman may operate in this area as in so many others with probabilistic as well as invariable attributes. The existence of a correlation, though it is less than perfect, between grammatical functions and semantic attributes would surely be discovered by native speakers if it could be of any use to them.

If words are to be used to refer it is obviously necessary to learn the referent categories and so there is a sense in which lexicon determines cognition* and inferences about cognition can be based on lexicon. It is much less clear how the formal practices of a language, the grammatical rules, can affect cognition. Yet it is just the grammatical differences, especially those of form class, that are most striking and it is their determining force which the anthropologist has stressed. The fact that a speaker observes the syntactical rules that place words in form classes does not alone constitute proof that he detects the semantic correlates of the form classes. The difference in the implications of referential and syntactical observances can be illustrated by imagining a simple game (and not a very entertaining one) that is a model for these aspects of language function.

There are ten different wooden counters in this imaginary game which are to be understood as utterances that make reference—like *dog* or *house* or *Ralph Jones*. There are ten different musical chords sounded on the piano and these are the referents of the ten counters. The rules of reference for the game are quite simple. When the tutor strikes a chord on the piano the player of the game is to name that chord by presenting the appropriate counter. This is like the situation in which a parent asks a child to name correctly dogs, cats, horses, and cows and it is also like the training procedure Itard used with Victor, described in the Introduction. In our simpler game it is clear that in order to play according to the rules one must be able to identify each of the ten musical chords and also to remember the counters that name them. There is a sense in which the game determines the player's cognition. It poses a set of problems in auditory recognition. In similar fashion the lexicon of a language poses a set of cognitive problems and differences of lexicon correspond to different cognitive problems. If we undertake to play the game that contains names for forty varieties of snow we undertake to learn to distinguish those forty varieties.

Now we add a syntactic rule to our game. The tutor will sound two chords and the player must present two counters to name them.

---

*See Chapter VI.

There is to be a rule of sequence for presentation of these counters. They are divided into two form classes, A and B, with five counters in each class. Counters of class A must always be presented before counters of class B, regardless of the sequence in which their referent chords have been sounded. The tutor will not judge a "reply" to be correct unless this rule of sequence is observed.

In order to be like the important form classes of natural languages, our classes A and B must have a semantic correlate. We might arrange things so that all counters of class A name chords in the minor mode while all counters of class B name chords in the major mode. If this were the case the classes could be defined in semantic terms quite as unequivocally as in syntactic terms. Class A would be the minor mode class as truly as the class of words that must precede words in class B. However, to make the analogy with natural languages exact, we shall give classes A and B a semantic correlate that is short of perfection. Four of the counters in A will refer to chords in the minor mode while one will refer to a chord of the major mode. Class B is the mirror image of A. There are now semantic features more probable in one form class than another but not perfectly predictable from the form class.

The player of the game is required to name each combination of two chords with the proper two counters in proper sequence. He could learn by rote the "reply" to each pair of chords and be completely unaware of major and minor modes. He could be aware of the two form classes, A and B, and not aware of their semantic. The fact that someone plays such a game according to the rules of the game is not evidence that he operates with the cognitive categories major and minor mode. And so it is in natural languages. One can make proper use of nouns without thinking of them as the names of substances. Gender can be an automatic appurtenance of nouns and need not suggest sexual categories. Grammatical rules do not compel the discovery of semantic correlates of grammatical classes and those anthropologists who move from grammar description to psychological conclusions move too quickly.

For someone learning our simple game, however, it would be useful to notice the semantic correlates of classes A and B. If he is told or discovers that counters of class A usually name chords in the minor mode then, for example, whenever he hears a minor chord he will know that its name is more likely to be a counter of class A than of class B. The semantic of the form classes cannot tell him exactly which counter to select and it will even occasionally happen that he will be led to select a counter from the wrong class since the semantic correlation is imperfect. Still, discovery of the semantics of form classes is potentially an aid to language learning, its usefulness increasing with the consistency of the semantic-formal correlation. Suppose these correlations were higher in the vocabulary of children than they are in the larger vocabulary of adults. We might, then, as children attend to the semantics of the form classes since this would aid us in learning the language.

For several months I sat in on the sessions of the Harvard Pre-School.* There were eight children in each class; two of the classes were limited to children between four and five years while a third class accepted those between three and four. As an observer, I sat on the side lines and let the Pre-School life swirl about me, recording verbatim all the conversation I could hear. From these records, I made vocabulary lists classified into the parts of speech. It was my impression, on examining this vocabulary that the nouns and verbs of children were more nearly consistent with the usual semantic definitions than are the nouns and verbs of adults. Nouns commonly heard were *truck, blocks,* and *teacher.* The non thing-like nouns were uncommon. There were no uses of *thought* or *virtue* or *attitude.* These observations suggested that as the form classes grow larger they decline in semantic consistency. Perhaps children develop firm, and temporarily reliable, notions about the semantics of nouns and verbs. These notions may stay with them as adults even though they retain only a probabilistic truth. It is even possible that such first semantic conceptions affect the formation of new meanings. When the word *justice* comes into one's vocabulary it comes as a noun and may, as a consequence, be endowed with thing-like attributes borrowed from blocks and trucks. It would then be quite natural to make statues and paintings of justice.

To compare the character of adult and child vocabularies I examined the first thousand most frequent words from the Thorn-

---

*This description of an experiment is adapted from "Linguistic Determinism and the Part of Speech," by R. W. Brown (24) with the permission of *The Journal of Abnormal and Social Psychology.*

dike-Lorge (225) list of adult usage and also the first thousand most frequent words from the Rinsland (194) list of the vocabulary of children in the first grade. The Rinsland list is based on 4,630 pages of conversation plus more than a thousand letters and stories. The Rinsland list is much the same as lists compiled independently by the Child Study Committee of the Kindergarten Union (37) and by Ernest Horn (96) for the 24th Yearbook of the National Society for the Study of Education.

The first set of contrasts deals with two reduced lists: nouns found among the first thousand for adults but not for children compared with nouns among the first thousand for children but not for adults. The set of nouns having clearest "thing" character would seem to be those that are called "concrete" and it is a commonplace to describe the language of children as more concrete than that of adults. One sense of the pair "concrete-abstract" is the same as "subordinate-superordinate." The more abstract term, the superordinate, includes in its denotation the denotation of the concrete or subordinate term but extends beyond it. Superordinate-subordinate relations between the two lists were all in one direction. The adult list included *action, article, body, experience,* and at least seven others which were superordinate to many words on the children's list. There were no nouns on the children's list superordinate to those on the adult list.

The concrete noun with the smaller denotation is likely to be more picturable than its superordinate and picturability is another common sense of "concrete." Of course the concrete noun, like the abstract, names a category rather than a particular instance. However, some categories have a more or less characteristic visual contour and size while others do not. Visual contour is a criterial attribute for *table* but not for *thing* or *experience.* Of the adult list 16 per cent named categories having a characteristic visual contour while 67 per cent of the children's nouns were of this kind. Nouns like *apple, barn,* and *airplane* name categories for which size is a criterial attribute while nouns like *affair, amount,* and *action* do not. On the adult list 39 per cent of the nouns were of the former kind while 83 per cent of the children's nouns had size implications. It appears that children's nouns are more likely to be concrete (in the sense of naming narrow categories with characteristic visual contour and size) than are the nouns of adults. As the number of nouns increases the semantic of the noun seems to become less consistently thing-like.

I also compared two lists of verbs, those among the first thousand for adults but not for children and those among the first thousand for children but not for adults. The question here was the percentage of verbs naming animal (including human) movement. Of the adult verbs 33 per cent were of this kind while 67 per cent of the children's verbs named actions. The common notion that verbs name actions seems to be truer for the vocabulary of children than for the vocabulary of adults.

These studies of word lists confirmed my impression that the nouns and verbs used by children have more consistent semantic implications than those used by adults. It remained a question as to whether children are, in any sense, aware of these implications. Adults often try to convey the sense of a word by speaking it in the presence of the object or event named. All such single namings are ambiguous. The adult who says "water" while looking at a glass of water may cause a child to attend to the glass itself as a container, to the glass as a transparent material, to the liquid character of its contents, to the height of the liquid, to the state of containment, and so on. Selection of the nonlinguistic attributes that govern proper denotative use of the word *water* cannot be guaranteed by a single naming. Repeated pointings can, of course, establish the invariant circumstances governing use of the word. If there were nothing to suggest to the child the probably relevant features of the nonlinguistic world, discovery of linguistic meanings would be a very laborious affair. However, a new word is ordinarily introduced in a way that makes its part-of-speech membership clear: "Look at the dog" or "See him running." If a part of speech has reliable semantic implications it could call attention to the kind of attribute likely to belong to the meaning of the word. A child who had absorbed the semantics of the noun and verb would know the first time he heard the word *dog* that it was likely to refer to an object having characteristic size and shape whereas *running* would be likely to name some animal motion. The part-of-speech membership of the new word could operate as a filter selecting for attention probably relevant features of the nonlinguistic world. It seemed to me that one could learn whether children experience any such filtering of attributes by introducing to them newly invented words assigned to one or another part of speech and then inquiring about the references the words seemed to make.

In the children's speech I had recorded, nouns and verbs were given proper grammatical treatment. In addition the children made correct use of a subclass of nouns—the mass nouns. These are words like *dirt, snow, milk,* and *rice* which are given different grammatical treatment from such particular nouns as *barn, house,* and *dog.* While we say *a barn,* for instance, we do not ordinarily speak of *a rice* but rather of *some rice.* The semantic difference between these two classes of noun is suggested by the designations "mass" and "particular." Mass nouns usually name extended substances having no characteristic size or shape while particular nouns name objects having size and shape. There are, of course, cases in which this semantic-formal parallel is not preserved. It would seem, for instance, that we ought to speak of *some martini* as we do of *some milk* or *some orange juice.* Instead, of course, we say *a martini* but, perhaps, that is because martinis regularly come in the following shape: Y Many nouns can function in either a mass or particular way with attendant shifts in the speaker's view of the referent. *Some cake* is a chunk of a mass while *some cakes* are either cupcakes or layer cakes arranged in a row. Many words in the vocabulary of psychology have this double potentiality. Although the personologist deplores such usage, the layman speaks of someone having *a lot of personality* or *very little temperament.* The professional insists that personality is not an undifferentiated substance of which one can have more or less. Personalities are like cupcakes—all of a size and one to a customer—with only their frostings to make them unique.

In the speech of the pre-school children *milk* and *orange juice* and *dirt* were the most common mass nouns. These were always given correct grammatical treatment. No one said *a milk* or *some dirts.* I decided to work with three functional classes; the particular noun, the mass noun, and the verb.

The experiment involved three sets of four pictures each. One of these sets will be described in detail. The first picture in the set shows a pair of hands performing a kneading sort of motion, with a mass of red confetti-like material which is piled into and overflowing a blue and white striped container that is round and low in shape. The important features of the picture are the kneading action, the red mass, and the blue and white round container. The motion would ordinarily be named with a verb (like *kneading*), the mass with a mass noun (like *confetti*), and the container with a particular noun (like *container*). It was assumed that children would have no readily available names for any of these conceptions. Each of the remaining three pictures of this set exactly reproduced one of the three salient features of the first picture, either the motion, the mass, or the container. In order to represent the motion a second time it was necessary to show also a mass and a container. However, the mass was here painted yellow so as not to duplicate the original and the container was of a different size, shape, and color from the original. The other two sets of pictures involved different content but always an action, a mass substance, and a particular object. In one case the first picture showed hands cutting a mass of cloth with a strange tool. In the third set, hands were shown emptying an odd container of a slushy sort of material.

In overview, the following use was to be made of the three sets of pictures. Children were to be shown the first picture in conjunction with a new word identifiable either as a verb, a mass noun, or a particular noun. Then they would be shown the remaining three pictures of the set and asked to point out the one that pictured again what had been named in the first picture. I anticipated that when the new word was a verb they would point to the picture of motion, when it was a particular noun they would point to the container, and when it was a mass noun they would point to the extended substance.

Three word stems were used: *niss, sib,* and *latt.* If the stem was to function as a verb I would begin by asking: "Do you know what it means to sib?" (Children do not always answer "no" as they ought). "In this picture" (first picture of a set) "you can see sibbing. Now show me another picture of sibbing" (presenting other three pictures of the set). If the stem was to function as a particular noun I began: "Do you know what a sib is?" and proceeded in consistent fashion. If the word was to function as a mass noun I began: "Have you ever seen any sib?" and went on accordingly.

Each child saw all three sets of pictures and heard each of the word stems—one of them as a particular noun, one as a mass noun, and one as a verb. The combinations of word stem, part-of-speech membership, picture set, and order of presentation were all ran-

domly varied. There were sixteen children in all, half of them between three and four years, and half between four and five. They
were all acquainted with me by the time the experiment was performed. The procedure was very like the familiar business of looking at a picture book and naming the things seen and was accepted
by the children as a kind of game. The game was always played
with one child at a time.

The quantitative results are very simple. When a new word
was introduced as a verb ten of the sixteen children picked out
the picture of movement. When the word was a particular noun
eleven of sixteen selected the picture of an object and when the
word was a mass noun twelve of sixteen selected the extended
substance. Of the fifteen responses that were not correct four were
simply failures to answer because of some distraction from the
task.

It is well known that children will sometimes do what an adult
wishes in a task of this kind though they do not understand the task
as the adult does. Consequently, I am more persuaded by the qualitative results than by the quantitative. These former leave little
doubt that some children, especially the more verbal and older
ones, were guided by the part-of-speech membership of the new
word. In the first trial with the first child I showed the picture of
cloth being cut by an odd tool and said that there was a *sib* in the
picture. Then went on with: "Can you show me another sib?" and,
while I still fumbled with the other three pictures, my subject
swung around and pointed to the steam valve on the end of the
radiator saying, "There's a sib." The pictured tool looked very like
the steam valve. In another case I showed the picture of confetti-
kneading and said, "There is some latt in this picture," whereupon
my subject said: "The latt is spilling." And it was.

It is an interesting feature of this experiment that children perform better than adults. To an adult it is inconceivable that there
should be something in this simple picture named with a monosyllable like *niss* with which he would not be familiar. The adult
does not believe that this is simply a naming situation. He attributes
some subtle purpose to the experimenter and responds in unexpected ways. The filtering action of names can be observed in
adults but a different sort of picture and name are required. Suppose we have a photograph of several men in shop aprons working

with a complicated and unfamiliar machine. If I tell you that this is a picture of a *ladiocinator* you will expect me to mean the machine, but if I say that the picture shows *ladiocinating* you will look to the process.

Even though form-class semantic is used in the language learning of both children and adults it probably drops from consciousness as language skills become smooth and rapid. There is no need to think of the moon as feminine when one says *"la lune,"* or of charity as a thing, or lightning as an event of brief duration. There is no functional reason to do so, no introspective evidence that one does so, and scarcely enough time in fluent speech for such thought to be possible. However, it does not follow that form-class semantic is inoperative in the accomplished speaker. Like other sorts of meaning it may exist as a disposition. Speakers of Hopi may be prone to think in terms of event-duration when the circumstances are right. They may be more prone to think along these lines than the speaker of English who is placed in like circumstances. Form-class semantic may leave its traces in the nervous system, facilitating thought in some directions, inhibiting thought in other directions. It is not that people are always thinking in terms of gender or substance or round objects, but that they are disposed to think in these terms. The different dispositions should come out in problem solving, poetry writing, painting, and creative thought in general. The effect of form-class semantic cannot be demonstrated with linguistic data alone but requires the study of extralinguistic behavioral data.

Cases of Forced Observation in Grammar

In order to play the naming game—to use words denotatively—one must be able to identify referent categories in the nonlinguistic world. This is a part of the total language game that forces certain observations and, as a consequence, differences of reference are an important clue to the psychology of those who speak the language. On the other hand, no part of the language game forces observation of form class-semantic and, as a consequence, the linguistic data alone have no clear implications for cognitive psychology. We turn now to a kind of grammatical difference that does involve forced observation.

In English we conjugate our verbs into tenses. To name an action is to place it in time as past, present, or future. An English verb must always occur in some tense and it would seem that a sense of time is constantly necessary for the speaking of English. Dorothy Lee (141) tells us that the Wintu verb conjugates for validity rather than time. In naming an action the Wintu must describe his grounds for believing in the action, the evidence for the action. Thus the event—Harry chops wood—can assume the following forms. If Harry is seen to be chopping wood the verb is conjugated for direct visual evidence. If the speaker has been told that Harry is chopping wood, he conjugates the verb for hearsay evidence—the gossip mode. This is the form, interestingly, in which a man speaks of his own drunkenness; presumably because he tells of events known to him by hearsay alone. If Harry regularly chops wood at a given time of day, one conjugates the verb for a lawful, predictable occurrence. There are other validity modes in Wintu but these three are enough to suggest that this verb system forces a different set of observations from that required by the usual European verb system. Whorf (246) has described somewhat similar validity modes for Hopi, while Kluckhohn and Leighton (126) tell us that the Navaho verb must rigorously specify whether an act is in progress or just about to start, or just about to stop, or habitually carried on, or repeatedly carried on. There are, then, a number of things, other than time of occurrence, to say about an action and some of these are more regularly expressed by some people than is time.

In speaking our own language we don't stop, whenever a verb is due, to check the time. A whole story may be in the simple past tense and, once begun, we need not pause to think again about tense. A tense-set will carry us along for sentence after sentence. Still in English speech or writing it is necessary to keep one's chronological bearings, to order events with regard to one another. Our verbs do not force a time observation for every statement but they do require that one who operates with the language should place himself and the objects of his discourse in some sort of temporal relationship. The Wintu and Hopi verbs seem to require, on the other hand, a continuing grasp of the evidence for every statement that is made. It remains to compare the roles of time and validity in these several cultures to see whether the nature of the verb predicts cultural emphasis. Whorf has made a beginning, but his work must be extended and more carefully controlled.

Relativity and a Complex Society

American character is not easily epitomized and neither is American cognition or language. I don't know about the Hopi, the Wintu, and Navaho. It may be that each of these societies is sufficiently homogeneous to justify discussion of the Hopi language and the Hopi mind. But in American society, and in modern states generally, there are many minds, many languages, and many cultures.

Consider the contrast between the Eskimo snow vocabulary and the English snow vocabulary. In English, the case has been put, we can express with a phrase, distinctions that the Eskimo codes with a word, and it has been proposed that the relevant categories of snow are less available to English speaking persons. Yet within the English speaking community there exists a group accustomed to distinguish many snows and having, among themselves, a well developed lexicon for the naming of these distinctions. Skiers know the meaning of *powder* and *slush* and *crust*. Their categories may not exactly duplicate those of the Eskimo but the skier's snow world competes in differentiation with that of the Eskimo. Substantive conclusions drawn for the English speaking community, as a whole, do not apply to skiers. However, the general principles worked out for category availability and codability do apply. Since they are concerned with snow, skiers make more distinctions than the rest of us and since they often speak of these distinctions among themselves, the names for them have abbreviated, in accordance with Zipf's Law, to single words.

Most of the cognitive and linguistic oddities turned up by Whorf and others can be found in some segment of our complex society. Cattle breeders recognize and name many kinds of cattle. Experts on kinship terminology know all the kinds of aunts there are. And Murdock, writing for other social scientists, abbreviates *father's sister* to *fasi* and *father's brother's wife* to *fabrwi*. Botanists do not stop with the large category *palm trees,* and ornithologists are not satisfied to speak of *parrots.* We have subcommunities for whom particular regions of experience are more differentiated than they are for the majority and, within these subcommunities, there is a special lexicon to meet special cognitive needs.

With the aid of some suggestions made by John Fischer (65) in his doctoral dissertation we can formulate some likely hypotheses with regard to these subcommunities. A society that distinguishes many roles will have many groups possessing special concerns not shared by the rest of society. If only the young go to battle only the young men will have a passionate interest in the details of weapons, combat techniques, and war ceremonials. To make fine distinctions in these areas of life will have a life-preserving importance for them but for the rest of society such distinctions can only be an avocation. It amazes us all when a policeman knows about first *folios* and second *quartos* in Shakespeare publication, or when a Shakespeare scholar knows about *muggers* and *bennies.* Our society differentiates into many roles, each having special concerns and a special vocabulary. To the degree that a group is socially homogeneous, with the same concerns shared by all, the same vocabulary should be shared by all.

Werner (240) and many others have pointed to the lack of a generic term *snow* among the Laplanders who have, however, many terms for kinds of snow. It is likewise true that the Guarani with all their palm trees and parrots lack generic terms like our *palm tree* and *parrot.* These frequently reported absences of the generic term have suggested to Werner and Goldstein (77), among others, that the primitive mind has not developed the capacity for abstractions to as great a degree as we have.* It seems more likely that the generic term is missing where every member of a society is so directly concerned with a region of experience that no one can afford to speak in clumsy and undifferentiated fashion of the region as a whole. To the majority in our society, a palm tree is a palm tree and snow is snow. Finer distinctions are left to specialists who care about such things. Within the same large language we have elaborate vocabularies for subgroups and generic terms for the group-as-a-whole who can afford to lump together what the spe-

_____
See Chapter VIII.

cialist must differentiate. Snows matter to all Laplanders and parrots to all Brazilian Indians. There is no one to stand outside and create the generic term. It is proposed, in short, that a more differentiated society will tend to develop both specific and generic terms for a given region of experience because the two kinds of terms correspond to the viewpoints of the insider and the outsider.

It can be charged against the above view that speakers of European languages who develop new special concerns always create the generic term as well as the detailed vocabulary. Shannon and Weaver (205), in their book on the mathematical theory of communication, give us "bits" and "redundancy" and "transition probabilities" but also "information theory" which embraces their subject and puts it on a level with other kinds of theory. They are specialists who need fine distinctions. Why should they coin a word that will serve outsiders as a tag for a vaguely comprehended realm of knowledge? In a society as differentiated as ours each man plays multiple roles, and develops agility in moving from one to another. Shannon and Weaver are not only information theorists; they are also mathematicians and scholars. Working in a new area they must see it from both the inside and the outside and make the linguistic inventions appropriate to both positions.

In the area of the grammatically forced observation, too, one can find in subgroups of our society parallels to the majority practice in other societies. Consider the validity modes of the Wintu verb and the concern they reveal with the evidence for an event. In the professional publications of scholars there is at least as great a concern with evidence and this concern finds linguistic expression—though not in the method of conjugating verbs. One can recognize a scholarly treatise by what someone (W. H. Auden, I think) has called the blueberries sprinkled through the text. After each statement, a name and year, to indicate the source or, perhaps, just a number to identify the source in a bibliography. Scholars work almost entirely within the hearsay or gossip mode but they cannot stop with the simple statement "I am told that Boswell never really liked Johnson"; they must go on to report who told them and when and sometimes who told the person who told them.

In the social sciences there is also great concern with evidence and an equally compulsory linguistic expression. One cannot simply report that 51 per cent of Catholics showed no fear of Communists in America while 48 per cent of Protestants showed no fear. One must say whether the difference is "significant." One cannot simply report that the stories told by a group of subjects contained aggression; one must specify the symptoms of aggression and the reliability with which these symptoms can be judged. We conjugate our verbs with "t" ratios and reliability coefficients. In this case, at least, the linguistic practice reveals a habitual mode of thought.

Linguistic relativity must take account of social complexity. It will not suffice to contrast the cognitive practices of one nation with those of another. We are likely to find that a manner of perceiving, thinking, and speaking that characterizes the majority in one society is found in only a minority of another society. When we know the psychology of children, of psychotics, of bureaucrats, of creative artists I shall be very much surprised if there will not be some segment of our society to match whatever strange cognitive modes the ethnolinguist may turn up.

Culture Area and Language Area

The doctrines of linguistic relativity and determinism would seem to be embarrassed by the imperfect geographic correspondence of culture areas and language areas. One would suppose that the cognitive categories held by all members of a society would comprise its culture, and if these categories are caused by the structure of the language then language and culture areas ought to coincide. There is, of course, some correspondence between the two but it is far from perfect. The Finnish people who are generally well assimilated to European culture speak a Finno-Ugric tongue unrelated to most other European languages. The Hopi and Hopi-Tewan share a general Puebloan culture but speak very different languages. How can these cases of noncorrespondence be reconciled with the doctrines of linguistic relativity and determinism?

To begin with, culture is not exhausted by shared cognitive categories. Culture, according to Kluckhohn and Kelly (125), includes "all those historically created designs for living, explicit and implicit, rational, irrational and non-rational, which exist at any time as potential guides for the behavior of man." These designs for living include values, ways of obtaining food and shelter, marriage practices, etc. Many of these are not cognitive categories likely to be determined by language. The assignment of a society to a culture area need not depend on the cognitive characteristics which are likely to be linked closely with language. There is room enough in the concept of culture for the possibility that the Finnish people are in certain cognitive respects (related to their language) unlike other Europeans and room for the possibility that the Hopi and Hopi-Tewan are cognitively unlike, though assigned to a common culture.

Secondly, and more importantly, the criteria for establishing family relationships among languages are not the aspects of language that seem likely to have the strongest determining effect on cognition. Considerations of phonology—particular phonemic repertories—enter into the determination of language kinship but are probably not indicative of any important cognitive differences. The distinctions between isolating, agglutinative, flexional, analytic, synthetic, and polysynthetic languages are important to the definition of language families but of doubtful significance for general cognition. In short, culture is not exhaustively defined by shared cognitive categories and language is not exhaustively defined by the features likely to be most directly related to cognition. Consequently criteria are available for the definition of culture areas and language areas that will result in imperfect correspondence of the two.

Whorf did not extend his thesis to a comparison of cognitive modes among the European peoples. He put all their languages together under the term Standard Average European and assumed them to have one "mind" and one culture. Certainly there are no differences within Standard Average European to equal the contrast of Hopi and English. Probably, however, there are smaller differences in cognition which go with the smaller differences in language. Everyone knows that the German's *Schadenfreude* has no single word equivalent in English and that the English *home* has no single word equivalent in French. These are differences of lexicon that may have cognitive significance. A more common sort of lexical difference is one of imperfect coincidence of partially overlapping terms. The German *Vaterland* is much like the American *fatherland*. The two words may have identical referents. If, however, we extend our notion of semantics to include all the contexts in which a word may be used—all the things said of it, all the adjectives applied to it, all the emotional slogans in which it appears—it will be clear that *Vaterland* and *fatherland* are not identical. Neither are *father* and *Vater* or *mother* and *mère*. A full description of the meaning of any one of these words would involve a description of the greater part of the culture to which the word belongs. Ruth Benedict (13) has actually presented the Japanese culture by attempting to give the full meanings of a few Japanese words. The Japanese equivalent of *elder brother,* for example, is partially identical with our term, but a full definition involves a description of Japanese law and family life.

When the notion of semantics is expanded in this way the correspondence between language and culture will improve. But this will be a truistic correspondence. For language, in the full, is nothing less than an inventory of all the ideas, interests, and occupations that take up the attention of the community. In this extended sense, the study of language cannot be distinguished from the general study of culture.

Relativity and Determinism in General

How stands the case for relativity and determinism? There cannot be a single answer because these terms do not name a single thesis. In general, linguistic relativity holds that where there are differences of language there will also be differences of thought, that language and thought covary. Determinism goes beyond this to require that the prior existence of some language pattern is either necessary or sufficient to produce some thought pattern. To evaluate any form of either thesis it is necessary to distinguish operationally between the language and thought in question.

There is a weak form of the relativity thesis that is very well established. In this case "language" is a formal system, a phonology, a morphology, and a grammar. "Thought" is a set of cognitive categories manifest in the discriminating use of names. The thesis that language (as phonology, etc.,) and thought (as selective linguistic response) covary is established if it is shown that formally distinct languages are also semantically distinct. Whorf and others have presented ample evidence that this is true on the level of the lexicon, of the form class and of certain grammatical categories. I have suggested that differences in the semantics of form classes are not alone evidence for differences in cognitive categories as differences in the referents of names are. However, there is reason to believe that such linguistic differences do correspond to cognitive differences in speakers of the language. It is useful in learning a language to detect the semantics of form classes and it has been shown that some American children learning English do so. The weak form of linguistic relativity serves to overthrow the notion that all languages code the same categories.

There is another form of undoubted covariation; the words and referents of a child correspond to the words and referents of his parents. Surely there is also a kind of determinism here since the linguistic behavior of the parent exists before that of the child. The "thought" of the child is, here, his referent categories as these are revealed in naming behavior. The "language" of the parent is the use of linguistic forms to mark out referent categories. It cannot be said that the language of the parents is the cause of the formation of referent categories in the child. The difficulty is that the referents that are distinguished by name are also distinguished by many other kinds of adult behavior. Cats are called *cat* and dogs *dog* but, in addition, the former are fed milk while the latter get bones. The referent categories revealed by the child in his naming behavior could have been learned from the nonlinguistic discriminating behavior of his parents. In the natural case linguistic behavior and other kinds of cultural behavior are always confounded and so the fact of cognitive socialization does not prove that the linguistic behavior of parents causes children to form the categories their speech reveals. Children might attach the name after the category has been learned from nonlinguistic parental response.

In Chapter VI certain properties of linguistic response have been brought forward which make it a more economical guide to the categories of a culture than is any other kind of response. This may mean that linguistic response is the preferred means for acquiring parental categories. It cannot be maintained that the language of parents is either a necessary or sufficient cause of the categories that develop in the thought of a child. The most that can be said at this juncture is that we can see how the language could fit into a matrix of factors so as to produce the categories of the child. It is possible to weave a plausible account of cognitive socialization in which the language of adults figures importantly.

A more exciting form of the relativity thesis would define "language" so as to include semantics and define "thought" in terms of some nonlinguistic behavior. In general, the thesis here would be that some nonlinguistic evidence of thought covaries with some linguistic evidence. For example, it might be maintained that making statues of justice goes with the membership of the word for this concept in a form class that has generally the "object" or "thing" semantic. The relativity thesis could then be checked by looking at the statues and form classes of social groups and of individuals. If an attempt is made to go beyond relativity to determinism we see at once that there are two possible kinds of chronological priority the linguistic form might have—either historical or biographical. One could see whether the linguistic practice preceded the making of statues in the history of a group and one could see whether knowledge of the linguistic practice came before the inclination to make a statue in the life of the individual. Very few independent definitions of language and thought, which are of the sort required by this kind of relativity and determinism, have been offered. An attempt was made in this chapter to provide multiple indices of a linguistic variable (codability) and to indicate general methods for assessing a thought variable (availability). The proposed relationships between these variables have some empirical support but nothing like adequate proof. I don't know of any attempts as yet to show that an independently defined linguistic pattern has either historical or biographical priority over the thought pattern it is supposed to determine. While this more ambitious form of relativity and determinism seems to be what many anthropologists have in mind they have scarcely taken the first steps toward demonstrating it.

Summary

Two things are well established. Languages differ in the referent categories they name and code grammatically as well as in such formal characteristics as phonology, morphology, and syntax. The referent categories that children learn to name and code grammatically vary with the categories used by their parents. That parental semantic rules determine the semantic rules of a child is not certain but is very probable. To what degree does nonlinguistic behavior (the formation of expectancies, problem solving, invention, and art) vary with the rules of reference for a language? It has been suggested that the more codable a category, the more available it will be for general psychological use. This kind of connection between language and thought has not yet been proved.

chapter viii Progressions
and Pathologies

T HE WORDS "concrete" and "abstract" are regularly used in five different fields of language study. Animals are said to function in a more concrete way than human beings. Children are said to have a more concrete mentality than adults. In the history of linguistic change abstract meanings are said to grow out of concrete meanings. Individuals suffering impairment of language function as a consequence of brain injury (aphasics) are said to be unable to adopt an abstract attitude; to function always in a concrete manner. Finally, the cognitive processes of schizophrenics have been called more concrete than the normal. This ubiquitous terminology suggests that there may be here a really grand generalization—nothing less than a law of linguistic progression and pathology.

There are three progressions: the evolution of the species from animal to man, the historical development of contemporary languages, and the recurrent transformation of children into adults. The early stages of all three progressions have been called concrete and their later stages abstract. If even this much be true we have a psychological equivalent of biology's famous: "Ontogeny recapitulates phylogeny." The psychological development of the individual duplicates stages in the development of his species.

The generalization implied by these literatures has still greater scope. Both aphasia and schizophrenia have been called psychological regressions. The aphasic has lost brain tissue. This loss presumably carries with it some acquired psychological functions and so returns the victim to an earlier developmental stage. Freud classified schizophrenia (he called it *dementia praecox*) as a narcissistic neurosis. This means that the schizophrenic's libido is concentrated on himself; he has none available for object cathexis. In a Freudian metaphor the schizophrenic is like an amoeba that sends out no pseudopodia. Its substance cannot be teased out from its center. Freud believed that the infant libido was also narcissistic and, consequently, that the schizophrenic was regressed to infancy. Since the cognitive processes of both aphasic and schizophrenic have been called concrete the total picture is consistent. Psychological and linguistic development are from the concrete to the abstract and regressive illness returns the human adult to the more primitive level.

I cannot pin the full span of this proposal on any single author. Part of it is contained in Locke's *An Essay Concerning Human Understanding* where he distinguishes man from beast and civilized man from primitive man by their powers of abstraction. G. Stanley Hall (82) specifically suggested that "Ontogeny recapitulates phylogeny" is as true for psychology as for biology. Heinz Werner (240) uses the concrete-abstract dimension to point up developmental parallels between children, primitives, aphasics, and schizophrenics but shies away from a strict recapitulation theory. I cannot recall that Kurt Goldstein (77) includes the early history of languages under his rubric of concrete function but he certainly includes all the rest. The words "concrete" and "abstract" have been used so as to imply the vast generalization I have stated. Most people, whether psychologists or not, subscribe to at least part of the generalization. It is well established in the popular mind that abstraction is a lofty cognitive process.

You will not be surprised to hear that the words central to this thesis, "concrete" and "abstract," have not always been understood in the same way and that the thesis is, on that account, of uncertain

truth and even uncertain meaning. It is not my purpose to make a
stale exposé of polysemy in the language of psychology. Instead I
plan to take one sense of "concrete-abstract," the clearest sense,
I believe, and one that is congruent with more usage than is any
other single sense, and examine the thesis as so defined.

A superordinate category is more abstract than its subordinate.
The subordinate is more concrete. The following categories are
listed in abstract to concrete order: living things, animals, vertebrates, primates, men, American men, Ralph Jones a particular
American. Each of these categories is superordinate to all of those
that follow it. One category is superordinate to another when it
includes the other and extends beyond it. When the categories are
named we will say that the more abstract name includes in its
extension all less abstract names but extends beyond any of them.
The attributes criterial for a more abstract category will always
also be criterial for the less abstract category. The attributes defining men in general also help to define Americans and the particular
Ralph Jones. Some attributes that are noisy for the more abstract
category must be criterial for the less abstract category. Nationality
varies for men-in-general but is defining of Americans. Within a
hierarchy of categories, then, as we move from the more abstract
to the more concrete the categories have smaller extensions and
more elaborate intensions.

Defined as subordination-superordination, concrete and abstract
are relative judgments that can only be applied within a hierarchy
of categories. The definition provides no method for deciding on
the relative abstractness of two categories not related to one another as subordinate and superordinate. The only absolute of
abstraction for which it provides is the all inclusive category—
everything, or perhaps the Universe. The only absolute of concreteness is the unique space-time point. Everything in between
is either concrete or abstract according as it is contrasted with a
superordinate or a subordinate. As we shall see, many authors have
used concrete and abstract as an absolute dichotomy applicable to
all categories whether or not these are in the same hierarchy. These
definitions can be shown to grow out of the relative sense we have
described.

The Three Progressions

The origin of the species and the history of language are chronologically continuous. In the beginning was the one-celled animal, then the mobile metazoa, the land dweller, the mammal, primate, and man—man at first without speech and finally speaking man. The discontinuities in this span are methodological. For a tiny fraction of the whole, the most recent period, there are written records. But the records begin some time after man began to speak, probably long after. The comparative philologist has a plausible method for reconstructing the languages of immediate pre-history from relations between the most ancient recorded languages, but the greater part of pre-history belongs to archaeology. From tools and potsherds and tombs much can be guessed about the economics of remote millennia and a little about social systems but nothing whatever of language and thought (38). Of course there are today a few societies whose economic life is of the Old Stone Age. It has sometimes been assumed that the languages of such societies reveal the character of language in the European Stone Age of 200,000 years ago but this is an untrustworthy assumption. Except for the last few thousand years the story of the development of speech and thought belongs to comparative zoology rather than the anthropological sciences.

Our expectation is that we shall find an increasing talent for abstraction in the phyletic scale. When man began to develop speech he ought to have had abstractive powers roughly on a par with the other primates. It may be that the pre-literate languages of today contain abstractions intermediate between those of which the great apes are capable and those to be found in the earliest languages known to philology. In the history of language, finally, we should discover that vocabulary grows increasingly abstract. If the historical developments were conceived to be a consequence of evolutionary changes in the species they ought to be very slight in comparison with the phyletic changes since the time span is comparatively short. It may be, however, that the development from concrete to abstract thought is greatly accelerated once language begins. From that point on we are dealing with a cultural evolution in which one generation builds on another even though there may be very little alteration in the inherited character of the species. Finally the development of the individual from child to adult is expected to recapitulate this progress. We will consider first the phyletic progression, then the historical, and finally the individual.

The Phyletic Progression. It has been said of the animals below the primate level that they function in an absolutely concrete fashion. According to our understanding of concrete this would mean that the animal reacts to all aspects of each unique situation. It can be said at once that this is false.

The unlearned reactions of very simple creatures are "released" by specifiable stimuli. The stimulus pretty well guarantees the reaction regardless of the concomitants of the stimulus. A male wasp for instance will attempt to copulate with a piece of paper on which a female wasp has been crushed. Copulation is not a reaction triggered by a particular wasp nor even by the female of the species. It is released by a certain odor wherever the odor is found. The odor defines the category of circumstances able to elicit the copulation response. There is no concern at all for the character of the unique object.

The male stickleback assumes its fighting posture when confronted with another male stickleback. Even this description indicates that the reaction is categorical, elicited by the class of males not by a particular rival stickleback. Experiment has shown that the category is even wider than we have indicated. The naturalist who said the stickleback reacts to the presence of another male stickleback appears to have been describing his own rather than the stickleback mind. For the fish will make the same response to wooden decoys having little resemblance to the stickleback or any other kind of fish so long as the decoy is marked with a blob of red paint resembling the red mark on the undersurface of the male stickleback. This creature's nervous system is wired to react to a releasing stimulus that ordinarily defines the class of his natural enemies. However, he will react in the same way to any other object manifesting the critical stigma.

There is an astonishing disregard of the unique object in the animal world, a rather bloodcurdling categorical equivalence in which one egg or one mate or one enemy will do as well as another. We are reminded of man in a race riot where one Negro will do as well as another or of man in heat where one woman will do as well as another.

The learned behavior of animals is just as categorical as their innate behavior. The simplest form of learning, one found at practically all phyletic levels, is classical conditioning in which a response (or response component) transfers from one stimulus to another. The conditioned stimulus (CS) is an abstraction from the total situation. It is the attribute defining the class of circumstances that predicts the unconditioned stimulus (UCS). There are certain features of the situation—perhaps the lighting in the room—which are always the same. The light is on whether the UCS is about to appear or not and so the light is a non-criterial silent attribute of the situations preceding the UCS. There are certain changing conditions—the level of extraneous sound, the postures of the experimenter—whose changes do not correlate with the onset of the UCS. Since the sound level attending the UCS varies this is a noisy but non-criterial attribute. The defining attribute of situations preceding the UCS is the CS. When a dog has learned to salivate to the sound of a buzzer he demonstrates that he has acquired the category "situations-preceding-UCS" by extending his response to new instances of that category. Classical conditioning is an achievement in abstraction, in learning to react to one stimulus regardless of its concomitants.

Actually the abstraction goes beyond this point. If the conditioned animal is presented with other stimuli similar to the CS he will extend his CR to these stimuli without further training. That fact suggests that he is not reacting to a particular buzzer but to an attribute of the buzzer which is found also in other stimuli. Lashley and Wade (137) say, "A definite attribute of the stimulus is abstracted and forms the basis of reaction; other attributes are either not sensed at all or are disregarded. So long as the effective attribute is present, the reaction is elicited as an all or none function of that attribute." The attribute abstracted from a conditioning experience can be such as to define a very general category. "In the early stages of conditioning any change in the environment may elicit the avoiding reaction. Even with human subjects, conditioned to the sound of a bell, the senior author has obtained the conditioned reaction without further training from the sound of a buzzer, of breaking glass, of clapping hands, from a flash of light, from pressure or prick on arm or face. The only dimension common to such stimuli is that all produce a sudden change in the environment."

It is very clearly the character of animal mind to abstract, whether these abstractions are built into the species or acquired in a conditioning experience. Possibly the very abstract categories are more difficult for animals on the lower phyletic levels but there is no good evidence that this is the case. We do not, for instance, have data on the ease of acquisition at various phyletic levels of such categories as 1) a particular equilateral triangle, 2) equilateral triangles, and 3) triangles. To be sure, the primates have acquired some very abstract categories that lower animals are not known to have acquired. Weinstein (238) has trained a rhesus monkey to select the object that matches the color of a sample object shown to him. Robinson (196) has trained chimpanzees to select the odd object of three shown to him. Others have trained chimpanzees to select the object of intermediate size, to distinguish triangles from circles, and even to match objects with their respective black and white line drawings (91). We do not know that animals below the primate would be unable to form such categories; in general they have not been given the opportunity and so it remains to be demonstrated that the level of abstraction to which an animal can attain is a function of phyletic position.

The Historical Progression. "The surface study of semantic change indicates that refined and abstract meanings largely grow out of more concrete meanings." This statement is from Bloomfield's *Language* (21), and its like can be found in most of the great works on the theory of language and comparative philology. This is a "surface" generalization because it requires considerable explication and qualification to make it clear and true. We will begin by eliminating several erroneous interpretations of this kind of statement.

It is not true, for instance, that all words or even the majority of words increase their generality of application. Vendryes (231) guesses that restriction of meaning is a more common historical change. A familiar example of restriction occurs in the etymology of the word *meat.* This term once named all manner of food, as in the phrase *meat and drink,* but it has come to have the restricted sense of flesh-food. Narrowing of extension is probably at least as common as widening, in linguistic change.

It is not true that the earliest known linguistic forms were proper names, the most concrete form known to us. F. Max Müller (166) defined a linguistic root as "whatever cannot be reduced to a simpler form." The roots have no known etymologies. They are a minimal set of primitive forms from which all other words can be derived and, for most languages and even language families, they number only a few hundred. The roots of Sanskrit were worked out by the ancient Sanskrit grammarians. The roots of Hebrew and Chinese and other languages have been worked out in modern times. In addition, philologists have reconstructed the roots of the presumed prehistoric ancestor of all the Indo-European languages. There are, of course, no Indo-European documents. The roots are abstractions from comparative study of many languages but especially Sanskrit, Greek, and Latin. Müller argued that they are more than an academic abstraction. "If then it is admitted that every inflective language passed through a radical and an agglutinative stage it seems to follow that at one time or other the constituent elements of inflectional languages, namely, the roots were to all intents and purposes, real words and used as such both in thought and speech." The premise of this argument—that inflectional languages must have passed through radical and agglutinative stages—cannot be granted today and so the conclusion is quite doubtful. However they may have functioned, these ancient roots qualify as the oldest forms of which we know anything. The meanings that have been worked out for them are not ultimately concrete. They seem to be predicates of a middling level of abstraction; such forms as *sar* (*to go*), *nad* (*to shout*), *angh* (*to choke*), and *yu* (*to join*).

The earliest known forms are probably extremely remote from the origins of speech and it may be that forms earlier than those we know were more concrete. History only goes back a few thousand years but speech itself may go back 300,000 or so. Vendryes says of the students of linguistic history: "Yet however far back they pursue their inquiries, they always find themselves dealing with highly developed languages possessing a past of which we know nothing. The notion that the reconstruction of the original language might be arrived at by a comparison of existing languages is chimerical, and though it may have been played with by the founders of comparative grammar, it has long since been abandoned." Linguistic history then cannot tell us the character of the earliest meaningful forms. Is there any other way to find out what they may have been like?

The languages of pre-literate or uncivilized peoples have often been interpreted as though they were fossilized pre-historic systems. In fact, of course, these languages have long, though largely unknown, histories. It is certain that the pre-literate languages are not primitive but it is probable that the people speaking these languages are nearer the primitive way of life than are the members of modern civilized states. Pre-literacy, narrow geographic range, the absence of industry, etc., must all have been characteristic of primitive societies. The modern languages of people living in societies of this kind may have something in common with actually primitive speech. But the pre-literate languages of today are not much alike. Some of them have as many grammatical complexities as Sanskrit; some are as simple as Chinese. What have pre-literate languages in common that might conceivably be a primitive trait?

Lévy-Bruhl (143), summarizing the reports of many travelers, says of the primitive mind: "It is a mentality which makes little use of abstraction and even that in a different method from a mind under the sway of logical thought, it has not the same concepts at command." Werner (240) drawing on many of the same sources reaches similar conclusions: "The more primitive the society the less interest there is in the generic name. Names are, above all, individual names." Vendryes (231), though more critical of the evidence, accepts this general conclusion of the languages of uncivilized peoples: "They abound, therefore, in concrete and special categories, and are thus strongly contrasted with our cultivated tongues where these have almost vanished, and in which there is an increasing tendency toward purely abstract and general categories." The evidence on which all of these authors build is typified by the following report. The Bakairi of Brazil are said to have names for many particular kinds of parrot but no generic term corresponding to our *parrot*. In general one language or another is reported to lack some generic term commonly found in western European languages or to habitually make some fine distinction that we usually overlook.

It is extremely difficult to tell whether there really is a partiality for the concrete in pre-literate languages. Many of the sources are untrustworthy. They include reports of missionaries and travelers, some of whose statements about phonology and grammar and religion and sex roles are demonstrably false or culture-bound. It seems unlikely that their semantic observations would be more reliable. One can easily imagine that the generic term may simply not have been elicited in conversation with a particular informant. Reporting could easily be selective. A few missing generic terms might be noticed and the field worker might overlook generic terms found in the uncivilized language and not found in his own. We have no word for fruit-and-nuts or for the slaying-of-a-son or for blue-and-green. All of these are found in one or another language. A really detailed comparison might show no over-all differences in the number of abstract terms but rather a difference of pattern, of the realms of experience covered by such terms. The number of field workers who agree that uncivilized languages are concrete is impressive but this agreement could derive from sources other than the data. For centuries it has been a tenet of European psychology that primitive minds are not given to abstraction and most travelers would be alert to find confirming evidence. When all these doubts are expressed I still conclude that pre-literate languages have fewer abstract terms than do the languages of civilized peoples and that this is likely also to have been true of primitive languages. This conclusion rests, in part, on theoretical considerations which are set forth at a later point in this chapter.

Now we must find our way back to Bloomfield's statement and try to make clear just what truth there is in it. We have discarded the notion that words invariably grow more abstract in meaning and have found no proof that the earliest words were the names of particular things. We are inclined to believe that primitive languages lacked words at a very high level of generality since pre-literate languages are reported to be deficient in such terms. It may be that there is a class of abstractions never found in the early history of a language and always named by terms that originally had a more concrete sense. I believe this is what Bloomfield intends to say. However, the exact definition of this class of abstractions is not easily found.

In part this class seems to be characterizable as words that are very nearly all-inclusive. They are either the absolute abstractions of *totality*, of the *Universe*, or only a step or two below that level. In 1952 I had the pleasure of hearing several lectures by Eric Havelock, the Harvard classical scholar, in which he proposed that the development of Homeric Greek into Socratic Greek was a progress from the concrete to the abstract. He described, for instance, the evolution of the concept of *cosmos*. The word originally named such things as a woman's headdress or the trappings of a horse's harness, generally a decorative moving cluster. It began the ascent toward abstraction in two different ways; by being applied adverbially in the sense of "decoratively" and by being stretched a little so as to identify the ranks of an army. In this latter use it came close to the sense *order* but was still restricted to particular picturable circumstances. The Ionian thinkers stretched it still farther to identify some over-all "world" they wished to talk about. They approached close to the concept of a (physical) order. These steps in abstraction did not involve neologism. Rather an existing word was placed in an enlarged context which generalized the application of the word. The word did not reach the ultimate of abstraction so long as it was *an* order, so long as there could be more than one. When it became *the* order it became single, total, all-inclusive, and could go no farther. Words of this order (Havelock mentioned also the Greek equivalents of *one, whole, all, quality* and *kind*) are not reported to be among the primitive roots of any language, are not common in pre-literate languages, and in Greek, at least, are known to have evolved from more concrete notions.

Bloomfield meant to include more than these ultimate abstractions in the class of late developing concepts. It will help us to grasp this class if we examine several distinguished antecedents of the Bloomfield statement. In *An Essay Concerning Human Understanding* (149) Locke wrote: ". . . *to imagine, apprehend, comprehend, adhere, conceive, instil, disgust, disturbance, tranquillity,* etc., are all words taken from the operations of sensible things and applied to certain modes of thinking." Müller (166), commenting on Locke's claims wrote: "All roots, i.e., all the material elements of language, are expressive of sensuous impressions, and of sensuous impressions only; and as all words, even the most abstract and sublime, are derived from roots, comparative philology fully confirms the conclusions arrived at by Locke." Finally, Whitney (243) has written: ". . . the whole body of our intellectual, moral, and abstract vocabulary; every word and phrase of which this is composed, if we are able to trace its history back to the beginning, can be shown to have signified originally something concrete and apprehensible by the senses. . . ." The claim is that a class of words variously characterized as sublime, intellectual, and moral has derived from another class of words characterized as concrete, sensible, sensuous, and apprehensible. This class of late developing abstractions appears roughly to be the vocabulary of folk psychology—*to comprehend, to adhere, to believe, the personality, thought,* and *emotion.* These are not ultimate abstractions. It is not clear that they have larger extensions than such roots as *to go* or *to join.* They are rather a special class of abstractions that seem to be slow to develop.

To the authors we have quoted, psychological abstractions are the antithesis of that which is sensible or apprehensible. Locke, we know, distinguished between ideas that arise from sensation and those that arise from reflection on the working of one's own mind. We may suppose that the other authors we have cited also believed that there were two kinds of knowledge; that gained by training exteroceptors on the real world and that gained by introspection. It is conventionally assumed, and may even be true, that a word like *understanding* names some distinctive mental state available only to the person who understands. It is not clear why such introspective quale should be more difficult to separate out than green and red and sweet and sour. However, if psychological terms had an exclusively introspective reference each of us would be able to use them to speak of himself alone. No one could challenge another's use nor would there be any shared use. Each man's employment of the terms would be exclusive of every other man's. I could speak of understanding where no one else could—concerning myself—but I could not speak of understanding where others could—concerning themselves.

In fact, of course, our psychological terms are confidently applied to others. I can say: "He understands but *he* does not." This vocabulary must then have reference to the behavior of others. However, most behavioral categories do not appear to have any invariant sensible attributes. Happiness is not always revealed in a smile. Understanding does not always cause people to "light up" and say, "Aha!" As behavior, the categories that we call psychological appear to be disjunctive and therefore, difficult to acquire. If understanding is this or that or the other kind of behavior then the category must be learned as a list of unrelated entities. It may be, of course, that these varying behaviors have a common mental correlate—the experience of understanding. Even if this is so the equivalence of the various behaviors of others could not be known until one had behaved in all those ways oneself and experienced understanding in each case. Some psychological terms probably name behavior categories having some common attribute but this is never a color or an odor or a visual contour. It is more likely to be some kind of relation that would be very difficult to see if it were not suggested by the concrete origins of the word. Consider the notion of adherence. A liquid that adheres to a surface sticks close to the surface and appears to resist efforts to dislodge it. A man who adheres to his beliefs persists in speaking and acting in a certain way and resists efforts to change him. Probably this relationship is not a very obvious or available abstraction. To make things even more difficult psychological terms are usually dispositional in character. A man who is described as dishonest is not necessarily breaking the law at that moment. He is rather categorized as a person who will break laws and rules under certain kinds of presently unrealized conditions. Dispositional concepts like honest, intelligent, and friendly involve not only enormously varied behavior but also a memory for what the referent person has done in various circumstances. In sum, there are many reasons why psychological categories should be late acquisitions phyletically, historically, and in the life of the individual.

Why should these psychological categories be called abstract? What has psychology in common with superordination? Consider the hierarchy: particular equilateral triangle A, equilateral triangles, triangles, and polygons. As we move to the superordinates the categories become less sensible in any single instance of the category. The more subordinate categories have more defining attributes and so more that one pictures is essential to the category. In a picture of a particular triangle every attribute counts and it can be truly said that the category is "sensible." Equilateral triangles must all have three equal sides and so this attribute of the category can be represented in a particular picture. Equilateral triangles vary in size, position, and color and so the values of these attributes represented in any particular picture should not be looked for in the category as a whole. Much that is sensed in any given instance is not characteristic of the category as a whole and so the category is less picturable than the particular triangle. As the number of noisy attributes increases (and this number increases as the categories move toward superordination) the possibility of representing the whole category in a particular instance declines. Within a hierarchy, then, picturability decreases with increasing abstraction. It is not surprising then that philologists have chosen to call "abstract" certain categories that are very difficult to represent. In the case of the psychological categories this unpicturability does not derive from the size of the extension. It is rather because any instance of honesty or understanding on which one can train his exteroceptors will contain little or nothing that is characteristic of the category. If there is a defining attribute it is not available to the exteroceptors. As behavior, which *is* available to the exteroceptors, these categories are so varied that it is doubtful whether anything characteristic of the entire category can be experienced in a single instance.

The Individual Progression. The vocabulary of pre-school children in the United States is less abstract than the vocabulary of adults. In studies comparing the most commonly used words in these two vocabularies it was found that the adult list contained more superordinates.* It included words like *article* and *action* which were not used by children. There were many more picturable words on the children's list, i.e., words naming categories having a characteristic visual contour. Without having made any controlled comparisons most adults are aware of this difference. The young child is likely to say *car* or *truck* but not *vehicle;* he will know *dog* and *man* and *bird* but not *mammal* or *quadruped.* Where he does use a very abstract term like *animal* or *flower* he does not usually possess the full category but only applies the terms to some restricted subclass of the whole.

Studies of free association also show the child to be relatively deficient in superordinate terms. Woodrow and Lowell (252) administered the Kent-Rosanoff list of stimulus words to 1,000 children. The responses of the children were classified and com-

---

*See Chapter VII.

pared to those of adults. In general, adult associations move within categorical hierarchies moving to subordinate, superordinate, or coordinate terms. *Dog* might elicit *cat* or *poodle* or *animal*. Children more commonly produce contiguous associations, i.e., they name something that is often experienced along with the first thing named. To *dog* a child might say *ball* or, perhaps, *tail*. Most directly relevant to our present concern, children produce fewer superordinates than do adults.

Vocabulary growth in children does show a progression from concrete to abstract, from smaller and more picturable categories to the wider, less picturable categories and to the psychological categories. Is this because the child can only function concretely or are there other causes? It can be said with confidence that children, like all other animals, characteristically abstract from the total situation. They do not show absolutely concrete behavior and, in fact, seem disposed to the formation of broad categories.

The child's conception of quantity as it is revealed in Piaget's beautiful studies (181) illustrates the kind of abstraction possessed by very young children (about three and a half). The experimenter ranged side by side two tumblers filled with water to exactly the same height and asked his young subjects whether the tumblers contained equal amounts or, if not, which one contained more. Under these circumstances even the youngest answered correctly. Then, while the child watched, Piaget poured the water from one tumbler into a container of different shape, narrower and taller. In this new container the water rose to a greater height than the water in the remaining tumbler. The child was asked whether the amounts of water were still equal. Now the younger children usually answered that they were not equal. Some thought there was more water in the new container. Piaget decided that such children were judging quantity by the height of the water in the container quite without reference to the size of the container. Other children thought there was more water in the tumbler and they seemed to be judging quantity by the size of the container without reference to the height of the liquid in the container. Older children and adults judge liquid quantity by taking account of both container size and the degree to which the container is filled. The vocabulary of liquid quantity has reference for us to a relationship between these two variables. Very young children attend to one or the other of the two but not to both. It is not difficult to understand how this misunderstanding could develop. The vocabulary of quantity is likely to be introduced with simplified comparisons where one of the variables is constant. With a set of glasses all the same size *more, less,* and *equal* are directly tied to the height of the contained fluid. With a set of canisters varying in size but all filled to the top, quantity varies with the volume of the container. Moving outside these simplified situations, the child, at first, makes an inappropriate extension of his semantic rule and has to learn to take account of two variables at once. He can also solve the problem, of course, by grasping the reversibility of the pouring process. Having seen water poured from one container to another we should know that the quantity had not changed because the process could be reversed restoring the original situation. For the very young child pouring seems to be an irreversible process altering the quantity of the fluid.

These fascinating observations from Piaget illustrate several important things about the categories of children. The words *equal amounts* name, for some children, a class of liquids rising to the same height in whatever container. This is clearly an abstraction. It is different from the abstraction that governs adult use of *equal amounts* but not subordinate to that abstraction. Finally, the abstraction the children possess is a function of the training adults have given them as much as it is a function of the child's abstracting ability. The vocabulary of children and their understanding of that vocabulary is largely determined by adult notions of the kinds of words and meanings that children are able to grasp. To see the natural tendencies of the child mind it is instructive to recall what they do with words of their own invention and with conventional words to which they give their own meanings.

There are many diaries reporting the day by day acquisition of language by particular children. It appears from these reports that the words invented by children do not name particular situations nor even, usually, narrow classes of situations. They are likely to generalize very widely. Wilhelm Stern's (217) son Gunther used "psee" for leaves, trees, and flowers (very near our notion of vegetation). Gunther used "bebau" to name all animals. Lombroso (150) tells of a child who used "qua qua" for both duck and water and "afta" for drinking glass, the contents of such a glass, and a pane of glass. When a conventional word is introduced to a child he commonly generalizes it at once. His usage is often incorrect but scarcely concrete. Jespersen (118) tells of a nephew who, when he saw a picture of a priest, was told the word *priest*. The little boy promptly applied the word to his aunt who happened to be wearing a collar rather like the priest's. He seems to have abstracted one characteristic from the picture and generalized the word to everyone possessing that characteristic.

The child, like the animal, habitually abstracts and there is no evidence that either abstracts less widely than the civilized adult. There is evidence that primitive man had a less abstract vocabulary than civilized man, and this suggests that primitive man is not to be grouped with child and animal. However, there is also evidence that children have less abstract vocabularies than civilized adults so, perhaps, we need to distinguish between the vocabulary possessed and the abstracting potential of the mind. We will now try to resolve these inconsistencies.

The Resolution. If the primitive mind (phyletically, historically, or individually) is concrete it must be a mind that can discern the unique qualities of every situation. The assumption is that discrimination is primitive and that one must learn to overlook differences, to *abstract from* unique situations so as to categorize them together. All the evidence on animals, primitives, and children argues that one might better make the opposite assumption. Mind begins with an absence of differentiation. Of course this is not a complete absence. Probably there are some distinctions made by all children and most animals. The difference between light and darkness may be one of these, and the difference between a loud noise and near silence may be another. Furthermore, each animal seems to have unlearned discriminations which are peculiar to its species. Barnyard fowl, for instance, distinguish a short-necked hawk-like shadow from a long-necked goose-like shadow. Doubtless the availability of various perceptual distinctions is a function of the animal's physical state and the situation in which he finds himself as well as his species membership. For a hungry dog odors may be prepotent. An accidental visual fixation may cause a child to notice one portion of a visual contour rather than another. I will assume that children and animals and adults do not usually detect all of the differences they are potentially able to detect. Instead they notice only one or a few features of most situations and so store their experience in categories. They do not place themselves in unique situation A but rather in a situation of type A.

These first categorizations operate with the attributes most available to the animal or child. A rat may notice the horizontal baseline in a triangle and so generalize its jumping response to all figures having such a baseline rather than to all triangles. A small boy may notice the collar on a priest and so generalize the word *priest* to all persons wearing such collars. The discrimination of additional features can be produced in either case with the proper corrective training. Eventually we learn to make a great many discriminations because they are all important to the gratification of our needs. The ability to appreciate a situation in its unique concreteness is a late development, a product of much learning, rather than the primitive state of mind. Even when we are able to appreciate many features of a situation we ordinarily remember it in terms of some categorical membership since it is only as category instances that situations recur. Categories are the terms of our expectancies.*

Abstraction is held to be a function of all minds—whether primitive or advanced. In one sense the primitive mind may be more abstract than the mind of the civilized adult since it makes fewer distinctions and has larger equivalence classes. How then shall we account for the relative lack of superordinate terms in primitive and child?

It is reasonable to suppose that the first attempts at language endured and developed because they aided the survival of the individual and the group. The predicate roots of Indo-European could have been used to elicit cooperative effort from others or to command others to act in some necessary way. The oldest concrete nouns could have been used to apprise others of something known only to the speaker, who may have been a lookout or a hunter, and so to enable others to act in the light of such knowledge. With a highly abstract verb one could instruct others to *act* or perhaps to *move* or *behave*. With highly abstract nouns one could tell the others that a *thing* was coming or that an *article* or *object* was to be found nearby. There is a sense in which such superordinate

---

*See Chapter VI.

terms carry less information than such subordinate commands as "Run!" or "Pull" or such announcements as "Tiger!" or "Deer!"

Information theory defines the amount of information carried by an item as a direct function of the number of equally probable alternatives from which it is selected. Where the alternatives are not equally probable the amount of information is an inverse function of the probability of the item. A symbol drawn from thirty equally probable alternatives carries more information than a symbol drawn from twenty such alternatives. It is more informative in the sense that it excludes more alternatives. In this strict sense *Act!* is probably about as informative as *Run,* perhaps a little more so. They are drawn from the same class of possibilities but *Act* is a little less probable. This is a definition of information in terms of empty symbols that takes no account of semantics.

We can, however, frame a semantic definition of information by analogy with the formal definition and when this is done we shall see that *Run* is vastly more informative than *Act.* The command to act is semantically consistent with all of its numerous subordinates; *run, walk, sit, talk, eat, etc.* The reference for *act* embraces the references for all of these subordinate terms. It excludes none of them. The utterance "Run," on the other hand, excludes most of the other subordinate references. It is not consistent with "Walk," "Sit," or "Lie down." As a phonemic sequence "Act" may be slightly more informative than "Run," but as a reference "Run" is vastly more informative. In general, a subordinate term will be semantically more informative than its superordinate. When the words are nouns it is clear that *lion* is more informative than *animal.*

This semantic sense of information may be more consistent than the formal sense with colloquial use of the term. In popular parlance I suppose that a person who has more information is in a better position to act than the person who has less information. This is true with the semantic definition of information. If I know that an animal is coming I hardly know how to prepare. It may be King Kong or a Pekinese. If, however, I hear a shout "Lion" I have some idea what to do. That generic preparedness which is aroused by *animal* might not do at all. Similarly, if I hear the command "Act" I don't know what muscles to contract but "Run" sets my legs going. The more subordinate concrete term has a narrower reference and calls for a more defined action from the auditor.

It seems, therefore, that when language is closely tied to vital needs, when it is an instrument for command, warning, and appeal, its usefulness would be proportional to its concreteness. Probably language is such a vital instrument in uncivilized communities today and was such a vital instrument in primitive communities. The primitive state of vocabulary could be concrete even though the primitive state of mind is not. For while primitive man may have perceived many abstract categories he would not have felt any pressing need to talk about them. A highly abstract vocabulary would only become important when man had gained some freedom from the daily subsistence grind—as the pre-Socratic Greeks had done. It would then be possible for some members of the community to stand back a little and try to understand the world. They might then want to talk about color, tone, quality, force, velocity, vertebrates, and the like. Boas (22) has similarly argued that the shortage of generic terms in the languages of pre-literate peoples does not stem from any impairment of the abstracting capacity and he has supported the argument with important field experiments involving the Indians of Vancouver Island. "After some discussion, I found it perfectly easy to develop the idea of the abstract term in the mind of the Indian, who stated that the word without a possessive pronoun gives good sense, although it is not used idiomatically. I succeeded, for instance, in this manner in isolating the terms for 'love' and 'pity' which ordinarily occur only in possessive forms like, 'his love for him' or 'my pity for you.'" Boas was doing for this Indian language what the pre-Socratic philosophers appear to have done for Greek.

Why should a psychological vocabulary come late? It is possible of course that behavioral attributes are less "available" to human cognition than other kinds of attribute. But this seems a doubtful assumption. Escalona (63) reports that infants empathize with the very subtly expressed food preferences of their nurses. Children in their first year are very sensitive to a cold tone of voice or a gesture of irritation. However, while a cold tone of voice is a behavioral attribute it is not yet a psychological category. *A cold tone of voice* is the name of a sensible attribute. *A cold disposition* is the name of a psychological category having no single reliable sensible attribute. The cold disposition will sometimes be manifest in tone of voice, sometimes in silence, sometimes in physical withdrawal, sometimes in a level unblinking stare, in a failure to smile, etc. The probability that someone will be identified as having such a disposition increases with each symptom but no one symptom is necessary and sufficient. Furthermore, since it is a dispositional category none need be present at the time of the categorization. The disposition may be inferred from remembered past performances. Probably the psychological vocabulary is late to appear because these categories are difficult to form. They are likely to be disjunctive, probabilistic, and dispositional.

Why is the vocabulary of children more concrete than the vocabulary of adults when their minds appear to be strongly disposed to abstraction? The immediate reason is that adults present them with concrete rather than abstract terms. The first procedure that occurs to most parents is to take some manipulable object and name it—*Ball*. The same entity might of course be called *thing* or *object* or *sphere* but the parental preference is for the more concrete name. Or the parent will name some moving figure—*Dog*—or some person who has come to visit—*Mrs. Brown*. A child will often generalize these names very broadly but the parent seldom gives him the correct names for his categories (e.g., *guadruped* and *older ladies*). Instead the child will be corrected in his use of *dog* and *Mrs. Brown* until he has cut back to the proper categories. Parents generally will not try to teach psychological terms. In part this may be because of the difficulty of forming such categories but in part, also, because it is difficult to present contrasts. One can pick up a ball and bat any time but a happy and unhappy person may not always be at hand and certainly will not always manifest the symptoms of their dispositions.

Everything in the world has many names and so when a parent names anything he selects from a number of equally correct alternative. The *ball* is also *a baseball* and even *your brother's newest baseball*. In the superordinate direction it is *a sphere* or *something used in a game* or *an object* or *a thing*. The parental choice usually falls on *ball,* and this is not just because *ball* is a simple monosyllable. I have heard parents name the set *television* and the bottle *vinegar*. There are no monosyllabic names for these articles that are anywhere near so common as the polysyllabic ones.

Why should one name for a thing be more common than another? It seems to me that objects are most commonly assigned to the category that reminds us of the attributes that are important for its most common use. To call a ball an *object* or a *sphere* or a *thing* is entirely too uninformative. To call it a *baseball* is more informative than calling it a *ball* but the longer word is not often necessary because the kind of ball intended can usually be recovered from context. For one thing baseballs and footballs have their distinctive seasons so that *ball* in the summer is baseball and in the fall football. For another thing they are used together with distinctive sets of equipment. If a catcher's mitt is in evidence the *ball* is base; if a helmet and spiked shoes are the uniform the *ball* is *foot*. Still narrower categories are so infrequent as not to be named with a single word. Individual variations in the cleanliness, stitching, and shape of baseballs are irrelevant to the purposes for which we use baseballs and so can go unnamed although of course a phrase name can always be constructed. With persons, on the other hand, individual names are needed because the interaction pattern for each one is somewhat unique. When there is a great status difference as with a slave caste or a captive population and an occupation force the most common name may become generic— *Joe* or *Nigger*. This is possible because one member of a group is treated in much the same way as any other. Patterns of interaction are prescribed for entire groups and so individual differences become irrelevant and need not be named. The suggestion, then, is that each entity is most commonly named so as to categorize it in the way that is most relevant to customary interaction with the entity. These categories will almost never be at the levels of highest abstraction. The common names are the ones children hear first and most often. It takes more time to hear the abstract words frequently enough to learn them.

It has been proposed that children and primitives and animals are all quite able to make high level abstractions and there is no evidence that they are less able to do so than civilized adults. There is evidence that vocabulary progresses from the concrete to the abstract in history and in the development of the individual but this has been attributed to the superior utility of concrete communications rather than to an incapacity for abstraction in primitive minds. Is there nothing at all, then, in the notion that high abstraction is an advanced process?

There is more to the thesis if it is restricted to abstraction with differentiation. The child who uses *bow-wow* to name the class of animals an adult would call *quadrupeds* has not grasped the adult concept. He generalizes from failure to distinguish dogs from cats from cows from horses. The adult classifies all of these as quadrupeds even though he sees their species and even their individual differences. The adult abstracts from many perceived differences to find a common quality. The child happens to notice the common quality in a single exemplar and generalizes where he has not differentiated. The same child who generalizes across the quadruped range may, as an adult, find this concept difficult to form. Similarly, the animal whose conditioned response generalizes to any abrupt stimulus gradient generalizes from failure to differentiate. While high abstractions may be a primitive process when they are accomplished in the absence of differentiation, they may be an advanced process after differentiation.

Think of such a pair of classes as *mammals* and *ants*. These categories are not related to one another as subordinate-superordinate and so, by our original criterion, we cannot say which is the more abstract. I think, however, that most of us feel mammals to be more abstract. Surely this is not because mammals are more numerous (as that is even doubtfully true) but rather because we are aware of more diversity within the mammal category than within the ant category. I could in two minutes time name far more subordinates of the class mammal than of the class ant. With humans, at least, this provides a test of the relative level of abstraction of various categories. It is a criterion that can be employed for categories not in the same hierarchy. It is relative, quantifiable, and geared to the individual though it might also be applied to a language community by sampling the dictionary for subordinates.

It is redundant to say that abstractions of this sort will be acquired later than their subordinates. The abstraction implies the differentiation of subordinates. Before differentiation there can only be the abstraction that is a failure of discrimination. However, there remains an empirical form of the thesis of a concrete-abstract progression. It may be that as one moves from animals to primitive men, children, and civilized adults one finds abstractions of advancing level. The level now is measured by the number of differentiated subordinates rather than by the range of the category.

Perhaps clear phyletic differences will appear in studies of animal behavior when we study abstraction after differentiation. Let the rat be trained to respond differently to triangle A than to triangle B and differently to B than C. Let him then learn to react in one way to all triangles and in another way to all polygons. Experiments of this kind will be laborious but they seem more likely to bear out the notion that abstraction is an exalted process than do present studies of abstraction without differentiation.

The Pathologies

Aphasia. Aphasia is the name for any impairment of language function which is caused by brain injury, created by accidents, tumors, and, especially, by wars. Surprisingly little has been learned about the cerebral localization of language functions from the study of aphasia. This is because natural experiments, the only kind possible with this problem, are not good experiments. The precise extent of the cerebral damage is often unknown. Damage is seldom localized just as it should be in order to answer the experimenter's questions. The language functions of the patient prior to injury have generally not been studied.

Language involves two sets of receptor organs (the ears for hearing speech and the eyes for reading) and two sets of effectors (the vocal apparatus for speaking and the hands for writing). Peripheral injury to these receptors or effectors will impair language function but is not an aphasia. However, many of the difficulties produced by cerebral damage can be classified as either receptive or motor symptoms. As our analysis of language function would lead us to expect, patients are sometimes found who are not only unable to understand language but are unable to perceive it. To perceive language means simply to recognize equivalent sequences and to discriminate distinctive sequences. Language perception is a problem in categorization which is independent of language understanding. We should also expect to find the language apraxias, difficulties with the motor aspect of speech or writing, which are sometimes found in patients who can perceive and understand language. The rudiments of the Original Word Game, described in Chapter VI, were found to be language perception and motor production. These are distinct rudiments because we can see how they might be independently learned. The classical division of aphasic symptoms into receptive and motor varieties confirms the functional independence of the two rudiments. Loss of one does not necessarily entail loss of the other.

There are other aphasias which are neither receptive nor motor but associative. These, too, are no surprise. Amnesic aphasia is impairment of linguistic reference. The patient cannot find the names for objects though he can pronounce these names if they are offered to him. When a patient is unable to name the socks that are pointed out to him he may be able to come up with the word as a completion of the sequence "shoes and . . ." Transition probabilities, the associations between words, are sometimes preserved when the associations to referents are weakened or destroyed. Such patients may be able to recite long overlearned sequences like the alphabet or an entire poem. Granich (79) sometimes helped amnesic patients to "find words" for familiar things by training them on lists of articles of clothing or items of furniture or kinds of food. The amnesic patient, helpless to produce the name for an object, could run through his list and "recognize" the correct word when it came along. There are also patients who are not amnesic, who can name objects, but suffer from agrammatism—an inability to construct proper word sequences. Such patients will sometimes produce a word that has the intended sense for a given position but is not the most probable word for that position. A patient of this kind might say "man and youth" rather than "boy" or, perhaps, "between the devil and the deep blue ocean." Errors of this kind like the symptom of agrammatism suggest a disorder of sequential probabilities. Jakobson (112) believes that aphasics can be divided into two types according to whether they suffer from impairment of associations between name and thing (reference) or impairment of associations between words (transitions).

Goldstein, the great modern student of aphasia, holds that, in addition to their specific symptoms, aphasics suffer from a general deterioration of the abstract attitude; they function concretely. In his earlier writings Goldstein espoused an extreme holistic view of cerebral function. He thought the impairment of abstraction would be a function of the amount of cerebral tissue destroyed rather than of the exact locus of the destruction. In his more recent writings he is disposed to believe that the frontal lobes may be more important to abstraction than are other parts of the cerebrum.

In at least one statement Goldstein and Scheerer (78) define the concrete attitude in a manner that is identical with our basic definition. They write: "In this attitude we are given over and bound to the immediate experience of the given thing or experience in its particular uniqueness." This is what we have called the extreme of concreteness. However, Goldstein and Scheerer continue: "Our thinking and acting are directed by particular claims made by one particular aspect of the object or situation in the environment." When only one particular aspect of an object is appreciated the object is not unique but a member of a category of objects manifesting the aspect. I cannot reconcile these two statements. They seem to me to define the concrete attitude in directly contradictory fashion. However, the first statement which agrees with our own definition is consistent with more of Goldstein's clinical examples than is the second.

One of the tests used by Goldstein and Gelb for the diagnosis of concrete attitude is a color matching task. The patient is shown a sample strand from the Holmgren color yarns and instructed to select from the collection of yarns (all varying slightly in hue) those that belong with the sample. A healthy person will, most commonly, pick up the yarns belonging to the same highly codable category as does the sample. If the sample is a variety of green it will be matched with the greens. An occasional aphasic patient will find it impossible to match the sample with any other yarns. He insists, quite correctly, that it is not exactly like any other hue in the collection. Such a patient seems to operate on a level of absolute concreteness, appreciating the uniqueness of the object. Other patients will match the sample with other yarns but with very few others, perhaps only those of immediately adjoining hue. This is a concrete performance in that the patient is operating with narrower categories, smaller extensions, than the normal.

Another of the Goldstein diagnostic tests requires the patient to match a pattern of colored squares with a set of colored blocks. The aphasic will sometimes be unable to match the printed pattern because it is small and the blocks are large. He shows an inability to abstract the pattern from its over-all size but insists on all attributes of the original. An occasional patient will pile blocks on top of the sample pattern, in an effort to match spatial loci as well as patterns. These, too, are concrete performances in our sense of the word.

Goldstein (76) also reports aphasic language performances that are concrete in the sense that the patient utilizes unusually narrow reference categories. A German lady, for instance, could not accept the polysemy of the word *Anhaenger*. This word has the very general sense of something dependent. It can be used to name a lavaliere, also someone who is a follower, and also a second street-car that is hitched to another. The aphasic could not accept the full extension of this word but preferred to limit it to one of its senses. The same lady was asked to name some animals. She produced "polar bear," "brown bear," "lion," and "tiger." On inquiry it was discovered that she thought of the Berlin Zoo and named animals in the order one encountered them on going into the zoo. She had not thought of generic names but of names of particular animals known to her.

Not all aphasic behavior, by any means, shows this kind of concreteness. On the color matching test, for instance, patients will sometimes pick up a very large collection of yarns. These are sometimes a little unusual, for instance a group of cold colors or of summer colors, but not strictly concrete. In amnesia the names that are lost first and last to be recovered (according to Granich [79]) are not highly abstract terms but are rather proper names. These would seem to be the most concrete terms in the language and ought to be retained by aphasics. The detailed case study of the patient Lanuti by Hanfmann, *et al.* (85), though it is described as a study of concrete behavior, does not conform to our sense of concreteness. Lanuti made many incorrect identifications. Shown an egg he called it a *ball;* shown a match he called it a *stick;* shown a lemon he called it a *carrot.* These mistakes seem to involve abstraction of a single attribute and neglect of others. The egg is shaped a little like a ball but the size, color, and surface texture are not like most balls. The lemon is a little like a carrot in color but not in shape. Certainly these performances do not suggest appreciation of the unique object.

Aphasic deviations from the norm cannot be subsumed under the simple rubric—a preference for narrow categories that take account of numerous attributes. Goldstein and Scheerer's full definition of the abstract and concrete attitudes goes far beyond our treatment of these terms. The abstract attitude, they say, is characterized by the following: 1) An ability to assume a mental set voluntarily; 2) an ability to shift voluntarily from one aspect to another of objects and situations; 3) an ability simultaneously to keep in mind several aspects; 4) an ability to generalize abstract common properties; 5) an ability to detach the Ego from the task. Apparently the Goldstein tests help clinicians to diagnose aphasia. However, I cannot believe that the clumsy conceptualizations of the abstract attitude are of much help in this task. The operations for recognizing the abilities listed above are not all clear. The logical relations between them are confused. It is not clear what empirical relations hold between them. Are these abilities in high mutual correlation? How high? Finally the various abilities do not seem to be subsumed under any common principle. They appear to be a collection of symptoms, a syndrome, which might better be called "non aphasia" rather than the "abstract attitude." The fact seems to be that the aphasic is less likely to show each of these characteristics than is the normal person. They are an empirical cluster of abilities defective in brain injured patients. Calling the cluster the *abstract attitude* suggests that they are also a logical group. It suggests that aphasics all show the same kind of impairment. In fact they seem to show one or another of a limited class of impairments. In a few words, I think the abstract attitude is a disjunctive category.

Since I have very little clinical acquaintance with aphasia the following suggestions are distinctly presumptuous. From the clinical literature, however, I believe that aphasic impairments can be described in a clear and consistent fashion using the terms of category theory. One common deviation in aphasic cognition is, clearly, the preference for more concrete categories than the normal would use. Another deviation is an inability to recategorize. The patient who is able to sort yarns into hue classes may not be able to re-sort them into brightness classes or into warm and cold colors. This is categorical rigidity. Lanuti's recognition errors have suggested to me an explanation that makes sense in terms of category theory but which may be quite mistaken. His errors were usually corrected when he experienced an additional criterial attribute of the object. Allowed to crack the egg he recognized it as an egg rather than a ball; allowed to light the match he correctly identified it; allowed to smell the lemon he correctly identified it. The visual attributes of these objects would have sufficed to identify them for the normal person. Lanuti required an additional highly criterial attribute in each case. It may be that he was less able to use probabilistic attributes. Possibly the aphasic requires attributes of near perfect criteriality in order to categorize correctly.

The amnesic patient's difficulty with proper names, especially first names, may derive from the fact that these words are felt to be arbitrary in a way that other words are not. A name like *James* is applied to a number of discriminated persons and these persons have no characteristic quality that makes them a category. *Chair* is also a name applied to many discriminated entities but these have common qualities which constitute the essence of "chairness." There is no essence of James. Furthermore many of us have the experience of finding a name for a person and so we feel the separability of name and referent. We are not namers of chairs and tables. Their names are given to us and are not felt to be susceptible of change. It may be that names which are not felt to be necessary and natural are most easily lost in aphasia.

In sum, I think that the varieties of aphasia can all be described in the consistent terminology of category theory but I see little evidence that aphasia always involves the same ability, the ability to abstract. Neither do I see evidence that aphasic behavior resembles the behavior of animals, primitives, and children.

Schizophrenia. Something like 50 per cent of the patients in mental hospitals have been diagnosed as schizophrenic. The behavior of these patients is enormously varied. Robert White (242) suggests that the only attribute characteristic of the entire group is a lack of interest in the environment. The clinician recognizes four principal varieties of schizophrenia. These are by no means alike in language behavior. The hebephrenic, for instance, produces neologisms like "prestigitis," "hydroscenic," "rodential," and the like. All of the neologisms I have heard conform to the phonology of the patient's native language. The disease does not seem to disrupt that very fundamental pattern. In addition most neologisms are constructed according to some standard morphological pattern. Their meanings can often be guessed from the constituent morphemes. This would simply be linguistic invention were it not for the fact that the patient seems to think his neologisms are conventional forms requiring no explanation. The hebephrenic may speak in what has been called "word salad," i.e., a senseless ungrammatical succession of words. Word salad resembles the agrammatism of aphasia but is not the same. The aphasic's sentence is telegraphic. It is cut back to a few most important words with the empty connectives left out. The sense of the message is usually fairly clear. Word salad is not an abbreviated conventional phrase. Decoding is not likely to be possible for anyone but the doctor who is thoroughly familiar with the preoccupations of the patient. Paranoid schizophrenics often produce perfectly intelligible grammatical speech. They may introduce occasional neologisms and these are likely to be of an elaborately technical nature. The abnormality of paranoid speech is primarily semantic rather than grammatical. What the patient says is fantastic. He expresses his delusions and hallucinations and we cannot believe in the propositions he voices. There are differences, then, in the language behavior of the various kinds of schizophrenic. In addition, however, Goldstein (76) and his students contend that schizophrenics show a general impairment of the abstract attitude.

Because some schizophrenics perform in a concrete fashion resembling the behavior of brain injured patients Goldstein has suggested that schizophrenia may sometimes involve organic damage. He makes a point of saying, however, that he does not think of schizophrenia as entirely organic in character. Since autopsies have failed to discover cerebral pathology in most schizophrenics it is commonly believed that this disease is "functional" in character. There seems to be some confusing mind-body dualism in the distinction between a "functional" and an "organic" psychosis. I take it for granted that schizophrenia is a disorder of the nervous system as well as of behavior and consciousness. The disorder need not be anything like the gross lesions of aphasia. It may be a matter of the microscopic structure of the cortex. To say that schizophrenia is an organic disorder is not to say that it was caused by a tumor or a blow on the head and can only be cured by "physical" therapies. Organic changes can be produced by experience. In learning to be schizophrenic the patient's nervous system may grow so as to facilitate the nervous connections that result in hallucinations and bizarre motor symptoms. It may be, too, that this unhealthy state of his nervous system can only be altered by a psychotherapy, a new set of experiences establishing a new set of connections. However, the belief that schizophrenia is primarily caused by experience and is most likely to be unlearned through psychotherapy need not commit us to the view that schizophrenia is a disembodied mental disorder. For that matter one can believe in the experiential origins of the disease and yet hold that some kind of physical therapy is best able to undo the consequences of bad experience. The upshot of this little digression is that the similarity of some schizophrenic behavior to aphasic behavior suggests that schizophrenia may sometimes involve the *same kind* of organic disorder as aphasia. That schizophrenia is an organic disorder I take to be as certain as the fact that it is a mental and behavioral disorder.

A number of studies of schizophrenics (usually paranoid) describe behavior that is abnormally concrete in our sense of the word. Benjamin (14), for instance, asked patients to tell him the meanings of familiar proverbs such as "a rolling stone gathers no moss." One schizophrenic said that this simply meant a moving object is not suitable for plant growth, and another said that the speed of the stone will prohibit the gathering of any substance. These are narrow readings. The "rolling stone" and "moss" of the proverb are intended to symbolize more widely. The person who moves about a great deal doesn't accumulate much property. The schizophrenics read the proverbs literally taking the narrow reference for each word. Another example of the same sort of thing is supplied by Eugenia Hanfmann (84). She tried to suggest to a patient the symbolic character of the proverb: "Don't cry over spilt milk." Hanfmann pointed out that this proverb might be said to someone who had lost money. What would it mean under these circumstances? The patient thought a bit and replied that it would mean: "Cheer up, you can buy more milk at the store." Milk is milk to this patient and cannot be money or anything else.

A number of experimental studies contrasting matched schizophrenic and normal persons report more concrete performances for the schizophrenics. They have been found less well oriented in space and time (de la Garza and Worchel [53]), less likely to give abstract definitions for words (Moran [162]), and less able to find abstract analogies (Moran). It is the general rule with these studies to find a statistically significant group difference but also to find that the two distributions have a large area of overlap. This means that these characteristics are not reliably diagnostic. Some of the performances of the schizophrenic clearly involve a preference for narrow categories (e.g., a failure to define a term by its superordinate) but many do not and it is often difficult to figure out the general definition of concreteness under which the performance is subsumed. Furthermore, there are some schizophrenic performances which must be judged abstract by our definition. Moran, for instance, found that schizophrenics would accept an abnormally large number of synonyms for words. They gave to words an exceptionally wide range of meanings. This is a preference for large categories which is in direct contrast to the aphasic lady who would only tolerate one meaning for *Anhaenger*.

Goldstein acknowledges that schizophrenic concreteness is not exactly the same as aphasic concreteness. He and his students have worked with both groups using the Vigotsky blocks. This is a set of wooden blocks varying in color, size, and shape. The subject is asked to group together those that belong together. Goldstein finds schizophrenic performances more varied than those of brain injured patients. The individual preoccupations of the patient operate to produce idiosyncratic groupings. One, for instance, combined a very heterogeneous set of blocks and called them "policemen."

Cameron (33) also used the Vigotsky blocks with schizophrenics and compared the results with those for children and organically deteriorated senile dementia patients. He found that each of these groups was different from the healthy adult but that they were also unlike one another. Cameron (31) directly denies that schizophrenic cognition is like that of children. He emphasizes a peculiarly schizophrenic difficulty with the Vigotsky task. The patient cannot maintain the limits of the problem. He wants to put the experimenter's yellow pencil with the yellow blocks or the experimenter's arm with the red blocks since the arm has red blood in it. There seems, in general, to be even less evidence that schizophrenics are concrete, in any consistent sense of concrete, than there is for aphasics. There are only isolated points of resemblance between schizophrenic cognition, aphasic cognition, and primitive or immature cognition.

Accurate observations concerning all or nearly all schizophrenics are bound to be very abstract since the patients in this category are so heterogeneous. One such observation comes to us from von Domarus (233) and has been elaborated on by Arieti (8). These authors find that schizophrenics see identities where we should see nothing more than a partial similarity. A short man has something in common with Napoleon. A virginal girl shares at least one attribute with the Virgin Mary. We would never go on to say that the short man is Napoleon or that the virginal girl is Mary. The schizophrenic may. The particular identities accepted will be a function of the particular life history of the individual patient but perhaps most patients believe in some such identities. This is not a concrete mental process. It involves neglect of individual characteristics. The false identities result from an abstraction that is excessive. Korzybski (129) has inveighed against the same tendency in persons who are only un-sane rather than insane. He calls it the "is of identity." The unsane are disposed to identify Negro "A" with Negroes or even table "A" with tables. There are no identities between subordinate and superordinate categories but only limited similarities. It seems to be true that schizophrenics accept false identities because they focus on single abstracted attributes which are selected for reasons peculiar to the individual disease process.

A Psycho-Genetic Law. Psychology's genetic law was created by faith and semantic confusion. The categories of the law are lower animals, primitive men, children, aphasics, and schizophrenics. Before these categories can be proved to be similar to one another we must know that there are psychological uniformities within each category. We don't know that. Perhaps we are nearer to knowing it for the first three than for the last two. Consequently we can feel fairly sure that in one sense of abstraction—generalization through failure to discriminate—animals, primitives, and children are quite prone to abstract. In another sense—generalization after differentiation—they may be less prone to abstract than the civilized human adult. Aphasia and schizophrenia are large, loose diagnostic categories. It is not at all clear what aphasics have in common beyond some kind of cerebral injury or what schizophrenics have in common beyond a lack of interest in the environment. It is, therefore, quite impossible to decide whether these categories resemble the first three categories.

The consistent descriptive terminology in these literatures suggests that the uniformity of the categories and their mutual similarity have been established. This is a consistency of pre-supposition rather than of data. Research workers believe in the psychological unity of children, in the mind of primitive man, in the animal mind. They believe in disease entities called *schizophrenia* and *aphasia*. And so they are disposed to unify each category through the use of a common descriptive term. All of these categories are fallen away from the healthy, civilized, human adult. Each category lacks one attribute of the category to which the researcher himself belongs. There is a beautiful simplicity in the notion that all departures from ourselves are basically the same kind of departure. *Abstract* is the word that has been chosen to name the special quality of our mind and *concrete* the word for all other minds. The words have been used so as to maintain the master preconception rather than with referential consistency. The result is that *concrete* and *abstract* name all sorts of behaviors having no clear common properties. These unwitting shifts in reference are responsible for the general agreement that all kinds of sub-human mind are concrete as opposed to the abstract mind of the healthy, civilized adult.

The law of progressions and pathologies is a vision not an achievement. It is a psychological solar system. Only we haven't seen it yet; we just think it is there. We cannot doubt that the mind of the healthy, civilized, human adult is the sun but the five planets are not so certainly identified, and their positions relative to one another and the sun are quite uncertain. A vision gives point and scope and excitement to the individual research. The vision precedes the research and motivates it but ought also to be sensitive to it.

Summary

The vocabularies of children and of pre-literate peoples have a smaller proportion of general terms than the vocabularies of literate adults. Probably this difference in vocabulary is not evidence of a difference in ability to abstract. Children, pre-literate peoples, and also the lower animals seem to be able to operate with very general categories. The shortage of very general *terms* is ultimately to be explained by their lesser utility for the purposes of children and primitive societies than terms on a more concrete level.

In languages whose histories are known, the vocabulary of psychological description is usually derived from a vocabulary describing spatial relations, colors, textures, etc. In the linguistic development of children the psychological uses of such vocabulary usually come later than the non-psychological. It may be that the categories of psychology are difficult to form, perhaps because they tend to be disjunctive, relational, and dispositional. Perhaps adults of the past and children today need the help of a metaphor from the world of objects to "see" the criterial attributes of psychological states.

It is not clear that aphasia and schizophrenia are regressions along the better established lines of progression. It is not demonstrated that persons suffering from these disorders lack either general or psychological categories. The cognitive symptoms of the two kinds of patient can be roughly differentiated in the category metalanguage. Aphasics are likely to show one or more of a set of defects including a preference for narrow categories, difficulty with recategorization of a collection of objects, inability to use multiple probabilistic attributes in categorization. Schizophrenics (especially the paranoid variety) differ from the rest of us in that certain categories are more available to them, available to the point of obsession, and in that they treat certain partial similarities as identities. The particular categories and identities that occupy a schizophrenic appear to be dictated by his personal life history. They are not the same in different patients but all patients are "odd" in that they use their favored categories when we should not use them and in that they use metaphor when we would accept a simile. The schizophrenic would not shock us if he said: "I am *like* Hitler" but if, in speech that does not advertise itself as poetry, he says: "I am Hitler" then we are surprised.

Future research that is inspired by the vision of a law of progressions and pathologies might do well to operate with a different definition of abstraction. Instead of studying breadth of generalization as an outsider sees it we probably should study the number of familiar differentiations from which a subject abstracts some similarity. In these terms abstraction may prove to be an advanced skill showing phyletic, historical, and biographical progression. It is less likely that it will also describe the regressions of aphasia and schizophrenia.

chapter ix

Persuasion, Expression,
and Propaganda

I<small>F</small> I <small>WANT</small> a table to move, I move it. If I want
a dog to move I will try to cajole him into moving. But if cajolery
fails I may, in exasperation, pick him up and throw him through
the hoop. Very young children are not much more persuadable
than a dog or cat but we try to resist the impulse to force the
spinach into the mouth. It isn't right to impose one's will on a child
as one does with a table and sometimes may with a dog. Most of
the movement we desire in adult human beings cannot be induced
by the direct application of force. It is seldom practicable to pick
someone up and move him to another room. Adults must usually
be persuaded by speech and gestures to undertake the movement
themselves. Occasionally, when all symbolic manipulation fails, we
may treat a human being like a thing and boot the drunk out of
the saloon. The fact that we may fall back on action directly applied when speech and gesture fail shows that the goal of some
linguistic behavior is action in another person. We may define
persuasive behavior as symbol-manipulation designed to produce
action in others. Persuasion depends for its effect on some kind of
psychological consent in the audience.

Persuasive efforts are labelled *propagandistic* when someone judges that the action which is the goal of the persuasive effort will be advantageous to the persuader but not in the best interests of the persuadee. There are no objective techniques for determining the best interests of the persons involved in a persuasive effort. Consequently the social psychologist does not decide whether or not a given effort is propagandistic. Propaganda comes into psychology as a judgment made by others. We can study propaganda as we can study good and evil. We don't make the judgment but we can study the phenomena so judged.

When the person making a persuasive effort believes the goal of this effort to be advantageous to himself but not to his audience he is a deliberate propagandist. When the person who is the object of a persuasive effort believes that the effort is designed to benefit the persuader more than himself then he is conscious of being subjected to propaganda. It is the sweetest dream of the deliberate propagandist that symbolic techniques exist which are as immediate and uncontingent in their effects as the direct force applied to a chair. It is the worst nightmare of the person propagandized that such techniques exist—techniques which will constrain him to obey. Since we are all both deliberate propagandists and witting objects of propaganda the irresistible persuasive technique is both wished for and dreaded.

In both popular and academic social psychology the "masses" are thought to be unable to resist certain kinds of persuasion. An unscrupulous propagandist can persuade the masses to act in a way that is not consonant with their own best interests. They can be manipulated with honeyed words, false promises, emotional appeals, flattery, unfounded threats, and irrelevant testimonials. Intellectuals have always enjoyed vilifying the masses. Emerson held that "A mob is man voluntarily descending to the nature of the beast"; Shakespeare called the mob: "The beast with many heads"; LeBon said: "The crowd is always intellectually inferior to the isolated individual."

In America the people believe that they have sometimes acted as masses and are afraid of doing so again. After the First World War analyses of anti-German propaganda convinced many Americans that they had been tricked into participating in a war that was none of their concern. In addition, books like *Fashion is Spinach* and *One Hundred Million Guinea Pigs* persuaded Americans that they were easy targets for smart advertisers. Muckraking novels by Upton Sinclair and John Dos Passos, and non-fiction by Lincoln Steffens, showed Americans to be the dupes of politicians, publishers, and big business. The success of Italian, Russian, and German dictators was generally credited to their skillful use of propaganda. Hitler and Dr. Goebbels were believed to have made a science of propaganda; a science set forth in Hitler's *Mein Kampf*. Sinclair Lewis wrote *It Can't Happen Here* to show that America could be turned into a police state by the skillful use of propaganda. For all these reasons Americans developed an attitude toward propaganda which William Empson describes as follows:

> They believe in machinery more passionately than we do and modern propaganda is a scientific machine, so it seems to them obvious that a mere reasoning man can't stand up against it. All this produces a curiously girlish attitude toward anyone who might be doing propaganda. Don't let that man come near. Don't let him tempt me, because if he does I'm sure to fall.

At the beginning of the Second World War American fear of being manipulated by propaganda grew even stronger. Many Americans judged that any effort to enlist them in the war would be propagandistic since it would not be in American interest to fight in Europe. Partly in response to this fear, an Institute for Propaganda Analysis was founded. The publications of the Institute were distributed to schools and libraries and were widely used in high school teaching. The Institute tried to treat propaganda as a kind of persuasive effort that could be recognized without making any judgments concerning the best interests of the people concerned. The defining characteristics of propaganda were held to be the following seven methods of irrational persuasion: 1) Name Calling, 2) Glittering Generality, 3) Transfer, 4) Testimonial, 5) Plain Folks, 6) Card Stacking, and 7) Band Wagon. The Institute exposed these propagandistic devices wherever they appeared, in the press releases of Germany or of England, in the speeches of Roosevelt, Churchill, Hitler, Lindbergh, or Father Coughlin. Of course the devices are actually ubiquitous. They appear in the Bible, the Declaration of Independence, in philosophy, psychology, physics, and biology—probably just about everywhere except perhaps in an exposition of formal logic or mathematics. The Institute's

effort to ignore the evaluative judgment in the propaganda concept
caused it to go out of business when America entered the war.
With the declaration of war we committed ourselves, as a nation,
to the belief that the persuasive efforts of the Axis were propagandistic (not in our best interests), while those of the Allies and
our own government were not propagandistic since they must represent our own best interests. However, the Allies made just as much
use of Glittering Generalities and Band Wagon effects as did the
Axis. But to label persuasion on the home front as propagandistic
would have been a disloyal act. The pejorative sense of the word,
its roots in the notion of persuasion to act against one's own interests, were too strong for the analysts who tried to make an objective
concept of propaganda.

The Institute for Propaganda Analysis presented its six persuasive techniques as powerful poisons bound to infect those not
inoculated with the antitoxin of propaganda awareness. I believe
they have exaggerated the power of these techniques. In the first
place very few people need to be taught that devices of this kind
are sometimes used in an unscrupulous effort to make us do what
is not in our own best interests. From childhood we have worked
at propaganda detection and have come to be pretty good at it.
This is evident in the fact that the famous techniques are not always effective. The first section of this chapter describes several
recent researches that disclose limitations of the techniques. Separating propaganda from good advice and useful information involves penetrating to the motives and knowledgeability of the
person originating the message (the source). We generally discover the character of another person from his actions and speech.
To use speech for this purpose is to treat it as an *expression* of the
speaker. Consequently, the second section of this chapter is a discussion of the *expressive* function of language. We will return then
to the techniques of persuasion in order to show that their effectiveness is primarily contingent on the expressive meanings carried
by the technique and its concomitants. Finally, three different
kinds of persuasion situation are defined and an effort is made, in
each case, to show the dependence of persuasion on expression. It
is the general purpose of this chapter to show that the "Power of
Propaganda" has been oversold and, in particular, to show the
ways in which it is limited by our habit of treating speech and all
behavior as revealing of character.

The Contingent Effectiveness of Persuasion Techniques

The social psychological experiments to be described have not been presented by their authors as studies of the rhetorical devices named by the Institute for Propaganda Analysis. However, the procedures clearly are examples of these devices and the results establish certain limits on their effectiveness.

Card Stacking. Card Stacking involves arguing unfairly in favor of a thesis, leaving out arguments on the other side. After the defeat of Germany in World War II, morale in the American Army began to decline. The troops anticipated that Japan would surrender very soon and so they were inclined to relax a bit. The War Department, however, believed there might still be a long war ahead and wished to convince the troops of this. An experiment, described by Hovland, Lumsdaine, and Sheffield (98), was performed to discover which of two persuasive techniques would be more effective. Some platoons were shown a film that presented all the arguments favoring the long war thesis but no arguments on the other side. Other platoons were shown a film that argued for the same thesis (a long war) but also discussed the reasons for thinking the war would not last very long. Which presentation was more effective, the one-sided or the two-sided? It proved to depend on the character of the audience. For instance, men who had graduated from high school were more affected by a two-sided presentation; men with less education were more affected by a one-sided presentation. Furthermore, men who initially opposed the thesis presented (a long war ahead) were more affected by the two-sided presentation, while men who were initially inclined to believe in the long war thesis were confirmed in this view by the one-sided presentation but disturbed by the two-sided presentation. The results contained one pleasant irony. The two-sided presentation was not strictly fair because it did not mention one of the most important opposition arguments, the possibility that Russia might declare war on Japan. Some of the men in the audience had thought of this possibility. For these men the two-sided presentation was not very effective.

What has become of the vaunted effectiveness of Card Stacking? However unscrupulous the propagandist, it will be difficult for him to know whether or not to stack the cards. If the audience is uniformly ill informed and uneducated he ought to use it, if the audience is well informed he ought not to use it. Most audiences are heterogeneous in these respects and so it must be difficult to know what to do.

Band Wagon. The technique called Band Wagon operates by convincing an audience that everyone believes or is doing something and that it behooves the audience to swing along. Relevant to this technique are experimental studies of Sherif and of Asch. If a pinpoint of light is exposed in an otherwise dark room to a subject who has no certain knowledge of the size of the room or the distance between himself and the light, the light will appear to the subject to move, though it is actually perfectly steady. This apparent movement is called the "autokinetic phenomenon." Its exact cause is not known. However, since individuals vary greatly in their estimations of the extent of movement it is called a subjective phenomenon, an ambiguous stimulus situation. This means, of course, that subjects disagree in their assessment of the effect. Sherif (208) used this phenomenon to demonstrate the operation of group norms. One subject, alone with the experimenter, was asked to make repeated estimates of the extent of movement. These estimates varied considerably at first, but eventually settled down to a rather narrow range of variation, the norm for this individual. Such a subject then joined a group of others making similar judgments. These others had been instructed by the experimenter to make estimates markedly different from those of the first subject but in close agreement with one another. Under these conditions the estimates of the first subject moved in the direction of those made by the collaborators. He conformed to a group norm; he got on the Band Wagon. Results of this kind suggest that it is indeed powerful persuasion to demonstrate to someone that everyone else disagrees with him.

Recent studies by Asch (9) show that the sort of pressure to group conformity demonstrated by Sherif is also only contingently effective. In the Asch procedure a subject arrives at the laboratory expecting to participate in an experiment in visual perception. It is a group experiment and some other subjects are already there. These others are all secret collaborators of the experimenter. The group is seated in one row with the single naïve subject jockeyed into a middle position. The problem is a very simple one in the estimation of size. The experimenter holds up two cards. On one is a single vertical line. On the other are three vertical lines, one of which is the same length as the single line while the other two differ slightly from the single line. The three comparison lines are labelled *A*, *B*, and *C* and each subject is to call out, in his turn, the letter of the line equal in length to the single test line. While the judgments vary somewhat in difficulty they can all be made correctly by anyone with normally good vision. For the first few trials the subject and collaborators all report the correct answer and are in perfect agreement. But then the collaborators begin to report incorrectly, though in agreement with one another. The subject who is reporting what he sees finds himself a minority of one. Will he continue to report what he sees or will his judgments conform to those of the group?

It all depends. It depends on many things, only a few of which have been identified. Asch intended this demonstration to show that when perceptual judgments were not ambiguous, group pressures would not be so effective as Sherif had found them with the autokinetic phenomenon and, in his first study, Asch found that more than half of his subjects continued to make true judgments in opposition to the Band Wagon. But there were also a number of subjects who conformed and in some replications of this procedure there have been more conformists than independents.

Asch has conducted many variations on the original procedure and found the effectiveness of the group pressure very sensitive to procedural changes. If, for instance, there is but one other subject who makes the same judgments as the naïve person the latter is far more likely to persist in his independent responses. The effectiveness of Band Wagon pressures is contingent on the behavior involved, the size of the majority arraigned against the individual, and the character of the individual. These experiments suggest that a Band Wagon will be likely to work when the individual stands alone in his assessment of an ambiguous situation. Conditions of this sort would be difficult to establish in anything short of a totalitarian state.

Prestige Suggestion. The techniques called "Testimonial" and "Transfer" by the Institute are much the same and are both subsumed in social psychology under the heading "prestige suggestion." This is the device so widely used in advertising—the doctors who prefer one brand of cigarette to others, the athletes who thrive on

corn flakes. Earlier studies supported the notion that prestige suggestion was an uncontingently effective device. It was shown by
Sherif (207) that evaluations of literary productions are influenced
by supposed authorship, and by Farnsworth and Misumi (64) that
judgments of beauty in paintings are influenced by the prestige of
the supposed artist. Saadi and Farnsworth (199) contend that the
acceptance of dogmatic statements on various topics depends on
the respect accorded the presumed author of the statement. It seems
that people were more impressed with a statement when it was
attributed to Charles Darwin than when it was attributed to Clara
Bow. These results have been quoted to prove that critical intelligence can be overcome by clever propaganda. After all it is the
same line of poetry whoever may be supposed to have written it
and the same political slogan whether attributed to Woodrow
Wilson or Al Capone. But the use of a highly prestigeful name
seems to compel approval regardless of the merits of the product.
If this were true we should indeed be at the mercy of the advertisers. However, Asch (9) and Helen Lewis (144) have shown that
changing the supposed authorship of a political slogan will not
work with subjects who are well informed about the politics of the
persons whose names are used. Not everyone is willing to believe
that Roosevelt would approve the slogan "America First!" or that
Hoover would applaud "Workers of the world, unite!". The information possessed by a subject sets definite limits to the effects
that can be achieved by prestige suggestion and the success of the
technique is clearly contingent on the probability and suitability
of a given endorsement.

Insofar as the propagandistic devices exposed by the Institute
have been empirically studied they are found to be contingently
rather than invariably effective. They do not constrain everyone to
produce the desired responses. The subject's consent must be won.
The effectiveness of any particular technique for winning consent
seems to depend on many things—the education and information of
the audience and all the characteristics we call "personality." Must
we be content to list an endless variety of contingent factors or is
there some general statement that will summarize what we know
of these and anticipate much that has not been proved? I think
there is such a statement but that its formulation involves our recognizing that language serves an expressive as well as referential
function.

Language as Expression

The subject of this book is the covariation of linguistic behavior with other kinds of events. When linguistic responses are categorized there are recurrences—of phonemes, morphemes, phrases, and the like. When the rest of the world is categorized there are again recurrences—of trees, clouds, running, red, and the like. Linguistic categories covary with nonlinguistic categories—it is this that I have called linguistic reference. We need now to differentiate several kinds of reference. Referent categories can be usefully divided into those in which the speaker himself has membership and all others. The utterance *I am a thief* goes with membership of the speaker in the class of people who have stolen things. The utterance *That is an apple* goes with apples but does not imply that the speaker is one. Speech is *expressive* to the degree that it covaries with characteristics of the speaker. Expression is a kind of reference in which the nonlinguistic category includes the speaker. We have used reference generically to include all kinds of linguistic and nonlinguistic covariation but we shall use it more narrowly in this chapter for covariation that is not expressive.

The semantic categories, the morpheme, word, and phrase, have correlates in the speaker as well as in the nonlinguistic world. In addition the empty categories that do not make reference are nevertheless expressive. A particular pronunciation of an English phoneme, for instance, goes with membership of the speaker in the class of persons born in France. All aspects of linguistic behavior are expressive. Indeed, all kinds of behavior are expressive. A gesture goes with Italian parentage; the choice of a necktie points to Ivy League schooling. The same utterance is simultaneously expressive and referential. The word *apple* refers to apples and expresses membership of the speaker in the class of people who speak English. In our efforts to cope with the present and anticipate the future we have learned to attend to both reference and expression. The lady who tells me that our friends are heading for divorce also, inadvertently, tells me that she herself is a gossip and can be expected to pass on anything I may say.

Language or any other sort of behavior *functions expressively* when someone treats it as a sign that the behaving person belongs in some category. If an infant's cry causes me to think of it as hungry, and so to feed it, then the cry has functioned expressively.

If an inflection in someone's speech causes me to identify the speaker as a person having a superior attitude then that inflection has functioned expressively for me. One way to find out whether behavior is functioning expressively for someone is to ask what the action or remark "means." Expressive interpretations will be statements about the speaker: "He thinks he is better than other people" or "He is hungry."

There is a second distinction among linguistic, nonlinguistic covariations that will be useful to us. Some linguistic categories are treated as signs of their referent categories but will not be used as names of them; we shall call these *symptoms*. A tremulous voice may be symptomatic of fear in the speaker but it is not the name of fear. A particular tone over the telephone may be symptomatic of the presence of eavesdropping parents or wife or pastor but it will not be the name of any of these. The linguistic categories with which this book has been concerned until now are both names and signs of their referents. The word *house* names the thing and may act as a sign of it. The word *thief* names the category and may also be a sign of the membership of the speaker in the category as in "I am a thief." When someone says, "I am afraid," his utterance *expresses* fear but is not a *symptom* of fear because it uses linguistic categories that can be used to name the referent. A tremulous voice, on the other hand, is an expressive symptom. What is the difference between expression by names and by symptom? It is ordinarily a difference in the intention of the speaker. The person who says, "I am afraid" means to place himself in the category of people who fear. If we interpret his utterance to mean "You are afraid," he will accept that interpretation as legitimate. The same interpretation of a tremulous voice may be denied, perhaps vehemently so, or it may be accepted as legitimate but not quite what the speaker had intended when he tremulously remarked: "Who's afraid?" Because we have learned the referents for certain expressive symptoms we can sometimes penetrate to a truth about a person which he has not intended to reveal. When the speaker is selfishly motivated we are likely to identify his persuasive messages as propagandistic and so will not act as he recommends. The unwitting expressive symptom often trips up the deliberate propagandist.

Expressions of Infants, Animals, and Adults. The vocalizations of an infant function as expressive symptoms. His audience assumes that he is not talking about anything. They use his vocalizations to discover his needs. Adults may interpret the infant cries to one another. The interpretations always take the form of a statement concerning the infant: "He is hungry" or "He isn't sleepy yet." Infant cries operate as symptoms of infant needs and cause action appropriate to these needs. As we saw in Chapter VI these cries have a built-in expressive value deriving from their isomorphism with the needs that set them off.

With pet animals, as with infants, we are primarily concerned with the expressive function of behavior. The adult human being is in the role of provider and protector for these creatures and so is anxious to discover their requirements. A sudden high pitched yelp from the dog instructs us to look for some sudden pain—he has been kicked or the rocker has squeezed his tail. Hunger does not have so sudden an onset. There are other expressive behaviors that are not uniform within an animal species. Their significance is built up between animal and owner. A dog that wants to go out of doors has no instinctive response to this need that will communicate to his master. Kept on the move by his desire, he will emit a variety of behaviors. Eventually one of these will catch his master's attention and suggest the correct expressive interpretation. Most likely to serve this function are actions in the vicinity of the door, barking or scratching or just standing there. Because these behaviors tend to be promptly reinforced by accession to his desire to go out, the dog will learn to perform them more promptly. The expressive act is selected from many acts for its ability to suggest to a human being the desire to go out the door. As a consequence, different dogs and cats have somewhat different "let me out" signals but most of these are performed in the vicinity of the door.

The speech of an adult human being has always an expressive potential. At the very least one can use it to categorize the speaker by nationality, social class, and sex. What we call a "foreign accent" is one of the most interesting expressive features of speech. If he is to avoid all misunderstandings of reference an immigrant to America must preserve in his spoken English all the phonemic contrasts used by native speakers. He must, for instance, pronounce [r] and [l] differently and consistently lest someone misinterpret his *route* as *loot* or *road* as *load*. If he is French he has an [l] almost exactly like the English but his [r] will be a uvular trill.

He can speak English using his [r] wherever we should use ours and his references will be perfectly understood. The feature distinguishing these two consonants is not a significant feature in English speech and so it can vary without signalling a change of reference. The feature not used for reference is freed for expressive use and we will register the deviant pronunciation as a symptom of foreign, perhaps of French, birth. It is likely to be perfectly agreeable to the Frenchman to be so categorized and downright gratifying to the Frenchwoman to be correctly identified so the accent is likely to remain.

Behaviors expressing nationality, sex, and social class fall into certain highly reliable clusters. It is always a shock to find attributes in the same person that are expressive of categories thought to be exclusive of one another. When a black man speaks with an upper-class British accent provincial Americans are stunned. When someone dressed as a man speaks with the inflections and vocabulary of a woman people are either amused or disgusted. I remember a man with a heavy German accent saying to a cab driver: "Step on the gas," and my amusement at the incongruous combination in one utterance of the phonetically exotic and semantically home grown. The sounds of his speech expressed German birth while the content expressed American birth. When travelling in Germany I have tried the effect of a well rehearsed, impeccably pronounced single German sentence. My auditor took this sentence to be a symptom of a fluent command of German. He categorized me as one who speaks the language like a native and he responded accordingly, with a flood of rapid colloquial German. He had categorized me incorrectly and I was overwhelmed. Excellence of pronunciation is often diagnostic of general competence in a language. There are linguists who claim to be able to judge the length of time someone has been speaking a second language by the state of his pronunciation—a kind of glottochronology of the individual speaker. But this cue is not perfectly reliable. An acquaintance of mine has an excellent grasp of the vocabulary and grammar of French. He can say just about anything he wishes in the language but, always, with a dreadful accent. The sounds of a language never interest him very much. But he complains that people often say that he speaks terrible French while so-and-so, who has little vocabulary and less grammar but a very Parisian pronunciation, is credited with beautiful French.

Expression in Scientific Language. While all human language is potentially expressive, not all language is equally likely to function expressively. J. Adams has shown, in an essay called "Expressive Aspects of Scientific Language" (1), that one who knows psychology can take an excerpt from the writings of a particular psychologist and use it to infer many things about the psychologist which are not specifically stated in the excerpt. And, of course, we all know that this is possible. The beliefs of psychologists like the beliefs of everyone else fall into clusters and the rest of a cluster can often be inferred from one item of belief. If a psychologist describes thought as a "cognitive re-structuring" I anticipate that he will not employ the concept of sensation, that he will be little interested in the study of individual differences, and will take more pleasure in the writings of Ernst Cassirer than of A. J. Ayer. Indeed, I think I can go beyond this cluster of professional preferences and make better than chance guesses about the values, tastes, and training of the psychologist. I expect him to believe that man is a rational being and, for that matter, that the higher animals are more rational than is usually supposed. I expect him to place high value on art and literature. To the degree that one can reconstruct the nonprofessional character of a scientist, his values, traits, and tastes, from his professional utterances, we have an undeveloped science. When propositions are clearly demonstrated they compel belief in men of all sorts. We can't tell much about a man's temperament from the fact that he believes $F = MA$ or $V = D/T$ or $DL/S = K$, though we can tell something about the nature of his education.

From Adams' demonstration that the statements of psychologists are intercorrelated it does not by any means follow (as he implies) that the language of science is the same as all other language. The statements of the most advanced sciences differ from other kinds of statements in their expressive potential. In general it would appear that values and temperament and the like are not expressed in these statements. Furthermore, I should suppose that while the language of social science and of scholarship in general may have considerable expressive potential, it is less likely to be treated as an expression than most other language. The reader of scientific and scholarly language is not so much interested in inferring the combination of beliefs held by a particular writer as in discovering what beliefs are tenable and what logical relations hold between beliefs. Some scientific language differs from some other kinds of language in the nature of its expressive potential, and probably all scientific language is unlikely to be treated as an expression. Adams has reminded us of a potentiality of scientific language that is often overlooked but, in the very fact that it is usually overlooked, we find one basis for distinguishing scientific language from other varieties.

Expression and the Freudian Interpretation. The language of the analysand on the couch is particularly likely to be treated as an expression. The expressive function of language is its principal function for the psychoanalyst. If his patient tells him that there is a plot against his life the analyst does not telephone the police, which would be an appropriate response to such a statement interpreted as a reference. However, the analyst treats the report as a symptom useful for categorizing or, if you like, diagnosing the patient. The Freudian revolution is, in a way, a revolution in the mode of responding to certain kinds of language.

You will remember that point in Freud's career when he attributed hysterical neurosis in women to the early trauma of incestuous seduction by their fathers. He came to this conviction from the recurrent reports of such episodes by his own patients. He took them at their word, that is to say he responded to their speech as reference. Further evidence convinced him that he was mistaken in this belief. His patients had deceived him. In despair at his own gullibility he found his way to another interpretation of these incest-reports. They expressed the speaker—not simply as a liar—but as unconsciously desiring the reported seduction. Incest was a wish-fulfilling phantasy, not an accomplished fact. All of Freud's clinical work from this point on may be accurately described as an effort to work out a new set of semantic rules for the expressive function of behavior, to discover the diagnostic significance of various actions and utterances.

When Pharaoh dreamed of seven lean kine devouring seven fat kine the correct interpretation of this dream was a prophecy that Egypt would have seven years of plenty followed by seven years of want. This was an interpretation of the dream report as reference. Freud looked to the dream to learn about the dreamer—not about the world. He found slips of the tongue expressive of more than fatigue and haste; they hinted at suppressed desires. The gesture language of neurotic symptoms—compulsive hand washing for instance—expressed more than a desire to be clean. Today we think that even a man's viscera may give him away. An ulcer expresses repressed submissive impulses. The analytic psychologist or layman listens with the "third ear" to a special language for which Freud provided the code book. Some kind of ultimate in the tendency to treat behavior as a personal expression is reached in Freud's judgment that, in dying, man expresses his desire to die. It is not at all clear how much of Freud's expressive semantic code is accurate but it seems to have provided many clinicians with an effective way of reacting to the language of the patient.

Freudian interpretations are excellent examples of the use of language and behavior as a set of expressive *symptoms*, not simply as expressive actions. For instance, a patient may say: "I have always been an awful liar." It is his intention that we use this utterance as a reason for categorizing him as a liar. If we say that we interpret his remark to mean that he is a liar he will accept that interpretation but this is hardly a Freudian interpretation. Suppose, however, that when a man expresses concern for his father's health we interpret this remark as an indication that the man hopes for his father's death. The speaker will indignantly reject this interpretation. He does not find it an adequate translation of his own remark. It does not jibe with his intentions. This *is* a Freudian interpretation. It does not accept the self-categorization named by the patient. The analyst whose patient says: "I am a liar," is likely to interpret this remark as indicative of a pathetic need for reassurance rather than a genuine tendency to lie. We might say that the analyst treats behavior as a *revelation*, rather than simply as a symptom. The word *revelation* is intended to suggest the disparity between the interpretation and the subject's statements about himself.

We commonly pick up expressive meanings at several levels of acceptability to the speaker and frequently also a referential meaning. Suppose a man returns home late to supper and not for the first time. His wife may be suspicious that the cause of these latenesses involves both women and alcohol. However, she may have no evidence of guilt and so be unwilling to make a direct accusation. She realizes too that she may be quite wrong in these suspicions. If that should be the case she would be sorry to add her accusations to his other burdens. All these impulses find expression in the inquiry with which he is greeted, "Working late?" The words express a simple concern but a special sort of hesitation; a sharp, rising glide of intonation puts a trace of insinuation into the question. If he has anything to feel guilty about he will realize from her tone that she is on to him. The poor man registers this whole complicated meaning and is faced with a response option. He may ignore the intonation and reply with great good humor: "That's right, dear, working late!" Alternatively, he may respond to the insinuating intonation with an abused and irritable intonation but keeping the words the same: "That's *right*, dear, *working late!*" Then again he may react to her insinuation in angry words. "What the hell do you think I've been doing?" This brings the latent expressive content to the surface. The difficulty with such a response is that his discussion partner may elect to pretend that no such latent content was part of her thoughts. She may react to his outburst with tears and the plaint: "What did I do—simply ask you if you were working late?" She changes the intonation, of course, and repeats the words without the insinuation. Since people do not write down intonation and are not fully aware of it she will probably be able to convict him of unjustified ugly temper.

Attendant expressive meanings commonly influence the major referential interpretation. As the expressive meaning changes so does the reference and also the overt reaction of the interpreter. Recall the story of the boy who cried "Wolf." He was a shepherd, bored with his sheep, who thought it would be fun to alarm the villagers. These latter took his call to refer to the presence of a marauding wolf and to express the boy's alarm at its approach and so, of course, they ran to his aid. As we know, this joke was repeated too often and grew so stale that the villagers stopped reacting—with unhappy results for the boy. But what caused this change in overt response to the call? We may suppose that the boy called with fully as much conviction on the last occasion as on the first—with even more I should think. There was no change in intonation or words. However, the utterance, as originally interpreted, predicted a frightened boy and a ravening wolf. Instead of these the villagers found a laughing boy and no wolf at all. The boy's cry came to express for the villagers his boredom and desire to be amused. The word "Wolf" no longer made a reference. Its whole meaning came to be expressive.

When we undertake to persuade others we always express something about ourselves as well as refer to something external to ourselves. These expressive meanings, this orchestral accompaniment to the referential theme, will help us to understand why persuasive devices are effective in some cases and not in others.

The Dependence of Persuasive Effects on Expressive Meanings

The cries of infancy are expressive of infant needs and, in addition, are wonderfully persuasive. Totally dependent on the actions of others, the infant has not the strength to constrain others to do his will. But he is set down in the midst of a community intent on learning what he needs and satisfying him. This is our Eden in which vocalization is persuasive as it never again will be.

The infant himself is not very responsive to persuasive efforts but is, nevertheless, subjected to them from the very beginning. Because he is so weak the community can easily impose its will upon him in many matters. He is moved and put to bed by the direct application of force but he cannot be made to eat or sleep or smile. These greatly desired reactions cannot be forced and an effort is made to wheedle them from him. He reigns as an absolute monarch. His casual utterances are studied so that he may be pleased. All about him, supplicants smile and entreat him to accept what is offered.

The serpent in Eden is a distinction parents make between what infants want and what is good for them. He may want to put the pins in his mouth but he had better not. We may assume that parents identify their own interests with what is good for the child rather than with his desires. In addition, adults have interests of their own which are only vaguely and, perhaps by rationalization, connected with the infant's best interests but which definitely conflict with his desires. Father does not want his watch broken and mother is too tired to carry a baby around by the hour. So there occurs a diversion of interests from the parental point of view and also from the child's point of view and consequently the opportunity for propaganda warfare.

When father tastes baby's food and smacks his lips over it baby may be led to taste. If the taste is pretty bad a propaganda analyst is born. When this persuasive device is used again he will feel himself to be the object of a propagandistic effort. However, father is no subjective propagandist. He believes that he is acting in the best interests of the child. Where parents repeatedly prove to be both wise and unselfish we may suppose that a child will not identify their persuasive efforts as propagandistic. He will feel that their interests are identical with his own but that they are better able to calculate these interests than he is. They know that fire burns, knives are sharp, and that cats will scratch. He can rely on them as an information source that is devoted to his welfare.

However, it is a rare parent who never tries to persuade a child to do something solely for the sake of parental comfort. Most parents are occasionally conscious propagandists trying to talk a boy out of a trip to the zoo on Sunday. So children discover that parents are not invariably selfless. It is a rare parent who is not sometimes proved wrong. Timid mothers overestimate the probability that dogs will bite and that cats will scratch, and children find that out. Consequently most parents are regarded as often reliable informers but as occasional propagandists. The trick is to discover when they are making propaganda.

Children, since they have little power, and many desires not shared by parents, are often conscious propagandists and parents are conscious of being propagandized. The little boy who tells his mother that the up-to-date lady next door lets her son have a dog uses prestige suggestion. Surely the primal use of Band Wagon is the one that begins: "All the kids have one." Most parents are resistant to such tactics because they discern the child's selfish motive and because they are not impressed with him as a source of information. With regard to his parents a child is in a position like that of one nation toward another when war has been declared between them. His motives are automatically suspect. Under these conditions children, like nations, resort to "black" propaganda—a persuasive effort where the true source is concealed. The boy across the street asks Mrs. Jones if Johnny can go swimming with him and his family. Johnny put him up to it rather as Nazi Germany got certain Austrians to clamor for unification with the Reich.

It is the aim of all these persuasive tactics between parents and children to convince the object of the effort that he has mistaken his own interests. Ideally the effort will be perceived as the disinterested introduction of new and relevant information. If everybody owns a dog it is important to have one despite the expense and trouble. If a psychologist says it is important for a small boy to have a pet then he had better have one. But if dogs bark and bite and have to be kept tied up they may not be worth having. For any of this new information to affect the calculation of self-interest it must make some appeal to the audience. If the Band Wagon theme is tried with parents who like to be different from their neighbors it will boomerang. But we seldom make gross errors of this kind. We usually know what kinds of appeals have a chance of moving our audience. The trick, then, is to get the audience to believe the new information.

A message will be credible, a recommendation to action will be persuasive, to the degree that the source of the message is thought to be trustworthy. In a study by Kelman and Hovland (124), groups of high school students listened to three different speakers recommend the same policy—extreme leniency in the treatment of juvenile delinquents. The speakers were differently characterized: one as a judge in the juvenile court, another as a neutral member of the studio audience, and a third as a former juvenile delinquent now involved in various shady deals. The first speaker was judged more trustworthy and was more effective in changing opinions than the second and the second more trusted and effective than the third. In a similar study Haiman (81) found that a speech on compulsory health insurance was more effective when attributed to the Surgeon General of the United States than when attributed to a Communist or college sophomore. Merton (158), in his analysis of the stunningly successful Kate Smith War Bond Drive, reports that many influenced members of the audience said that they were chiefly affected by the evident sincerity and altruism of Miss Smith's action. There seem to be two principal ingredients in trustworthiness: (1) the source must be either disinterested or devoted to the welfare of the audience, and (2) the source must be knowledge-able. To the degree that the perceived source of a message is be-lieved to have these qualities the message will be effective.

Sometimes a source is identified by name (Kate Smith), some-times by role (Surgeon General of the United States) and judged to be trustworthy or not on the basis of popular reputation or past performance. In the prestige suggestion experiments names or titles are attached to statements and the changing evaluations of the statements can be explained by the perceived trustworthiness of the source. In addition, however, a source expresses or reveals the trustworthiness of its character through the style and content of the message. In the Card Stacking experiments the message re-vealed to some subjects the biased, interested character of the source. In the group conformity experiments the situation caused subjects to categorize the source of the persuasive message as lack-ing in knowledge. In all of these cases the effectiveness of the mes-sage proves to be contingent on one thing—the perceived trust-worthiness of the source.

Card Stacking and the Character of the Source. In the wartime study of the effectiveness of presenting both sides versus one side of an issue, conducted by Hovland, Lumsdaine, and Sheffield (98), facts were presented that argued for a long war ahead to any rational person. Members of the audience who already believed the war would be long and who had not thought much about the argu-ments on the other side could be strengthened in their conviction by a one-sided presentation. Since this presentation did not con-flict with their own beliefs, and since no important contrary argu-ments were omitted as far as they could see, the film expressed a disinterested desire to inform. Other men who opposed the long war thesis or knew about arguments on the other side identified the one-sided film as either biased or uninformed. They felt them-selves to be the target of a propagandistic effort. The two-sided film expressed disinterested concern for the truth and so the same facts were more persuasive than in the one-sided film, except, of course, for those men who noticed the omission of the possibility that Russia might declare war on Japan. This omission made the two-sided presentation suspect and so less persuasive. It is the agree-able implication of these results that when people are well informed a persuasive effort can only succeed when it is truly advantageous to the audience. The contingencies governing the effectiveness can be summarized by saying that a biased presentation will be effective to the degree that the bias is not detected. When the bias is visible the source is judged to be interested, the message is identified as propaganda, and the audience is not persuaded.

Band Wagon and the Character of the Source. In the group conformity studies of Sherif (208) and Asch (9) no persuasive effort seems to be directed at the subject. A group of other people, in the same position as the subject himself, seem to be trying to make accurate perceptual judgments. This is the "blackest" sort of propaganda. The source of the persuasive judgments, the experimenter, is concealed. In addition, these judgments are directed to the experimenter not the subject. In a way he overhears information that is relevant to his problem. It comes therefore with all the persuasive power of a stock market tip accidentally picked up from someone else's conversation. There is no conceivable way in which the source can benefit by his behavior. The source cannot have meant to influence him since it has not directed its remarks to him. The source is unimpeachably disinterested and so this is potentially a very persuasive situation. However, while the source is certainly honest, it may not be knowledgeable.

The evidence of the subject's own vision leads him to suspect that the source may not be knowledgeable. In the case of the autokinetic phenomenon this evidence does not seem to be very strong and so subjects usually get on the band wagon. In the judgments of visual extent set up by Asch the sensory evidence is stronger and so subjects sometimes report contrary to the group. It is not possible that the subject's judgment should be correct and also that the persuasive source should be both disinterested and well informed. Something has to give way. The situation is designed so as to make it very unlikely that any subject will consider the possibility of a motivated group distortion. Usually the subject does not recognize the group for the collaborators they are but, instead, tries to explain their conflicting reports as a consequence of visual defects, different positions in the room, or misunderstanding of the experimental instructions. He tries to find out why the group is not knowledgeable. When a single member of the group makes the same judgments as the subject, the probability that the others are wrong greatly increases and so the persuasiveness of the band wagon decreases.

Prestige Suggestion and the Character of the Source. In the prestige suggestion experiments a usually disinterested or altruistic and knowledgeable source is said to have endorsed or even proposed a given view. Then, in a control situation, a usually interested or uninformed source is linked with the same view. Where subjects know little about either the view or the source, prestige suggestion works and that is as it should be if the categorization of the source is an important determinant of the persuasiveness of a message. This result and our own theory would suggest that a presentation can be made effective by the simple device of attributing it to a source that is categorized as trustworthy. However, the results of Asch (9) and Helen Lewis (144) show that there are definite limits to what can be achieved by this device. When a subject is well informed, and a statement is credited to someone who could not possibly favor it, the endorsement is not believed. This is a case in which "black" propaganda is unmasked by knowledge.

Even where subjects do not actually deny the experimenter's linkage of source and statement, even where they have very limited knowledge of the source, Asch has shown that prestige suggestion accomplishes little. He used, for instance, the following sentence by Thomas Jefferson: "I hold that a little rebellion, now and then, is a good thing, and as necessary in the political world as storms are in the physical." Some subjects were told that Jefferson was the author; others were told that it came from the works of Lenin. Sure enough the statement found more approval when attributed to Jefferson, and one is unfavorably impressed by these subjects who ought to have evaluated the saying on its own merits. However, Asch went beyond a simple demonstration of the effect to try and discover its causes. He had each subject write out in his own words exactly what the statement meant. When the author was thought to be Jefferson, subjects understood the statement to recommend political revolt whenever government no longer represented the people. The statement was thought to have specific reference to the American Revolutionary War. When Lenin was understood to be the author the statement seemed to recommend social and economic upheaval, on the model of the Russian Revolution, as a generally salutary thing. Change in authorship seemed to change the meaning of the statement. Asch emphasizes the rationality of this response. It is not a stupid yielding to prestige but a Gestalt effect in language comprehension. Only in a very unimportant sense is it correct to say that the *same* statement has been attributed to two different authors. The same series of words was involved but not the same proposition. The meaning of any utterance depends on its context and the source of the utterance is highly relevant context. Subjects quite intelligently "consider the source" in interpreting a statement. The different evaluations made in experimental and control conditions are not made of the same proposition. Asch has beautifully demonstrated that the prestige suggestion effect, when it is studied closely, argues for the rationality rather than the irrationality of man.

There is another aspect of the Asch results which interests me very much. Prestige suggestion is supposed to change social attitudes. In Chapter III I described the "social attitude" as a dispositional concept. We usually assess attitudes from paper and pencil scales but we do not think that the attitude is identical with the answers to a few questions. The attitude is a disposition to behave in many ways with reference to the social category that is its focus. Anti-Semitism involves a readiness to say unpleasant things about Jews, to complain to the manager of any hotel that receives Jews, to be rude to Jews in person, to subscribe to restrictive housing covenants, etc. An attitude scale samples a small fraction of verbal behavior from the total behavior disposition that is the attitude. We believe we can predict much else in the population of behaviors from this sample. Each of us has a lot of incidentally gathered evidence that certain remarks about a social category predict other remarks and action with reference to that category. The studies that have demonstrated a prestige suggestion effect have shown that a name can alter reaction to a particular statement. It is assumed that this represents a change of attitude. But does it?

Most American college students will disagree with the statement recommending rebellion when it is attributed to Lenin and agree when it is attributed to Jefferson. Believers in the extreme manipulative power of propaganda will say that attitudes toward rebellion have been changed. Strong endorsement of the Lenin statement implies approval of the Russian revolution and readiness to support an uprising of the proletariat in other countries. Can American college students be prepared for such action by the simple device of affixing Jefferson's name to his own statement? Social change is not so easily accomplished. The interpretations of the statement, obtained by Asch, indicate that approval has different action implications when Jefferson is supposed to be the author. The new focus of the attitude is the American Revolution, or more generally any war in which abused colonies try to become independent of the mother country. Subjects applauding this proposition will be disposed to support such wars for independence. The unfavorable reaction to the Lenin statement and the favorable reaction to the "same" statement presented as the work of Jefferson does not represent a change of attitude. We have in these reactions measures of two different attitudes with two different foci. The "same" statement acquires a new primary reference and new action implications with a change in its presumed source.

A message can be made more persuasive by attributing it to a source of good character. However, in making this change the behavior to which the audience is persuaded is also likely to be changed. Soviet agents may sometimes persuade or compel respected Americans to make pro-Communist statements and so win approval for the statements. But this approval will not have the same action implications as approval of the statements when they are known to come from a Communist. Christ said: "Lay not up for yourselves treasure on earth; where the rust and moth doth corrupt." The same advice if it came from the president of the local bank might mean: "Don't put your money where moths and rust can get it, put it away safely in the bank." (This is the interpretation of the text made by Sinclair Lewis' Elmer Gantry in his sermon before a wealthy congregation.) With a change in source the action implications are reversed.

Propaganda is not limited to politics and advertising. We usually talk in order to obtain some reaction from someone else and such talk is often judged to be propagandistic. We are conscious propagandists and analysts of propaganda from earliest childhood. It is absurd to suppose that persuasive tricks like Band Wagon, Card Stacking, and Prestige Testimonial put us at the mercy of unscrupulous propagandists. We have all used and exposed these techniques. We are a tough audience. The conscious propagandist who would persuade us to act in his interests rather than our own will have a difficult time. Since the action is not really to our advantage he has got to stack the cards by lying or omitting facts. If we are at all informed we will identify his presentation as biased and will not be impressed. If he tries to convince us that the action is desirable because "everybody's doing it" he must somehow prevent us from finding anybody who isn't. Even if he controls our social contacts so as to give an "impression of universality" we may decide that everybody else is wrong. Where the propagandist is known to us as a propagandist he will have to conceal the source of his presentation. He can make it more acceptable by creating the illusion of a creditable source. But he is limited here by the fact that we know what kinds of things people we respect are likely to say. When they are supposed to have said something very unlike themselves, and contrary to what we believe, we will doubt they ever said it. In short we can be persuaded of ideas that might be held by people we admire but these will generally be ideas we already approve. The rather cramped operating space that remains to Prestige Testimonial is further reduced by the fact that a change in source often changes the significance of a statement and so the action implications of approval. The immediate response to a sentence can be rather easily altered but attitudes have more inertia.

Three Kinds of Persuasion Situation

The expressive function of speech and action is important in all persuasive efforts but it operates differently with different kinds of effort. The most important distinctions I have been able to find are the following: (1) The persuasion monopoly, (2) The persuasion competition with a most favored source, (3) The persuasion competition with no favored source.

The Persuasion Monopoly. Probably no single source ever has a complete monopoly of the persuasive influences operating on an audience. A parent may have a near monopoly with a young child and the leaders of a totalitarian state with the people they govern. Monopolies of this kind are difficult to maintain because there will usually be other sources, with conflicting points of view, anxious to influence the audience. Parents may be "undermined" by teachers, television, or other children; dictators have to contend with short wave broadcasts, leaflets from balloons, and rumor campaigns. Persuasive monopolies are incomplete and unstable.

The monopoly involves a role differentiation into those who present messages and those who receive them. To be ideally effective the monopolist must be perceived by his audience as one who informs the uninformed for the benefit of the uninformed. Parents and dictators would like to be thought more knowledgeable than their audience but completely identified in interests with that audience. Because the roles are differentiated it is always possible that the audience will find that the informer has goals of his own which are in conflict with those of the audience. We are dealing with the near monopoly and so it may be assumed that outside forces are not able to reach the audience to suggest such a divergence of interests. In the near monopoly the principal dangers lie with the expressive behavior of the monopolist himself and with the course of events. If things go wrong the monopolist will be categorized as a selfish manipulator and his presentations will become propaganda rather than information.

The persuasive force in a totalitarian state ordinarily labels itself a Ministry of Information and this is, of course, the way it would be thought of. It places its persuasive messages with usually disinterested and knowledgeable sources—newspapers, radio commentators, and the like. In Germany under the Nazis, and Czechoslovakia under the Communists, the precise wording of radio and newspaper releases was not dictated. Instead these sources were informed of the general lines of governmental policy and then encouraged to vary in unimportant ways while conforming only to major policy decisions. In this way the hand of the government is less visible, the audience has some illusion of a variety of informative sources. In Czechoslovakia during World War I it was customary to blank out sections of the newspaper considered unsuitable for general circulation even as the army censor clips forbidden sentences from letters. The newspapers are never handled in this way any more. It conveys to the audience too strong a sense of control. Where there is obvious control one inevitably considers the possibility that it may not be exercised in the interests of those controlled.

The Nazi and Communist parties were smaller groups within

the state. It was important that party members be identified as exceptionally devoted patriots and not as a privileged élite. The behavior of party members and government officials sometimes suggests that they have interests divergent from the welfare of the people. Hitler realized in World War II how important it was that no division of interest should develop between governed and governing.* In his funeral oration for General Lutze on May 7, 1943, Hitler stressed the sacrifices party members were making for the war: "From the National Socialist Reichstag down to the mature age groups of the Hitler Youth the numbers of our dead from our movement proportionately far exceed the average of the share of all the rest of the people." [General Lutze himself was killed when his automobile skidded in Germany.] The Nazi leaders at Christmas time took Christmas dinner at the front with their troops and Goebbels publicized this act of identification. The German people remembered that in the last war their Kaiser had gone into exile and saved his skin. In home front releases Goebbels often returned to the theme that Hitler was not that sort of leader, he was the soul of his people and lived only for them. Rumors of government leaders having funds abroad and private airplanes in readiness are destructive of unity and must be combatted by any wartime government. Of course the enemy is aware of the great advantage to be derived from a division of interests between leaders and people. Propagandists always distinguish between the leaders and the people—whether the leaders are described as "Wall Street Bankers" or as "the men in the Kremlin."

At the beginning of World War II Goebbels could tell the truth and at the same time persuade the German people to work and fight. German troops were victorious everywhere and the German radio celebrated their triumphs. Major victories were announced by interrupting all radio broadcasts with a great trumpet fanfare. Everything confirmed the truth of the government's announcements. Returning soldiers and plunder from France and Norway testified to quick victories. When the *Wehrmacht* was slowed down, stopped and turned back in Russia, Goebbels had a new problem. He could not tell the truth and maintain the optimistic view that this would

---

*Much of the information in this chapter concerning Nazi propaganda comes from the book *German Radio Propaganda* by Kris and Speier (133).

be a war of quick victories with the German army welcomed everywhere by the common peoples. There were some lies, some failures to report defeat, in fact some card stacking. But even in a near monopoly this technique proved unwise. Wounded men returning home told different stories, depleted stocks of food and clothing told of hardship, and defeats had to be admitted at last. Eventually Goebbels found it better policy to admit to troubles and defeat so that his agency should not be discredited.

When the war began to go strongly against the Germans the danger was that the people would desert their leaders. Allied propaganda insisted that the criminal German leaders were their real enemy. The individual soldier could save his own life by surrender. Goebbels publicized the Morgenthau plan to reduce Germany to an agrarian state and assured the people that the Russians would send the German population into Siberian slavery. He pictured German defeat as the end of everything for every German so that the people might prefer to die defending the Reich rather than to surrender.

A great deal of nonsense has been said and written about the high science of Nazi propaganda. A study of Goebbels' wartime diaries by Doob (57), and analyses of German radio propaganda by Kris and Speier (133), show that Goebbels' was a hunt-and-peck system. He tried one thing and another, seldom knowing what worked well and why. The success of Nazi propaganda undoubtedly owes more to the police system that backed it up than to the science of the propaganda itself. In a police state persuasive efforts are in large measure only a courtesy. If the audience does not do what it is asked to do it can usually be made to comply. Force stands ready to accomplish what persuasion cannot. Persuasive principles credited with Nazi success might not work so well when not backed with force. It must be stressed that the persuasive techniques that seem to work in a monopoly situation are likely to be less effective where there is a competition of persuasive efforts.

The Persuasion Competition with a Most Favored Source. This is the situation that applies in propaganda warfare between nations and in political campaigns in this country. Different sources try to persuade one audience to take mutually incompatible actions. The German is urged to fight to the death by his own radio and to surrender by the Allied short wave broadcasts. The American citizen is urged to vote either Democratic or Republican. Of the several competing sources one is most favored because it is believed to have the same interests as the audience. The German trusts his own government, the Republican trusts his own party leaders. The communications of the favored source are identified as informational; opposed communications are propagandistic. Which of two competing forces will be favored? The source with which the audience member categorizes himself. The Democratic Party in America has tried very hard in recent years to establish itself as the party of working-class people and to present the Republican party as a party of privilege. Since most Americans think of themselves as working-class people they would assume that the Democratic party works in their interest. All parties will present themselves as spokesmen for the ordinary people who are the majority. If the Democrats have been more successful than other parties in this effort it is probably because much of their legislative and executive behavior has *expressed* a concern for working people. However, many Americans do not think of their working-class membership as their most important membership. They may also categorize themselves with intelligent people, with non-radicals, with proponents of honest government. So, even though one party may establish itself as the spokesman for the working class, the candidates of that party will not be elected invariably. If another party can propose candidates who express all the virtues of good citizenship, the electorate may feel that it shares more important interests with those candidates than with the working class. We may guess that these values of honesty, economy, traditionalism, and the like are relatively high in the hierarchy of human motives and not likely to dominate the individual unless more basic motives are satisfied. In very prosperous times one's membership in the working class may be unimportant. In difficult times when one's livelihood is not assured, when one economic class competes with another for government favor, the working-class membership might be the most important self-categorization.

Political presentations not originating with the parties themselves are likely to be effective to the degree that the sources are believed to share the interests of the audience. Lazarsfeld and his co-workers (138) found that in the 1943 election Erie County voters mentioned the *Farm Journal* as frequently as *Colliers Maga-*

zine as a force influencing their vote. While *Colliers* has the greater
circulation, the *Farm Journal* is a source more closely identified
with the interests of the audience. Similarly the Townsend publication was mentioned as often as *Life* or the *Saturday Evening
Post*.

Since the messages of one source are identified as informational,
while all others are propagandistic, the first problem confronting
the unfavored source is to get its message to the audience. So long
as the audience operates on self-selection it is unlikely to expose
itself to the presentations of unfavored sources. Why listen to a lot
of propaganda? It has been shown more than once that in America
Democrats expose themselves to Democratic speeches, articles, and
editorials, while Republicans tune in on Republican presentations
(138). In a study for NORC of the effectiveness of an information
campaign on the subject of international relations, Hyman and
Sheatsley (102) found that internationally-minded people com-
prised the majority of the audience reached.

There are some well-known methods for reaching the audience
that will not select your message. One technique is to package the
message with something the audience will select—entertainment in
the case of the advertiser and sometimes in the political rally. Another method is to go directly to your audience—the highly effective personal approach in electioneering. In wartime the appetite
for news is so great on the home front that a certain number of
radio listeners will expose themselves to propaganda in the hope of
learning something not in their local papers. Among the troops
there is a great need for entertainment as well as news and so
Tokyo Rose and Lord Haw Haw had sizeable audiences.

If the message reaches the audience the problem is to cause
it to be categorized as information rather than propaganda. The
enemy in wartime has, by definition, interests opposed to those of
the audience. The opposition in politics similarly has its own goals.
This division in American politics is not, of course, as strong as the
national alignments of wartime. There are many voters whose
political identification is uncertain and they will consider the possibility that the other side has their advantage at heart.

One method for causing the message to be favorably categorized
is to conceal the source: e.g., to represent a preference for one
presidential candidate as the disinterested decision of a great

national magazine; to broadcast Allied messages as though they originated within Germany from rebellious Germans; to recommend pro-Soviet policies in a local newspaper. It is sometimes possible successfully to conceal a source. The La Follette Committee found that very little of the persuasive material originating with the National Association of Manufacturers was known to originate there (140). In 1934 the Federal Trade Commission found that much of the argument favoring private ownership of utilities in America originated with the utilities themselves but was not known to have this source. Messages of this kind would be much less effective if it were known that they originated with interested parties.

The chief difficulties with "black" propaganda are that it is difficult to make convincing, it is often unmasked, and likely to boomerang. Consider only the language of the presentation. One of the newspapers in Austria favored a Communist government but hoped that its campaign would be perceived as a local movement rather than as a Russian effort. The writers repeatedly betrayed themselves by the use of Soviet jargon—"collectivization," "bourgeois decadence," and the like. During the war the Japanese sometimes presented broadcasts supposed to be the testimony of American soldiers who had defected. These testimonies often involved errors in English usage that unmistakably *expressed* their Japanese origin. The Voice of America has found that the nationals of a country are more persuasive than American experts. It is difficult for an outsider to avoid expressing his membership in the outside group.

As an alternative to "black" propaganda the unfavored source can work to discredit the favored source and establish itself in that position. In the book of instructions to Nazi agents in North and South America appears a directive to plant lies in the publications of the opposition, lies which the Germans could expose. In this way the home presentations could be made to appear more propagandistic than those of Germany. During the war both the Allies and the Axis accused the other side of lying. It came to be the policy of Allied radio to tell the truth in the hope that the Axis would lie itself into the position of unfavored source with its own people. As Allied victories were becoming more frequent and Axis victories less frequent this was an easy policy to follow. We must add the proviso, however, that to tell the truth does not always express a truthful source. Where the truth is incredible the source will be categorized as lying. Herz (92) writes that it was actually the case that German prisoners of war interned in Canada had eggs for breakfast. This might seem to be a powerful argument for surrender to use on the individual Axis soldier. However, in pre-testing the story with captured Germans, it was found to be so incredible that the source was identified as a liar. Subjective or apparent truth expresses a truth-teller. Actual truth does not invariably do so.

While much may be done to shift the balance from one favored source to another it is unlikely in wartime that any people will actually put more trust in another government than in their own. For that to happen the fortunes of war must create some genuine common interest between a people and the enemy government. When it became clear that Germany would be defeated such an interest developed between the German common soldier and the Allied command. The German government was guilty and would have to be punished but the soldier would not be held responsible. Herz says that the most effective pamphlet used against the Germans was one that very simply documented the fact of imminent German defeat and then offered a safe-conduct to the soldier who would save himself. Having established a reputation for truth through their news broadcasts the Allies were thought trustworthy (as indeed they were) in this offer. Now that a real split of interest had developed between the German leaders and the people the Allies could capitalize on their long effort to establish themselves as a credible source. The split of interest was created by two things, the defeat of German arms, which no propagandist could control, but also the Allied insistence on distinguishing between guilty leaders and gullible people. This latter was a genuine persuasive achievement.

In persuasive competition with a most favored source the sources that are not favored can try to conceal the source of their messages or can try to shift the balance of favor. Competing sources are always alert to expose "black" propaganda and, in addition, it is always difficult not to reveal the true source of a message. Shifts in the balance of favor are best achieved by telling the truth but that is difficult to do when the truth is not favorable. The realities of victory and defeat are usually so evident that a genuine shift of favor must wait upon a genuine shift of interests. Once again we find the propagandist severely limited in what he can accomplish.

The Persuasion Competition with no Favored Source. In American advertising all sources are known to be interested. They may have some concern for the public welfare but they have more concern for the company's profits. A large number of equally interested sources urge the audience to take mutually exclusive actions. They are generally concerned with areas in which some action is sure to be taken. We all buy some kind of dentifrice, some toilet soap, some bread, some milk. Most of us buy some brand of cigarette, of beer, and hair tonic. Within a category of action we can move in any of a variety of directions—toward Pepsodent, Iodent, Colgates, Dr. Lyons, or Chlorodent. Most advertising aims at increasing the advertiser's share of a given action category. Occasionally, however, advertising aims to build a whole category—to increase consumption of milk, to make men feel the need of a deodorant. In this latter case the source can sometimes get away with a relatively disinterested tone since it is less evident that action will benefit a specific company.

The advertiser may dream of "black" propaganda but cannot easily accomplish it. However much his newspaper copy resembles a news story the Bourne Publicity Law of 1912 still requires that the copy be labelled "advertisement" which is to say "propaganda." The message presented may incidentally benefit the public but that is not its primary intent. The advertiser may cause his message to be spoken by a famous entertainer or athlete but as soon as the product name is mentioned the audience knows that money has changed hands and propaganda is being made. No doubt there are some innocent adults and very young children who are not aware of the hard facts of advertising, but the majority of the audience knows an ad when it sees one and knows also that the aim of advertising is not to benefit the audience.

Yet it is perfectly certain that advertising pays. The brand that advertises increases its share of the market. I will summarize only one recent and very convincing proof of the effectiveness of advertising: *The Hofstra Study—A Measure of the Sales Effectiveness of Television Advertising* by Coffin (42). The study was financed by the National Broadcasting Company. There were two matched groups of consumers—one group owned TV sets and the other did

not. Products in twelve categories were studied: gasoline, ciga-
rettes, razor blades, dentifrice, coffee, tea, cheese, soap, watches,
lighters, radios, and refrigerators. Within each category a study
was made of matched brands, one advertised on TV and the other
not. There were 3,270 interviews. Several of the results will give
the picture. More set-owners than non-set-owners used each of the
advertised brands. Fewer owners than non-owners used the brands
not advertised on TV. When a brand began to advertise on TV its
sales went up with set-owners while holding at a constant level for
non-owners. Persons buying TV sets increased their purchases of
advertised brands but not of brands unrepresented on TV. This is
a very cleverly designed study and it establishes a causal connection between television advertising and increased sales.

How is the effectiveness of advertising to be understood if
persuasive messages are effective only to the degree that the source
is believed to be disinterested, or identified with the audience, and
knowledgeable? All advertising is known to be interested and much
of it is disliked. Lazarsfeld and Kendall (139) found that 26 per
cent of their sample listed commercials as one thing they disliked
in radio.

Listening to TV owners, you form the impression that TV advertising is even more unpopular. The fact that advertising works
even though it is known to be interested, and even though it is
often disliked, has frequently been cited to prove the uncontingent
power of persuasive devices. Because Testimonial, Glittering Generality, Band Wagon, and Card Stacking are used in advertising,
and because advertising is effective, it has been assumed that these
dangerous techniques will be effective everywhere. To understand
the effectiveness of advertising we must examine the properties of
a persuasion competition in which all sources are known to be interested to see how this persuasive situation differs from others we
have examined.

The first important fact is that the kinds of action in which the
advertiser is interested are actions we all feel bound to make—the
purchase of some kind of food, drink, clothing, transportation, and
entertainment. We are presold on the action category, pre-sold by
our cultural experience and our animal necessities. Even the new
kinds of product are usually only new on the instrumental level.
They are aimed at familiar goals—health, comfort, and personal

attractiveness. To understand the effectiveness of advertising we must understand, then, that it is usually a competition to persuade us to move in various directions *one of which we are bound to take*. Some choice must be made between Pepsodent, Iodent, Chlorodent, and the others. It is a rare man who can let his teeth go unwashed.

Some choice must be made between equally interested advertisers. The man in the drug store will insist on knowing what kind of toothpaste I want. I have no convictions about any toothpaste so I am likely to say the name that comes most readily to mind. And that name will, of course, be the one I have heard most often. It is like a free association test. If you say *hot,* I think *cold*. Not because I like *cold* but because *hot and cold* is such a very familiar pairing in my experience. Although the druggist's question is worded as a request to state a preference it seems likely that the mechanism is often that of free association. Owners of TV sets belong to a linguistic subcommunity from which non-owners are excluded. In this community certain words, the names of TV advertised brands, have a higher frequency of occurrence than they enjoy outside the community. TV set-owners may say *Pepsodent* and non-owners *Colgates* just as inhabitants of Minneapolis say *Minnesota* in free response to *state* while inhabitants of Detroit say *Michigan*.

Where all sources are equally untrustworthy but where some choice must be made, *repetition* is the first law of persuasion. This is why all brands—whatever their merits, and whatever their persuasive techniques, increase their share of the market when they begin to advertise. In the Hofstra study it is reported that when a commercial is seen and *disliked* the set-owner buys more of the advertised brand than when he does not see the commercial. The one thing characteristic of all advertising is frequent mention of the brand name and that seems to be the pre-eminently effective technique.

The second important way in which the advertising effort differs from other efforts is in its concentration on a particular act rather than on an attitude. The advertiser wants us to buy his product. He would like us to think well of it too, no doubt, but what we think, say, or do is of no use to him if we don't buy. To buy one brand in preference to many others suggests a generally favorable attitude toward the brand. We would normally expect the buyer to praise the brand, argue for its merits, contribute money to its advertising campaign. The preference for one presidential candidate over another predicts such general favoring action. However, the purchasing act may be only an apparent preference. It may really be an act of associative memory. Although I think *Michigan* when I hear *state* it does not follow that I like Michigan; similarly, the act of buying one brand rather than all others is often not drawn from the population of behaviors defining a favorable attitude to a brand.

The indications are that while repetition increases the probability of buying a brand it is not a very good technique for building favorable attitudes. A person will often be well disposed toward an advertiser who pays for a program he very much likes. I feel that way about the Texas Company because it has broadcast the Metropolitan Opera for many years. However, when I buy gasoline I don't trouble to look for a Texaco station even though I have sometimes told myself that I ought to. My attitude centers on the Texas Company as a patron of the arts rather than as a gasoline. I speak well of it in this role but really have no opinions about Texaco gasoline. I know of many cases in which radio or television listeners have written to a sponsor or network to praise them for presenting a much enjoyed program. However, as often as not, these letter writers do not buy the advertised product. Their favorable attitude does not center on the product but on the sponsor as sponsor. Favorable attitudes toward products, as evidenced by more than perfunctory buying, by proselytizing for the product, usually grow out of a personal conviction that the product has merits. Such conviction ordinarily develops from use of the product. Repetition may serve to cause us to buy, but favorable attitudes and persistent buying seem to depend on the quality of the product.

It would be a mistake to suppose that repetition and the qualities of the product are the only effective devices in advertising. An effort is constantly being made to improve source credibility. Many of the transparent propagandistic devices used today were once effective means for suggesting a disinterested knowledgeable source. Probably the first time a famous baseball player endorsed *Wheaties* the audience thought he must be sincere. So famous and wealthy a man would not take money to endorse a product. But as different baseball players endorsed different cereals, and as rumors spread that baseball players didn't eat any cereals, the athletic endorsement came to express a sponsor's contempt for his audience, except, of course, for each new generation of youngsters—great cereal eaters—who are probably gullible for a short time. Probably, too, the first medical preference for one cigarette over others was effective; now it is a joke. Recently advertisers have tried to connect their messages with disinterested, knowledgeable sources by quoting the findings of "an independent survey." Sometimes developments in science precede commercial sales and dispose the audience to believe a message. It was fairly well known that ammonia retarded tooth decay and so the first ammoniated toothpastes were given serious attention.

The Great Public has a dim notion that there are legal limits on the degree of misrepresentation permitted an advertiser. Aren't there laws which prevent out-and-out lying? The advertiser is obviously interested first of all in selling his product and so might be inclined to lie without limit, but the sense of legal restraints holding him back gives some credibility to the message. Where a new brand makes bold new claims it may win some belief. This is especially probable where individuals in the audience greatly desire to believe. The need for an acne cure in teenagers, for relief from rheumatism in older people, increases their credulity and literally leads them to "try everything."

Finally, there is the persuasive technique that puts the theory of expressive behavior to work for the advertiser, the technique that undertakes to sell a product for its expressive value rather than for its utility or its intrinsic ability to give pleasure. Our very acuteness in absorbing incidental associations is used to induce us to buy. Hathaway shirts are pictured on an exceptionally civilized and distinguished looking chap with a patch over one eye who does nothing but spend conspicuous leisure time. Not surprisingly the Hathaway shirt becomes in our minds the badge of such persons and if we don such a shirt we feel rather like the Hathaway man and expect others to see us that way. In like manner a pipe can be made to suggest meditative masculinity and a streamlined cigar can seem to put a man in the class of up-and-coming junior executives. The astute advertiser today does not bribe a noble lord to endorse his walking sticks; he hires a model who looks like a peer to be photographed with the stick and makes no further comment. He saves the cost of the endorsement and gets round our suspicions of explicitly stated preferences and exhortations to buy. The habit that is our safeguard against so many unscrupulous efforts to persuade, the picking up of incidental associations among persons and things and actions, delivers us into the advertiser's hands. We buy his walking stick because it makes us feel aristocratic.

The Motivation Research people have used several familiar psychological methods to find out the expressive meanings of products, packages, and brand names. One such firm, for instance, found out for prune-growers that their product was widely thought of as the favorite food of crotchety, constipated, "prunesy" people and advised them to associate it with vigorous, youthful, healthy types. Motivation Research can also find out what kind of impression potential consumers of a product would like to make on the world and on themselves. Word association tests and the TAT story-telling technique are sufficiently indirect to get past the misleading rationalizations that may be elicited by direct consumer research questioning. If you ask a man what factors he takes into consideration in buying a car he is likely to talk about engines and economy when in fact he wants to wrap his ego in a long strip of chrome. It is the long chrome job that he will buy even if it has a rubber band for an engine.

Personally, I rather like the advertising that sells a product for its expressive value; it is so nicely adapted to our symbol-making habits. Some of those who rail against this kind of advertising seem to feel that it is necessarily a cheat to sell the consumer a symbol, as if the only real goods in the world were those that satisfy hunger and thirst. Behind this view too is that stubborn dualism which thinks of anything psychological as insubstantial and unreal. But we are not animals that we should select food for its nutritive value alone, or buy clothing for its ability to keep out the cold. The symbol that helps me to think well of myself may do me as much good as the meal that keeps me alive.

The selling of a symbol is not necessarily a cheat. If the makers of Hathaway shirts can sell the world on the expressive meaning of its product then I will get what I pay for—a mark of quality. But what if the product does not have the expressive value it is supposed to have? What if the buyer of Hathaway shirts sees them on middle-class drones like himself? What if the schoolteacher who saved up for a leisure-class trip to Bermuda meets only school-teachers on the boat? They will judge themselves to have been persuaded against their best interests, to have been propagandized. This is the point at which the technique becomes reprehensible but it is also the point at which our usual defenses come into action.

To be sure, we will absorb the associations between a product and a kind of person that an advertiser sets up for us, but we will also absorb the "real-life" associations between the product and persons and that limits what the advertiser can accomplish. In France the sale of Coca Cola has met an obstacle in that it is widely thought to be the favorite drink of undiscriminating American tourists with whom the Frenchman may not care to be identified. In an effort to change this meaning billboards went up in Paris picturing a hostess of evident distinction pouring a coke and remarking that it advertises one's good taste. Most people smiled at this ad. There are far too many boobs in sport shirts ordering cokes for the drink to be accepted as the choice of the discerning few. Indeed, a manufacturer's wish for large sales is in essential contradiction with the "select-few" variety of expressive advertising. What would happen if Hathaway shirts sold so well that men began wearing them to the factory and on beer picnics? The shirt could not effectively continue to represent itself as a symbol of the leisure class. The best way to get a product accepted as a symbol of high status is to charge a high price for it but, in that case, it probably will in truth be associated with people of high status and so its advertising does not lie and people get what they pay for. If a product has nothing of the expressive meaning it pretends to have its pretensions are likely to be "seen through."

Persuasion Situations in General. Sources of persuasive messages always hope to be perceived as disinterested and knowledgeable. They frequently present themselves as such—in so many words. Insofar as they can control their expressive behavior they intend it to express altruism. However, it frequently proves difficult to express a good character and, at the same time, pursue one's goals. The public finds that their goal-directed behavior *reveals* selfish motives. When that happens the audience identifies the message as propaganda and its effectiveness is reduced. Far from being helpless dupes of persuasive effort human beings are extremely alert to discover the motives of such effort and are often more interested in the motive than the message.

In practice we nearly always treat language as an expression of the speaker, but when we think about language we are quite likely to miss its expressive function. Even if the expressive function is detected it is likely to be credited with much less importance than the referential function. For this reason many mistakes are made in judging the persuasive value of messages. In the recent past, *Life* magazine published an editorial deploring the preoccupation of American novelists with degeneracy and unhappiness. The editorialist judged that a literature of this kind lowered American prestige abroad since it presented so grim a picture of American life. *Life* asked for an affirmative literature presenting the truth about this prosperous and happy country. Robert Penn Warren replied to the *Life* editorialist in the *New York Times* Literary Supplement for December 11, 1955. Mr. Warren shows that he is aware of the expressive value of behavior and of the ways in which it affects the persuasive value of a message. The following quotation contains much of Mr. Warren's argument. "I shall tell a story. A little while after the war in Europe I became acquainted with a young Italian who, in the first year of the war, as an officer in the Fascist Army, had deserted and taken to the mountains, to fight on our side. I once asked him what led him to this drastic step. He replied that American novelists had converted him. 'How,' I asked. 'Well,' he said, 'the Fascists used to let us read American fiction because it gave, they thought, a picture of a decadent America. They thought it was good propaganda for Fascism to let us read Dreiser, Faulkner, Sinclair Lewis. But you know, it suddenly occurred to me that if democracy could allow that kind of criticism of itself, it must be very strong and good. So I took to the mountains.'"

A point of view like that of the *Life* editorialist caused Ambassador Luce to withdraw the movie *The Blackboard Jungle* from the 1955 Venice Film Festival. It was felt that Europeans ought not to be told about juvenile delinquency in America. The withdrawal action had an expressive value of its own. Parisian and Roman newspapers ridiculed this sanctimonious, suppressive action. It gave us the character of a propagandist, trying to sell a bad bill of goods by concealing facts.

In addition to neglecting the expressive function of behavior the public usually also fails to distinguish between various kinds of persuasive situations. They do not make even the rudimentary distinctions of this chapter and, as a result, there is much faulty reasoning about persuasion and propaganda. For instance, there are those who tremble at the idea of a single Communist teacher in the schools. Since Communist propaganda appears to hold all the Russias in its grip they believe that it is also able to overwhelm a student body. This judgment ignores the difference between a persuasion monopoly backed by force and a persuasion competition with no favored source. An American student is the object of many persuasive efforts and that greatly reduces the power of any single one. Because Hitler said repetition was a powerful persuader, and because it appears to work in advertising, there are those who believe it is the sovereign technique for all persuasive effort. These people would dread exposing our soldiers to the enemy's repetitive lies. They ignore the fact that, in wartime, there is one most favored source while in advertising there is not.

Bruce Lannes Smith (213) has said that training in propaganda analysis of the type promoted by the Institute breeds a disturbing amount of cynicism in students. To identify particular styles of linguistic expression as propagandistic is, in effect, to say that people who talk or write that way are selfishly motivated. This is a disturbing and untrue generalization. The works of Christ, Buddha, Kierkegaard, and Laotse are filled with emotional expressions and glittering generalities. It is a strange teaching that all such literature is an effort to persuade us to act against our own best interests.

The consequences of propaganda analyses exposing techniques of propaganda can be described as a change in the expressive function of the technique. At one time a trembling voice and impassioned delivery probably expressed a sincere conviction that one's message was right for the audience. They may still do so if done just right on certain occasions. But in the Fourth of July orator, the political candidate, or the advertiser it is usually taken for hokum. A certain kind of tremolo in the voice has become the very stigma of insincerity, of deliberate propaganda. There is some indication that efforts at propaganda analysis have altered the expressive value of certain kinds of linguistic style. In 1936, for instance, Hartmann (89) found that an emotionally worded political pamphlet was more effective than one of less emotional tone. In recent studies, however, the two styles have been found about equally effective by Dietrich (54) and Hovland, Lumsdaine, and Sheffield (98). I am inclined to think that with better educated audiences today the dispassionate modest delivery has become most effective. We may be entering an era of calm, self-belittling commercials, of reasonable unemotional political speeches. The British manner is beginning to appear in magazine advertising and in "high class" radio and TV. Emotionality has begun to express falsity and a dispassionate tone to signify sincerity. To my mind this does not mean that propaganda is disappearing from our lives It is rather a change in the expressiveness of rhetorical styles. One can be quiet, modest, tweedy, and yet a villain.

Summary

We often speak in order to persuade others to take some action. Speech is not directly instrumental, it does not compel action. The consent of the audience is won by convincing them that the recommended action is in their own best interests. When someone judges a persuasive effort to be not in the best interests of the audience, though clearly to the advantage of the source, he identifies the effort as propagandistic. Everyone, all his life long, is the target of persuasive efforts and everyone, all his life long, tries to figure out when such efforts are propagandistic. It is instrumental to this goal to learn to make accurate judgments about the character (motives, values, knowledge, etc.) of other people. Such judgments are founded on observed covariations between what a person says or does at one time and what he will say and do in other circumstances; accurate judgments of character develop out of the habit of treating speech and other behavior as expressions of character. It is especially valuable to learn to interpret expressive symptoms since they often convey information the other person has not intended to reveal.

The effectiveness of various techniques of propaganda appears to be contingent on the presumed character of the message source. The informed person can detect Card Stacking and behind it the unscrupulous propagandist and that makes the message ineffective.

A unanimous Band Wagon can influence a lone subject on ambiguous matters, matters on which he has no conviction. However, if the subject has a confederate, or if he sees clearly the matter in question, he will come to doubt the motives or knowledgeability of the Band Wagon and so reject its suggestions. Prestige Suggestion is a technique of persuasion whose effectiveness is predicted by the fact that people habitually consider the character of the source. However, the possibilities of this technique are greatly limited by the fact that people can often detect a false linkage of message and source and by the fact that even a believable change in source will usually alter the reference of a message and therefore the actions that are implied by acceptance.

In a Persuasion Monopoly there is a necessary division of labor into the communicators and their audience. The principal danger to the effectiveness of the communicator is the possibility that the audience, having separated itself from him in terms of social function, may go on to detect a division of interests. Monopolies usually turn into Competitions With One Favored Source. The first problem for the source out of favor is to get its message to an audience that ordinarily will not select it since it has been identified in advance as propaganda. When the message has reached the audience the problem is to get it reclassified as information rather than propaganda. This involves establishing a good character and is only, in small part, in the control of the source itself. In a Persuasion Competition With No Favored Source the appeal and soundness of the message itself will count if the subject cares about the matter in question and if the sources all have a fairly good reputation. This seems to be the case of education in American society. In an open competition where all sources are discredited, and the actions to which the audience is urged are not important to the audience, repetition is probably the cardinal principle of persuasion.

The study of mass persuasion and propaganda should be brought within the general psychology of language. The first connection may lie in the expressive function of language and of all behavior. Evaluating the source of a mass communication is continuous with the expressive interpretation of behavior. There is a set of cognitive checks on persuasive efforts deriving from a habitual concern with propaganda detection.

chapter x   Linguistic Reference
in Psychology

Psychology is a curiously reflexive business. The design of experiments and the construction of theory are cognitive and linguistic labors and so, for the psychologist, they are both method and subject matter. Experimentally founded propositions of the form: "If X then Y," are, after all, *expectancies*—more trustworthy, perhaps, than those we acquire casually. The X and Y of the expectancy are categories. Should someone care to make practical use of this expectancy he must know how to recognize instances of X and Y. Should someone wish to repeat the experiments that gave rise to the expectancy, or perhaps to modify an experiment so as to refine the expectancy, he too must be able to identify instances of X and Y. For all these reasons, psychological writing must communicate concepts so that reader and author can reach extensional agreement. This requirement on psychological definitions is ordinarily called the requirement of *reliable* measurement. In the simplest case the "measurement" involved is only nominal, the assignment of instances to categories X and Y. Sometimes X and Y are dimensions to which ordinal or interval or ratio scales are applied and reliable measurement then requires that author and reader reach extensional agreement on the assignment of numbers to referents.

The categories or variables of psychology are never called X and Y. They are given names which belong to some larger language than that of psychology, probably to English, French, German, or Russian. When X has a name it becomes possible to ask whether the category or measurement and the name are well paired. Is the Stanford-Binet test really a measure of *intelligence?* Do the problems that Maier set his rats really involve *reasoning?* Are sociometric ratings a true index of *group morale?* In psychology this is usually called the requirement of *validity* in measurement. Does the operation in question measure what it "undertakes" to measure? From the point of view of linguistic reference this is a problem of the suitability of the match between a referent and its name. What the experimenter has "undertaken" to measure is revealed in the name he applies to his category or variable.

Social psychology adds one more reflexive contortion to those of laboratory psychology. The concerns of science grow out of the concerns of everyday life. A science seems never to originate interest in a range of phenomena but, rather, to professionalize a prior general interest. When the concepts and methods for dealing with the stars became sufficiently precise, specialized men began to speak of a science of astronomy. The science of psychology is still in its first century but men everywhere must always have worked on the problems of psychology. In the first days or decades, even centuries, of its scientific status a study will be using concepts and terms that are also to be found in general popular use. *Force* and *work, intelligence* and *human nature* are older words and concepts than the sciences of physics and social psychology. In physics, though the names are the same, the concepts have moved far from their popular origins and, indeed, are far from their contemporary popular equivalents. Physics can discard its popular origins and ignore its popular equivalents. The lay conception of gravity or of atomic energy is of no concern to the physicist; it does not affect his data. The social psychologist, on the other hand, must be concerned with popular notions about the character of the races or with popular notions about human nature in addition to being concerned with real ethnic character and real human nature. He may even be interested in popular ideas about atomic energy. Folk science, generally, belongs to the subject matter of social psychology and, when the folk science in question is social psychological, matters get particularly confusing. In certain cases what people believe has proved to be more accessible and perhaps more important than what is true. We know more about popular ethnic *stereotypes* than about the real character of ethnic groups, and we know more about popular beliefs concerning human nature than about *human nature* itself. Everyone has beliefs about racial and human nature and most people set great store by these beliefs. They are not lightly exchanged, for an alteration in such beliefs is itself an instrument of social change. What social psychologists say about the realities of their subject matter is itself a social force. This is a temptation to the reformist zeal in their nature and a discouragement to the scientific objectivity.

The first two sections of this chapter discuss the problems of *reliable* and *valid* linguistic reference in psychology. The last two sections discuss the concepts *human nature* and *stereotype* and the difficulties they pose for social psychology.

Reliability in Technical Linguistic Reference

By experiment we discover expectancies linking categories or variables. If X occurs can Y be far behind? Expectancies founded in science compel respect because they can be and are repeatedly checked. For that to be possible the terms of the expectancy must be defined so that others can identify instances or assign numerical values. We have become familiar with two methods for communicating concepts or categories: by pointing to instances and non-instances, the method of denotation; by naming the criterial attributes, the verbal method.

In an experimental report it is seldom possible to do the whole job of definition by the method of denotation. Suppose a clinical psychologist has been checking the Freudian notion that adults who have a psycho-sexual fixation at the anal level are likely to be pedantic, neat, and thrifty. He will not help the reader very much by including photographs of a sample of "anal characters" since these probably have no very trustworthy facial stigmata. To make a worthwhile empirical study of his Freudian hypothesis he must have independent definitions of such critical terms as *anal fixation* and *thrifty*, and it must be possible for others to apply these terms as he does. Probably this psychologist will have worked from behavior rather than physiognomy, with such things as answers to questions, reminiscences of parents, stories told about ink blots or pictures, preferences in profanity, proportion of earnings saved, etc. In his experimental report he may help us by pointing to certain behavior products—examples of "anal" stories or interviews. Piaget, we know, has studied the causal explanations of very young children. In his report (180) of this research he distinguishes seventeen varieties of causal explanation, and to help us understand these, he includes numerous "typical" verbatim examples of each variety. McClelland and his associates (155) have devised a technique for measuring the strength of achievement motivation and have used this technique in many studies. The measure works from stories told about pictures and involves the identification of "achievement imagery" in such stories. To help the reader understand what achievement imagery is like the book includes many examples from actual stories. Denotation in psychological writings seldom provides us with the full range of contrasts to teach the category or to enable us to measure the variable, but such a range will ordinarily be available in a scoring manual, a more detailed report elsewhere, or upon inquiry from the authors. Denotation is most often used to fill out a verbal definition with a few examples. In many cases the definition is entirely verbal with no denotation whatever.

A verbal definition can communicate a concept when the terms of the definition are reduced to familiar experiences for everyone. This is so obviously the case with certain definitions or measures that the reader who undertakes to work with them feels no requirement to demonstrate his extensional agreement with the author. This is true of those laboratory methods that put physical instruments to some psychological use. If a psychologist chooses to he may take a given deflection of a string galvanometer which is arranged so as to measure galvanic skin reaction as evidence of "guilty knowledge." In his report it will be enough to describe the wiring of the apparatus and to specify the numerical deviation defining guilt. No one likely to apply this definition feels the need for pictures teaching how to read the galvanometer. The basic perceptual operation involves recognizing the coincidence of a pointer and a line on a scale and that is a thoroughly familiar operation on which high agreement is guaranteed. The psychologist's "reliability" problem here is no different from, or greater than, that of the physicist, and that is true of all physicalistic psychological methods —reaction time taken from a chronoscope, for instance. There are, in addition, many behavior observations not involving physical scales which have a prior familiarity and a known reliability. No denotative training is required to teach us to tote up the number of correct answers on a fixed alternative paper and pencil test, or the number of trials taken to learn to recite a list of nonsense syllables, or the number of trials required before a maze can be run without error. The perceptual judgments involved in all these measures have familiar unequivocal names and so words alone will suffice to define them.

There is another class of psychological categories where extensional agreement cannot be assumed to exist, where the experimenter must report a reliability coefficient. This coefficient is a statistic describing the degree of extensional agreement between the experimenter and someone else. If the measure or concept is not the experimenter's own invention he usually compares his judgments with those of the inventor and reports their degree of agreement. If the measure or concept is the invention of the present experimenter he correlates his own judgments with those of several colleagues to whom he has supplied a definition. A high correlation is a guarantee to the reader that the definition communicates enough extensional agreement so that others can work with the same category or variable. It is a guarantee that the terms of the expectancy established in the experiment need not be the private property of the man who did the experiments.

Verbal definition alone will often fail to bring others to adequate extensional agreement. Even verbal definition with examples may not do it. In his study of the causal explanations of children Piaget offers no reliability coefficient and so no guarantee that his system of classifying explanations can be used by others. J. M. Deutsche (52) undertook to check the Piaget stages in the development of the notion of causality with a large sample of American children. To do this he had to be able to classify new causal statements into Piaget's seventeen classes. He naturally wondered whether his classification would be the same as Piaget's. Deutsche abstracted the best definition of each category given by Piaget and combined these with examples from the original work. After studying these definitions, Deutsche and two other psychologists independently classified a collection of new statements. There was much disagreement among the three judges; only 21.76 per cent of the items being classified in the same way by all of them. In effect, Deutsche tested the Piaget definitions by the method of extensional agreement and found them deficient. What Piaget wrote about his seventeen classes does not convey the ability to identify new instances in a reliable fashion. With content analysis of this kind, building reliability is an important part of the procedure and a high coefficient an essential guarantee that the categories can be shared.

It sometimes happens that much training is necessary to bring a new judge into that state of grace where he can reliably categorize. This is the case with McClelland's Achievement Motive. The authors of the measure supply verbal definitions of the types of imagery to be scored and, in addition, a set of sample protocols with their approved scoring. An experimenter who wishes to work with this variable practices scoring on some of the stories, then checks himself against the answers. When his agreement with the authors reaches a high level he is ready to operate. In a sense the experimental instrument has been constructed in his own mind.

It sometimes happens in psychology that an experimenter wants to work with variables that cannot be reliably assessed even with considerable training, and yet the variables are believed to be capable of assessment by a particular class of judges. Suppose subjects are to be rated on "ego strength," or "therapeutic improvement," or "narcissism." The experimenter may despair of setting up definitions that communicate and yet he may be convinced that professionals can apply the terms in a consistent fashion. If so, the variable may be assessed by clinical ratings. In this case the application of the term is held to be so esoteric a business that no short training course will suffice. To be a judge of "ego strength" one must have the experiences guaranteed by a degree in psychiatry or clinical psychology.

Society as a whole recognizes that some terms involve semantic rules whose appreciation requires a lifetime of study. The general population may bandy these terms about but when their application is important everyone else stands back to hear professional counsel. The judgment of "legal insanity" is this kind of judgment. The law holds that some men are morally responsible and that others are not. Only the sane can be held accountable and only the sane ought to be punished. Psychiatrists are a class of beings equipped to judge whether a penal or a custodial-therapeutic code should be applied to a man. Frederic Wertham (241), who has often been asked to advise on murder cases in New York City, describes the difficulty the psychiatrist has in diagnosing "legal insanity." These arise from the fact that "insanity" is not a psychiatric concept. Psychiatry does not find that the behavior of some men is determined and the behavior of others free. The law has compromised the free will-determinism issue and handed psychiatry the job of drawing the line. Not surprisingly, extensional agreement is low. In many cases (e.g., the Leopold-Loeb murder) prosecution and defense have been able to find conflicting expert testimonies. This experience warns the experimenter that when he uses expert testimony he is still bound to obtain high reliability coefficients to rule out the possibility that understanding of a term is entirely idiosyncratic. If experts can be described, and if experts can agree, new experimenters can find new experts and work with the same variable.

Validity in Technical Linguistic Reference

Psychological variables are not called X and Y. They have names, usually names not invented by the psychologist, names possessed of a considerable history and a more or less well known semantic. What relations hold between the psychologist's use of the term and the usage of the larger community? His new rule of reference must respect established rules. The particular community whose usage commands most respect changes with the character of the research.

Research for an Employer. When an experiment is paid for, the employer's usage defines the validity of a measure. Suppose a psychologist has been hired to improve "morale" in a factory unit. His major problem will be discovering what "morale" means to his employer. Is it possible to speak of good "morale" in a factory where production is low? Do workers with good "morale" develop a particularly militant union? Do workers with good "morale" plan their recreation together? By attending to the employer's usage of "morale" the psychologist may discover that the word reduces to low absenteeism, high production, and an absence of strikes. In some cases the psychologist may discover an internal contradiction in management's aims. Perhaps certain concessions in wages or safety devices or rest periods are essential to the attainment of more important goals. He may succeed in selling the "farsighted" meaning of "morale" if this semantic shift simply involves recognizing the expediency of temporary, small losses as a means to lasting, large gains. There is room for some creative interpretation at this point. Still the validity problem is basically solved by the expectations of the person paying for the research. "Morale" has been improved when desired changes have occurred.

Professor John Carroll of the Harvard Graduate School of Education has recently developed a test of "linguistic aptitude." Many questions might be asked about the validity of any such measure. Is not aptitude innate and should not the test, therefore, yield scores that do not change with age? Should all great writers have high scores on such a test? The validity problem, in this instance, is greatly simplified by the fact that the organizations interested in the test and Professor Carroll, himself, want to be able to predict performance in college foreign language courses. That is the meaning of "linguistic aptitude" to them and the measure will be a valid index of such aptitude when it predicts such academic performance. General English usage of *linguistic aptitude* is of no concern here.

Research Testing Existent Theory. Psychologists have often performed experiments to test some existent theory. When that theory is Hullian the problem of valid measurement is not likely to arise because the constructs of this theory have been turned into measures by the author. When the theory is Freudian, however, the terms have not been operationalized by the author and validity is a problem for anyone who undertakes to test the theory. Cameron (31, 32), for instance, attempted to check the Freudian idea that schizophrenic thought is regressed. He reasoned that schizophrenic thought, if regressed, should resemble the thought of children. He therefore compared the causal explanations for physical phenomena given by children, normal adults, and schizophrenic adults. Cam-

eron found that schizophrenic thought processes were unlike the
thought processes of children. He took this to be a disconfirmation
of Freudian views on schizophrenia. Consider now the impact of
this result on one who is an adherent of Freudian theory. It recommends that he revise statements he has been disposed to make
about schizophrenia and regression. Alternatively he can let these
statemes to stand if it seems that Cameron's experimental treatment
of such terms as "schizophrenia," "thought," and "regressed" does
not jibe with his own usage. In the present instance the treatment
of "regression" is the likeliest point of attack. Freud described the
schizophrenic ego as regressed to the stage of primary narcissism.
However, he places that stage in earliest infancy while Cameron's
children were between seven and nine years of age. The results
of this experiment need not be interpreted as a disconfirmation of
Freudian theory since the problem has not been posed in a way that
validly represents the theory.

In the empirical testing of Freudian theory the following sequence has been often repeated: a term is turned into a reliable
experimental procedure; the experimental definition is criticized by
those who know the theory well; the definition is refined into a
more valid index. Psychologists once thought they could test for
"repression" by asking subjects to recall as many events as possible
from the previous summer and then to label them "pleasant" or
"unpleasant." If fewer unpleasant memories were reported it was
thought that repression would have been demonstrated but, in fact,
much more is required to satisfy informed referential use of this
term. For instance, repression must be motivated by anxiety and
there must be evidence that repressed material survives in the unconscious. Taylor (222) attempted to test "sublimation" by inquiring into the sex lives of forty brilliant, healthy, esthetically refined,
and unmarried young men to see if they were diverting sexuality
into the sublime channels that lead to undergraduate eminence. He
discovered that all of his subjects enjoyed direct sexual satisfactions
of one sort or another. A disconfirmation of sublimation? Not
necessarily. To mention only one deficiency, sublimation is concerned with pre-genital sexuality and Heaven only knows what
Taylor's subjects were doing about that. In all these studies the
validity of a definition is judged by an élite that knows the theory
well. Satisfying them has not proved easy. Freud used his terms

with a grand carelessness and when to this we add the exegetical variations among his disciples it is not easy to determine informed usage.

The experimenter cannot be eternally obliging about this business of refining definitions, for there are some psychoanalytically-inclined folk who cannot be pleased unless the experiment confirms the master. Their attitude may be revealed in a parable. Suppose a non-literate people to have developed a rain dance. It is their expectation that when this dance is performed rain is constrained to fall. Perhaps this expectation has been fulfilled on a great many occasions. Now there comes a time, or a number of times, on which the dance is ineffective. What will be done? Will society yield to the pressure of empirical evidence and cease to believe in the rain dance? Probably not. By this time the dance has been institutionalized; there is a priesthood, a ceremony for consecrating dancers, a temple for performance of the dance itself. Nobody feels like recognizing a disconfirmation of this fundamental belief. Under these circumstances the "dance" may be redefined. In order to be effective it must be performed with a properly "reverent" frame of mind. The priest may point out that this was written down from the beginning but had been overlooked. The recent disappointments have not diminished the rain dance but have proved the dancers guilty of irreverence. The variable has moved inward. It is now a more spiritual faith and also a less vulnerable one; less vulnerable in the sense of being able to be disproved. This is a direction in which religious beliefs often move. The Christian law is in part such a spiritualization of the Mosaic Law. Sins are not only such overt acts as theft, adultery, and blasphemy; a man sins who thinks evil. As a man is in his heart so is he. This is an exalted but not an operationalized morality. Christ told his disciples that if they had faith enough they could move mountains. He did not describe to them any technique for determining whether or not one had such faith except the moving of mountains. In these terms the statement is incapable of disproof since the requisite faith is inferred from the effect it is presumed to have caused. When scientific theories become religions they tend to become invulnerable in this same way. It is difficult, for instance, to get psychotherapists to describe the prerequisites or characteristics of successful therapy in terms that do not involve the outcome of such therapy—remission of symptoms. In refining an empirical definition to meet the usage of a theorizing élite, one must beware of the vicious circularity which may be the unwitting goal of that élite.

Research Involving Terms from Common Parlance. Many of the basic terms in psychology come to us from colloquial speech. *Reason, intelligence, emotion, learning,* are none of them terms coined by psychologists. When experimental variables are named by words like these the problem of validity is especially interesting.

Suppose we were to set about developing a measure of intelligence. We might decide that intelligence should be proportional to the circumference of the cranium at the trans-orbital ridge. This is a physical measure and presents no problem of judgmental reliability. However, it presents a serious problem of validity. Have we a measure of intelligence?

The word *intelligence* is imbedded in popular discourse. People who speak English are disposed to ascribe more *intelligence* to boys who get good grades, build racing cars from soap boxes, and win essay contests than to boys who do not do these things. Speakers of English are disposed to find intelligence in animals to the degree that they behave like man. These are a few rough rules for the denotational use of the word. The validity question here asks how well the cranial circumferences of men and animals predict the application of the term. Is it true that, of two individuals with different cranial measurements, the one with the larger head will be the one people are likely to call more *intelligent?* Unfortunately for this definition there is no such clear relation. There are macrocephalic idiots whom no one will call *intelligent.* There are the hippo and elephant whom few will think more *intelligent* than the chimpanzee. And the dinosaurs, we understand, were not clever enough, despite their great heads, to survive a change of climate. In short, the cranial measure does not rank people and animals in anything like the order in which we commonly rank their intelligences.

Speakers of English are disposed to form utterances like "A man's intelligence is native to him" or "Intelligence is inherited." If head size is an indication of intelligence, and intelligence is native, an individual's relative standing should be fixed at birth and continue unchanged. This is not the case. Heads grow with age and not all at the same pace. The operation for measuring intelligence falsifies a common assertion using the word. In general, then, the definition is invalid because it is inconsistent with common usage.

To validate a measure of intelligence or achievement motivation one must demonstrate that the measure in question relates to other measures in a way that generally fulfills expectations derived from popular discourse. Binet (18) put together a test that predicts school performance, produces low scores from the mentally retarded and high scores from the outstandingly creative. Furthermore an individual's score does not change very much with age. This measure satisfies our discourse and, therefore, is an *intelligence* test. McClelland and his associates (155) developed a measure that predicts endurance in problem solving and which yields high scores for outstanding campus "achievers." The picture is not quite so clear as with Binet's test but the McClelland measure appears to be correctly named.

In the case of the McClelland measure it seems to me that "validation" has turned into something more interesting. In addition to finding out whether or not their measure has been correctly named the authors are finding which of several familiar senses of *achievement motivation* best describes the measure. There is a kind of achievement motivation which is mainly concerned with meeting external standards, an "Other Directed" motivation in David Riesman's terms. A person motivated in this way is anxious to do well but what constitutes "doing well" is decided by others. Another sort of achievement motivation is problem centered, the goal is not easily revised by social pressures. A person motivated in this way is "Inner Directed," at least in the sense of being relatively independent of the values of others. It has been discovered that a high score on the McClelland measure predicts an independent performance in the Asch group pressure situation described in the last chapter and it predicts also resistance to prestige suggestion. Winterbottom (155) found that the mothers of children who earned high scores on the McClelland measure expected their children to become independent in many ways at an earlier age than the mothers of children who earned low scores on the measure. From these and other indications it appears that the authors have measured a kind of independent or problem centered achievement motivation.

Most of the vocabulary of folk psychology has been given operational translation. *Reasoning, emotion, learning, motivation* are the names of experimental chapters in modern psychology. Of the classical terms, only *will* or *volition* cannot now be found in psychology. English speakers are disposed to make the following sentences using *will:* "The will is free and undetermined," "A man exercises his free will." Sentences predicating freedom and indeterminacy of the *will* are among the most probable utterances involving the word. What operation can be devised that will not falsify this disposition which is so essential a part of ordinary usage? The psychologist is usually committed to determinacy in human behavior. Any behavior that validly translates *will* can have no reliable antecedents. It must be unpredictable behavior. Those few psychologists who have used the term are men whose commitment to determinism is not wholehearted. For the rest the functions of the *will* have been absorbed by *motivation* or *ego strength* or *expectancy*—terms not so committed to freedom in popular discourse.

The psychologist who borrows words from common usage is not inevitably required to abide by that usage. It is possible to distort the sense of a familiar word and to have one's personal semantic prevail. Savory (201) points out that the words *force, work, power,* and *weight* taken by physics from ordinary speech have acquired stable scientific meanings that depart from their originals. Because the physicist has decided that a *force* does *work* only when it moves something, "I may push and pull in vain at some unmovable obstacle, make myself hot and tired by my efforts and yet find that mathematically I have done no work" (201). In the world of physics metals can "fatigue" and oils "crack" though these assertions seem odd to the man in the street. If a concept is powerful enough, if a measure has enough predictive power, it can persuade a profession, even a society, to use an old term with a new meaning. It would not, ultimately, matter whether the Binet test measured *intelligence* so long as it measured something important.

There is a famous theoretical controversy, one that has been doing well in the psychological literature for about twenty-five years, in which the relations between popular and technical usage of a word have been very important. The word is *hypothesis* and the controversy concerns the continuous or non-continuous nature of discrimination learning. The story may be said to begin with Lashley's (135) suggestion that "in the discrimination box responses to position, to alternation, or to cues from the experimenter's movements usually precede the reaction to light and represent attempted solutions that are within the rat's customary range of activity." He further suggested that the actual correct association might be formed very quickly and that the practice preceding the solution might be irrelevant to its formation.

Shortly after the publication of Lashley's book *Brain Mechanisms and Intelligence* Krechevsky (131) proposed that these "attempted solutions" be called "hypotheses." He demonstrated by appropriate analysis of discrimination learning records that the rat does systematically run through a series of behavior patterns during which his responses are always selective with respect to one or another of the stimuli present in the situation. Thus the animal may begin with a position preference, then drop that in order to respond to other differentia, eventually hitting upon the important discrimination. "Hypothesis" meant "response consistency"—a simple, reliable definition.

The non-continuity theory of discrimination learning, championed by Krechevsky, held that the animal learns something about the significance of the stimulus to which he is responding but nothing about stimuli to which he is not "paying any attention." The stimulus to which he is paying attention was to be inferred from his response consistencies; it would be the stimulus that regularly predicted the response.

Spence (216), serving as spokesman for the continuity view, held that the excitatory tendency of the positive stimulus increases in strength with each reinforced pairing with the response. Learning will occur if the stimulus impinges on the animal's sensorium. It need not be attended to.

These two viewpoints generate opposed predictions which make possible crucial experimentation. The paradigm for such experimentation occurs in the study of McCulloch and Pratt (156) requiring monkeys to make a weight discrimination. For an experimental group the investigators reversed the significance of the cue stimuli during the presolution period in which the animal was not responding more than 50 per cent of the time to the positive cue stimulus. A control group did not have the cues reversed but continued throughout on the same problem. If continuity theory were true it would seem to follow that the experimental group, handicapped by reversed cues, should learn less rapidly than the control group which would receive positive reinforcements from the beginning. Since non-continuity theory holds that the animal only learns what it is attending to, the events of the presolution period should have no bearing on the solution of the problem. Consequently the control group would not be expected to learn more rapidly than the experimental group.

McCulloch and Pratt in their original study "found" for continuity theory—that the control group excelled the experimental. Subsequent variations on this paradigm have turned up data favoring both sides. In the interpretation of these data there is a problem relevant to the interest of this chapter. As originally defined, "hypothesis" was to mean response consistency and the presolution period was to include those trials prior to the testing of the correct hypothesis. In his experiments, however, Krechevsky employed varying numbers of reversed cue trials and then interpreted these as presolution trials if that would make the data suit his theory. When the experimental group suffered from the reversed cue trials these were assumed to have encroached upon the solution period. If this assumption were correct the non-continuity theorist could explain the data obtained since the animal would have been subjected to a reversal of cues to which it was attending. However, the assumption was not checked against the learning record but was invoked wherever convenient. This, as Spence quickly pointed out, was not playing the game.

The word *hypothesis* was not, of course, created by Krechevsky, nor was its meaning exhausted by his index of response consistency. Speakers of English will say of a *hypothesis* that it is a tentative proposition, a working theory, an idea to be tested. They will not hesitate to say that someone "may entertain a hypothesis without acting on it." Under the pressure of unfavorable experimental results Krechevsky's understanding of hypothesis fell back to this popular meaning. He deserted response consistency as an index of hypothesis testing and suggested that the rat might "have in mind" hypotheses he was not, at a given moment, doing anything about. The opposition has been quite willing to let *hypothesis* stand as response consistency even though this index does not adequately represent ordinary usage. In this case they have been willing to forget about the usual sense of the word because if *hypothesis* be response consistency continuity theory has scored a victory. The noncontinuity theorist, acting in accordance with neo-Gestalt laws, prefers to revise his operational index rather than his theoretical framework. While it may be true that animals can learn about a stimulus to which they are not responding in consistent fashion, it certainly is not true that animals can learn about a stimulus to which they are not attending. It remains for the continuity theorist to find a more valid indication of what it is the animal has in mind.

Research Involving Newly Created Technical Terms. It is finally possible to invent a name for a measure or a concept. There is some feeling that this possibility has been overdone in the social sciences and there is a certain amount of disdain for our "jargon." I would like to propose a definite meaning for the word "jargon": that it be applied to any unfamiliar term created to name a concept that is already familiar and has a familiar name. Thus if *super-ego* is nothing but *conscience* Freud is guilty of having written some "jargon." The terminology of the social sciences can now be called "jargon" if the concepts are familiar. It is a question whether this be the case or whether those who accuse the social sciences of "jargon" have not understood them well enough to distinguish their concepts from certain familiar ideas.

Actually the linguistic creations of science are never really new. The scientist could, to be sure, select some phonemes from his language, arrange them in a unique but permitted sequence, and call his new test an index of *Sloff*. The ability to create such words is a part of knowing English. We saw in Chapter I that anyone can do it. However, there are difficulties with *Sloff*. For one thing it resembles certain English words—*sloth, laugh, soft*. These resemblances will suggest the nature of *Sloff* before the scientist has a chance to define it carefully and the suggestion may be misleading. An unfortunate name could equip the concept with a permanent, misleading connotation.

Ordinarily any sequence of sounds will call up some meaning. The only way around this is to have a rule for the naming of concepts that is known to guarantee arbitrary sound-meaning correlations. If a set of test factors be named by the letters of the alphabet no one will be misled by these names. In the biological sciences new specimens are tagged with the discoverer's name and knowledge of this rule causes us to neglect any possible phonetic symbolism. Where no such rule exists, as in psychology, the name will inevitably suggest a meaning. Therefore we do not leave this matter to chance but select sounds so that their prior semantic is congruent with the sense we wish them to have.

New words could be made from English resources by the controlled arrangement of phonemes or by the novel combination of English morphemes. Neither of these techniques of invention is common in science. The former method is not common anywhere. Probably this is because the semantic value of novel phoneme combinations is not clear enough to guarantee the desired meaning. The method of combining English morphemes to create new words is common in advertising but not in science.

In the physical and natural sciences, at least, new names are customarily drawn from Greek or Latin. In many cases the word is simply imported without any change. *Bacillus, cerebrum, corolla,* and *focus* are all borrowed from Latin; *soma, larynx, cotyledon,* and *genesis* are from Greek. In other cases the scientist makes a new combination of Greek and Latin morphemes: *ectoderm* and *photosynthesis* are from the Greek, *univalve* and *quadruped* are from Latin; *haemoglobin* mixes the two. Since these scientific terms are borrowed from natural languages, it would seem appropriate to ask the validity question. Is this concept or operation really what it purports to be? However, the validity question is not raised for *octopus* or *annelida* or *cybernetics.* Instead here is a different question. Has the concept or operation been aptly named? Scientists often set great store on finding a good word for whatever it is they have to name. Why should the validity question be displaced by a question about the suitability of the name?

Apparently the important difference is that the word has been imported from abroad. Its meaning can depart from previous usage without interfering seriously with anyone's linguistic habits. Where the word has been put together by the scientist there is no customary use of the term to worry him. In the modern community of scientists Greek and Latin derivatives will often be quite unfamiliar. The form is free to take on new meaning and, yet, because we know it to be a borrowed word we discount the phonetic sym-

bolism that might have misled us in a free invention. Sooner or
later someone will acquaint us with its etymology and the half
appropriate original meaning almost will seem to be a witticism
of the author.

The Persuasive Power of the Human Nature Concept

The concept *human nature* has a powerful persuasive force in
human affairs. This force makes the concept a particularly interesting social psychological datum and, at the same time, makes it extremely difficult to use in a consistent technical fashion. With one
term, *human nature,* used by both the profession and the people,
it has been difficult to separate what they think from what we think
and to remember who thought it first.

Human nature is generally understood to be a listing of qualities
common to all mankind because they are innate-unlearned. Un-
deniably a part of this universal human nature are the vital drives
that maintain the organism. In our experience these drives have
always proved ultimately irresistible. It is possible to hold one's
breath for seconds, to retain urine for hours, to fast for days, but
all these acts of control have limits which have not been exceeded
by anyone living. In our experience whatever resists the vital drives
must eventually yield.

We have also found that any scheme that does not allow for
the vital drives is bound to fail. If a man plans to walk across the
desert he had better think about water supplies. If a man intends
to take a safari into the jungle, to climb a mountain, or rocket to
the moon, his first concern must be to guarantee that the vital needs
can be met in these exotic settings. Any undertaking that does not
make such provision is foredoomed.

The next step is to suppose that there are psychological motives
which are also a part of human nature. I use *psychological* to refer
to functions of the organism, that are presumed to involve primarily
the central nervous system, but which it is not at present possible
to describe in any neurological detail. It is my conviction that the
psychological characteristics of the organism are no less physical,
no more disembodied than the biological characteristics. The difference lies in the fact that we may learn about biological matters

by studying the tissues and juices of the body, while the psychological aspects are only revealed in behavior. *Learning* is now studied by way of performance. It may be, however, that *learning* corresponds to neuronal growth across the synaptic gap in accordance with the theory of neurobiotaxis, and some day it may be possible to study *learning* on that level. It follows from such a view that psychology may be an interim science destined to wither away as neurology advances. I think this is about as imminent as the withering away of the Soviet dictatorship but I would not deny the possibility.

Without all these qualifications most people will assume that human nature involves psychological motives as well as biological drives. These motives are credited with the same universality, insistence, and innateness as the vital drives. Suppose, for a moment, that one is living under a tyranny or that the social system is, for whatever reason, felt to be restrictive or oppressive. It will be useful to believe that there is in human nature a yearning toward freedom. To call this yearning a part of human nature is to suggest that it is universal, insistent, and certain to be satisfied. Such a need can be bottled up as one can bottle up one's breath but it must eventually burst its container. This is excellent revolutionary rhetoric. It exhorts a man to feel what all feel, to join a cause that must triumph.

Rousseau's "natural man" loved freedom and equality as did Rousseau himself. It is far more persuasive to be told that these are "natural" desires than it is to be told that they are the desires of one man—Rousseau—conceivably a malcontent. The empiricist analysis of the human mind begun by Locke, and followed through by Berkeley, Hume, and many others, is an epistemologist's way of declaring that all men are created equal. We cannot suppose it accidental that this philosophy dominated the century of the French revolution. When men are interested in changing society they are able to construct a view of human nature which predicts the desired change.

If, on the other hand, one is content with the social status quo it is convenient to discover a different set of social motives—motives which the present society perfectly satisfies. The apologist for capitalism finds in human nature a profit motive or a competitive instinct or a natural desire for private property. Radical schemes that do not assume such motives are "harebrained." Socialism, we are told, simply "does not jibe with human nature."

The persuasive value of the human nature concept is not limited to political argument. It can also function in the internal arguments that constitute personality dynamics. Nancy Mitford's little novel *The Blessing* illustrates this area of usefulness. The heroine of the novel has married a dashing French nobleman who loves her intensely but not exclusively. She discovers one of his infidelities and is made desperately unhappy. Friends of her husband assure her that he is behaving quite "naturally." Man is not "naturally" monogamous, she is assured. Why not forget what she knows and go on as before? He is grieved to have distressed her and feels a fool for having been so careless. Except for his indiscretion, she has not suffered any lack of attention or felt any lessening of his devotion. The lady tries to reason herself into this civilized frame of mind but cannot manage it. The pain of the knowledge is too great to be suppressed. At this juncture she suddenly sees—almost as a revelation—that it is "human nature" to be jealous of a lover. This formulation is gratifying. It says, in effect, that jealousy is like hunger—universal and irrepressible. She cannot be expected to change. If anything is to be done he must make the adjustment. Lovers in such a situation may dispute for the possession of a phrase—"human nature." In this case the disputant who gains the phrase finds his conduct justified and himself established as the fixed quantity to whom adjustment must be made.

Most generalizations about our psychological human nature run into contradictory instances. Motives we had thought universal and innate prove to be parochial and acquired. However, popular conceptions of human nature can be quite resistant to evidence. Contrary instances are handled as super- or sub-human, as glorifications or degenerations of the type. In spite of the common belief that the first law of human nature is self-preservation, our society includes both suicides and martyrs. The second law is probably preservation of the race and yet there are both homosexuals and members of chaste religious orders who do not subscribe to it. All such cases are defined as "unnatural"—some admirably so, others execrably so. Once an individual has been labelled in this fashion we are relieved of the responsibility to understand him. The man who defies human nature defies comprehension. Around every society there is a fringe of "unnatural" persons who violate the local conception of human nature and are denied understanding.

If it should eventually be proved and accepted that most of the psychological motives that have been called "natural" are not common to all men but are, rather, the creation of particular social systems, it will not follow that they are either feeble or easily changed. These expectations derive from a lingering dualism that finds anything psychological rather vapourous. Men have sought torture and death for psychological reasons. The profit motive created by a capitalist economy may resist any socialist efforts to eradicate it. It is probable that an urge to freedom will not be destroyed by any amount of persecution. If we think of the acquisition of psychological motives as involving actual structural changes in the nervous system, we will better estimate their force and endurance. Revolutionists know that not everyone can be persuaded. With some people one must wait for death. We certainly need not believe that only natural motives are strong.

In one particular, however, it may be very important whether certain psychological motives are believed to be "natural" or "cultural." For what is natural is supposed to be innate while the cultural is acquired. Innate qualities will recur with each generation of children. If the same qualities are acquired each child begins— to colloquialize Locke—with a clean slate. American political theory, growing out of British and French philosophy, has a strong environmentalist slant. Our experience of the rapid acculturation of immigrants seems to confirm this theory. Our indigenous psychologies have all constructed a picture of human nature that is congruent with American political doctrine.

John Watson (236) is, of course, the extreme environmentalist in our recent history. His assertion that any normal child, with proper environment and training, can be made into "any type of specialist I might select—doctor, lawyer, artist, merchant-chief, and, yes, even beggarman and thief, regardless of his talents, penchants, tendencies, abilities, vocations, and race of his ancestors" is a famous extreme. The appeal of Watson's writings is, in part, attributable to the fact that they rephrase the sentiment "All men are created equal."

Freud, in his last years, constructed a rather pessimistic model of human nature. Thanatos—the death instinct—compelled man to destroy others and eventually to destroy himself. Crossing the Atlantic, psychoanalysis underwent a sea change and in America we find little mention of its gloomier instinctivist side. It emerges as a theory and a therapy dedicated to human perfectibility. It affords a rationale for drastic revisions of child training practice— revisions aimed to improve the adult product. Psychoanalysis blends nicely with Pavlovianism in the work of Miller, Dollard, Mowrer, Whiting, Sears, etc., and there emerges an American psychology dedicated to the view that man's nature is created in society. This is, of course, just the right psychology for a democratic, equal opportunity, melting-pot society. The fit is as good as that between the requirements of the Soviet society and its scientific psychology, though we believe it has been accomplished by different means.

The term *human nature* is forceful, both politically and personally. The social scientist, like Hobhouse, Murdock, or Klineberg, who attempts an objective examination of the cross-cultural evidence to determine what is universal and innate must cope with his own prior commitments and the commitments of his society. The psychologist who constructs a view of human nature from his studies in the genesis of behavior has also his own loyalties and predilections. Where the evidence is incomplete, as it now is, the theorist's prior convictions must be expected to exert an influence on his construction. It will not be easy to arrive at technical definitions that are independent of popular definitions when the term is as persuasive as *human nature*.

The psychological profession and the larger linguistic community are engaged in a constant interchange of verbal materials. The linguistic stream that feeds us sometimes poisons us. We have little opportunity to refine a technical vocabulary because our words quickly pass through the semipermeable membrane separating us from the larger society and then return to us substantially altered.

The Definition of Stereotype

Human nature is the name of a conception in professional psychology and also of a conception in folk psychology. No linguistic distinction is made between what most people believe and what social science has established. Perhaps the failure to use different names is the cause of some of our confusions, making it easy for scientific notions to affect social processes and for popular notions to move into science. In the study of racial or ethnic nature we do make a linguistic distinction between the scientific and the popular conception. Social scientists have ideas about *national character* whereas the general public has *national* or *racial stereotypes*.

From the writings of social scientists it is clear that they have a poor opinion of racial stereotypes. They think it is at least irrational and probably wicked to subscribe to them, and today a large part of the American public agrees with this judgment. This was not the case in 1933 when Katz and Braly (122) established a method for studying stereotypes. They asked Princeton undergraduates to characterize a dozen ethnic groups (German, Jew, American, Turk, Negro, etc.), drawing from a list of eighty-four trait names. Their subjects found the task congenial and were generally agreed in reporting Jews to be "shrewd," "mercenary," and "industrious"; Turks to be "cruel," "very religious," and "treacherous"; Negroes to be "superstitious," "lazy," "happy-go-lucky," etc. Similar studies in many parts of the country turned up a few regional specialties like the Texan conception of Mexicans and the Californian conception of the Chinese. However, beliefs about most ethnic groups were uniform across the country. In the years since these early studies were conducted the stereotypes have changed in a manner consistent with America's shifting military and diplomatic alliances. The Japanese got more "treacherous" for a few years and the Germans more "militaristic" but they are now returning to their pre-war "intelligence" and "industry." In 1950 Gilbert (72) repeated the Katz and Braly procedure with a new generation of Princeton men. He found them much less willing than their predecessors to generalize about ethnic groups. Some simply rejected the task, others gave answers but insisted that they were only describing group trends to which there were numerous individual exceptions, still others who characterized the groups insisted that they were simply reporting "what people said" not what they themselves believed. The social scientist's judgment that stereotypes are bad has affected the stereotypes themselves. Educated people in America have become very suspicious of generalizations about races or nationalities or religions. Advertisements in the subway train adjure us all not to "infect" children with the poisonous stereotypes. The mass circulation magazines are contemptuous of "stereotyped thinking" about ethnic groups. What is wrong with *stereotypes* that is not also wrong with notions of *national character?*

There have been attempts to define the *stereotype* as a special kind of mental construction containing fundamental illogicalities that make it undesirable. It has been said, for instance, that a stereotype is a generalization; it overlooks individual differences. To react to a person as a German is to forget that no two Germans are exactly alike. Stereotypes are "bad" because they are indiscriminate. This characterization is insufficient because it does not distinguish stereotypes from any other categories. The notion of a right triangle is also a generalization; it overlooks differences of size and color and location. And so are all categories generalizations that overlook differences. However, this is not necessarily a bad business. Right triangles are all equivalent in that they satisfy the Pythagorean theorem. Walter Lippmann (147) invented the word *stereotype* and he defined it as a mental picture. It is not, of course, clear whether the individual who manifests a stereotyped conception of the Turk has in his head a generic image of the Turk. The "picture in our heads" notion is not only uncertain but, in addition, does not help to distinguish stereotypes from other concepts. We are as likely to have a generic image of the right triangle as of the Turk.

Definitions of the *stereotype* as a generalization or as a mental image have had unfortunate effects. Some people have been led to believe that every sort of generalization about national or religious groups is untenable and morally reprehensible. The ability to entertain such notions is for some the hallmark of Fascistic proclivities. Among social scientists there are some who suspect the study of *national character* of being a step toward black reaction. Sometimes a college student who has been talked out of his *stereotypes* in a psychology course is amazed to discover, on his first trip abroad, that the Germans really are different from the Italians. He may then develop new, "empirically founded," tourist conceptions of national groups. These often reverse the evaluations in the home grown *stereotypes* with the childlike Italians currently ranking very high. Sometimes a college graduate will feel that his business experience compels him to believe that Jews really *are* mercenary or Negroes lazy or Swedes stupid and he becomes a little contemptuous of the Ivory Tower psychologist. At the same time every educated person knows that it is bad form to express racist notions. The prevalent opinion is that decent people are partners to an agreement to pretend that ethnic groups are all alike but realistic men of experience privately know better.

For Katz and Braly the stereotype was bad but not just because it was a generalization or a mental image. It was bad because it was a false generalization. This is certainly a better direction for the definition to take: *stereotype* to be the name for false ethnic beliefs and *national character* the name for valid generalizations. However, this definition commits the social scientist to demonstrate the falsity of the beliefs he intends to label as *stereotypes*. Katz and Braly described their work as a study of verbal stereotypes and yet they offered no data to prove that the beliefs of their undergraduate subjects were false. Is it possible that the social psychologist has used the word *stereotype* to stigmatize beliefs of which he disapproves but which he does not know to be false? Has he perverted his science to achieve a moral purpose?

If popular conceptions of ethnic groups were proposed as exceptionless generalizations there would be no need to report data proving them false. Only a single exception would be necessary and everyone is acquainted with exceptions. Certainly not all Jews are mercenary; neither are all Negroes superstitious nor all Germans militaristic. The most limited experience with a group falsifies almost any exceptionless generalization. However, there is no reason to suppose that Princeton men in 1933 thought that the traits they ascribed to a group were true of all members. There is every reason to suppose from work done since 1933 that people seldom believe in the exceptionless ethnic generalization. The popular notion is not that all Germans are militaristic but that Germans *tend to be militaristic*. The falsity of such a qualified belief is much more difficult to demonstrate than the falsity of an exceptionless generalization.

Perhaps, then, stereotypes are false in that a trait is believed to be more characteristic of an ethnic category than it actually is. This is difficult to prove. We should need, in the first place, to know just how characteristic of the ethnic group a given trait is believed to be and the literature on stereotypes does not provide such data. In the second place we should need to know just how characteristic the trait really is and we have very little information on that point. There are, to be sure, reports of IQ averages in various ethnic groupings. In most cases, as Allport states (6), the Jewish IQ has run a little higher and the Negro a little lower than the average of other groups. But this confirms the stereotype that Jews are intelligent and that Negroes are not. We also know that Jews are underrepresented on the stock exchange in Wall Street and in the banking profession (6). This contradicts the stereotyped belief that Jews are usually financiers and money lenders, for while we do not know just how distinctive this trait is held to be of Jews it could not be distinctive at all unless the group was somewhat above average in this regard. There is very little more known about the truth of stereotyped beliefs. It follows that the term *stereotype* has not been used to label beliefs of demonstrated falsity.

How, then, can the social scientist justify his attack on *stereotypes?* There can be no question of the attack. *Stereotype* is not just the name for any popular conception of the character of an ethnic group; it is the name for conceptions that are undesirable because they are false. The falsity has not been directly proved. The best we can say is that certain things we know about these popular beliefs tend to discredit them, to suggest that they are false or, at any rate, not well founded.

Many of the traits attributed to ethnic groups are logically incapable of being proved or disproved. This is because the adjectives used express attitudes as often as they make verifiable assertions. To say that the Chinese are "superstitious" is to say that they hold certain supernatural beliefs *and to express our contempt* for these beliefs. The prevalence of the beliefs can be determined but not whether these beliefs are "superstitious," "spiritual," "religious," or "magical." Many Americans who have been abroad report that the Italians and French and British are all "dirty." The frequency with which the population of a country bathes can be determined but not whether that frequency makes them "dirty." The adjectives used in ethnic stereotypes are commonly evaluative in nature and the propriety of applying them cannot be determined in any absolute sense. It is possible, however, that the empirical core of the attribution might be demonstrated.

The individual who believes that Chinese tend to be conservative cannot possibly know all the Chinese in the world. How then can he support his generalization? It may be contended that he has noted the prevalence of conservatism in the sample of the Chinese population that he does know. But is that sample representative? Perhaps his sample of Chinese acquaintances is biased in the direction of conservatism. Probably no one ever knows a random sample of an ethnic population and so no one is ever in a position to generalize about that population. It is even sometimes true that an individual holds stereotyped beliefs concerning a group when he is acquainted with no members of the group. The readiness with which Katz and Braly's subjects characterized the Turk is a notorious example. Many studies have shown that stereotypes are not necessarily abstractions from personal experience. They are often learned verbally. The trait-adjectives are linked with the group-noun until the child puts them together in his own conversation and thoughts. This fact does not succeed in demonstrating that stereotypes are ill-founded beliefs. Much that we know comes to us by report only. The whole past history of the world, the description of unvisited lands, the biographies of people we have not met—all stock our minds with knowledge that must be taken on faith. Parents are the source of much information that is true and useful. It may be that the ethnic stereotype is the distilled wisdom of many people made available to us by our parents.

However, those individuals who are in a position to know best about an ethnic group often do not subscribe to the stereotype. B. M. Kramer (130) has shown that the belief that Negroes are unclean is stronger in residential areas remote from Negroes than it is in areas adjoining Negro dwellings. In one housing project described by Deutsch and Collins (51) there were some buildings in which both Negroes and whites lived and others in which these groups were segregated. In the unsegregated buildings 80 per cent of the whites thought the Negroes were the same as themselves, while in the segregated buildings only 50 per cent held this belief. During the Second World War, according to the Information and Education Division, United States War Department (103), white men in the army were asked how they would feel about companies in which Negro platoons were combined with white platoons; 62 per cent of these men disliked the idea. The idea was put in practice in several companies, and of the men in these companies only 7 per cent thought it a bad idea. There is then some evidence that people who contact members of an ethnic group as equals do not subscribe to popular stereotypes concerning the group.

Finally, the truth of the stereotype is made doubtful by data showing that belief in the stereotype serves personal needs. In some cases the content of the stereotype is too patently a wish fulfillment to be believed. This is the case when a European nation decides that the natives of an oil-rich little island are just naturally incapable of handling their own affairs. Sometimes the content of the stereotype is too obviously a rationalization to be taken seriously. This is true of the belief of some Southern white men that Negro women are just naturally sensual, amoral creatures. This is a particularly dubious claim when we note that the men who make it have been in the habit of making casual sexual use of Negro women. Campbell's study (34) showing that anti-Semitism is strong among men who are dissatisfied with their own achievements argues against the notion that stereotypes are rationally founded. The extensive work with the authoritarian personality by Adorno, *et al.* (2), argues the same way as does the everyday observation that people who strongly believe in stereotypes do not change them when they meet exceptions to the ethnic rule. Stereotypes are seldom revised under the impact of new evidence. None of this work proves that the content of stereotypes is false. It only shows that belief in stereotypes can be motivated behavior, highly gratifying to the one who believes, and, therefore, that there are reasons to look for distortion of the truth.

A case has been made for defining the "stereotype" as a false generalization. In making the case, however, we have had to argue indirectly from evidence not collected for this purpose and, at best, have only shown that the stereotype is ordinarily not founded on trustworthy evidence. It seems to be clear that social scientists carelessly adopted Lippmann's ill-defined word and used it as a term of opprobrium for beliefs linked with ethnic prejudice.

A distinction should definitely be made between popular conceptions of racial or national character and the conceptions of social science. The distinction cannot at present be made in terms of demonstrated falsity and validity. It ought not to be made in terms of the persons subscribing to the belief. Much of the work described in the literature on national character has no greater claim to validity than the beliefs of the layman. The "impressions" of a social scientist seem to me to have little more value than the "impressions" of anyone else. We ourselves conform to the laws of human behavior. Even anthropologists are "culture-bound," even psychiatrists are influenced by unconscious needs, even experimental psychologists show the effect of motivation on perceptual selection. Training in a social science does not lift a person above the laws revealed by that science. The study of national character has a right to be distinguished from popular impressions and its conclusions have a claim to greater validity insofar as this study observes canons of evidence not observed by the layman. The student of national character must be concerned to have a representative sample, to make reliable observations, to distinguish culture-bound judgments from ascertainable facts, and to recognize that a trait characteristic of a national or religious group is not necessarily innate in the group.

Social scientists feel very strongly about ethnic stereotypes and there is no reason why they should not. It is a commonplace saying that values have no place in science. This is sometimes foolishly taken to mean that a scientist ought not to be disposed to form sentences of the type: "X" (name of a scientific concept) "is good (or bad)." Is there a physician who will not say that cancer is bad or an intelligence tester who will not say that intelligence is good? These judgments present no problem for medicine or psychology, and neither does the judgment that ill founded, rigidly maintained, culture-bound judgments about supposedly innate characteristics of national groups are bad.

The trouble begins when the scientist cannot give an entity its scientific name without consulting his attitude toward the entity; when his feelings for or against a thing affect its scientific classification. The intelligence tester can diagnose individuals as *moronic* or *average* or *very intelligent* without regard to his liking for these individuals and different testers will agree on the classification of subjects though they may disagree in the way they feel about the subjects. The layman, on the other hand, is inclined to describe a new acquaintance as *intelligent* if he finds him congenial.

Suppose the actual rule of reference governing the word *stereotype* is that it shall be the name of any statement about an ethnic group with which I do not agree. Suppose, in addition, that the rule of reference is "represented" to be that *stereotype* shall be the name of any demonstrably false statement about an ethnic group. To the degree that social scientists have the same values they can agree on the application of the word *stereotype* and can use it to attack a set of popular beliefs. The attack may boomerang if the public checks the beliefs and finds some of them true. To the degree that social scientists have different values they will not be able to agree on the use of the word *stereotype*. A belief about Negroes that is a *stereotype* in the northern United States may not be a *stereotype* in the southern United States. A belief about Germans that is a *stereotype* to German social scientists may be a statement about *national character* to American colleagues. The social scientist is certain to feel strongly about his subject matter. His values are part of his motive force. But the value must not figure in the rules of reference governing the use of technical terms. Values vary and scientists must speak a common language.

Summary

There must be reliably applied rules of reference linking scientific terms to scientific categories. Where there is any doubt of reliability a test of extensional agreement should be made. Because scientific terms are ordinarily borrowed from some existent vocabulary it is possible to ask the validity question: "Has the scientist measured what the name commits him to measure?" It seems always to be necessary to worry about prior understanding of the name by one or another linguistic community though the particular community that matters changes with the nature of the research.

The concepts and language of social psychology are powerful social forces. Popular notions of human nature have always been sensitive to popular aspirations and fears. So long as the evidence is incomplete, the conception of human nature developed by a social scientist is likely to be sensitive in the same way to his personal values. In the study of ethnic natures a linguistic distinction has been made between the *stereotypes* of the people and the notions of *national character* held by scientists. The popular stereotypes have not been proved false, but it has been proved that they are not well founded in direct experience, that they sometimes serve to "rationalize" selfish actions, that they often take the form of untestable, culture-bound judgments, that they are not sensitive to contrary evidence, and that they ascribe to racial inheritance what may be a cultural acquisition. In short the intellectual respectability of the popular stereotypes has been convincingly impugned. Conceptions of national character can be distinguished from stereotypes when they are based on superior evidence and reasoning.

chapter xi Conclusions

IT IS UNFORTUNATE, in a way, that so many
people have been interested in the psychology of language. Most
of them have had a say in this book and in the resulting polyphony
it will not have been easy to keep track of the set of propositions
championed by the author. I would, therefore, state the major
themes of the volume—without corollaries, qualifications, or dissent-
ing opinions.

1. *Both linguistic forms and referents are categories and can be
described with a single metalanguage.* Every language unit,
whether phoneme, word, phrase, letter, or paragraph, is identified
by certain attributes while freely changing in numerous other attributes, and this is also true of the referents of language units.
Just as there is some essential invariance in the many pronunciations of the word *book,* so there are invariant properties in the
many publications that can be labelled with that word. Here, of
course, is our major premise from which many other things follow.
Its tenability can be judged in the first three chapters where speech,
writing, and referents are analyzed in the category metalanguage.

2. *Since they are apprehended as instances of categories rather*

than as unique events, both linguistic forms and referents recur and give rise to expectancies. An event appreciated in all its detail occurs but once and so affords no basis for expectancy. The past repeats only when it is categorized, i.e., when some detail is disregarded. The uses of expectancies are familiar enough. They help us to identify each event as it occurs because not all events are expected to be equally probable. If I hear "Bell, Book and . . ." I can anticipate "Candle" since that completes the familiar title of a play. With so strong an expectancy I can identify the next word even if I do not hear it very clearly. Furthermore, when it is desirable to take action in the present, expectancies enable us to make that action appropriate to a probable future. If someone sets a cocktail glass on a polished table I can quickly lift it and forestall the probable ring.

3. *Since both linguistic forms and referents are categories they can share criterial attributes; i.e., there can be phonetic symbolism.* This is most obvious with an onomatopoeic word like *cock-a-doodle-doo* where the bursts of noise that constitute the referent are matched by bursts of noise constituting the linguistic form. However, there is a less obvious phonetic symbolism where the referent is not acoustic. The segmentation of the centipede is matched in the reduplication of the word *ongololo.*

4. *Since referents are categories they can share criterial attributes, and so the name of one category may be extended to the other, thereby creating a metaphor.* There are similarities between a person tightly laced into his clothing and a person tightly bound by a sense of propriety. When the latter sort of person was first called *strait-laced* a metaphor was created, a metaphor that has outlasted the style of clothing that generated it.

5. *While animals make selective response to numerous categories of stimulation, this performance is not the same as linguistic reference.* The animal response lacks many characteristics of the linguistic "name." It does not belong to a set of responses sharing a fairly simple phonological structure in which there is a distinctive response referring to each of the categories known to the social group. The animal's performance is not governed by the sorts of contingency that operate with linguistic names.

6. *Because linguistic invariance is much simpler than invariance of reference, language guides the child in his cognitive socialization.* Whether speech is analyzed into phonemes or distinctive

features, its significant attributes are not numerous. Referents, on the other hand, have an endless and ever expanding variety of criterial attributes. After a few years of hearing his native language a child can at once recognize the invariant aspects of a new linguistic form and be guided by their repetition to the discovery of a coordinate invariance of referent. A child hearing the word *desk* for the second time knows it to be a repetition because its criterial attributes are preserved and he can compare the two occasions to discover the characteristics of the non-linguistic world that govern the occurrence of the word.

7. *Referent categories may not be equally codable for all persons or for all communities. The level of codability is probably an index of cognitive availability.* Codability can be measured in several different ways: a) by the length of a name; b) by the amount of agreement on a name; and c) by the delay in producing a name. To the degree that a category is available it will be utilized in forming expectancies. Within one language community different professional groups have their special vocabularies to go with their special constructions of reality. Physicians have an elaborate nomenclature for diseases and we may guess that they apprehend persons as instances of disease categories and prognosticate accordingly. Different language communities may have different codability scores for categories of kin, for personality types, for livestock, for kinds of weather, even for the basic classes of sensation such as colors, tastes, and smells. It is hypothesized that the terms of their expectancies are correspondingly unlike.

8. *Parts of speech are best defined as classes of syntactically equivalent linguistic forms, but it must be recognized that these classes also tend to be differentiated semantically and that naïve speakers are aware of the semantic differences.* It was shown in an experiment that very young American children use the part-of-speech membership of a new word as a clue to the word's meaning. Perhaps our notions of the fundamental categories of reality—process, object, substance, quality—are derived from the semantics of the English parts of speech. Perhaps languages having different semantic distinctions among their parts of speech teach a different metaphysics.

9. *Language forms covary with characteristics of the person producing them as well as with characteristics of the external world, i.e., language is expressive.* Speech is treated as an *expres-*

sion whenever we use it to categorize the speaker. When someone says: "I am afraid," and his audience concludes that he is, in fact, afraid, his statement has been treated as an expression. In this case the speaker probably intended that his statement should be so interpreted since he uses words that explicitly categorize himself as afraid. On the other hand he might have said: "I am brave," and yet been categorized as afraid because of a telltale quaver in his voice. In this case one aspect of his speech is treated as a *symptom;* it indicates that a speaker belongs in a certain category but does not name that category. The speaker had not intended to create that impression. Whenever anyone tries to persuade us of something for selfish reasons of his own, i.e., whenever anyone propagandizes us, he will intend to conceal his private purpose and to express an altruistic character. However, we are all very skilled at picking up symptoms of true character and so there is a good chance that the propagandist will unwittingly give himself away. This is the great cognitive check on the power of propaganda and advertising. It can be temporarily circumvented by one device or another but eventually such devices are seen through and deprived of their effectiveness.

10. *The vocabularies of children and of pre-literate peoples probably have a smaller proportion of very general superordinate terms than do the vocabularies of literate adults.* Probably this difference in vocabulary is not evidence of a difference in ability to abstract. Children and pre-literate peoples seem to be able to operate with very general categories. The shortage of very general *terms* is ultimately to be explained by the fact that they are less useful for the purposes of children and primitive societies than are terms on a more concrete level.

11. *Very abstract categories (in the sense of categories having many distinct subordinates) are probably more difficult to acquire than relatively concrete categories.* While it has not been demonstrated that the ability to form such abstractions increases in the phyletic scale this is likely to be the case. It is also likely that as children grow older they become increasingly capable of such abstractions. If abstraction is to be an exalted mental function it is better defined in terms of the number of distinct subordinates than in terms of the number of entities included within a category.

12. *With respect to category attainment and utilization, the performances of schizophrenics and aphasics are in many ways unlike*

those of normal persons. However, the performances of individuals belonging to the same disease group are not the same and the various performances reported seem to have no common characteristics. The schizophrenic who interprets the proverb "A rolling stone gathers no moss" to mean that "moving objects are unsuitable for plant growth" understands the words more narrowly than does the ordinary person. On the other hand the schizophrenic who puts the doctor's yellow pencil with the yellow Vigotsky blocks understands this task more broadly than does the ordinary person. The schizophrenic who puts one set of blocks together because they are all policemen has a different order of availability for his categories than does the ordinary person. The aphasic who does not recognize an egg on sight but must see it cracked requires more attributes of high criteriality than is normal. The aphasic who cannot change his classification of a set of color yarns is abnormally rigid about recategorization.

13. *The problems of reliability and validity in psychological measurement translate respectively into the problems of consensual agreement on the identification of referents and the appropriateness of a measure to its name.* Where consensus cannot be taken for granted an experimenter must demonstrate his ability to identify new instances correctly. The reliability coefficient is a measure of the amount of agreement in the referential use of a term. Because psychological terms are usually borrowed from some existent vocabulary it is necessary to ask whether the psychologist has measured what the name commits him to measure. The relevant prior understanding of the term may be that of an employer subsidizing research, a theorist whose theory is to be tested, or the linguistic community at large from whom the term has been appropriated. Ultimately it will not matter whether the measure satisfies prior understanding so long as it measures something important. Except in the case of subsidized research the validity problem is only a badly formulated version of the problem of discovering the properties of a measure. The authors of the measure of the Achievement Motive, for instance, are not by now worried about whether their measure gets at what most people mean by achievement motivation. They simply want to know what kind of personal characteristic it is that they are measuring.

14. *The psychologist can feel as strongly evaluative about his subject matter as the physician does about his. However, if there is*

*to be agreement on the referential use of psychological terms the
value must not figure in the definition.* Conceptions of "human
nature" are themselves a powerful social force and have been more
closely related to the values of the social scientist than to the state
of the evidence at any given time. There is reason to believe that
the term *stereotype* has been used by American social scientists to
stigmatize beliefs of which they disapproved. The emergence of a
set of approved generalizations about ethnic groups under the title
national character requires that the social scientist distinguish the
two sets of beliefs in terms of their demonstrated truth value or, at
least, in terms of the trustworthiness of the procedures by which
they are attained.

References

1. Adams, J. "Expressive Aspects of Scientific Language," in H. Werner (ed.), *On Expressive Language*. Worcester, Mass.: Clark University Press, 1955, pp. 47-52.
2. Adorno, T. W., Frenkel-Brunswik, Else, Levinson, D. J., & Sanford, R. N. *The Authoritarian Personality*. New York: Harper, 1950.
3. Agnew, D. C. *The Effect of Varied Amounts of Phonetic Training on Primary Reading*. Durham, N. C.: Duke University Press, 1939.
4. Allport, F. H. *Social Psychology*. Boston: Houghton Mifflin, 1924.
5. Allport, G. W. "Phonetic Symbolism in Hungarian Words." Unpublished manuscript, Harvard University, 1935.
6. ———. *The Nature of Prejudice*. Cambridge: Addison-Wesley, 1955.
7. ———, & Kramer, B. M. "Some Roots of Prejudice," *Journal of Psychology*, 22: 9-39, 1946.
8. Arieti, S. "Some Aspects of Language in Schizophrenia," in H. Werner (ed.), *On Expressive Language*. Worcester, Mass.: Clark University Press, 1955, pp. 53-67.
9. Asch, S. E. *Social Psychology*. New York: Prentice-Hall, 1952.
10. ———. "On the Use of Metaphor in the Description of Persons," in H. Werner (ed.), *op. cit.*, pp. 29-39.
11. Bateson, F. W. *English Poetry and English Language*. Oxford: Clarendon Press, 1934.

12. ——. English Poetry; A Critical Introduction. London: Longmans, Green, 1950.

13. Benedict, R. F. The Chrysanthemum and the Sword; Patterns of Japanese Culture. Boston: Houghton Mifflin, 1946.

14. Benjamin, J. D. "A Method for Distinguishing and Evaluating Formal Thinking Disorders in Schizophrenia," in J. S. Kasanin (ed.), Language and Thought in Schizophrenia. Berkeley: University of California Press, 1946, pp. 65-90.

15. Bentley, M., & Varon, Edith J. "An Accessory Study of Phonetic Symbolism," American Journal of Psychology, 45: 76-86, 1933.

16. Berelson, B. "What Missing the Newspaper Means," in P. F. Lazarsfeld and F. N. Stanton (eds.), Communications Research 1948-1949. New York: Harper, 1949, pp. 111-28.

17. Berkeley, G. A Treatise Concerning the Principles of Human Knowledge. Dublin: A. Rhames (printer), 1710, pp. 4, 9, 10.

18. Binet, A. L'étude Expérimentale de L'intelligence. Paris: Schleicher, 1903.

19. Birdwhistell, R. L. Introduction to Kinesics: An Annotation System for Analysis of Body Motion and Gesture. Washington, D. C.: Foreign Service Institute, Department of State, 1952.

20. Bloch, B., & Trager, G. L. Outline of Linguistic Analysis. Baltimore: Linguistic Society of America, 1942.

21. Bloomfield, L. Language. New York: Holt, 1946, p. 429.

22. Boas, F. The Mind of Primitive Man. New York: Macmillan, 1938, p. 217.

23. Brown, R. W. "Language and Categories." Appendix to J. S. Bruner, J. J. Goodnow, & G. A. Austin, A Study of Thinking. New York: Wiley, 1956.

24. ——. (1957), "Linguistic Determinism and the Part of Speech," Journal of Abnormal and Social Psychology, 55: 1-5, 1957.

25. ——, & Lenneberg, E. H. "A Study in Language and Cognition," Journal of Abnormal and Social Psychology, 49: 454-62, 1954.

26. ——, Black, A. H., & Horowitz, A. E. "Phonetic Symbolism in Natural Languages," Journal of Abnormal and Social Psychology, 50: 388-93, 1955.

27. ——, & Hildum, D. C. "Expectancy and the Identification of Syllables," Language, 32: 411-19, 1956.

28. ——, Leiter, R. A., & Hildum, D. C. "Metaphors from Music Criticism," Journal of Abnormal and Social Psychology, 54: 347-52, 1957.

29. Bruner, J. S., Goodnow, J. J., & Austin, G. A. A Study of Thinking. New York: Wiley, 1956.

30. Bühler, K. "Tatsachen und Probleme zu einer Psychologie der Denkvorgänge," Archiv für die Gesamte Psychologie, 12: 1-92, 1908.

31. Cameron, N. "Reasoning, Regression, and Communication in Schizophrenics," Psychological Monographs, 50, No. 1, 1938.

32. ——. "A Study of Thinking in Senile Deterioration and Schizophrenic Disorganization," American Journal of Psychology, 51: 650-64, 1938.

33. ———. "Deterioration and Regression in Schizophrenic Thinking," *Journal of Abnormal and Social Psychology* 34: 265-70, 1939.

34. Campbell, A. A. "Factors Associated with Attitudes Toward Jews," in T. M. Newcomb and E. L. Hartley (eds.), *Readings in Social Psychology.* New York: Holt, 1947, pp. 518-27.

35. Carnap, R. *The Logical Syntax of Language.* London: Kegan Paul, Trench, Trubner, 1937, p. 12.

36. Cattell, J. M. "Uber die Zeit der Erkennung und Benennung von Schriftzeichen, Bildern, und Farbern," *Philosophische Studien,* 2: 635-50, 1885.

37. Child Study Committee, International Kindergarten Union. *A Study of the Vocabulary of Children Before Entering the First Grade.* Washington, D. C.: The International Kindergarten Union, 1928.

38. Childe, V. G. *Man Makes Himself.* London: Watts, 1936.

39. Church, R. M. "Factors Affecting Learning by Imitation in the Rat." Doctor's thesis. Cambridge: Harvard University, 1956.

40. Clarke, Helen M. "Conscious Attitudes," *American Journal of Psychology,* 22: 214-49, 1911.

41. Clemens, S. L. "The Horrors of the German Language," in *Mark Twain's Speeches.* New York: Harper, 1910, pp. 43-52.

42. Coffin, T. E. *The Hofstra Study: A Measure of the Sales Effectiveness of Television Advertising.* New York: N.B.C. Research Division, 1950.

43. Committee on Reading. *Studies in Reading,* Vol. II. Publications of the Scottish Council for Research in Education, 34, London: University of London Press, 1950.

44. Comstock, Claire. "On the Relevancy of Imagery to the Processes of Thought," *American Journal of Psychology,* 32: 196-230, 1921.

45. Crosland, H. R. "A Quantitative Analysis of the Process of Forgetting," *Psychological Monographs,* 29, No. 130, 1921.

46. Cummings, e. e. *I; Six Nonlectures.* Cambridge: Harvard University Press, 1953, p. 46.

47. Currier, Lillian B. "Phonics or No Phonics?" *Elementary School Journal,* 1916.

48. Dashiell, J. F. *Fundamentals of General Psychology.* Cambridge: Riverside, 1937.

49. Davis, K. "Extreme Social Isolation of a Child," *American Journal of Sociology,* 45: 554-65, 1940.

50. ———. "Final Note on a Case of Extreme Social Isolation," *American Journal of Sociology,* 52: 432-37, 1947.

51. Deutsch, M., & Collins, Mary E. *Interracial Housing: A Psychological Evaluation of a Social Experiment.* Minneapolis: University of Minnesota Press, 1951.

52. Deutsche, J. M. "The Development of Children's Concepts of Causal Relations," in R. G. Barker, J. S. Kounin, and H. F. Wright (eds.), *Child Behavior and Development.* New York: McGraw-Hill, 1943, pp. 129-45.

53. De La Garza, C. D., & Worchel, P. "Time and Space Orientation in Schizophrenics," *Journal of Abnormal and Social Psychology*, 52: 191-95, 1956.

54. Dietrich, J. E. "The Relative Effectiveness of Two Modes of Radio Delivery in Influencing Attitudes," *Speech Monographs*, 13: 58-65, 1946.

55. Dolch, E. W., & Bloomster, Maurine. "Phonic Readiness," *Elementary School Journal*, 38: 201-205, 1937.

56. Dollard, J., & Miller, N. E. *Personality and Psychotherapy; An Analysis in Terms of Learning, Thinking, and Culture.* New York: McGraw-Hill, 1950.

57. Doob, L. "Goebbels' Principles of Propaganda," *Public Opinion Quarterly*, 14: 419-42, 1950.

58. ———. *Social Psychology.* New York: Holt, 1952.

59. DuShane, G. "Of Books and Reading," *Science*, 123: 703, 1956.

60. Ebbinghaus, H. *Uber das Gedachtnis: Untersuchungen zur experimentellen Psychologie.* Leipzig: Duncker and Humblot, 1885.

61. Eberhardt, Margarete. "A Study of Phonetic Symbolism of Deaf Children," *Psychological Monographs*, 52: 23-42, 1940.

62. Erdmann, B., & Dodge, R. *Untersuchungen über das Lesen.* Halle: M. Niemeyer, 1898.

63. Escalona, S. K. "Feeding Disturbances in Very Young Children," *American Journal of Orthopsychiatry*, 15: 76-80, 1945.

64. Farnsworth, P. R., & Misumi. "Further Data on Suggestion in Pictures," *American Journal of Psychology*, 43: 632, 1931.

65. Fischer, J. L. "Language and Folktale in Truk and Ponape: A Study in Cultural Integration." Doctor's thesis. Cambridge: Harvard University, 1955.

66. Flesch, R. *Why Johnny Can't Read.* New York: Harper, 1955.

67. Fries, C. C. *Teaching and Learning English as a Foreign Language.* Ann Arbor: University of Michigan Press, 1945.

68. ———. *The Structure of English; An Introduction to the Construction of English Sentences.* New York: Harcourt, Brace, 1952.

69. Galton, F. *Inquiries into Human Faculty and its Development.* London: Dent, 1907.

70. Garner, R. L. *The Speech of Monkeys.* London: Heinemann, 1892.

71. Gelb, I. J. *A Study of Writing.* Chicago: University of Chicago Press, 1952.

72. Gilbert, G. M. "Stereotype Persistence and Change Among College Students," *Journal of Abnormal and Social Psychology*, 46: 245-54, 1951.

73. Gleason, H. A. *An Introduction to Descriptive Linguistics.* New York: Holt, 1955.

74. Gleason, Josephine M. "An Experimental Study of Feelings of Relation," *American Journal of Psychology*, 30: 1-26, 1919.

75. Glenn, E. S. "Semantic Difficulties in International Communication," *Etc.*, 11: 163-180, 1954.

76. Goldstein, K. "The Problem of the Meaning of Words Based upon Observation of Aphasic Patients," *Journal of Psychology*, 2: 301-16, 1936.

77. ———. *Language and Language Disturbances: Aphasic Symptom Complexes and Their Significance for Medicine and Theory of Language.* New York: Grune and Stratton, 1948.

78. ———, & Scheerer, M. "Abstract and Concrete Behavior: An Experimental Study with Special Tests," *Psychological Monographs*, 53, No. 2, 1941.

79. Granich, L. *Aphasia: A Guide to Retraining.* New York: Grune and Stratton, 1947.

80. Gray, W. S., & Iverson, W. J. "What Should be the Profession's Attitude Toward Lay Criticism of the Schools? With Special Reference to Reading," *Elementary School Journal*, 53: 1-44, 1952.

81. Haiman, F. S. "An Experimental Study of the Effects of Ethos in Public Speaking," *Speech Monographs*, 16: 190-92, 1949.

82. Hall, G. S. *Youth its Education, Regimen, and Hygiene.* New York: D. Appleton, 1917.

83. Hall, R. A. *Hands off Pidgin English.* Sydney: Pacific Publication, 1955.

84. Hanfmann, Eugenia. "Analysis of the Thinking Disorder in a Case of Schizophrenia," *Archives of Neurology and Psychiatry*, 41, 1939.

85. ———, Rickers-Ovsiankina, Maria, & Goldstein, K. "Case Lanuti: Extreme Concretization of Behavior Due to Damage of the Brain Cortex," *Psychological Monographs*, 57, No. 264, 1944.

86. Harlow, H. "The Formation of Learning Sets," *Psychological Review*, 56: 51-65, 1949.

87. ———. "Primate Learning," in C. P. Stone (ed.), *Comparative Psychology*, (3rd ed.) New York: Prentice-Hall, 1951, pp. 183-238.

88. Harris, Z. S. *Methods in Structural Linguistics.* Chicago: University of Chicago Press, 1951.

89. Hartmann, G. W. "A Field Experiment on the Comparative Effectiveness of 'Emotional' and 'Rational' Political Leaflets in Determining Election Results," *Journal of Abnormal and Social Psychology*, 31: 99-114, 1936.

90. Hayes, Cathy, *The Ape in our House.* New York: Harper, 1951.

91. Hayes, K. J., & Hayes, Catherine. "Picture Perception in a Home-Raised Chimpanzee," *Journal of Comparative Psychology*, 46: 470-74, 1953.

92. Herz, M. F. "Some Psychological Lessons From Leaflet Propaganda in World War II," *Public Opinion Quarterly*, 13: 471-86, 1949.

93. Hilgard, E. R., & Marquis, D. G. *Conditioning and Learning.* New York: Appleton-Century-Crofts, 1940.

94. Hockett, C. F. "Chinese Versus English: An Exploration of the Whorfian Theses," in H. Hoijer (ed.), *Language in Culture.* Chicago: University of Chicago Press, 1954, pp. 106-23.

95. Holt, E. B. *Animal Drive.* London: Williams and Norgate, 1931.

96. Horn, E. "The Commonest Words in the Spoken Vocabulary Up To and Including Six Years of Age," in National Society for the Study of Education, *Twenty-fourth Yearbook*. Bloomington, Illinois: Public School Publishing Co., 1925, pp. 186-98.

97. Horowitz, A. E. "The Effects of Variation in Linguistic Structure on the Learning of Miniature Linguistic Systems." Doctor's thesis. Cambridge: Harvard University, 1955.

98. Hovland, C. I., Lumsdaine, A. A., & Sheffield, F. D. *Experiments on Mass Communication*, Vol. III. Princeton, N. J.: Princeton University Press, 1949.

99. ——, & Weiss, W. "The Influence of Source Credibility on Communication Effectiveness," *Public Opinion Quarterly*, 15: 635-50, 1951.

100. Hull, C. L. "Knowledge and Purpose as Habit Mechanisms," *Psychological Review*, 37: 511-25, 1930.

101. Humphrey, G. *Thinking: An Introduction to its Experimental Psychology*. New York: Wiley, 1951.

102. Hyman, H. H., & Sheatsley, P. B. "Some Reasons Why Information Campaigns Fail," *Public Opinion Quarterly*, 11: 412-23, 1947.

103. Information and Education Division, United States War Department. "Opinions about Negro Infantry Platoons in White Companies of Seven Divisions," in G. E. Swanson, T. M. Newcomb, and E. L. Hartley (eds.), *Readings in Social Psychology*. New York: Holt, 1952, pp. 502-06.

104. Irwin, O. C. "Infant Speech: Consonantal Sounds According to Place of Articulation," *Journal of Speech Disorders*, 12: 397-401, 1947.

105. ——. "Infant Speech: Consonant Sounds According to Manner of Articulation," *Ibid.*, 402-04.

106. ——. "Infant Speech: Development of Vowel Sounds," *Journal of Speech and Hearing Disorders*, 13: 31-34, 1948.

107. ——, & Chen, H. P. "Infant Speech: Vowel and Consonant Frequency," *Ibid.*, 123-125.

108. Itard, J. M. G. *The Wild Boy of Aveyron* (trans. by G. and M. Humphrey). New York: Century, 1932.

109. Jacobson, E. "Electrophysiology of Mental Activities," *American Journal of Psychology*, 44: 677-94, 1932.

110. Jaensch, E. R. *Der Gegentypus*. Leipzig: Barth, 1938.

111. Jakobson, R. *Kindersprache, Aphasie, und Algemeine Lautgesetze*. Uppsala: Almqvist and Wiksell, 1941.

112. ——. "Aphasia as a Linguistic Problem," in H. Werner (ed.), *On Expressive Language*. Worcester, Massachusetts: Clark University Press, 1955, pp. 69-81.

113. ——, Fant, G. M., & Halle, M. *Preliminaries to Speech Analysis; The Distinctive Features and Their Correlates*. Cambridge: Acoustics Laboratory, Massachusetts Institute of Technology, Technical Report No. 13, 1952.

114. ——, & Halle, M. *Fundamentals of Language.* Gravenhage: Mouton, 1956, p. 37.

115. James, W. *The Principles of Psychology,* Vol. I. New York: Holt, 1890, p. 471.

116. Javal, L. E. "Essai sur la Physiologie de la Lecture," *Année d'Oculistique,* 82: 242-53, 1878.

117. Jenks, A. E. "Bulu Knowledge of the Gorilla and Chimpanzee," *American Anthropologist,* 13: 56-64, 1911.

118. Jespersen, O. *Language; Its Nature, Development, and Origin.* London: Allen and Unwin, 1922.

119. Jones, L. "Visual Message Presentation," *Part I of Final Contract,* AE 19 (122)–17 item *I,* February 5, 1954.

120. Joos, M. "Acoustic Phonetics," *Language Monographs,* No. 23, 1948.

121. Katona, G. *Organizing and Memorizing: Studies in the Psychology of Learning and Teaching.* New York: Columbia University Press, 1940.

122. Katz, D., & Braly, K. W. "Racial Stereotypes of 100 College Students," *Journal of Abnormal and Social Psychology,* 28: 280-90, 1933.

123. Kellogg, W. N., & Kellogg, Louise A. *The Ape and the Child.* New York: McGraw-Hill, 1933.

124. Kelman, H. C., & Hovland, C. I. " 'Reinstatement' of the Communicator in Delayed Measurement of Opinion Change," *Journal of Abnormal and Social Psychology,* 48: 327-35, 1933.

125. Kluckhohn, C., & Kelly, W. H. "The Concept of Culture," in R. Linton (ed.), *The Science of Man in the World Crisis.* New York: Columbia University Press, 1945, pp. 78-106.

126. ——, & Leighton, Dorothy. *The Navaho.* Cambridge: Harvard University Press, 1946.

127. Köhler, W. "Die Methoden der psychologischen Forschung an Affen," in E. Abderhalden, *Handbuch der biologischen Arbeitsmethoden.* Berlin: Urban and Schwarzenburg, 1921, pp. 69-120.

128. ——. *The Mentality of Apes* (2nd ed.). New York: Harcourt-Brace, 1927.

129. Korzybski, A. *Science and Sanity; An Introduction to Non-Aristotelian Systems and General Semantics.* Lancaster: Science Press, 1933.

130. Kramer, B. M. "Residential Contact as a Determinant of Attitudes Toward Negroes." Doctor's thesis. Cambridge: Harvard University, 1951.

131. Krechevsky, I. " 'Hypotheses' in Rats," *Psychological Review,* 39: 516-32, 1932.

132. ——. "A Study of the Continuity of the Problem-Solving Process," *Psychological Review,* 45: 107-33, 1938.

133. Kris, E., & Speier, H. *German Radio Propaganda: Report on Home Broadcasts During the War.* London: Oxford University Press, 1944.

134. Langer, Susanne K. *Philosophy in a New Key*. New York: Penguin, 1942.

135. Lashley, K. S. *Brain Mechanisms and Intelligence*. Chicago: University of Chicago Press, 1929, p. 135.

136. ——. "Conditional Reactions in the Rat," *Journal of Psychology*, 6: 311-24, 1938.

137. ——, & Wade, Margaret. "The Pavlovian Theory of Generalization," *Psychological Review*, 53: 72-87, 1946.

138. Lazarsfeld, P. F., Berelson, B., & Gaudet, Hazel. *The People's Choice*. New York: Duell, Sloan, and Pearce, 1944.

139. ——, & Kendall, Patricia L. *Radio Listening in America*. New York: Prentice-Hall, 1948.

140. Lee, A. M. *How to Understand Propaganda*. New York: Rinehart, 1952.

141. Lee, Dorothy D. "Conceptual Implications of an Indian Language," *Philosophy of Science*, 5: 89-102, 1938.

142. Lenneberg, E. H. "Cognition and Ethnolinguistics," *Language*, 29: 463-71, 1953.

143. Lévy-Bruhl, L. *Primitive Mentality* (trans. by Lilian A. Clare). New York: Macmillan, 1923, p. 147.

144. Lewis, Helen B. "Studies in the Principles of Judgments and Attitudes: IV. The Operation of Prestige Suggestion," *Journal of Social Psychology*, 14: 229-56, 1941.

145. Lewis, M. M. *Infant Speech*. London: Kegan Paul, 1936.

146. Lindzey, G., & Rogolsky, S. "Prejudice and Identification of Minority Group Membership," *Journal of Abnormal and Social Psychology*, 45: 37-53, 1950.

147. Lippmann, W. *Public Opinion*. New York: Macmillan, 1922.

148. Livingstone, D. *The Last Journals of David Livingstone in Central Africa* (ed. by H. Waller). New York: Harper, 1875.

149. Locke, J. *An Essay Concerning Human Understanding*, 1905 edition. London: Routledge, 1690.

150. Lombroso, P. "Das Leben der Kinder," *Pedogogische Monographien*. Leipzig: Nemnich, 1909.

151. Lorenz, K. *King Solomon's Ring*. New York: Crowell, 1952.

152. Maerz, A., & Paul, M. R. *A Dictionary of Color*. New York: McGraw-Hill, 1930.

153. Maltzman, I., Morrisett, L. Jr., & Brooks, L. O. "An Investigation of Phonetic Symbolism," *Journal of Abnormal and Social Psychology*, 249-51, 1956.

154. McCarthy, Dorothea. "Language Development in Children," in L. Carmichael (ed.), *Manual of Child Psychology*. New York: Wiley, 1946, pp. 477-581.

155. McClelland, D. C., Atkinson, J. W., Clark, R. A., & Lowell, E. L. *The Achievement Motive*. New York: Appleton-Century, 1953.

156. McCulloch, T. L., & Pratt, J. C. "A Study of the Pre-Solution Period in Weight Discrimination by White Rats," *Journal of Comparative Psychology*, 18: 271-90, 1934.

157. McDowell, J. "A Report on the Phonetic Method of Teaching Children to Read," *The Catholic Educational Review*, 51: 506-19, 1953.

158. Merton, R. K., assisted by Marjorie Fiske and Alberta Curtis. *Mass Persuasion*. New York: Harper, 1946.

159. Mill, J. S. *Examination of Sir William Hamilton's Philosophy*. London: Longmans, Green, 1865.

160. Miller, N. E., & Dollard, J. *Social Learning and Imitation*. New Haven: Yale University Press, 1941.

161. Miller, R. L. "Auditory Tests with Synthetic Vowels," *Journal of the Acoustical Society of America*, 25: 114-21, 1953.

162. Moran, L. J. "Vocabulary Knowledge and Usage Among Normal and Schizophrenic Subjects," *Psychological Monographs*, 67, No. 20, 1953.

163. Mosher, R. M., & Newhall, S. M. "Phonic Versus Look-and-Say Training in Beginning Reading," *Journal of Educational Research*, 21: 500-06, 1930.

164. Mowrer, O. H. "On the Psychology of 'Talking' Birds—A Contribution to Language and Personality Theory," in O. H. Mowrer, *Learning Theory and Personality Dynamics; Selected Papers*. New York: Ronald, 1950, pp. 688-726.

165. Müller, H. *Experimentelle Beiträge zur Analyse des Verhältnisses von Laut und Sinn*. Berlin: Müller and I. Kiepenheuer, 1935.

166. Müller, M. *The Science of Language*. London: Longmans, Green, 1891.

167. Murdock, G. P. *Social Structure*. New York: Macmillan, 1949.

168. Newman, S. "Further Experiments in Phonetic Symbolism," *American Journal of Psychology*, 45: 53-75, 1933.

169. Nida, E. A. *Morphology: The Descriptive Analysis of Words*. Ann Arbor: University of Michigan Press, 1946.

170. Norris, C. *Signs, Language and Behavior*. New York: Prentice-Hall, 1946.

171. Okabe, T. "An Experimental Study of Belief," *American Journal of Psychology*, 21: 563-96, 1910.

172. Optical Society of America, Committee on Colorimetry. *The Science of Color*. New York: Crowell, 1953.

173. Osgood, C. E. *Method and Theory in Experimental Psychology*. New York: Oxford University Press, 1953, p. 396.

174. ——, & Suci, G. E. "Factor Analysis of Meaning," *Journal of Experimental Psychology*, 325-38, 1955.

175. Padilla, S. G. "Further Studies on the Delayed Pecking of Chicks." Doctor's thesis. Ann Arbor: University of Michigan, 1930.

176. Paget, R. *Human Speech*. New York: Harcourt, Brace, 1930.

177. Pechuël-Loesche, E. *Die Loango-Expedition ausgessant von dem deutschen Gesellschaft zur Erforschung Aequatorial-Africas 1873-1876. Ein Reisewerk in drei Abtheilungen*, Vol. 3. Leipzig: P. Frohberg, 1882.

178. Pfungst, O. *Clever Hans, The Horse of Mr. Von Osten*. New York: Holt, 1911.

179. Piaget, J. *The Child's Conception of the World.* New York: Harcourt, Brace, 1929.

180. ——. *The Child's Conception of Physical Causality.* New York: Harcourt, Brace, 1930.

181. ——. *The Child's Conception of Number.* London: Routledge, 1952.

182. ——. *The Origin of Intelligence in the Child.* London: Routledge, 1953.

183. Pike, K. L. *Phonetics; A Critical Analysis of Phonetic Theory and a Technic for the Practical Description of Sounds.* Ann Arbor: University of Michigan Press, 1943, pp. 15, 143.

184. ——. *The Intonation of American English.* Ann Arbor: University of Michigan Press, 1946.

185. ——. *Phonemics; A Technique for Reducing Languages to Writing.* Ann Arbor: University of Michigan Press, 1947.

186. Pillsbury, W. B., & Meader, C. L. *The Psychology of Language.* New York: Appleton, 1928.

187. Pittman, D. *Practical Linguistics.* Cleveland: Mid-Missions (314 Superior Avenue), 1948.

188. Plato. "Cratylus," in B. Jowett (ed.) *The Dialogues of Plato,* Vol. 1. Oxford: Clarendon, 1892, pp. 253-389.

189. Potter, R. K., & Steinberg, J. C. "Toward the Specification of Speech," *Journal of the Acoustical Society of America,* 22: 807-20, 1950.

190. Razran, G. H. S. "Studies in Configural Conditioning; Historical and Preliminary Experimentation," *Journal of General Psychology,* 21: 307-30, 1939.

191. Rich, Susannah. "The Perception of Emotion." Honors thesis. Cambridge: Radcliffe College, 1953.

192. Richards, I. A. *Practical Criticism.* New York: Harcourt, Brace, 1929.

193. ——. *Speculative Instruments.* Chicago: University of Chicago Press, 1955.

194. Rinsland, H. D. *A Basic Vocabulary of Elementary School Children.* New York: Macmillan, 1945.

195. Riopelle, A. J., & Copelan, E. L. "Discrimination Reversal to a Sign," *Journal of Experimental Psychology,* 48: 143-45, 1954.

196. Robinson, E. W. "A Preliminary Experiment on Abstraction in a Monkey," *Journal of Comparative Psychology,* 16: 231-36, 1933.

197. Rothmann, M., & Teuber, E. "Einzelausgabe aus der Anthropoidenstation auf Teneriffa. I. Ziele und Aufgaben der Station sowie erste Beobachtungen an den auf ihr gehaltenen Schimpansen," *Abhandlungen der preussischen Akademie der Wissenschaften,* 1-20, 1915.

198. Russell, D. H. "A Diagnostic Study of Spelling Readiness," *Journal of Educational Research,* 37: 276-83, 1943.

199. Saadi, M., & Farnsworth, P. R. "The Degrees of Acceptance of Dogmatic Statements and Preferences for their Supposed Makers," *Journal of Abnormal and Social Psychology,* 29: 143-50, 1934.

200. Sapir, E. "A Study in Phonetic Symbolism," *Journal of Experimental Psychology*, 12: 225-39, 1929.

201. Savory, T. H. *The Language of Science.* London: Deutsch, 1953.

202. Seashore, R. H., & Eckerson, L. D. "The Measurement of Individual Differences in General English Vocabularies," *Journal of Educational Psychology*, 31: 14-38, 1940.

203. Seroshevskii, V. R. *Iakuti.* St. Petersburg: Royal Geographical Society, 1896.

204. Shannon, C. E. "The Redundancy of English," in H. Von Foerster (ed.), *Cybernetics; Transactions of the Seventh Conference.* New York: Josiah Macy, Jr. Foundation, 1951.

205. ——, & Weaver, W. *The Mathematical Theory of Communication.* Urbana: University of Illinois Press, 1949.

206. Shepard, J. F., & Breed, F. S. "Maturation and Use in the Development of an Instinct," *Journal of Animal Behavior*, 3: 274-85, 1913.

207. Sherif, M. "An Experimental Study of Stereotypes," *Journal of Abnormal and Social Psychology*, 7: 386-402, 1935.

208. ——. *The Psychology of Social Norms.* New York: Harper, 1936.

209. Sherman, M. "The Differentiation of Emotional Responses in Infants. II The Ability of Observers to Judge the Emotional Characteristics of the Crying of Infants and of the Voice of an Adult," *Journal of Comparative Psychology*, 7: 335-51, 1927.

210. Singh, J. A. L., & Zingg, R. M. *Wolf-Children and Feral Man.* New York: Harper, 1942.

211. Sitwell, Edith. *Poetry and Criticism.* London: Hogarth, 1925, p. 18.

212. Skinner, B. F. *The Behavior of Organisms; An Experimental Analysis.* New York: Appleton-Century, 1938.

213. Smith, B. L. "Propaganda Analysis and the Science of Democracy," *Public Opinion Quarterly*, 5: 250-59, 1941.

214. Smith, K. U. "Discriminative Behavior in Animals," in C. P. Stone (ed.), *Comparative Psychology*, 3rd ed. New York: Prentice-Hall, 1951, pp. 316-62.

215. Smith, M. K. "Measurement of the Size of General English Vocabulary Through the Elementary Grades and High School," *Genetic Psychology Monographs*, 24: 311-45, 1941.

216. Spence, K. W. "Continuous Versus Non-Continuous Interpretations of Discrimination Learning," *Psychological Review*, 47: 271-88, 1940.

217. Stern, Clara, & Stern, W. *Die Kindersprache.* Leipzig: Barth, 1920.

218. Stetson, R. H. *Motor Phonetics; A Study of Speech Movements in Action.* Amsterdam: North-Holland, 1951.

219. Stevens, S. S., & Volkmann, J. "The Relation of Pitch to Frequency," *American Journal of Psychology*, 53: 329-53, 1940.

220. Stevenson, C. L. *Ethics and Language.* New Haven: Yale University Press, 1944, p. 54.

221. Tate, H. L. "The Influence of Phonics on Silent Reading in Grade I," *Elementary School Journal*, 37: 752-63, 1937.

222. Taylor, W. S. "A Critique of Sublimation in Males: A Study of Forty Superior Single Men," *Genetic Psychology Monographs*, 13, No. 1, 1933.

223. Thorndike, E. L. "Animal Intelligence. An Experimental Study of the Associative Processes in Animals," *Psychological Monographs*, 2, No. 8, 1911.

224. ———. "The Origin of Language," *Science*, 77: 173-75, 1933.

225. ———, & Lorge, I. *The Teacher's Word Book of 30,000 Words.* New York: Bureau of Publications, Teachers College, Columbia University, 1944.

226. Tinbergen, N. *The Study of Instinct.* London: Oxford University Press, 1951.

227. Titchener, E. B. *Lectures on the Experimental Psychology of the Thought Processes.* New York: Macmillan, 1909, pp. 17-19.

228. Triggs, Frances O. "The Development of Measured Word Recognition Skills, Grade Four Through the College Freshman Year," *Educational and Psychological Measurement*, 12: 345-49, 1952.

229. Tsuru, S. "Sound and Meaning." Unpublished manuscript on file with Gordon W. Allport, Harvard University, 1934.

230. Usnadze, D. "Ein experimenteller Beitrag zum Problem der psychologischen Grundlagen der Namengebung," *Psychologische Forschung*, 5: 24-43, 1924.

231. Vendryes, J. *Language.* New York: Knopf, 1925.

232. Vigotsky, L. S. "Thought and Speech," *Psychiatry*, 2: 29-54, 1939.

233. Von Domarus, E. "The Specific Laws of Logic in Schizophrenia," in J. S. Kasanin (ed.) *Language and Thought in Schizophrenia.* Berkeley: University of California Press, 1944.

234. Von Frisch, K. *Bees, Their Vision, Chemical Senses, and Language.* Ithaca, New York: Cornell University Press, 1950.

235. Watson, J. B. "The Place of the Conditioned-Reflex in Psychology," *Psychological Review*, 23: 89-116, 1916.

236. ———. *Behaviorism.* New York: People's Institute, 1924, p. 82.

237. Watt, H. J. "Experimentelle Beiträge zu einer Theorie des Denkens," *Archiv für die Gesamte Psychologie*, 4: 289-436, 1905.

238. Weinstein, B. "Matching-From-Sample by Rhesus Monkeys and by Children," *Journal of Comparative Psychology*, 31: 195-213, 1941.

239. Werner, H. *Grundfragen der Sprachphysiognomik.* Leipzig: Barth, 1932.

240. ———. *Comparative Psychology of Mental Development.* Chicago: Follett, 1948.

241. Wertham, F. *The Show of Violence.* Garden City, N. Y.: Doubleday, 1949.

242. White, R. W. *The Abnormal Personality.* New York: Ronald Press, 1948.

243. Whitney, W. D. *Language and the Study of Language.* New York: Scribner, Armstrong, 1867, p. 112.

244. Whorf, B. L. *Language, Thought, and Reality,* with an introduction by J. B. Carroll. Cambridge: Technology Press, 1956.

245. ——. "The Relation of Habitual Thought and Behavior to Language." *Ibid.,* pp. 134-59.

246. ——. "Science and Linguistics." *Ibid.,* pp. 207-19.

247. ——. "Linguistics as an Exact Science." *Ibid.,* pp. 220-32.

248. ——. "Languages and Logic." *Ibid.,* pp. 233-45.

249. Wilson, R. A. *The Miraculous Birth of Language,* with a preface by G. B. Shaw. New York: Philosophical Library, 1948, p. 23.

250. Wissemann, H. *Untersuchungen zur Onomatopoiie: 1 Teil, die sprachpsychologischen Versuche.* Heidelberg: Carl Winter Universitätsverlag, 1954.

251. Wittgenstein, L. *Philosophische Untersuchungen* (Translated by G. E. M. Anscombe). Oxford: Blackwell, 1953.

252. Woodrow, H., & Lowell, F. "Children's Association Tables," *Psychological Monographs,* 22, No. 97, 1916.

253. Woodworth, R. S. "A Revision of Imageless Thought," *Psychological Review,* 22: 1-27, 1915.

254. ——. *Experimental Psychology.* New York: Holt, 1948, p. 744.

255. Wundt, W. *Volkerpsychologie; eine Untersuchung der Entwicklungs- gesetze von Sprache, Mythen, und Sitte,* 3 vols. Leipzig: Engelmann, 1900-1909.

256. Yerkes, R. M. *Chimpanzees; A Laboratory Colony.* New Haven: Yale University Press, 1943, p. 192.

257. ——, & Learned, Blanche W. *Chimpanzee Intelligence and its Vocal Expressions.* Baltimore: William and Wilkins, 1925.

258. ——, & Yerkes, Ada W. *The Great Apes,* 3rd ed. New Haven: Yale University Press, 1945.

259. Zener, K. "The Significance of Behavior Accompanying Conditioned Salivary Secretion for Theories of the Conditioned Response," *American Journal of Psychology,* 50: 384-403, 1937.

260. Zipf, G. K. *The Psycho-Biology of Language.* Boston: Houghton Mifflin, 1935.

Index

Abstract cognitive functioning, 264-297
Abstract ideas, 61, 85
Achievement motive, 345, 347, 353
Adams, J. K., 311, 312
Adorno, T. W., 369
Advertising, 305, 331, 339, 340, 358
Agnew, D. C., 75-77
Agrammatism, 288
Algren, N., 226
Allokinesic, 168, 169
Allophone, 31-34, 40, 41, 52
Allport, G. W., 123, 124, 127, 226, 367
Amentia, 187, 188, 191
Amnesic aphasia, 288, 292
Anna, an isolated child, 191, 192
Aphasia, 264, 287-292, 296, 297
Arieti, S., 296
Aristotle, 10
Articulational similarity, 30, 31
Asch, S., 145, 146, 148, 149, 304-306, 319-321, 353
Attitude, 321-323, 334, 367
Attribute, introduced, 10
    articulational, 25, 26
    formal, 14, 15, 28, 51, 145
    functional, 14, 15, 28, 42-53, 141, 145, 207, 208
    noisy, 12, 13, 85, 87, 88, 217, 218, 266, 277
    quiet, 12, 13, 266
Auden, W. H., 257
Austin, G. A., 9
Autokinetic phenomenon, 304, 305, 319
Automobile names, 216-218, 234
Auxiliary language, 229
Availability of a category, 236, 237, 241, 255, 262
Avoidance conditioning, 197
Ayer, A. J., 311

Babbling, 198-201
Band Wagon, 301, 302, 304, 305, 316, 317, 319, 320, 322, 332
Bateson, F. W., 138, 143
Bechi, G., 147
Behkterev, V. M., 182
Benedict, R. F., 260

Benjamin, J. D., 294
Bentley, M., 136
Berelson, B., 79
Beritov, I. S., 182
Berkeley, G., 85, 88, 89, 360
Berko, J., 120, 129, 218
Bilingual, 232
Binet, A., 89, 91, 353, 354
Birdwhistell, R. L., 168
Black, A. H., 124, 125, 127-130, 136
Blackboard Jungle, 338
"Black" propaganda, 316, 319, 320, 329-331
Bloch, B., 25, 35
Bloomfield, L., 270, 273, 274
Bloomster, M., 74
Boas, F., 283
Borst, 40
Boswell, J., 257
Bourne Publicity Law, 331
Bow, C., 306
Braly, K. W., 364, 366, 368
Brown, R. W., 45, 124, 125, 127-130, 136, 146, 148, 151, 152, 239
Bruner, J. S., 9
Bucephalus, 220
Bühler, K., 91

Callas, M. M., 147
Cameron, N., 295, 349, 350
Campbell, A. A., 369
Caniglia, M., 147
Capone, A., 306
Capp, A., 43, 49
Card Stacking, 301, 303, 318, 322, 323, 326, 332
Carnap, R., 165
Carroll, J. B., 349
Cassirer, E., 311
Category, defined, 6
    centrality, 238-241
    conjunctive category, 14, 42, 210, 225
    disjunctive category, 14, 42, 54, 276, 284, 291
    identity category, 8, 55, 84, 86
    relational, 14, 38
Cattell, J. M., 67, 70
Charades, 208

14759983R20234

Made in the USA
Middletown, DE
11 October 2014